THE
FEMALE
THERMOMETER

IDEOLOGIES OF DESIRE

David M. Halperin
Series Editor

THE FEMALE THERMOMETER
*Eighteenth-Century Culture and the Invention
of the Uncanny*

Terry Castle

THE
FEMALE
THERMOMETER

Eighteenth-Century Culture and the Invention of the Uncanny

TERRY CASTLE

New York   Oxford
OXFORD UNIVERSITY PRESS
1995

Oxford University Press

Oxford New York
Athens Auckland Bangkok Bombay
Calcutta Cape Town Dar es Salaam Delhi
Florence Hong Kong Istanbul Karachi
Kuala Lumpur Madras Madrid Melbourne
Mexico City Nairobi Paris Singapore
Taipei Tokyo Toronto

and associated companies in
Berlin Ibadan

Copyright © 1995 by Terry Castle

Published by Oxford University Press, Inc.
200 Madison Avenue, New York, New York 10016

Oxford is a registered trademark of Oxford University Press

Library of Congress Cataloging-in-Publication Data
Castle, Terry.
    The female thermometer : eighteenth-century culture and
the invention of the uncanny /
Terry Castle.
        p.   cm. — (Ideologies of desire)
    Includes bibliographical references and index.
    ISBN 0-19-508097-1. — ISBN 0-19-508098-X (pbk.)
    1. English literature—18th century—History and criticism.
    2. Gothic revival (Literature)—Great Britain.
    3. Women and literature—Great Britain—History—18th century.
    4. Romanticism—Great Britain—History—18th century.
    5. Femininity (Psychology) in literature.
    6. Sex (Psychology) in literature.
    7. Supernatural in literature.
    I. Title. II. Series.
    PR448.G6C37 1995   820.9′37—dc20   94-34700

    "'Amy, Who Knew my Disease': A Psychosexual Pattern in Defoe's Roxana," from *ELH*, 46 (1979). Copyright
1979 by the Johns Hopkins University Press. Reprinted by permission of the publisher.
    "Lovelace's Dream" from *Studies in Eighteenth-Century Culture*, 13 (1984). Reprinted by permission of the
American Society for Eighteenth-Century Studies.
    "'Matters Not Fit to be Mentioned': Fielding's *The Female Husband*," from *ELH*, 49 (1982). Copyright 1982 by
the Johns Hopkins University Press. Reprinted by permission of the publisher.
    "The Spectralization of the Other in *The Mysteries of Udolpho*," from *The New Eighteenth Century*, ed. Laura
Brown and Felicity Nussbaum (New York: Methuen, 1987). Reprinted by permission of Methuen & Co.
    "Phantasmagoria and the Metaphorics of Modern Reverie" from *Critical Inquiry* 15 (Autumn 1988) © 1988 by
The University of Chicago. All rights reserved. Reprinted by permission of The University of Chicago.
    "Contagious Folly: *An Adventure* and Its Skeptics" from *Critical Inquiry* 17 (Summer 1991) © 1991 by The
University of Chicago. All rights reserved. Reprinted by permission of The University of Chicago.

9 8 7 6 5 4 3 2 1

Printed in the United States of America
on acid-free paper

To Paul Alkon, with gratitude

ACKNOWLEDGMENTS

I would like to thank the editors of *PMLA, Critical Inquiry, ELH: Journal of English Literary History,* and *Studies in Eighteenth-Century Culture* for allowing me to reprint essays that originally appeared in those journals, and Routledge and Manchester University Press for letting me reprint "The Spectralization of the Other in *The Mysteries of Udolpho*" and "The Culture of Travesty," both of which originally appeared in published anthologies. I am also very grateful to the Society of Fellows at Harvard University, the Stanford University Humanities Center, and The Guggenheim Foundation for generous grants-in-aid.

It would be impossible for me to thank all of those—colleagues and students—who have offered me intellectual support and encouragement over the past ten years. Nonetheless I would especially like to express my gratitude to Paul Alkon, Doree Allen, John Bender, Bliss Carnochan, David Halperin, Herbert Lindenberger, Elizabeth Maguire, Diane Middlebrook, Nancy K. Miller, Stephen Orgel, Ronald Paulson, Rob Polhemus, Beverley Talbott, and Ian Watt. All inadequacies and errors that remain, needless to say, are my own.

CONTENTS

THE
FEMALE
THERMOMETER

CHAPTER 1

INTRODUCTION

f I may start with a paradox: the crucial essay in this volume, containing articles I have published over the past ten years about eighteenth-century English literature and culture, is not to be found in the table of contents. It isn't to be found there, I'm chagrined to say, because I didn't write it. I refer to Sigmund Freud's magnificent, troubling, and inspired essay of 1919, "The 'Uncanny.'" It's not here and yet—like an optical illusion, or one of those strange retinal "ghosts" that seem to float up in space after one stares too long at a word or line of type—Freud's essay haunts this volume, its magus-pages everywhere interleaving with my own. For after ten years, I discover, it is precisely Freud's unsettling, unflinching meditation on the problem of enlightenment—so profound in its implications—that most deeply shapes my own thinking about the eighteenth century and links the various essays in this book, one to one another.

How so? one may ask. The essays here were not written in concert, nor did I have "The 'Uncanny'" in mind (though I had certainly read it) when I began working on them over a decade ago. It is true, I find now, that I cite Freud's essay—fleetingly—in my title-piece, "The Female Thermometer" from 1986, and in an essay on Ann Radcliffe's Gothic fiction from 1989. But anyone searching for something more substantial—some extended reading or contestation—

Figure 1.1. Images of the uncanny. (a) Goya's "Que biene el Coco" [Here comes the bogey-man] and (b) "Duendecitos" [Hobgoblins] from *Los Caprichos*, 1799. Courtesy of the British Museum.

will be disappointed. Given this disarming paucity of references, why invoke "'The Uncanny'" at all?

The simple (if not simplistic) answer might be themes. As anyone who has ever taken it up it will know, "The 'Uncanny'" is first and foremost a sort of theme-index: an obsessional inventory of eerie fantasies, motifs, and effects, an itemized tropology of the weird. Doubles, dancing dolls and automata, waxwork

figures, alter egos and "mirror" selves, spectral emanations, detached body parts ("a severed head, a hand cut off at the wrist, feet that dance by themselves"), the ghastly fantasy of being buried alive, omens, precognition, déjà vu—all of these, says Freud, are "uncanny themes" par excellence. What makes them uncanny is precisely the way they subvert the distinction between the real and the phantasmatic—plunging us instantly, and vertiginously, into the hag-ridden realm of the unconscious.

Yet such are themes, I confess, to which I have myself ineluctably been drawn. I have always been attracted by the "irrational" or "gothic" side of eighteenth-century culture: by Mrs. Veal, Cagliostro, the Cock Lane Ghost, Mesmer, and Piranesi as much as by Toland, Hume, or Voltaire. Those "Night-visions" and "Antic Shapes," the "wild Natives of the Brain" eulogized by Edward Young in *Night Thoughts*, have typically engrossed me more than "the self-given solar Ray" of classic Enlightenment rationalism. And in the essays that follow I positively revel in the morbid, the excessive, and the strange: in prophetic dreams, doppelgängers, primal scenes, and sexual metamorphoses ("Amy, Who Knew my Disease," "Lovelace's Dream"); in disguises, estrangements, and carnivalesque assaults on decorum ("Matters Not fit to be Mentioned," "The Culture of Travesty," "The Carnivalization of Eighteenth-Century English Narrative"); in auras, detached body parts, and inanimate objects coming mysteriously to life ("The Female Thermometer"); in optical illusions, magic lantern shows, and hallucinatory reveries ("Phantasmagoria"); in corpses, tombs, and wandering apparitions ("The Spectralization of the Other in *The Mysteries of Udolpho*," "Spectral Politics"); and in monomania, *folie à deux*, time travel, and visionary "sightings" of the dead Marie Antoinette ("Contagious Folly").

But it is not merely a matter of sharing themes, or of using Freud to license my own sometimes peculiar divagations. "A scholar's mind," wrote Natalie Clifford Barney in *Adventures of the Mind*, "is a deep well in which are buried aborted feelings that rise to the surface as arguments."[1] My own ongoing obsession with the eighteenth-century "uncanny" is no doubt the result of a host of submerged emotional impulses—some of them embarrassingly personal. But changes in intellectual fashions have also had a lot to do with it. I am hardly the first recent literary critic or historian to find a phantasmagoric side to eighteenth-century literature and culture—or to sense in the myriad transformations of the epoch something other than the unproblematic, unassailable triumph of Reason's "sufficient light." Ever since the publication of Max Horkheimer and Theodor Adorno's magisterial *Dialectic of Enlightenment* over forty years ago, it has been difficult to maintain—without a devastating infusion of Swiftian irony—the once-conventional view of the eighteenth century as an era of unexampled social, political, and philosophical progress. The venerable notion of "Enlightenment rationalism" has itself come under pressing ideological attack, as a phalanx of historians and social theorists—from E. P. Thompson to Michel Foucault—have described ways in which appeals to reason can be used "instrumentally": "to control and dominate rather than to emancipate."[2]

The result has been the promulgation of an image of the eighteenth century profoundly unlike the one memorialized in Macaulay's *History of England from the Accession of James the Second* (1849–61) or Sir Leslie Stephen's *History of English Thought in the Eighteenth Century* (1876). No more the expansive, unruffled, serenely self-confident "Age of Reason" commemorated in nineteenth-century

Whig historiography: we now see the period more darkly—as riven by class and social tensions, as brutal and often neurotic in underlying character, and fraught with political, moral, and psychic instabilities. The "new" eighteenth century is not so much an age of reason, but one of paranoia, repression, and incipient madness, for which Jeremy Bentham's malign, all-seeing Panopticon, grimly refurbished by Foucault, might stand as a fitting, nightmarish emblem.

One might well ask, of course, how we have come to regard the eighteenth century in a manner so different from the nineteenth-century historians. How to reconcile—or even begin to relate—two such radically divergent images of the same epoch?

Yet here, I find, is where "The 'Uncanny'" offers a vital insight. Let us briefly recall Freud's argument. Defined as a feeling of "dread and creeping horror" manifest in the presence of "certain persons, things, sensations, experiences and situations," the uncanny arises whenever "infantile complexes which have been repressed are once more revived by some impression, or when the primitive beliefs which have been surmounted seem once more to be confirmed."[3] The Freudian uncanny is itself a sort of phantom, looming up out of darkness: an archaic fantasy or fear, long ago exiled to the unconscious, that nonetheless "returns to view"—intrudes on ordinary life—but in a form so distorted and disguised by repression that we fail to recognize its psychological source. Indeed, says Freud, the uncanny is "in reality nothing new or foreign, but something familiar and old-established in the mind": some "secretly familiar" thing, "which has undergone repression and then returned from it" (245).

What allows the repressed fantasy to come again into view? Metaphorically speaking, we notice, the Freudian uncanny is a function of *enlightenment:* it is that which confronts us, paradoxically, after a certain *light* has been cast. Freud quotes repeatedly (and famously) from the late eighteenth-century philosopher Schelling: everything is uncanny "which ought to have remained hidden but has come to light" (241). ("*Unheimlich sei alles, was ein Geheimnis, im Verborgenen bleiben sollte und hervorgetreten ist.*") Freud's own justly celebrated reading of E. T. A. Hoffmann's "The Sandman"—in which the hero Nathanael's hysterical fear of losing his eyes is interpreted as a displaced return of the infantile dread of castration—confirms the association: Hoffmann's fantastic tale unsettles so profoundly, Freud suggests, precisely because it brings to light—by way of a host of strange yet refulgent inventions—one of the darkest secrets of the psyche.[4]

But what if we lean on the "enlightenment" metaphor? What if we give it (so to speak) a capital letter—and treat it as a mode of historical assertion? Might one argue, extrapolating from Freud, that the uncanny itself first "comes to light"—becomes a part of human experience—in that period known as the Enlightenment? That the uncanny itself has a history, originates at a particular historical moment, for particular historical reasons, and that this history has everything to do with that curious ambivalence with which we now regard the eighteenth century?

Figure 1.2. The uncanny fear of losing one's eyes. Untitled engraving by George
Woodward, 1797. Courtesy of Houghton Library, Harvard University.

Obviously, as my subtitle suggests, I think we can. The assumption (tacitly Freudian) underlying all the essays in this volume is not simply that the eighteenth
century is "uncanny"—though that may be true—but that the eighteenth century
in a sense "invented the uncanny": that the very psychic and cultural transformations that led to the subsequent glorification of the period as an age of reason or
enlightenment—the aggressively rationalist imperatives of the epoch—also produced, like a kind of toxic side effect, a new human experience of strangeness,
anxiety, bafflement, and intellectual impasse. The distinctively eighteenth-century

impulse to systematize and regulate, to bureaucratize the world of knowledge by identifying what Locke called the "horizon . . . which sets the bounds between the enlightened and dark parts of things," was itself responsible, in other words, for that "estranging of the real"—and impinging uncanniness—which is so integral a part of modernity.[5]

This will seem an ambitious claim perhaps, but it is one that I think a careful reading of Freud's essay makes inevitable. True, we don't usually regard "The 'Uncanny'" as a historical allegory, let alone as a historical allegory having to do with the eighteenth century. Freud was hardly an intellectual historian in the conventional sense and often appeared impervious to matters of historical specificity. The diachronism structuring "The 'Uncanny'" might seem, on the face of it, of the loosest and vaguest sort—merely a version of the familiar psychoanalytic distinction between the archaic and the contemporary, the "primitive" and the civilized. Witness, for example, Freud's remarks on the uncanniness felt by many in relation to "death and dead bodies, to the return of the dead, and to spirits and ghosts":

> We—or our primitive forefathers—once believed that these possibilities were realities, and were convinced that they actually happened. Nowadays we no longer believe in them, we have *surmounted* these modes of thought; but we do not feel quite sure of our new beliefs, and the old ones still exist within us ready to seize upon any confirmation. As soon as something *actually happens* in our lives which seems to confirm the old, discarded beliefs, we get a feeling of the uncanny; it is as though we were making a judgement something like this: "So, after all, it is *true* that one can kill a person by the mere wish!" or, "So the dead *do* live on and appear on the scene of their former activities!" and so on. (247–48)

Or his colorful theory of the *doppelgänger:*

> [The] "double" was originally an insurance against the destruction of the ego, an "energetic denial of the power of death," as Rank says; and probably the "immortal" soul was the first "double" of the body. This invention of doubling as a preservation against extinction has its counterpart in the language of dreams, which is fond of representing castration by a doubling or multiplication of a genital symbol. The same desire led the ancient Egyptians to develop the art of making images of the dead in lasting materials. (235)

What makes the *doppelgänger* now seem uncanny (a "ghastly harbinger of death") is precisely the fact that we have grown out of that "very early mental stage" when the double functioned as a figure of existential reassurance—just as human culture as a whole has moved beyond the animistic beliefs characteristic of "primitive" or magic-based societies like that of the ancient Egyptians. Thanks to the estranging force of repression, says Freud, the historic "surmounting" of an older, atavistic way of thinking, the double "has become a thing of terror, just as, after the collapse of their religion, the gods turned into demons" (236).

And yet one can nonetheless detect at various points in "The 'Uncanny'" both a more refined sense of historical transformation and a powerful evocation of the uncanny's relatively *recent* origins. The crucial developmental process on which the Freudian uncanny depends is rationalization: the "surmounting" of infantile belief. Yet as ontogeny recapitulates phylogeny, so the individual repudiation of infantile fantasy simply recapitulates the larger process by which human civilization as a whole—at some paradigmatic juncture in its history—dispensed with "primitive" or "animistic" forms of thought and substituted new, rationalized modes of explanation. When did this crucial internalization of rationalist protocols take place? At least in the West, Freud hints, not *that* long ago. At numerous points in "The 'Uncanny'"—though perhaps most strikingly in the sections dealing with literary representations of the uncanny—it is difficult to avoid the conclusion that it was during the eighteenth century, with its confident rejection of transcendental explanations, compulsive quest for systematic knowledge, and self-conscious valorization of "reason" over "superstition," that human beings first experienced that encompassing sense of strangeness and unease Freud finds so characteristic of modern life.

It is not simply that Freud fixes on E. T. A. Hoffmann (1776–1822)—who began his literary career in the last decade of the eighteenth century and drew heavily on the rich traditions of late eighteenth-century Gothic and fantastic fiction—as the archetypal exponent of what might be called uncanny consciousness. For Freud, Hoffmann is the first and "unrivalled master" of the uncanny— the "writer who has succeeded in producing uncanny effects better than anyone else" (227). But that Hoffmann's characteristic uncanniness was decisively bound up with the evolution of Enlightenment philosophical and technological innovation will be immediately apparent to anyone familiar with his stories. (One cannot imagine Hoffmann writing his curious tales in any other epoch than his own.) As Freud himself observes, one of the most uncanny (yet typical) of Hoffmann's themes is that of the "dancing doll" or automaton—the mechanical doll Olympia in "The Sand-Man" being the obvious case in point. Freud explains its uncanniness in the light of the theory of psychic recurrence:

> We remember that in their early games children do not distinguish at all sharply between living and inanimate objects, and that they are especially fond of treating their dolls like live people. In fact, I have occasionally heard a woman patient declare that even at the age of eight she had still been convinced that her dolls would be certain to come to life if she were to look at them in a particular, extremely concentrated, way. (233)

In infancy, Freud continues, "the child had no fear of its doll coming to life, it may even have desired it." Hence "the source of the feeling of an uncanny thing would not, therefore, be an infantile fear in this case, but rather an infantile wish or even only an infantile belief." Once again, because the infantile wish has been distorted by repression, we now react with horror and uneasiness at the thought of a doll moving like a human being.

In the most literal sense, however, Hoffmann's uncanny effect is also the result of a distinctively "eighteenth-century" urge toward technological mastery and control. The first working automata (designed by the brilliant French scientist Vaucanson) were exhibited in England in the 1740s in the Long Room of the Opera House, Haymarket, and similar displays—of mechanical chess players, musicians, dancers, draftsmen, and so on—were a prominent feature of scientific exhibitions, fairs, and popular shows held across Europe into the early nineteenth century.[6] As Hoffmann's editor E. F. Bleiler remarks, "For us much of the emotional power of Hoffmann's story may be lost since the late 18th-century and early 19th-century automata are now mostly destroyed or inoperative. We can have no real idea of their remarkable performances nor can we regain their emotional impact, since robots and mechanized intelligence have become part of our daily life. During Hoffmann's lifetime, however, Maelzel's chess player (which was a fraud) aroused a sensation in Europe, while Vaucanson's mechanical duck (a remarkable mechanism that would grace any era) and his speaking head and similar marvels of mechanics were held to be almost miraculous."[7] Hoffmann's uncanny piece of literary invention, therefore, was thus dependent on an *actual* invention: a specific technological innovation, closely linked with the developing science of clockmaking, which at once galvanized public interest and made possible the curious reactivation of unconscious fantasy Freud describes so well. The eighteenth-century invention of the automaton was also (in the most obvious sense) an "invention" of the uncanny.

Yet Freud hints even more explicitly at the eighteenth-century "invention of the uncanny" in a set of comments near the end of his essay on why certain things are *not* uncanny. Restating his central presupposition, that the uncanny is nothing else than "a hidden, familiar thing that has undergone repression and then emerged from it, and that everything that is uncanny fulfils this condition," he notices that the proposition is not convertible, at least in the purely literary or imaginative realm. Fairy tales, he observes, often contain episodes that, strictly speaking, should strike us as uncanny, but generally do not. In the Grimm brothers' story of "The Three Wishes," for example, "the woman is tempted by the savoury smell of a sausage to wish that she might have one too, and immediately it lies on a plate before her. In his annoyance at her forwardness her husband wishes it may hang on her nose. And there it is, dangling from her nose. All this is very vivid but not in the least uncanny." Indeed, he notes,

> Fairy tales quite frankly adopt the animistic standpoint of the omnipotence of thoughts and wishes, and yet I cannot think of any genuine fairy story which has anything uncanny about it. We have heard that it is in the highest degree uncanny when an inanimate object—a picture or a doll—comes to life; nevertheless in Hans Andersen's stories the household utensils, furniture and tin soldiers are alive, yet nothing could well be more remote from the uncanny. And we should hardly call it uncanny when Pygmalion's beautiful statue comes to life. (246)

Figure 1.3. Two views (front and back) of a late eighteenth-century automaton by Jaquet-Droz. Reproduced from J. C. Beaune, "The Classical Age of Automata."

Figure 1.4. Anonymous engraving of eighteenth-century automata on display. From Richard Altick, *The Shows of London* (Cambridge, Mass., 1978).

By their very factitiousness, Freud suggests, fictional events are exempt from the sort of automatic "reality testing" we would apply were they to occur in the course of everyday life. As a result the story teller "has this license among many others"—

> [He] can select his world of representation so that it either coincides with the realities we are familiar with or departs from them in what particulars he pleases. We accept his ruling in every case. In fairy tales, for instance, the world of reality is left behind from the very start, and the animistic system of beliefs is frankly adopted. Wish-fulfilments, secret powers, omnipotence of thoughts, animation of inanimate objects, all the elements so common in fairy stories, can exert no uncanny influence here; for, as we have learnt, that feeling cannot arise unless there is a conflict of judgment as to whether things which have been "surmounted" and are regarded as incredible may not, after all, be possible; and this problem is eliminated from the outset by the postulates of the world of fairy tales. (249–50)

Even in a "less imaginary" setting, writes Freud, the depiction of marvelous events or supernatural entities still may not faze us. "The souls in Dante's *Inferno*, or the supernatural apparitions in *Hamlet, Macbeth* or *Julius Caesar*, may be gloomy and terrible enough," he allows, "but they are no more really uncanny than Homer's jovial world of gods." As long as such beings "remain within their setting of poetic reality" they do not strike us as uncanny: "we adapt our judgement to the imaginary reality imposed on us by the writer" (250).

The situation alters dramatically, however, as soon as the story-teller rejects the possibility of supernatural influence and "pretends to move in the world of common reality." Once a writer "accepts as well all the conditions operating to produce uncanny feelings in real life"—most important, the rationalist assumption that there is a nontranscendental cause for every effect and that natural laws cannot be violated—everything "that would have an uncanny effect in reality," Freud concludes, "has it in his story." Not only that, the writer "can even increase his effect and multiply it far beyond what could happen in reality, by bringing about events which never or very rarely happen in fact."

> He is in a sense betraying us to the superstitiousness which we have ostensibly surmounted; he deceives us by promising to give us the sober truth, and then after all overstepping it. We react to his inventions as we would have reacted to real experiences; by the time we have seen through his trick it is already too late and the author has achieved his object. (250–51)

Thus it is for Freud that literature offers "more opportunities for creating uncanny sensations than are possible in real life"—where, after all, natural causes and the laws of probability appear (most of the time) to hold sway.

Yet what has Freud outlined here if not that momentous "disenchantment" of the creative imagination that a host of historically minded critics—from Georg Lukacs and Ian Watt to Michael McKeon and Tzvetan Todorov—have informed us took place across Western Europe during the late seventeenth and eighteenth centuries? A familiar genealogy is implicit in the transformation delineated here—in Freud's careful rhetorical shift from the anonymous, archaic "story-teller," disseminator of supernatural tales and legends, to Dante and Shakespeare, refining artistically on the marvelous devices of myth and oral tradition, to the unnamed modern writer who, taking the rationalist premise for granted, "pretends to move in the world of common reality" and "deceives" us with his sober impersonation of the truth-teller. Reading Freud's half-rueful description of the latter—of the author-hoaxster whose realistic inventions lull us into a sort of trance of belief, only to shift abruptly into the register of the uncanny—one may think indeed of the pioneering eighteenth-century novelist Daniel Defoe, who in his preface to *Roxana* (1724) affirms that his fiction "is laid in Truth of Fact; and so the Work is not a Story, but a History," then confronts us, in the novel itself, with a tale crowded with uncanny effects. Precisely at the moment that the "marvelous" is dislodged and "sober truth" elevated in its stead, the possibility of the uncanny, Freud says, comes into being. Yet if the hidden literary chronology suggested here is any guide, then the profound cultural shift producing the uncanny in the first place—the "enlightening" turn from magic to reason—seems to have taken place, paradigmatically, during the eighteenth century.

Obviously Freud does not develop the "invention of the uncanny" idea in so many words: it remains, as it were, a sort of specter in his argument—shadowy, at times inchoate, more an intellectual potentiality than an easily recuperable presence. One would want to fill out what he says with much else—with related observations from *The Future of an Illusion* (1927) and *Civilization and Its Discontents* (1930), with supporting material drawn from sociology and the history of religion (Max Weber's celebrated work on "rationalization," and the cognitive discrepancies that result whenever a body of knowledge is systematized, would seem immediately relevant) and, above all, with some of the rich cultural contextualization we find in the work of modern intellectual historians. W. E. H. Lecky was the first great historian of secularization: the first to describe in microscopic detail how a new "spirit of rationalism" gradually rendered the age-old system of European magical belief and folk superstition mostly obsolete between 1650 and 1800. "There is no change in the history of the last 300 years more striking, or suggestive of more curious enquiries," he wrote in the first chapter of his monumental *History of the Rise and Influence of the Spirit of Rationalism in Europe* (1865),

> than that which has taken place in the estimate of the miraculous. Yet, a few centuries ago, there was no solution to which the mind of man turned more readily in every perplexity. A miraculous account was then universally accepted as perfectly credible, probable, and ordinary. There was scarcely a village or church that had not, at some time, been the scene of supernatural interposition. The powers of light and the powers of darkness were regarded as visibly struggling for the mastery. Saintly miracles, supernatural cures, startling judgments, visions, prophecies, and prodigies

of every order, attested the activity of the one, while witchcraft and magic, with all their attendant horrors, were the visible manifestations of the latter.[8]

With the "decline of theological passions" toward "the close of the eighteenth century," argued Lecky, men were finally able "to discuss these matters in a calmer spirit, and when increased knowledge produced more comprehensive views, the historical standing-point was materially altered."[9]

In our own day the historian Keith Thomas has brilliantly supplemented Lecky's central findings. In his magisterial *Religion and the Decline of Magic* (1971) Thomas too sees a profound historical transformation in the years between 1650 and 1800, as long-established magical beliefs—in ghosts, witches, demonic possession, astrology, divination, omens, and the like—were gradually supplanted by new kinds of knowledge. Though he attributes this "abandonment of magic" to changing patterns of social organization rather than the waning of "theological passions," he agrees with Lecky about its dramatic effect on human consciousness. Tracing Thomas's meticulous account of the process by which various occult beliefs were disarmed and discredited—the English Parliament, for example, made accusations of witchcraft and sorcery illegal in 1736—one develops an increasingly refined sense of how supernatural modes of explanation were "surmounted" in actual practice, and how widely, if also somewhat superficially, the rationalist perspective had triumphed across Western Europe by the beginning of the nineteenth century.[10]

But in another sense what Freud *has* said is suggestive enough. His central insight—that it is precisely the historic internalization of rationalist protocols that produces the uncanny—not only sheds light, it seems to me, on the peculiar emotional ambivalence the Enlightenment now evokes in us (it has both freed us and cursed us), it also offers a powerful dialectical model for understanding many of the haunting paradoxes of eighteenth-century literature and culture. In the most literal sense "The 'Uncanny'" has given me a model for my own historical investigations. Despite local differences in range and tone, all the essays here tell a similar Freudian story: the more we seek enlightenment, the more alienating our world becomes; the more we seek to free ourselves, Houdini-like, from the coils of superstition, mystery, and magic, the more tightly, paradoxically, the uncanny holds us in its grip.

My title-piece, "The Female Thermometer"—on the history of the so-called weather-glass—presents the story in what might be considered its emblematic form. Like the microscope, the "ingenious weather-glass" was one of the early triumphs of the New Science: a superb technical accomplishment and a bold manifestation of the urge toward the rationalization of the unseen. (Via the delicate fluctuations of mercury in a calibrated glass tube, thermometers and barometers measured, respectively, minute changes in the temperature and pressure of the air.) Yet precisely on account of its responsiveness—its almost "nervous" sensitivity to the environment—the weather-glass, like the automaton, also subverted the putative distinction between bodies and machines. Contemporary writers and artists were quick to make surreal connections between mercury and blood, glass and flesh. In comico-macabre fantasias such as Joseph Addison's *Spectator* 281 (1712), in which liquid from a dissected "coquette's Pericardium" is used to make a thermometer measuring feminine lasciviousness, or Hogarth's satirical engraving "Credulity, Superstition, and Fanaticism" (1762), in which a gruesome "Spiritual Thermometer" measuring religious fanaticism rises out of the anatomized brain of Wesley, the impinging strangeness of the weather-glass was revealed: its body was a living body, its "blood" our own vital, pulsing fluid.

One might call this a case of the uncanny made flesh: the urge to obtain a new and objective knowledge of the world makes it, at another level, all the more bewildering, inscrutable, and grotesque. Yet I find similar ironies elsewhere. In "'Amy, Who Knew my Disease'" and "Lovelace's Dream," for example—on Daniel Defoe's *Roxana* and Samuel Richardson's *Clarissa*—I find a version of the same dialectic in the early eighteenth-century novel. In *Roxana*, as I noted a moment ago, the supposed authenticity of the narrative conditions—vertiginously— that novel's almost Hitchcockian plunge into terror and uncanny dread. (The book begins with an unnerving parody of a primal scene and ends with the heroine's free-fall descent into alienation and madness.) But the same is true of *Clarissa:* both within the fiction and without, the quest for enlightenment ends in nightmare. The process is epitomized—or so I argue in "Lovelace's Dream"— in the novel's singlemost uncanny episode: when the villainous rake Lovelace attempts to possess the heroine Clarissa (whom he has already raped once) for a second time—by setting in motion a bizarre seduction-plot that comes to him in a "waking dream." The rational underpinnings of Richardson's fictional world seem to fly loose here, as the real and the phantasmatic merge in a dizzying sequence of sexual metamorphoses, doublings, disguises, and psychic exchanges. The reader ends up as helplessly benighted as Clarissa herself—lost in a logic-defying world where things repeatedly become their opposites and the truth remains a simulacrum.

In the three essays that follow, "'Matters Not Fit to be Mentioned': Fielding's *The Female Husband*," "The Culture of Travesty," and "the Carnivalization of Eighteenth-Century English Narrative," I relate the invention of the uncanny to the important eighteenth-century themes of masquerade and sexual impersonation. In the first essay, on Henry Fielding's anonymously published anti-lesbian pamphlet of 1746, *The Female Husband*, I suggest that it was Fielding's eminently "enlightened" approach to the world, his yearning for categorical distinctions and differences (particularly with regard to sex), that produced his curious obsession with Mary Hamilton, a notorious male impersonator who married a succession of women in the 1730s and 1740s. Because Hamilton doesn't "fit" comfortably into Fielding's rationalized cosmology—mediating as she does, oxymoronically, between two sexes—she becomes for him a kind of living embodiment of the uncanny: a dream-figure or totem, whose curious double nature, like that of the hermaphrodite, evokes a host of anxious fantasies and fears. And in "The Culture of Travesty" and "The Carnivalization of Eighteenth-Century English Narrative" —on the history of public masquerades—I suggest that it was the Enlightenment rigidification of conceptual hierarchies and atomized view of personal identity that made the saturnalian "Midnight Masque"—popularized in London in the 1720s and 1730s—so deeply unsettling to contemporaries. With its shocking travesties and mad, Dionysiac couplings, the masquerade represented a kind of "uncanny space" at the heart of eighteenth-century urban culture: a dream-like zone where identities became fluid and cherished distinctions—between self and other, subject and object, real and unreal—temporarily blurred.

In my last four essays, "The Spectralization of the Other in *The Mysteries of Udolpho*," "Phantasmagoria and the Metaphorics of Modern Reverie," "Spectral Politics: Apparition Belief and the Romantic Imagination," and "Contagious Folly: *An Adventure* and Its Skeptics"—all on the subject of ghosts—I connect my Freudian story, finally, with the history of eighteenth-century attitudes toward the spectral. What I argue here, among other things, is that the historic Enlightenment internalization of the spectral—the gradual reinterpretation of ghosts and apparitions as *hallucinations,* or projections of the mind—introduced a new uncanniness into human consciousness itself. The mind became a "world of phantoms" and thinking itself an act of ghost-seeing. Literature allegorized the change: in late eighteenth-century Gothic fiction, as I suggest in the essay on Radcliffe's *Udolpho,* the self-conscious debunking of stories of ghosts and apparitions coincides with an uncanny "spectralization" of human psychology. (While Radcliffe's characters condemn the traditional belief in spirits as "vulgar superstition," they speak obsessively of being haunted—in fancy—by the images of dead or absent loved ones.) In "Spectral Politics" I find similar paradoxes at work in late eighteenth- and early nineteenth-century medical writings on reverie and daydreaming, and in "Phantasmagoria"— on the history of magic lantern shows—in the realm of image-reproducing technology and popular spectacle. Lastly, in "Contagious Folly"—on two Oxford lady dons who claimed to have seen an apparition of Marie Antoinette at the Petit Trianon in 1901—I pursue the issue of spectralization into the twentieth century. Though not, technically speaking, "about" the eighteenth century, the essay nonetheless represents a kind of uncanny return to eighteenth-century problems. For just as the two ladies in question claimed to have traveled back in time (telepathically, they thought) to the era of Marie Antoinette, so their adventure—as would-be skeptics quickly discovered—simply raised in a new and perplexing form the classic Enlightenment conundrum: how to explain away the supernatural without "inventing the uncanny" in its place.

I do not claim, of course, that the "invention of the uncanny" is the only subject in the ten essays that follow. I am aware of various "shadow" themes here,

Figure 1.5. The nightmares of reason. Goya's "El sueño de la razon produce monstruos" [The sleep of reason produces monsters], from *Los Caprichos*, 1799. Courtesy of the British Museum.

surfacing from piece to piece, suggesting other rubrics under which the essays might be grouped. Befitting a work in a series entitled "Ideologies of Desire," I offer a number of speculations on the history of sexuality—especially female sexuality in its various real and imagined forms. The eroticized female body—in life and death, in relation to other bodies, in relation to the phantasmatic—has been a recurrent motif. This is perhaps not so surprising, given my overall psychoanalytic orientation. (No more *unheimlich* place, says Freud, than the female genitals—that "entrance to the former *Heim* [home] of all human beings, to the place where everyone dwelt once upon a time and in the beginning" [245].) Homosexuality has also been a recurring "shadow" theme. But certain formal topics, I find, have also been ongoing preoccupations: how narrative is shaped to produce meaning, the nature of genre and generic transformation, the relationship between emotion and literary form. Others will undoubtedly notice further points of connection between the essays that I am blind to.

But the link with "The 'Uncanny' " is the one I *can* see, the one that helps me find the pattern in a decade's worth of speculation. I hope it will also prove illuminating for the reader—if only in the (admittedly paradoxical) Freudian sense. What sense is that? Let us return to Freud's essay one last time. "[E. T. A. Hoffmann's] *Elixire des Teufels* [The Devil's Elixir] contains a whole mass of themes," writes Freud, "to which one is tempted to ascribe the uncanny effect of the narrative; but it is too obscure and intricate a story to venture upon a summary of it. Towards the end of the book the reader is told the facts, hitherto concealed from him, from which the action springs; with the result, not that he is at last enlightened, but that he falls into a state of complete bewilderment." At best, says Freud, even the canniest interpreter can only seek a partial clarification: "we must content ourselves with selecting those themes of uncanniness which are most prominent, and with seeing whether they too can fairly be traced back to infantile sources" (234).

One might call the paradoxical state that Freud aims at here that of "enlightened bewilderment." The more one understands, the less clear—one finds—things are. But one can nonetheless organize what one doesn't understand. Bewilderment may be modified, or lightened. In the case of the Hoffmann tale, with its mind-boggling surplus of uncanny themes, Freud looks for, and finds, a crucial link between them:

> These themes are all concerned with the phenomenon of the "double," which appears in every shape and and in every degree of development. Thus we have characters who are to be considered identical because they look alike. This relation is accentuated by mental processes leaping from one of these characters to another—by what we should call telepathy—, so that the one possesses knowledge, feeling and experience in common with the other. Or it is marked by the fact that the subject identifies himself with someone else, so that he is in doubt as to which his self is, or substitutes the extraneous self for his own. In other words, there is a doubling, dividing and interchanging of the self. (234)

There is indeed a "bringing to light" here—not least of Freud's own fantasized relationship to his reader. (What else is that "transfer" of mental processes from one person to another—"so that the one possesses knowledge, feeling, and experience in common with the other"—but an idealized image of the act of reading and writing?) In the following essays I have aimed at precisely this sort of light-bringing: at the enlightenment that is really only the apprehension of a greater, more far-flung, bewilderment.

CHAPTER 2

THE FEMALE
THERMOMETER

And what, pray, asks a Shandean voice, is a Female Thermometer? The essayist Bonnell Thornton described this egregious device in *The Connoisseur* no. 85 (11 September 1754). Perfected by an "ingenious friend" Mr. Ayscough, the optician and scientific instrument-maker of Ludgate Hill, the "FEMALE THERMOMETER" Thornton wrote, was an invention for measuring "the exact temperature of a lady's passions." It consisted of a glass tube filled with a chemical mixture derived from distilled extracts of lady's love and maidenhair and "wax of virgin-bees." When acted on by "the circulation of the blood and animal spirits," this liquor would invariably "rise and fall according to the desires and affections of the wearer." Some ludicrous verse explained the principle:

> As the frail dame now love, now reason guides,
> The magic mixture rises or subsides.

The calibrations on the Female Thermometer were as follows:

Abandoned IMPUDENCE.
—Gallantry.
—Loose Behaviour.
—Innocent Freedoms.
—Indiscretions.
Inviolable MODESTY.

Experiments had shown, wrote Thornton, that the rise and fall of the liquor in the tube bore "an exact proportion to the rise and fall of the stays and petticoats." At the playhouse, its actions corresponded to "the lusciousness of the dialogue and the ripening of the plot." At the opera house, "we observed that the Thermometer constantly kept time (if I may say so) with the music and singing," while at the Haymarket masquerade, "the temperature of the climate always proved so exceeding hot, that on the moment of our coming into the room the liquor has boiled up with a surprising effervescence to ABANDONED IMPUDENCE." Transported to Vauxhall and held in proximity to some "raw unpolished females, who came only to eat cheese-cakes and see the cascade and fireworks," the thermometer remained fixed at Modesty, but quickly rose to Loose Behaviour and Gallantry when other subjects advanced toward the dark walks. The Thermometer, Thornton observed, might prove a useful regulator of the passions when carried on one's person; his friend had offered to supply the public. In the meantime female readers were reminded that "the gradations, as marked on our Thermometer, naturally lead to each other; that the transitions from the lowest to the highest are quick and obvious; and that though it is very easy to advance, it is impossible to recede." Men could not use the Thermometer, it turned out, because they failed to register any intermediate states between Modesty and Impudence.

Thornton touted the Female Thermometer as a novelty, but the same cannot be said of his joke, which in 1754 was already more than fifty years old. True, the Ayscough mentioned in his piece was indeed a contemporary maker of meteorological instruments, the designer of an exquisite standing barometer in the rococo style now in the Victoria and Albert Museum, who may or may not have conspired in the facetious project described here.[1] But the idea of the "moralized" thermometer or barometer (both instruments appear interchangeably in early metaphoric contexts) was as old as such instruments themselves. With their curious, seemingly animate capacity to "feel" alterations in the atmosphere, weatherglasses, as they were known in the seventeenth century, lent themselves from the start to metaphoric adaptation. In the hands of eighteenth-century wits, they became registers for measuring fanciful changes of all sorts—fluctuations in sexual desire, physical or emotional excitement, religious enthusiasm and so forth. Similar adaptations survive today, as any contemplation of twentieth-century popular culture and vernacular metaphors will show. Joke thermometers and barometers indicating sexual prowess, susceptibility to liquor, or golfing handicaps are a kitschy staple of shopping mall gift stores, while on a slightly more elevated plane, journalists regularly invoke meteorological instruments like the barometer when speaking of mysterious processes of political, social, or economic change.[2]

We might take this as an early, somewhat vulgar example of the humanization of technology and leave it at that. Devices like the Female Thermometer were perhaps not what Wordsworth had in mind in the preface to *Lyrical Ballads,* when he praised modern poets for "carrying sensation into the midst of the objects of science itself," but they suggest nonetheless a deep tendency in Western culture since the Enlightenment to animate the unfamiliar products of modern scientific technology with human sentiments or capabilities. But the image works the other way too, suggesting that since the late seventeenth century we have increasingly conceptualized human nature, including the human body, with reference to our machines. In this respect the moralized thermometers and barometers of the eighteenth century continue to be revealing, for they altered their nature significantly over the course of the century. I want to outline here what I see as an important transformation in later eighteenth-century consciousness—one bearing both on the theme of sexuality and the modern life of the emotions—but I must do so by sketching first the history of a drollery.

Like the microscope, the weatherglass was one of the great theoretical and technical triumphs of the New Science. Galileo made a primitive air thermoscope in 1612, using long, open glass tubes and cisterns of water; similar experiments were carried out by Sanctorius, the Paduan doctor of medicine, in the same year. In England Francis Bacon wrote instructions for the construction of a simple heat-measuring device in 1620. Essential to the development of the modern thermometer and barometer, however, was the celebrated "Torricellian Experiment" of 1644—Torricelli's discovery of the variability of the pressure of the air. The thermometer, which had previously indiscriminately registered changes in temperature and air pressure, was now refined by sealing the glass tube, allowing for the measurement of heat alone, while its sister instrument, the barometer, was developed separately as a device for measuring changes in the weight of the air.[3]

Weatherglasses were much improved in the second half of the seventeenth century, largely as a result of experiments carried out by members of the Royal Society. Robert Boyle and Robert Hooke made important modifications in the design of the stick barometer (subsequently the most common form of barometer in the eighteenth century); Samuel Moreland invented the angled glass barometer in 1670. Mercury gradually replaced alcohol spirits as the customary fluid in the glass columns of both thermometers and barometers. Fixing a uniform scale posed a difficult technical problem for early thermometer makers, and as many as seventy different heat-calibrating scales were used in the late seventeenth century. The problem was more or less settled, however, by the introduction across Europe of the Fahrenheit scale in 1717, and later by the addition of the Réaumur and Celsius scales in the 1730s and 1740s. Barometer markings were simpler, being calibrated in inches, though the descriptive terms on the register plate ("Settled Fair," "Much Rain," etc.), introduced by John Smith in 1688, were never used very consistently from instrument to instrument.[4]

These refinements dramatically increased the availability and portability of

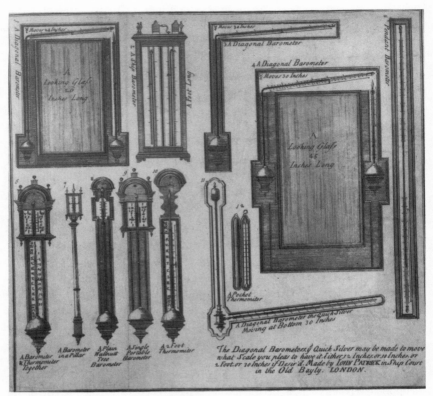

Figure 2.1. John Patrick, advertisement for barometers and thermometers, c. 1710.
Courtesy of the British Museum.

such instruments, and a vogue for weatherglasses developed quickly among the
wealthy, especially in England, where many of the best instruments were made.
Barometers and thermometers were first sold for domestic use in London in the
1670s and 1680s.[5] By the first two decades of the eighteenth century, such devices
(frequently combined in a single cabinet) had become an essential part of up-
wardly mobile middle-class decor. "Most houses of figure and distinction" had
one, wrote Edward Saul in 1735.[6] A stick barometer can be seen on the wall of the
fashionable drawing room depicted in Marcellus Laroon's painting *A Musical
Conversation* (1760). Contemporary domestic instruments were beautifully designed and crafted, and numerous examples survive. Case ornaments included
floral decoration and marquetry, scroll pediments, engraved register plates, mirrors, and sometimes even allegorical figures—Mercury, or the Sun and Moon—
surmounting the whole, as can be seen in John Patrick's advertisement from 1710
(Fig. 2.1).[7]

From the start thermometers and barometers exerted a powerful imaginative appeal. This charisma derived in part from the seemingly magical nature of mercury, that strange semiliquid medium that in the eighteenth century still preserved (after Pliny's *argentum vivum*) the evocative name of quicksilver, or "living silver." In an age of machines and automata we have become accustomed to the sight of inorganic things moving by themselves, but we must try to imagine the curious fascination mercury held in earlier centuries for people whose ordinary definition of life—like that of young children—was often simply anything having the power of independent movement. Mercury, the celebrated volatile principle of the alchemists, lent the weatherglass some of its own elemental physical mystery, as well as ancient symbolic associations with magic, change, and metamorphosis.[8]

Mercury also established a connection with the theme of human temperament. The "mercurial personality" was well known in the Renaissance and the eighteenth century, if not always esteemed as an ideal psychological type. Women were usually considered the primary embodiments of mercuriality—witnessed by their purported fickleness, emotional variability, and susceptibility to hysteria.[9] The delicate, ever-changing movements of the weatherglass suggested its seemingly feminine sensitivity and unpredictability. The language of late seventeenth- and eighteenth-century meteorology occasionally echoed the new and increasingly feminized language of sensibility emerging in popular fiction and journalism of the time. Hooke, for example, describing the device of the fixed zero temperature scale in his *Micrographia* (1665), wrote of bringing the sealed thermometer to greater "tenderness" by such a means, and the words *tender, sensible, sensitive,* and *nice* are used frequently in the papers of the Royal Society to refer to the accuracy of weatherglasses.[10] Gustavus Parker's *Account of a Portable Barometer* (1710) sometimes reads like one of Eliza Haywood's popular romances, with its torrid account of the "Terrene Emotions," "Effervescencies," "Subterraneous or Submarine Eruptions," "Copious Effluviums," and subtle "Protrusions of Exotick Force" one might detect with the aid of the barometer.[11]

The idea of a link between the movements of the weatherglass and the vagaries of human feeling developed quickly in the early eighteenth century and was reinforced by a host of scientific and pseudoscientific beliefs. On the most abstract level, traditional theories describing the effect of weather on human nature provided a philosophical basis for connecting human emotions with the state of the air. Hippocrates had spoken of the effect of climate on the mind and body, and the Greek belief in an interaction between the "ambient air," or "ethereal medium," and the so-called animal spirits—never completely disappeared. (The etymological relationship between temperature and temperament preserves the link.) Leo Spitzer has documented the history of the idea in his well-known essay on milieu and ambiance, and Arden Reed has traced its literary treatments in his fascinating book *Romantic Weather* (1983).[12] Certainly the early barometer makers, like Montesquieu after them, were convinced that atmospheric changes produced physical and emotional changes. In his *Horological Disquisitions,* containing "Rules for the Ordering and Use Both of the Quick-Silver and Spirit Weather-Glasses" (1694), John Smith asserted that on account of the increased moisture in the air, "the lower the *Quicksilver* descends, the more listless and out of order Men's Bodies are, because the Air is then full of that which is disagreeable to the Nature of Man, who was not made to live in a Watry Element." "Disorder and Melancholy" ensue.[13] Similar notions persisted a hundred years later: in *A Short Dissertation on the Barometer, Thermometer, and Other Meteorological Instruments* (1790), George Adams wrote that a falling barometer produced "depression and relaxation," as well as putrid sore throats and impoverishment of the blood. In contrast, rising air pressure strengthened the fibers, increased vital heat, and "promoted secretions."[14]

But even more influential, perhaps, in fixing the connection with human psychology was the purported resemblance between the fluctuations of the mercury in the weatherglass and the recently discovered movements of the blood in the bloodstream. A visual association had been made since the mid-seventeenth century. "His colour . . . sanke downe," declaimed a character in Sir John Suckling's *Brennoralt* (1646), "as water in a weather-glasse/Prest by a warme hand."[15] Early makers of weatherglasses unconsciously registered the analogy: Robert Hooke, in an effort to make the spirits in his first thermometer easily visible, tinted them "the lovely colour of cocheneel." The liquid in other instruments was sometimes colored with kermes, dragon's blood, or red wine spirits.[16] By the time of Joseph Addison and William Hogarth, the association between the quicksilver in the glass tube and the blood in blood vessels was a satiric commonplace. Once the phenomenological connection had been made, it was easy to draw out the comparison by linking the various emotional conditions traditionally associated with circulatory fluctuations—erotic passion, embarrassment, languor, and so forth—with the gradations on the new instruments. In the joke thermometers of the eighteenth century, for example, the rapid shooting up of the mercury was often treated as a symptom analogous to the blush or the racing pulse in the popular science of emotions—a sign of fevered spirits, sexual availability, or otherwise heightened sensibilities. In such pseudo-organic fancies, the weatherglass came, so to speak, alive.

Not surprisingly, writers and artists soon adopted the weatherglass as a figure for sexual desire. Indeed, it was not far to go from the scientific treatises, with their fantastical imagery of tender instruments, moisture, heat, blood, and excited animal spirits, to symbolic conceptions of a sometimes comically suggestive nature. Female sexuality—and its supposed irrationalism—was a special focus in many of these whimsical flights. In Restoration and early eighteenth-century writing, for example, images of barometers and thermometers typically appear in highly rhetorical evocations of feminine desire, or in passages describing the mercurial love-moods brought on by the presence of women. The spirit of metaphysical wit lingers on in these formulations. In Dryden's *Conquest of Granada* (1672), the passionate and fickle Lyndaraxa, hesitating between two suitors, exclaims:

> O! could I read the dark decrees of fate,
> That I might once know whom to love or hate,
> For I myself scarce my own thoughts can guess,
> So much I find them varied by success.
> As in some weather-glass, my love I hold;
> Which falls or rises with the heat or cold.[17]

In Susannah Centlivre's *The Gamester* (1723), Hector, hearing that his master, the gamester Valere, has fallen in love, remarks: "Ah! that's an ill sign. Now do *I* know he has not a Penny in his Pocket. Ah, Sir, your Fob, like a Baromiter, shews the Temper of your Heart, as that does the Weather."[18]

Addison developed the feminine association in two rather grotesque caprices in *The Spectator* of 1712. Two years earlier Swift had observed in *A Discourse Concerning the Mechanical Operation of the Spirit* that "profounder Chymists inform us, that the Strongest *Spirits* may be extracted from *Human Flesh.*"[19] In *The Spectator* nos. 275 and 281 (15 and 22 January 1712), Addison elaborated on Swift's satiric premise by describing the imaginary dissections of a *"Beau's Head"* and a *"Coquet's Heart"* by a group of virtuosos. The new imagery appears in embryonic form in the first essay, when an operator dissecting the head of a deceased beau discovers—along with *"Antrums* or Cavities" stuffed with "invisible Billet-doux, Love-Letters, pricked Dances, and other Trumpery," bladders containing "Froth," and a pineal gland smelling of "Orange-Flower Water"—certain pipes and tubes in his subject's brain "filled with a Kind of mercurial Substance, which he looked upon to be true Quick Silver." The presence of this volatile liquid betokens the beau's compromised masculinity: his brain is not like that of "another Man" but only "Something like it."[20]

In *The Spectator* no. 281, a second "visionary dissection" produces a related discovery. The opening of a coquette's "Pericardium" discloses "a thin reddish Liquor, supposed to be bred from the Vapours which exhale out of the Heart, and being stopt here, are condensed into this watry Substance." This liquor is found to have in it "all the Qualities of that Spirit which is made Use of in the thermometer, to shew the Change of Weather." One of the virtuosos describes making a weatherglass using this substance, which, when tried, did not show changes in the atmosphere but registered instead "the qualities of those Persons who entered the Room where it stood." The instrument proves to be as man-crazy as the woman who provides its vital fluid. It danced up, recalls its inventor, at the approach of "a Plume of Feathers, an embroidered Coat, or a Pair of fringed Gloves" and dropped abruptly in the presence of an "ill-shaped Perriwig, a clumsy pair of Shooes, or an unfashionable coat." Likewise, it rose flirtatiously when he giggled and fell when he looked serious.

Figure 2.2. William Hogarth, *Masquerade Ticket*, 1727. Courtesy of the British Museum.

In his satiric *Masquerade Ticket* of 1727 (Fig. 2.2), Hogarth transformed Addison's licentious weatherglass into a visual motif. Here, the orgiastic Haymarket masquerade room, ruled over by Venus and Priapus, is prominently decorated with two barometerlike instruments identified as "Lecherometers." These devices, calibrated "Expectation—Hope—Hot desire—Extreem Hot—Moist—Sudden Cold" and "Cool—Warm—Dry—Changeable—Hot—moist Fixt," register "ye Companys Inclinations as they approach em." The image perfectly summarized the masquerade's reputation as a modern Bacchanal. Assisted by a diminutive Cupid with a bow and arrow, Venus watches the Lecherometers slyly, while the lewd crowd of masqueraders disports beneath her.

Hogarth revived the sexual weatherglass in two subsequent plates, the unpublished *Enthusiasm Delineated* (c. 1761) and *Credulity, Superstition, and Fanaticism,* the engraving derived from it in 1762 (Fig. 2.3). In both pictures large instruments to the right of a ranting Methodist preacher and his congregation ostensibly measure fluctuations in religious enthusiasm. The crowd's spiritual elevation is shown to be indistinguishable, however, from more primitive forms of excitement. In the 1762 engraving, the calibrations "Love Heat," "LUST," and "EXTACY" are placed on a level with the lower bodies of the lubricious couple

Figure 2.3. William Hogarth, *Credulity, Superstition, and Fanaticism,* 1762. Courtesy of the British Museum.

immediately to the left of the larger instrument, while other figures writhe in indecent postures nearby. Under the influence of the throbbing scene, the mercurial fluid appears to be rising rapidly from "Luke Warm" to "Love Heat." Hogarth's meteorological wit was much imitated: the many moralized barometers and thermometers that appeared in religious tracts and pamphlets of the late eighteenth and early nineteenth centuries are adaptions of the Hogarthian emblem. It is worth noting that when David Hockney reworked Hogarth's imagery in the stage designs for Stravinsky's *The Rake's Progress,* he rediscovered the Lecherometer, placing two in the bedroom of Mother Goose's brothel (Fig. 2.4).[21]

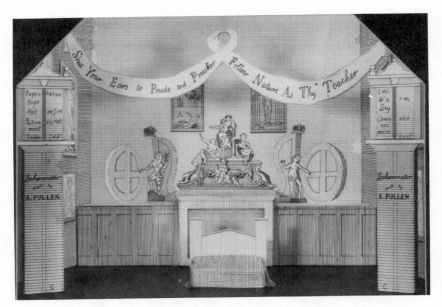

Figure 2.4. David Hockney, "Mother Goose's Brothel," from designs for Stravinsky's *The Rake's Progress*. Photo © David Hockney 1975; used by permission.

Granted, the weatherglass image was not invariably connected with carnal themes in the first half of the eighteenth century. Steele, in *The Tatler* no. 214 (22 August 1710), described a "Political Barometer" that had measured changes in English political "weather" since the time of Queen Elizabeth, and Horace Walpole used a similar metaphor in a letter in 1742 describing his uncle as a "political weather-glass" whose "quicksilver rises or falls with the least variation of parliamentary weather."[22] In John Arbuthnot's *The History of John Bull* (1712), the blustery spirits of the prototypical English citizen rise and fall "with the Weatherglass."[23] "Interest," wrote Hume in his *Political Discourses* (1752), "is the true barometer of the State."[24] An "Eccelesiastical Thermometer," again in *The Tatler* (11 September 1710), measured "heat" in religion, and this undoubtedly influenced the spirit gauges in Hogarth's *Enthusiasm Delineated* and *Credulity, Superstition, and Fanaticism*. Other imaginary instruments of the time registered degrees of literary merit and philosophic genius.[25]

It is safe to say, however, that at least for the first part of the century the instrument's popular connotations were feminine and amorous. Thornton's Female Thermometer, gaily registering impudence in 1754, typified a host of figures. The impulse behind such devices—in England at least—was almost always satirical. However whimsically, the moralized weatherglass played a part in the eighteenth-century male satirist's familiar assault on women's purported incorrigibility, licentiousness, and emotional instability. Men—as we see in the case of

Addison's beau, or the male Methodists in Hogarth's plates—were sometimes included in these misogynist fantasias, but only when they were also obviously effeminate, or had somehow appropriated the excitability and moral irresponsibility stereotypically associated with the opposite sex.

Images of the feminized weatherglass carried through into the second part of the century. In Richardson's *Clarissa* (1747–48), the figure is associated with the heroine's volatile friend, the gifted but capricious Anna Howe. Chastened by sorrow after Clarissa's death, Anna condemns herself for treating a faithful lover imperiously: "When the weather-glass of my pride got up again," she says of a conversation with Hickman, "I found I had gone too far to recede."[26] In France, Diderot used the image in his remarkable philosophical essay, *Sur les femmes* (1772). Here, a striking description of women's sexual hysteria, hypersensitivity, and primitive susceptibility to "émotions epidémiques" resolves into a plea for a proper emblem of their natures: "Il ne suffit pas de parler des femmes, et d'en parler bien, Monsieur Thomas, faites encore que j'en voie. Suspendez-les sous mes yeux, comme autant de thermomètres des moindres vicissitudes des moeurs et des usages" (It is not enough to speak of women, and to speak of them well, Monsieur Thomas, make me see them again. Suspend them before my eyes, like so many thermometers showing the smallest ups and downs in morals and customs).[27] In Mary Wollstonecraft's equally memorable *Vindication of the Rights of Woman* (1792), the female thermometer recedes from actual view yet nonetheless informs several important passages. "As a sex," wrote Wollstonecraft, "men have better tempers than women, because they are occupied by pursuits that interest the head as well as the heart; and the steadiness of the head gives a healthy temperature to the heart."[28] It reappears in classic form, however, in a late eighteenth-century painting by Michel Garnier called *La Douce résistance* (1793), in which a woman on the verge of yielding to her lover briefly struggles against him, while a barometer directly overhead hovers at "Variable" (Fig. 2.5).

None of which is to say that the sexual weatherglass is an entirely straightforward symbolic object. There is a basic ambiguity, for instance, in the very idea of a "female thermometer." Does the adjective in the phrase refer to the sex of the device? Or does it simply point to a relationship—i.e., that the thermometer, though not itself female, responds to a female presence? If it is possible to be precise about something so phantasmagorical, what can we say is the gender of such an instrument?

Certainly in a number of cases the weatherglass is indisputably a *femme-machine*. Addison's description of the thermometer made out of fluids in a coquette's heart is the obvious example: the instrument here is literally constructed from a woman's body. The fluctuations of the quicksilver match the sexual responses of the coquette exactly—for they *are* her sexual responses. Through a kind of macabre synecdoche, satiric objects and symbolic objects fuse in a single living thermometer-woman. Likewise, in other uses of the image—Lyndaraxa's

Figure 2.5. Michel Garnier, *La Douce résistance,* 1793. Courtesy of Stair-Sainty Matthiesen Gallery, New York.

barometrical passion, Anna Howe's rising and falling pride—the weatherglass is the woman. Its life is her life, and the range of "emotions" it displays simply a meteorological code for her desire.

But at other times the fantasy instruments of the eighteenth century seem to function in a way precluding any intrinsic femininity. Many contemporary weatherglass jokes parody the ancient idea of the aura—the belief in the power of certain objects to work on other objects through the medium of the atmosphere. That women's bodies, like celestial bodies, sometimes had an aura, an ethereal emanation or quasi-meteorological ambiance that could act on those who came into their presence, was a concept well known to the medieval poets and theologians. The familiar halo of the Virgin Mary, a light emanation, was one version of the idea. Leo Spitzer has found similar images of the aura in medieval love mysticism, when poets like Dante and Petrarch describe their lovers' sighs as emanations from a perfect soul. In Neoplatonic philosophy, the woman's *aria,* or atmosphere, was conceived of as a manifestation of her internal spiritual climate. In Goethe's *Faust,* there is a passage in which Mephistopheles calculates the effect on Faust of the sensuous air (*Dunstkreis*) surrounding Gretchen's bed.[29]

Thus when Thornton wrote that the Female Thermometer responded when it came "within the atmosphere of a lady's affections"—and was acted on by them in the same way as "the spirits are by the impulse of the air in the common Thermometer"—he was well aware of the traditional physics of femininity. Like a Newtonian gravitational force, the female body acted across the ether, attracting and elongating the mercurial fluids in the weatherglass tube.

In such situations, however, the "dear instrument" (to borrow John Cleland's language) was not, obviously, female itself. On the contrary, its tumidity in the presence of a female atmosphere was distinctly virile. The point was not lost on the eighteenth century. Descriptions of early experiments with the weatherglass had invited obscene imaginings: "The warm hand laid upon the Head of the Glass," wrote the author of a work on "Natural Motions" from 1677, "will depress the Water, by expanding the included Air two or three inches, but the Hand being removed, the Air will contract it self to its former Staple."[30] Likewise, experiments with medical thermometers reinforced the symbolic connection with the *membrum virile*.[31] Thornton made the nature of the Female Thermometer clinically obvious when he described it rising in response to the lifting of a woman's "stays and petticoats." But it was Hogarth who exploited the weatherglass's suggestive potential most fully. The larger thermometer in *Credulity, Superstition, and Fanaticism* is as phallic in design as it is in sensibility. To be sure, the object has a dreamlike kind of overdetermination: the scrotumlike brain of Wesley from which the mercurial fluid rises is also a demented face, and the drummer at the very top has associations with the Tedworth Drummer as well as with masturbation and copulation. The little apparition of the fortuitously named Cock Lane Ghost, hovering inside the pulsing head of the instrument, completes the Freudian overlay of verbal and visual scandal.[32]

Like Pope's Sporus, the weatherglass was thus something of a sexual *ambigue*. The point is worth remarking because it suggests similar ambiguities at a deeper level of conceptualization. Indeed, one might argue that, historically speaking, the maleness of the Female Thermometer was always there, just under the surface, waiting to be discovered. Despite the eighteenth century's satiric obsession with women and their sexuality, the nature of the image was ambiguous—as was, ultimately, the traditional metaphysics of gender on which its comedy relied. In the second half of the century, this ambiguity became increasingly pronounced. It testified to changing conceptions of masculinity and femininity, and, by degrees, to a profound alteration in the Western conception of human nature itself.

The developments of the later eighteenth century were twofold. While some older-style metaphors persisted, as in Garnier's painting, the weatherglass gradually ceased to be primarily a ribald or misogynist image. At the same time, not surprisingly, it came more and more to be associated with the psychic life of men. In historical terms, the new link pointed to a growing feminization of the male subject in the second half of the century. Terry Eagleton has spoken of the "feminization of discourse" in the late eighteenth-century novel; we might speak of the feminization of human nature itself. The Western image of masculinity has altered strikingly over the past two centuries, gradually absorbing many once exclusively feminine modes of experience.[33] Characteristics once seen as belonging only to women—moodiness, heightened sensitivity, susceptibility to hysteria, and so on—have come increasingly to be perceived as belonging to both sexes. In the eighteenth century, the cult of sensibility was an early sign of the weakening of sexual polarities; popular psychological and medical theories contributed further to the symbolic alignment of male and female.[34] Modern civilization has inherited the historic blurring of boundaries. In a remarkable incorporation of otherness, the inner life of twentieth-century man has increasingly come to resemble the emotionally fluid life of woman in earlier periods.

Beginning in the 1760s and 1770s, the weatherglass bore witness to this dramatic reinterpretation of the male psyche. Samuel Johnson's *Idler* no. 33 (2 December 1758) anticipates the new paradigm. Here Johnson presents the purported journal of a Cambridge don and "Genuine Idler." Over the course of three days the don records various meals he has eaten, a brief visit to his wine cellar (with a memorandum to move the port), an attack of gout, a victory at backgammon. Much given to hypochondria, he keeps track of the weather, compulsively consulting his barometer:

> Monday, Nine o'clock. Turned off my bed-maker for waking me at eight. Weather rainy. Consulted my weather-glass. No hopes of a ride before dinner.
>
> Ditto, Twelve, Mended a pen. Looked at my weather-glass again. Quicksilver very low. Shaved. Barber's hand shakes.
>
> Tuesday, Nine. Rose squeamish. A fine morning. Weather-glass very high.[35]

The Richardsonian parody is obvious: Johnson's idling don lives in what might be considered "female time." His days are divided into the same minute temporal segments that Richardson first used in *Pamela* to represent the richly textured and constantly changing psychic life of his heroine. What is missing, of course, is any real Richardsonian interiority: squeamishness hardly counts for much emotional depth. Yet this register of seeming banalities, with its hint of Baudelairean ennui, is also the preliminary accounting of a new male type—of the man who must abide in the nonheroic realms of bourgeois existence, and whose internal "weather," so to speak, obsessively charted, has become his sole remaining source of interest. Acute self-consciousness, symbolized by barometrical fixation, displaces the world of external incident. By invoking the familiar emblem of volatile femininity, Johnson projected the traditional mercuriality of women onto his antihero. The result, though undeveloped in any philosophical sense, was a novel psychic entity: the male hysteric.[36]

That Johnson was critical of such self-absorption is clear: in *Idler* no. 11 (24 June 1758) he had already condemned a sensitivity to weather—inner or outer—

as "the cowardice of idleness, and idolatry of folly." Only men give up to "fanciful credulity," he wrote, relate their private experiences to meteorological forces and seek to "regulate their lives by the barometer." Only twenty years later, however, another writer took up the same motif in a very different spirit:

> I shall perform upon myself the sort of operation that physicists conduct upon the air in order to discover its daily fluctuations. I shall take the barometer readings of my soul and by doing this accurately and repeatedly I could perhaps obtain results as reliable as theirs. However, my aim is not so ambitious. I shall content myself with keeping a record of my readings without trying to reduce them to a system.[37]

The striking voice here is Rousseau's, announcing the revolutionary auto-biographical project of *Reveries of a Solitary Walker* (1776–78). Rousseau's audacity lay in the fact that he internalized the voyeuristic metaphor of early eighteenth-century satire and transformed its nature. No longer do we have a male virtuoso taking readings on pathological female subjects: Rousseau makes himself both the observer and the observed—masculine "physicien" and mood-driven woman. This newly self-regarding, ambisexual being might justly be called a female man. He is a network of sensitivities: a vibrant if humorless conduit for deep sensations. The soul-barometer is his revolutionary emblem—the palpable sign of Rousseauean autoeroticism—but its history has been erased. Indeed, the cooptation of stereotypically feminine emotions is so subtle that it passes by almost unnoticed: we have heard a great deal about Rousseau's invention of a new "human" psychology. His imagery, however, shows a far more complex cultural process at work—the historic incorporation of the feminine, in all its volatility and pathos, into the inner life of man.

With Rousseau, of course, the floodgates of Romanticism open. And predictably, images of male mercuriality proliferated as the new movement swept through England and Europe. By 1820 the weatherglass motif had been seemingly universalized—which is to say it had become part of a new metaphorics of explicitly masculine feeling.

Keats's memorable "Pleasure Thermometer," mentioned in a letter to John Taylor, is undoubtedly the most famous—and ineffable—of such transvaluations. Describing the composition of these lines from *Endymion* (1818),

> Wherein lies Happiness? In that which becks
> Our ready Minds to fellowship divine;
> A fellowship with essence, till we shine
> Full alchymized and free of space. (1.777–80)

Keats describes seeing a wonderful vision of "the gradations of Happiness even like a kind of Pleasure Thermometer."[38] The poet may or may not have encountered the well-known plate of the "Spiritual Barometer," with its "Scale of the progress of SIN and GRACE," which first appeared in the *Evangelical Magazine* in De-

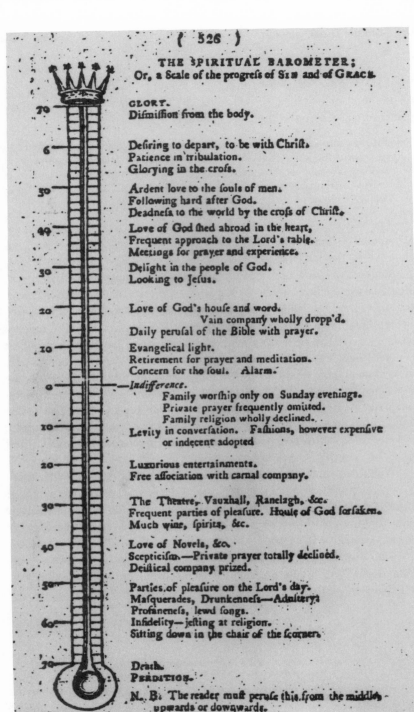

(526)

THE SPIRITUAL BAROMETER;
Or, a Scale of the progress of Sin and of Grace.

GLORY.
Dismission from the body.

Desiring to depart, to be with Christ.
Patience in tribulation.
Glorying in the cross.

Ardent love to the souls of men.
Following hard after God.
Deadness to the world by the cross of Christ.

Love of God shed abroad in the heart.
Frequent approach to the Lord's table.
Meetings for prayer and experience.

Delight in the people of God.
Looking to Jesus.

Love of God's house and word.
                    Vain company wholly dropp'd.
Daily perusal of the Bible with prayer.

Evangelical light.
Retirement for prayer and meditation.
Concern for the soul.   Alarm.

—Indifference.
        Family worship only on Sunday evenings.
        Private prayer frequently omitted.
        Family religion wholly declined.
Levity in conversation.   Fashions, however expensive
        or indecent adopted

Luxurious entertainments.
Free association with carnal company.

The Theatre, Vauxhall, Ranelagh, &c.
Frequent parties of pleasure. House of God forsaken.
Much wine, spirits, &c.

Love of Novels, &c.
Scepticism.—Private prayer totally declined.
Deistical company prized.

Parties of pleasure on the Lord's day.
Masquerades, Drunkenness—Adultery;
Profaneness, lewd songs.
Infidelity—jesting at religion.
Sitting down in the chair of the scorner.

Death.
PERDITION.

N. B. The reader must peruse this from the middle
    upwards or downwards.

Figure 2.6. "The Spiritual Barometer." From *The Evangelical Magazine*, December
1800. Courtesy of the British Museum.

36

cember 1800 (Fig. 2.6) and which charted the soul's redemptive spiritual movement toward "GLORY" and "Dismission from the body." His own image is similarly euphoric, though far more heterodox. The Pleasure Thermometer preserves a comic tinge of eighteenth-century eroticism, despite the thrust toward transcendental forms of bliss. But Keats also divorced the image from conventional moral and misogynistic judgments—implying instead a marvelous continuum between the sexes, as well as between earthly and mystical pleasures. Like Rousseau, he embraced the feminine device, transforming the eighteenth-century satiric motif into an image of ecstatic union with the muse.

But other writers also adopted the weatherglass as an emblem of new-felt masculine sensitivity. "Taste," wrote Byron in *Don Juan* (1824), "is the thermometer/By whose degrees all characters are classed" (16.48). In "A Rainy Day" (1820), Leigh Hunt spoke of the volatile actor Tate Wilkinson as an "old barometer." This "mimetic antique" had ever been a creature of moods, having cultivated "much hypochondriacal knowledge in his time, and been a sad fellow in a merry sense before he took to it in its melancholy one."[39] Even the satiric idea of the mercury in the female bloodstream received a new translation. "Thou hast quicksilver in the veins of thee to a certainty," a character in Scott's *The Abbot* (1820) says of the impetuous hero Roland Graeme.[40] Complaining of his "mismanaged sensibility" in *Biographia Literaria* (1817), Coleridge described himself as "delving in the unwholesome quicksilver mines of metaphysic depths"—as though searching for the elusive element with which to constitute Rousseau's weatherglass of the soul.[41]

One of the most subtle Romantic appropriations of the image occurs in E. T. A. Hoffmann's "The Sandman" (1816–17). There, Coppola, the evil figure who awakens in the hapless hero Nathanael those terrifying childhood memories that ultimately drive him to his death, first appears in the story as a horrible peddler selling barometers and thermometers. Nathanael identifies the "repulsive vendor of weather glasses" with the hated lawyer Coppelius, a mysterious old friend of his family, whom he had imagined in childhood to be the frightful monster known as the Sandman, who tore out children's eyes. During Coppola's strange visit, Nathanael is thrown into a panic of confused recollection. He refuses several weatherglasses, then buys a perspective glass simply to get rid of the man. Still later, haunted by the Coppola/Coppelius/Sandman image, he gradually descends into suicidal madness.

In Hoffmann, the weatherglass is associated for the first time with full-blown male neurasthenia. In a famous analysis of "The Sandman," Freud connected the character of Coppola with the uncanny—the unsettling emotional sensations prompted by the return of the repressed.[42] Coppola's weatherglasses may be taken indeed as a metonymic sign of those wild mood-swings and disturbing sensitivities he provokes in his victim. Nathanael's fits and horrors, his demented poetry and uncontrolled fantasy life, bespeak the new masculine interiority—characterized by violent emotional flux and those quasi-psychotic "vapours" associated in earlier periods with hysterical women. The process of feminization begun in Johnson and Rousseau is completed.[43] Interestingly enough, Hoffmann himself seems to have shared something of his hero's hypersensitivity. As Baudelaire wrote of *Kreisleriana*, "Hoffmann avait dressé un singulier baromètre psychologique destiné à lui représenter les différantes températures et les phenomènes atmosphériques de son âme" (Hoffmann had erected a curious psychological barometer designed to display for him the differing temperatures and atmospheric phenomena of his soul).[44]

Similar images appear off and on throughout the nineteenth century. We might call these "bisexual" metaphors, but only if we keep in mind the historical process that they encapsulate: the masculinization of a once primarily feminine motif. Indeed, as soon as the female paradigm was appropriated, women themselves figured less and less explicitly in the schemes of symbolic meteorology. A device like John Coakley Lettsom's "moral and physical thermometer," for example, in which a series of complex overlapping scales documented the physiological and spiritual effects of alcohol, might seem on the surface to apply to both sexes, but it unmistakably emphasized male pathology. The drinking of "Whisky in the Morning," for example, was correlated with perjury, burglary, and murder on the scale of "Vices"; epilepsy, melancholy, and madness on that of "Disease"; and jail, whipping, and "The Hulks" on that of "Punishments"—a distinctly masculine pattern of moral turpitude (Fig. 2.7).[45] Likewise, in Sir David Wilkie's painting *The Reading of the Will* (c. 1819), the barometer hanging on the wall over a crowd of will disputants has lost its feminine connections, monitoring instead the economic psychodramas of nineteenth-century patriarchy.

Several tendencies converge in Flaubert, who must be considered the great virtuoso of barometer and thermometer imagery in the nineteenth century.[46] To be sure, unlike some of his contemporaries Flaubert possessed a self-conscious, even sly awareness of the weatherglass's older association with female sexuality. In *Madame Bovary* (1857), when Emma meets Rodolphe in her drawing room just before their fateful ride in the woods, the familiar object is there, subtly responding to the scene: "She was alone in the fading light. The short muslin curtains along the windowpanes intensified the twilight; the gilt on the barometer, touched by a ray of sunlight, was reflecting sparks onto the mirror hanging between the fretted coral." The same barometer appears later in another crucial scene, when Emma is furious with Charles for his botched operation on Hippolyte's foot: " 'Enough!' she cried with a terrible look. And she ran from the room, closing the door so violently that the barometer fell from the wall and crashed into pieces on the floor."[47]

But Flaubert was also aware that the imagery of emotional flux had attached itself to men as well. We need not appeal to Flaubert's own neurasthenia, or his famous statement, "Madame Bovary, c'est moi," to convey his personal sense of

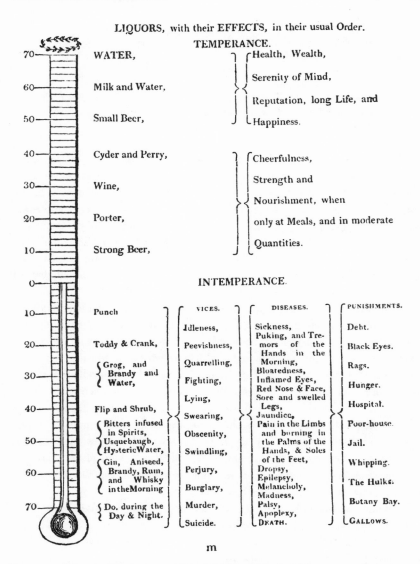

Figure 2.7. John Coakley Lettsom, "The Moral and Physical Thermometer" (early nineteenth century). Courtesy of the Wellcome Institute Library, London.

modern man's unstable inner weather. In *Bouvard and Pécuchet* (1881) he used the weatherglass very obviously to suggest the novel self-absorption of the bourgeois fantasist. Early in the book his two ridiculous heroes purchase for their new house "a thermometer and even a barometer, 'Gay-Llussac type' for experiments in physics, should the fancy take them." Later, in their hypochondriacal phase, they obsessively monitor each other's body heat in the bathtub with a thermometer.

"Move your limbs about," said Pécuchet.

He moved them, with no effect on the thermometer.

"It's decidedly cold."

"I'm not warm either," replied Pécuchet, shivering himself, "but shake your pelvic members, shake them!"

Bouvard opened his thighs, twisted his flanks, wobbled his stomach, puffed like a grampus, then looked at the thermometer, which was still falling:

"I don't understand it at all! I am moving though!"[48]

Reveling in hysterical symptoms, Bouvard and Pécuchet are like two halves of the same disordered consciousness, a consciousness in endless neurotic conversation with itself. Flaubert wished to parody, of course, the pitiful hobby-life of the bourgeoisie, with its collections of scientific gadgets, home experiments, and encyclopedias of learning. But we sense too his identification with the new self-consciousness. In Flaubert, Rousseau's soul-barometer has become banal, consumerized, an object available to all. Yet its fluctuations remain powerfully interesting nonetheless, for they have come to register the ineluctable psychopathology of everyday life.

I will not dwell long on the twentieth century. Freud, not surprisingly, invokes the meteorological motif, updating it slightly to reflect technological developments. In the case history *Dora* (1905), he describes how repressed ideas in the unconscious contend with conscious thoughts like "the two needles of an astatic galvanometer."[49] It makes sense that Freud should recreate the old mechanical image, for he more than any other modern thinker embraced the nineteenth-century discovery that profound emotional fluctuations could characterize the male as well as the female psyche. Freud followed the lead of the imaginative writers by universalizing hysteria and attributing neurotic symptoms to both sexes equally.[50] Indeed, the Freudian psyche itself might be described as a kind of androgynous, universal weatherglass: continually in flux, polymorphous in response, ever dominated by irrational moods and desires.

Generally speaking, however, the weatherglass metaphor has become a cliché in the twentieth century. True, it has occasionally prompted inspired parody and revision: Man Ray's dadaist photograph of the poet Mina Loy wearing a thermometer earring (1920) reworked eighteenth-century comic themes in an ironic modern mode (Fig. 2.8). A famous exchange in Virginia Woolf's *To the Lighthouse* (1927) seems to play subliminally on the old imagery of femininity:

There wasn't the slightest possible chance that they could go to the Lighthouse tomorrow, Mr. Ramsay snapped out irascibly.

How did he know? she asked. The wind often changed.

The extraordinary irrationality of her remark, the folly of women's minds enraged him. He had ridden through the valley of death, been shattered and shivered; and now, she flew in the face of facts, made his children hope what was utterly out of the question, in effect, told lies. He stamped his foot on the stone step. "Damn

Figure 2.8. Man Ray, portrait of Mina Loy wearing thermometer earring, 1920. Courtesy of the Man Ray Trust. Copyright 1992 Man Ray Trust-ADAGP-ARS.

you," he said. But what had she said? Simply that it might be fine tomorrow. So it might.

Not with the barometer falling and the wind due west.[51]

And more recently, the lesbian feminist poet Adrienne Rich has once more invoked the Female Thermometer—to put paid to it. Traveling with a lover, she finds that

> The rules break like a thermometer,
> quicksilver spills across the charted systems,
> we're out in a country that has no language
> no laws.[52]

What, in the end, to deduce from such transformations? Certainly, one can always use the fluctuating symbolism of the weatherglass to underwrite a more or less standard version of cultural history. The changing nature of the image, as we have seen, reinforces at least one familiar intellectual theme: the idea that "sensibility"—considered in its most expansive sense—has in the past two centuries assumed unprecedented importance in the life of the West. Indeed, the motif shows just how profoundly the private realm of feeling, carefully monitored, has become part of modern bourgeois self-consciousness. For a curious combination of reasons, some having to do with traditional psychological and philosophical theories and some with the nature of the instrument itself, the weatherglass seemed the perfect emblem of the emotionally volatile human subject that began to emerge, definitively, in the late eighteenth century. I have added a twist to the familiar story by suggesting that the discovery of sensibility had a sexual dimension, and that it was a preexisting cultural image of femininity that led to the formation of the new mercurial human subject. But the basic explanatory fiction holds. It is always possible to treat the humanized thermometer or barometer as the symptom of a greater cultural change.

But we might turn such predictable hypothesizing on its head and arrive, at least speculatively, at a more profound conception of our relations with objects. It seems equally likely that the sudden appearance of "mercurial objects" like the barometer and thermometer in the domestic life of the eighteenth century not merely reified but may have actually prompted this historic development of a new conception of the emotions. One cannot underestimate the subliminal charisma of the material world, or the unsettling power of certain objects to create a new human life around them. Mirrors, gradually introduced into household use during the Middle Ages, may have influenced the rise of bourgeois individualism, for instance, more than any unfolding philosophical or religious dogma. Twentieth-century technology provides many examples of the "intimate machine"—devices such as telephones, televisions, and computers—that have so penetrated human consciousness that they now seem to live almost within us and shape our very desires. Changing "structures of everyday life"—and not the abstract formulations of philosophy—may in fact provide the basic phenomenological impetus for shifts in the realm of ideas.[53]

One might borrow a term from object-relations theory and call the weatherglass a "transitional object" in the psychic life of the West. Not only did the instrument come to symbolize the feminization of human nature, it may in fact have facilitated the process. The strangely motile inner life of the weatherglass, as we have seen, was initially feminine: the new object gave comic form to traditional beliefs about women's hypersensitivity and irrational sexual moods. But the continued presence of such objects in everyday life—with their animated responses to the world—encouraged the universalization of sensibility. Barometers and thermometers acted out, so to speak, the future of the psyche.

Such a theory, while not perhaps susceptible of proof, is not entirely whimsical either. In 1700 the instrument maker John Patrick was already offering weatherglasses to the public that incorporated "a looking glass commodiously plac'd on the same frame, between the barometer and thermometer, whereby gentlemen and ladies at the same time they dress, may accommodate their habit to the weather." "An invention not only curious, but also profitable and pleasant," wrote Patrick of his creation.[54] But the material association was fateful: the emblem of mercuriality had been fused with the emblem of self-consciousness. Inner and outer weather merged. Significantly, the barometer-mirror made no distinction between the sexes; it invited universal self-contemplation. It is perhaps not too much to suggest that once absorbed into the realm of everyday objects, such a device, and others like it, had the power to alter the shape of human self-awareness.

To be sure, satirists like Bonnell Thornton tried to preserve the feminine paradigm for decades. But eighteenth-century technology was already hinting at something new, and producing the material ground from which different metaphors could emerge. By 1800 the symbolic transformation was complete. To judge by twentieth-century psychological theory, we have entirely internalized the universalist model of emotional flux.[55] All of us, male or female, have become Female Thermometers. Yet this humiliation (if indeed it is one) may conceal a truth more shocking: that we owe our much vaunted human feelings—ever shifting, unpredictable, and alive—to the flamboyant moods of a machine.

C H A P T E R 3

"AMY, WHO KNEW MY DISEASE": A PSYCHOSEXUAL PATTERN IN DEFOE'S *ROXANA*

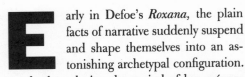

Early in Defoe's *Roxana*, the plain facts of narrative suddenly suspend and shape themselves into an astonishing archetypal configuration. Roxana is disclosing incidents that took place during the period of her ménage with her first lover, the English landlord/jeweler. She tells the events of one evening:

> At night, when we came to go to-bed, *Amy* came into the Chamber to undress me, and her Master slipt into Bed first; then I began, and told him all that *Amy* had said about my not being with-Child, and of her being with-Child twice in that time: Ay, Mrs *Amy, says he,* I believe so too, come hither, and we'll try; but *Amy* did not go: Go, you Fool, *says I,* can't you, I freely give you both Leave; but *Amy* wou'd not go: Nay, you Whore, *says I,* you said, if I wou'd put you to-Bed, you wou'd with all your Heart: and with that, I sat her down, pull'd off her stockings and Shooes, and all her Cloaths, Piece by Piece, and led her to the Bed to him . . . (46)[1]

After this exchange, Roxana continues, Amy and the landlord went on to have intercourse "before my Face," while she herself "stood by all the while." The sexual geometry of this scene, so oddly engineered by the narrator, suggests immediately a more profound symbolism than any Roxana herself assigns to it. Explaining the bizarre removal of Amy into the arms of her own bed-mate, Roxana says simply that "as I thought myself a Whore, I cannot say but that it was something design'd in my Thoughts, that my Maid should be a Whore too, and should not reproach me with it" (47). Yet the impulses at work here strike us, perhaps, as more subliminal in nature, more deeply regressive. Might one venture that the human pattern constructed by Roxana alludes, on some level, to a dimly recollected family arrangement? Is it not possible that Roxana, enacting an obscured version of what Freud calls the "phantastic repetition," attempts to place Amy, her ubiquitous companion, in the posture of the female parent, while she herself assumes the role of a child in the scene? Standing off to one side, Roxana is a mute observer to the sexual act. She recapitulates, it might seem, the child's primary exposure to sexuality. Defoe's normally garrulous speaker "cannot say," then, at this point, for she re-lives the basic content of the dream. Roxana has set up a sexual act involving Amy: her voyeurism is patent. Yet we do well to recall that the voyeur stands, wordlessly, at the apex of a more ancient triangle.

I would hesitate to hint at such a potentially arcane redaction of the foregoing scene were I not convinced that the abstract psychosexual pattern it suggests—particularly in regard to the displacement of the female participants—actually reappears in *Roxana*, and informs an important level of the novel's meaning. With perhaps inappropriate tactfulness, commentators on Defoe's final major fiction have, for the most part, avoided looking too intensely at the description of Amy's corruption. Monk, for one, is content to leave the incident simply as a "glance into hell," "the most appalling scene in serious eighteenth-century fiction, except for one or two in *Clarissa*."[2] Both Maximillian Novak and G. A. Starr point to Amy's bedding as a focal moment in Roxana's moral decay or "hard'ning," but do not linger on the specific nature of the role exchanges and sexual substitutions involved.[3] Again, in one of the most recent extended studies of the novel, John J. Richetti admits that the bedchamber scene is, emotionally, one of Defoe's "moments of intense coherence," yet warns us against extrapolating too much from it and thus falling into "superficial psychologizing." Richetti discounts the possibility that Roxana's activity here is linked, in terms of psychological content, to other events in her discourse, or that the manipulation of her servant indicates any kind of "sexual pathology": "[Its] implications for Roxana's sexual personality are completely ignored."[4] However helpful these various remarks and readings, they tend generally to underplay the psychic force Defoe's tableau holds for the reader, and, by extension, deflect us from its tremendous emblematic relevance to the entirety of Roxana's "secret history." For all its intentional sensationalism, Defoe's highly complex fiction may be read too as a consistently organized symbolic plot—one involving enigmatic emotional relations between parents and children, and, especially, between mothers and daughters. This "latent" plot is worked out, in the main, by the two female figures here so notably shifting roles, Roxana herself and Amy, the surrogate. The bedchamber scene draws the reader's attention, early on and in striking fashion, to these two figures, and to the possibilities held in their mysterious, passionate and destructive partnership. As one approaches the extremely problematic symbolic aspects of *Roxana* (above all, perhaps, the sinister and elusive "conclusion") there lies at each head this Roxana/Amy duality. Any gestures we make toward solving the extensive riddle posed by Defoe's text must necessarily include an untangling of this "Complication of Crime"—the maid on the bed, the projection of identity, the curiously intricate relation of fortunate mistress and able servant.

Indeed, who is Roxana's "indefatigable Amy," and how do we account for her strange proximity—within the bedchamber, within the structure of the fiction —to Defoe's narrator? The "ingenious helper," the character who acts as agent for the hero or heroine, is not of course an unfamiliar type in Defoe's novels. Leo Braudy has called attention to the tendency of Defoe's narrators to "spawn partners": Crusoe and Friday make up an obvious pair, so too "Captain Bob" and Quaker William in *Captain Singleton*.[5] In *Moll Flanders* (which, of the earlier fictions, bears the greatest surface resemblance to *Roxana*) we recall Moll's "old Governess," who guides and assists her during her criminal period. This woman, like Roxana's Amy, helps the heroine in her dealings with society, and functions as prudent advisor and accomplice. She likewise arranges Moll's final removal to America. Standing behind Moll's "old Governess," surely, is the conventional literary figure of the *eiron*—the tricky servant or vice. Frye has defined the *eiron* thus: "A self-deprecating or unobtrusively treated character in fiction, usually an agent of the happy ending in comedy and of the catastrophe in tragedy."[6] Amy, in one sense, fulfills functions similar to those performed by the governess-*eiron* in *Moll Flanders*. (She too is responsible for the heroine's final physical flight— though in a rather more ghastly manner.) It is hard to say in *Roxana*, however, that Amy retains ultimately an "unobtrusive," purely contingent or accidental role. Like the traditional vice figure, she is fully implicated in the mechanics of the plot and its (happy or catastrophic?) resolution. Yet she transcends the conventional identity she seems at first to assume, just as *Roxana* itself transcends conventional genres such as the picaresque.

From first to last, Amy's presence infiltrates Roxana's narrative in a curiously intense way, and modifies its complicated psychological structure. ("*Amy* was always at my Elbow" [238].) The reader thus experiences a double focus in the fiction: we receive not, as in other, perhaps more straightforward Defoe novels, simply the primary history of the speaker, but this history as transformed by the persistent presence of an other, an alternate self, indeed—in Roxana's case—an ideal self. Amy is the secret sharer in Roxana's life: she acts out her mistress's fantasies, she accepts the functions Roxana projects, both consciously and unconsciously, onto her. In Roxana's own chilling phrase, she is "*Amy*, who knew my Disease" (239). Defoe's onomastics suggest, possibly, something of the psychological complexity involved in the type of intimacy the narrative reveals. Amy is of course the *amie*—the perfect friend, the familiar. Likewise, she is also, perhaps, a "me"—an oddly displaced and altered version of the speaker herself. We must be alert, I suspect, to both possibilities in our readings of *Roxana*. Like mother and daughter, Amy and Roxana share a paradoxical relation of sameness and otherness. In that Roxana's ostensible "autobiography" incorporates a simultaneous history of Amy, the other, it recapitulates the psychological paradox on the level of narrative.[7]

Amy's complicity in the life of the narrator is, we find, established in the opening pages of the novel, and intensifies as Roxana's strange story unfolds. (The very continuity of Amy's presence in *Roxana* suggests already that she has an importance not shared by, say, Friday in *Robinson Crusoe* or William in *Captain Singleton:* these "partners" enter midway or later in the discourses in which they appear, while Amy is influential from the start.) Roxana introduces the servant into the narrative with powerful and suggestive images of intimacy. She characterizes her as being as "faithful to me, as the Skin to my Back" (25). Already Roxana, whether consciously or no, points to an almost physical bonding between her servant and herself. Again, the narrator speaks of their inseparability: "the Girl lov'd me to an Excess hardly to be describ'd" (31).

> I must remember it here, to the Praise of this poor Girl, my Maid, that tho' I was not able to give her any Wages, and had told her so, nay I was not able to pay her the Wages that I was in Arrears to her, yet she would not leave me. . . . (16)

The sense we receive early on of the emotional collusion that exists between the two women is heightened by a series of references—begun here and continued through the novel—to Roxana and Amy sharing a bed; the erotic ambiguity of these asides contributes to an initial effect of merging, or complementary identities.

Roxana likewise identifies for us in the crucial opening scenes of the novel what will become, apart from her utter devotion, Amy's most salient personal trait: her adroitness, her competence in all manner of social interaction. Amy is Roxana's "cunning Wench," her "resolute Girl." During the crisis after Roxana's abandonment by the brewer-husband, Amy demonstrates her skill variously: she works as a food-gatherer at the time of their near-starvation, advises Roxana (who remains inert through most of the upheaval—"I was in a Parlour, sitting on the Ground . . . and had been crying ready to burst myself" [17]), disposes of her mistress's children, and, perhaps most significantly, suggests and arranges the liaison with the landlord. Amy has, before, offered to prostitute herself to him; Roxana writes of the necessary fall from virtue, "the Jade prompted the Crime" (40). On all these occasions, Amy's role is intensely purposive: she functions as Roxana's surrogate in the social sphere—she mediates, in effect, between her mistress and the world of other people.

In this first stage of narrative, this transference of function results already in some decidedly odd effects. Roxana's discourse itself seems to lose focus at times. During the momentous seduction of the landlord, for instance, Amy is present.

Amy waited at the Table, and she smil'd, and laugh'd, and was so merry she could hardly contain it. . . . As soon as Dinner was over, *Amy* went up-Stairs, and put on her Best Clothes too, and came down dress'd like a Gentlewoman. (31)

Roxana tends to fade out of view here. Her ostensibly central place in the scene is momentarily subsumed. It is as if Amy, rather than Roxana, were the seductive mistress, the entertainer and sexual instigator. This scene of course foreshadows the actual sexual contact between the maid and landlord, as well as Roxana's later voyeurism. The immediate consequences, however, for the narrative are disconcerting; Roxana's "autobiography" seems even here to be shading into the story of someone else—a vibrant, ever-present other.

Early in the fiction, thus, we introduced to a certain basic pattern, an abstracted form of the relationship between the two women. Roxana's discourse suggests, via several interesting metaphors and asides, a profound emotional bonding of mistress and maid: they are physically identified, their lives and careers are, from the start, so nearly mingled that the success or failure of one results in the same for the other. Beyond this primary "doubling," however—conveyed by motifs of physical merging—there is a further dynamic aspect to the relation. In crisis Amy asserts herself as the prudent manager of affairs, while Roxana tends to devolve into passivity. Roxana remains the contemplative central consciousness, who observes and records, yet she is also completely dependent on Amy's manifold maneuvers in the larger world of the novel.

This contrast between Roxana's passivity and Amy's activity is expanded in the total context of *Roxana*. Reviewing the progress of the fiction as a whole, one is struck indeed by the fact that virtually all the significant shifts in the plot—the manifest alterations in Roxana's "fortune"—are occasioned not by the speaker herself, but by the facilitations of her familiar. Amy, Roxana tells us, was "precipitant in her Motions" (209). She arranges; she lubricates. I have mentioned already Amy's literally life-saving pragmatism after the disappearance of the brewer-husband: it is Amy's powerful maxim *"Comply and live; deny and starve"* of course which incites Roxana's all-important choice of career. Presupposing the truth of Roxana's account at this point, it is dubious indeed what would have been her course had she not heeded initially the timely arguments of her friend. Yet the examples of Amy's agency abound at all points—in France, at the Pall Mall household (where she assumes the role of "Companion" and begins to dress like her mistress), in those events which surround the "remove" to the Quaker lodgings. Amy appears in each situation as the "clever Manager"—as spy, accountant, housekeeper, procuress. Near the end of the novel her "management" takes on an additional feverishness: as we will see, she is focal in the almost unbearably tense scenes with Susan, Roxana's daughter. Her initial failure to help her mistress out of the deeply troubling difficulty that develops here is obviated by the fact that ultimately she does arrange things once more, though in dire fashion. The last action performed by "diligent *Amy*," "indefatigable *Amy*," the "ambitious Jade," is, of course, the gravest and potentially most significant act in all of *Roxana*.

If Amy's "management" is shown as more and more frenetic in the course of Roxana's history, and her affective power more absolute, we are invited to contrast this with Roxana's deepening inertia and powerlessness. One of her narrative asides is of special interest here. Describing the period of the *amour* with the Prince Roxana says,

> I have, I confess, wonder'd at the Stupidity that my intellectual Part was under all that while; what Lethargick Fumes doz'd the Soul; and how it was possible that I, who in the Case before, where the Temptation was many ways more forcible, and the Arguments stronger, and more irrisistable, was yet under a continued Inquietude on account of the wicked Life I led, could now live in the most profound Tranquility, and with an uninterrupted Peace, nay, even rising up to Satisfaction, and Joy. . . . (69)

Just before she has spoken of how the conscience, "once doz'd, sleeps fast, not to be awaken'd while the Tide of Pleasure continues to flow, or till something dark and dreadful brings us to ourselves again." And again, she notes that with her Prince, "I enjoy'd myself in perfect Tranquility" (70). Roxana's metaphors of somnolence operate on several levels. She uses the traditional imagery of sleep, restfulness, even stupor, to evoke her devolution, on an abstract plane, into moral quiescence. Yet the choice of words here attests also to a deeply-grounded general tendency in the character of Roxana—a psychological lethargy, a willingness to skirt responsibility, to evade direct action and conscious choice.

Analyzing plot in Roxana, we must point to the heroine's long career as kept mistress, of course, as the most immediately visible mark of her "Lethargick" tendency. Her involvements with men represent a kind of paradoxical 'work' that is not really work at all. Roxana reaps wonderful cash benefits despite a minimal expenditure of energy and an almost total lack of self-direction. One notes, at times, the strange resemblance of her history to a type of wish-fulfillment dream. (Indeed, Roxana's own couplet

> In Things we wish, 'tis easie to deceive;
> What we would have, we willingly believe (68)

gives, perhaps, a secret psychological emblem-motto for her 'autobiography.') Men initiate affairs with her without her apparently encouraging or premeditating such situations; once involved, they anticipate her economic needs with superabundant generosity. A kind of telepathy, for instance, seems to exist between Roxana and her eager Prince: "his Bounty always anticipated my Expectations, and even my Wishes; and he gave me Money so fast, that he rather pour'd it in upon me, than left me room to ask it" (75–76). But just as Roxana happily accepts the wild material rewards of being kept, so it would seem she finds the generalized passivity of the mistress-role satisfying on a more profound level. Her "Lethargy," after all, modulates into a "Fullness of Humane Delight" (68). The numerous seduction scenes which dot the text repeat in little the greater shape of Roxana's experience. Whatever her spoken protestations, she relinquishes control easily enough.

A pattern of physical symbolism, finally, reinforces the contrast implied at all points in Roxana's history. Her degree of physical mobility becomes—as it does, oppositely, in Amy's case—an index to her increasing lack of personal integrity and power. Again, we are invited to visualize a disparity between the two women, the speaker and the double. As Amy becomes more and more mobile throughout *Roxana* (engaging at last in a flurry of cross-Channel journeys), so the narrator accepts, indeed seems almost to seek, a greater and greater physical restriction. The motionless posture Roxana displays in the early scenes after her abandonment, when she is typically indoors and inactive, is assumed again, for example, when she becomes a full-fledged prostitute. She readily agrees to "Confinement" as a necessary part of her relationship with the Prince, and characterizes her living arrangement with him, pleasantly enough, as a "Prison." During the affair, as in her later liaisons, Roxana stays virtually entirely within doors. Suspended inside a series of cocoon-like interiors—the secret lodgings she is supplied with—her one function is to await her lover's visits. The later shift from the life of mistress to life in the Quaker woman's household is perfectly understandable if we see Roxana as a character who takes a perverse pleasure in self-limitation. Her longing for stasis, for "Tranquility," resolves into a persistent reduction of the space around her. The small clandestine rooms she takes with the Quaker are the final form this reduction takes ("I went but little Abroad" [213])—though one might look too to the binding Quaker habit itself, donned at this time, as a further emblem of self-restricted movement.

On both narrative and symbolic levels, then, the history Roxana provides us shows the contrast between Amy and herself to be a more basic contrast between action and evasion, movement and stillness. The myth Roxana thus effectively creates for us—beneath the surface of her discourse—is that of Amy's complete competence and energy and of her own incompetence and weakness. In the strange unit she describes, the Roxana/Amy mutuality, the primary self is debilitated, fixated, unable to move—the double is vigorous, effective, free. I would like to suggest here, however, a more specific structure for the speaker's fixation in *Roxana*. Might not Amy's persistent modulation into powerful female, archetype of competence, possibly bespeak her closeness to a maternal *persona?* Likewise, does not Roxana express herself in relation to her companion essentially as child to parent? Amy and Roxana appear to enact, most profoundly, a metaphorics of motherhood and childhood. Roxana's life, easeful as it is, recapitulates the prerogatives of the infant. She lies asleep at the center of the fiction. Watchful Amy travels its circumference.

The equation may seem a bald one at first, but it is strangely confirmed by the text. Roxana, one finds, repeatedly projects Amy into the role of a phantom mother—literally, of course, in regard to her children, but also, by a simultaneous symbolic extension, in regard to herself. This seems undoubtedly the most significant of the many displacements she makes onto her maidservant and friend.

The projection arises, necessarily, out of those aspects of her personality already examined. Roxana, predictably enough, is herself a distinctly "unmaternal" woman. Michael Shinagel has discussed the "maternal paradox" in the character of Moll Flanders—i.e., the contrast between Moll's fertility and her apparent emotional disconnection from her offspring.[8] A similar paradox informs Roxana's life, though with even more sinister and disconcerting reverberations. Her generalized evasion of adult responsibility—her "Lethargy"—shows itself most shockingly to the modern reader, perhaps, in those parts of the narrative in which she mentions her many pregnancies and how she treats the resulting children. Early on she abandons the offspring of the first marriage, summarily and under oddly ambiguous circumstances. Her son by the jeweler appears once at birth and then vanishes from the narrative, as he does apparently from Roxana's life. Her children by the Prince are delivered, again, into the care of others, and Roxana observes complacently, "nor did the Children ever know anything of their Mother" (80). Roxana's casual treatment, indeed, rejection of her various children —eleven in all—seems to stem from more than just the shame she professes to feel when she considers the circumstances of their births. Underlying the heroine's discussion of her childbearing is what appears to be a powerful ambivalence, even an anxiety regarding the maternal function. She speaks at one point, for example, of making her will before the birth of one of the Prince's children: "I had a strange Apprehension that I should die with that Child" (78). She feels relief when another child does not survive the Italian journey, and her discourse takes on a rather chilling tonelessness. "[N]or, after the first Touches of Affection (which are usual, I believe, to all Mothers) were over, was I sorry the Child did not live, the necessary Difficulties attending it in our travelling, being consider'd" (104). Finally, she expresses on occasion an even more primal and frightening kind of hostility toward her offspring. Concerning the soon-to-be–born son of the merchant, she notes ominously,

> I wou'd willingly have given ten Thousand Pounds of my Money, to have been rid of the Burthen I had in my Belly, as above; but it cou'd not be; so I was oblig'd to bear with that part, and get rid of it by the ordinary Method of Patience, and hard Travel. . . . (163)

"Getting rid" of the child is an underlying *leit-motiv* in Roxana's discourse—the most noteworthy of her evasions.

If Defoe's narrator is not amenable herself to motherhood, she has no qualms about transferring its responsibilities to someone else. And here we come back upon the primary importance of the "double" in her history. In the classical pattern of fixation described by Freud and others, the traumatized self is unwilling to take on those conventional adult functions associated with the parent. Rather, it seeks to retain its basic dependency on the parent, or through displacement, on a significant other. But is this not Roxana's procedure in regard to herself and her ever-present companion? Amy is indeed Roxana's "significant other." In the latter half of *Roxana*, we see that Amy's "clever Management" extends most memorably to the care of her mistress's grown children, Susan and the rest. This transfer of function—coupled with what we know of Roxana's anxiety and hostility regarding birth and children—intimates the specific psychological content of her "Lethargy." Roxana demonstrates elements of a syndrome involving trauma, emotional retrenchment, and projection. For reasons repressed in the surface discourse, Roxana eliminates her own maternal functioning in various ways. (Might one note here in passing the death of Roxana's own mother, the subject of one terse paragraph on the fifth page of narrative?) In further accordance with a pattern of psychological fixation, she then impels Amy to become a surrogate to the living children, thus confirming the friend unconsciously, it seems, as maternal surrogate for herself too. To the extent that Amy deals with Roxana's offspring, she symbolically nurtures Roxana herself: Roxana tends in the book to become, paradoxically, one of her own children. The competent servant resolves into the greatest *amie* of them all—the projected ego-ideal, the female parent. Amy takes care of her mistress in the most fundamental way: she participates with a kind of ultimate readiness in the dynamics of fixation. Roxana writes, "*Amy,* knew all the secret History of my Life" (317)—that is, she is comprehended within the hidden life of the speaker, the realm of unconscious need.

The basic configuration of mother and child that lies just under the conscious surface of the narrative in *Roxana* transforms the fiction into symbolic plot. Otherwise unaccountable vignettes in Roxana's story reveal themselves as emblematic instances in the history of this primally shaped relation. The triangulation between Amy, Roxana, and the landlord, as I suggested at first, shows one such archetypal transference of maternal function. Roxana, acting out, elevates Amy into a position of magnified power; she incorporates her into the regressive fantasy. The conversation that immediately precedes the scene deals, we recollect, with Amy's greater fertility. In the bedchamber exploit itself, Roxana suppresses her own sexual maturity and reverts to the impassive voyeurism of an earlier stage. Freud writes in *Three Contributions to the Theory of Sex,* "the sexuality of the psychoneurotic preserves the infantile character or has returned to it. May there not be a connection between the infantile and hysterical amnesias?"[9]

If *Roxana* presents itself, in one reading at least, as the self-portrait of a fixated individual, it invites us also to contemplate, finally, the consequences of this fixation. These are dire. As she approaches the last third of her discourse, Roxana seems to have achieved a precarious personal balance. She is maintaining the wish-fulfillment dream, prolonging it. Her past is hidden, she is wealthy, she will marry at last because she is safely past "breeding" and the prospect of further maternity is obviated. Most important, perhaps, Amy remains ever-faithful, a ubiquitous shadow version of the self—"*Amy* was now a Woman of Business, not a servant, and eat always with us" (245). Yet this balance is disastrously upset, precisely as a result of the role substitution she and Amy have acted out in their "Complicity of Crime." Roxana is shocked from her sleep.

The murder of Roxana's daughter Susan by Amy is at once a logical function of plot in *Roxana* and a devastating symbolic revelation of the types of destruction wrought by the heroine's deep-seated transference onto Amy. Amy, the speaker tells us, has played her part of mother-surrogate to the children so well that Susan, the cook-maid daughter, believes the servant to be her real parent. Amy's denial prompts Susan to an agonized search for Roxana, whom Susan correctly discerns as the true mother hidden behind the "double." Susan's pursuit becomes importunate: Amy hints that she will kill the girl, Roxanna cannot openly tolerate this suggestion. Amy leaves—as she has left so many times before on errands—and the daughter is silenced.

In these events Roxana and Amy enact their characteristic dynamic, but in its most terrifying form. Despite Roxana's conscious outrage at Amy's murderous suggestions, it is hard not to see Susan's killing as an act that Roxana in some sense desires. Amy, typically, becomes her mistress's instrument; she preserves Roxana's security. The friend acts out Roxana's fantasy of violence—the fantasy which, as we have seen, has always been a hidden aspect of her feeling for her children. The intense confusion in Roxana's surface narrative when she tries to discuss the killing testifies to her psychic implication in Amy's movements.

> It is true, I wanted as much to be deliver'd from her, as ever a Sick-Man did from a Third-Day Ague; and had she dropp'd into the Grave by any fair Way, *as I may call it;* I mean had she died by any ordinary Distemper, I shou'd have shed but very few Tears for her: But I was not arriv'd to such a Pitch of obstinate Wickedness, as to commit Murther, especially such, as to murther my own Child, or so much as to harbour a Thought so barbarous, in my Mind: But, as I said, Amy effected all afterwards, without my Knowledge, for which I gave her my hearty Curse, tho' I cou'd do little more; for to have fall'n upon *Amy,* had been to have murther'd myself. . . . (302)

Seen from one perspective, the murder is then a simple effect of the structure of relationship we have already seen between Roxana and her maid. Amy is doubling for her and protecting her. Roxana herself admits that the terrible deed has been done "owing to her Excess of Care for my Safety," "her steddy Kindness to me" (317). Yet the meaning of the event goes much deeper. Roxana's anxiety that she will be found out by her daughter seems far to exceed the stated reason for her fear—the shame she will face before her husband. Rather, we suspect that this anxiety—which becomes almost unbearable to read about—is a consequence of her abbreviated psychic development. Susan confirms Roxana's past role as mother—the role she rejects. To accept maternity is in the social realm to accept responsibility and adulthood; existentially, it is to affirm one's implication in the world of shared human suffering, and, ultimately, the fact of one's own death. Roxana thus confronts in her daughter an unintegrated aspect of her own being, the aspect she has until now successfully displaced. Yet even now, in her fifties, is Roxana willing to integrate Susan and what she represents into her life? Indeed not. The murder of the child is, it seems, the last possible act of psychological retrenchment. It is Roxana's most desperate attempt to maintain herself, with Amy's vital help, in a condition of stasis, imperviousness, centrality. The act consolidates fixation, makes integration impossible. In analytic terms, the trauma is repressed once more, not mastered.

As such, homicide modulates inevitably into a convoluted form of self-slaughter. This is perhaps the ultimate thematic complication in Defoe's novel. Roxana's fixation means "death" not just to Susan alone. We recollect the disarming concurrence of names in the fiction: as we learn Susan's name, we hear then that it is also really Roxana's too. "Roxana" is a later superimposition. The symbolic implication is hardly to be avoided: Roxana is engaged in a kind of self-destruction when she fantasizes the murder of her child. Part of the self cannot be repressed without great damage to the whole. The type of security, of archaic "Tranquility," that the heroine desires seems only to be mediated through death.

Is Amy, killing Susan, then "killing" Roxana? Susan, seeking the parent, is a "motherless child": yet so, always, has been Roxana herself. Roxana, fixated by trauma (one hesitates to say by the early death of her mother, but Roxana provides the fact, with details suppressed), transforms Amy into maternal surrogate. Yet the process is regressive, implies a perpetually disintegrated state of personality, and finally enforces a death of self. Susan's murder by the Mother figure (Amy) recapitulates on a literal level Roxana's own soul-destroying involvement with the same figure. The tremendous power the narrator has projected onto Amy—the power to save her—resolves into the power to kill her. "Susan" is the secret name of the self: she seeks out the Mother only to die at her hands.

Roxana's irrevocably damaged state of being is conveyed, one finds, in the increasingly oppressive tone of the latter part of her narrative. Witness indeed the frequent references to guilt, her obsessive returns to the crime she and Amy have committed, her frightening intimations of further disaster not recounted in the existing text. The picture we receive finally of Roxana after the removal to Holland is of a woman caught in a hell of her own design. Existentially, her attempt to block out anxiety through displacement has resulted in a complete, paralyzing takeover by anxiety at the end of her life.

> Not all the Affluence of a plentiful Fortune; not a hundred Thousand Pounds Estate; (for between us we had little less) not Honour and Titles, Attendants and Equipages; *in a word,* not all the things we call Pleasure, cou'd give me any relish, or sweeten the Taste of things to me; *at least,* not so much, but I grew sad, heavy, pensive, and melancholy; slept little, and eat little; dream'd continually of the most frightful and terrible things imaginable: Nothing but Apparitions of Devils and Monsters; falling

into Gulphs, and off from steep and high Precipices, *and the like;* so that in the Morning, when I shou'd rise, and be refresh'd with the Blessing of Rest, I was *Hag-ridden* with Frights, and terrible things, form'd meerly in the Imagination; and was either tir'd, and wanted Sleep, or overrun with Vapours, and not fit for conversing with my Family, or any-one else. (264)

She tells how "former things" which had "gnaw'd a Hole in my Heart before," now "made a Hole quite thro' it; now they eat into all my pleasant things" (264). This startling image describes, of course, Roxana's lack of resolved selfhood—she is hollow at the core.

The final mysterious paragraphs of *Roxana* detail the inevitable return of Amy to her mistress's side after the murder, and hint at deeper complications of guilt occurring outside the present discourse ("after some few Years of flourishing, and outwardly happy Circumstances, I fell into a dreadful Course of Calamities, and *Amy* also; the very Reverse of our former Good Days; the Blast of Heaven seem'd to follow the Injury done the poor Girl, by us both"). Roxana's incon-clusiveness here, the distressing gap in her narrative, suggests more profoundly than any specific conclusion would the unresolved condition of being in which she lives. The catastrophe befalling her and Amy is not to be "Related" (cf. "This Tragedy requires a longer Story than I have room for here" [302]). It, like the actual murder of Susan, is unspeakable. In the symbolic reading I have been applying to the text, all these unnamed events are equivalent. Roxana, one might presume, is doomed, with Amy, to act out over and over her acts of destruction and self-destruction, and never to find relief thereby. She is suspended in a lethal matrix of fixation; she has failed to birth herself.

To read *Roxana* as a parable of motherless children, of doubling, projection, and fixation, is, of course, to debilitate utterly our conventional sense of the novel and its characters. Yet the text admits such a reading. Indeed, at the level of deep structure, Roxana's narrative seems shaped by profound configurations of which she is apparently unaware. The double is in a sense so close to Roxana herself that she cannot really see her. She merely assumes her eternal presence.

The question of Defoe's place in all of this, one must admit, remains a problematic one. He has been in fact the missing man in this tale of female bonding. As the Preface shows, he stands behind the narrative as its "Relator," though what his precise relation to Roxana's "unspoken" history is is still ob-scure.[10] To what extent is Defoe consciously organizing the "double-talk" in Roxana's piece? Likewise, how do we reconcile the curiously realistic psychologi-cal patterns in her life-story with what we know of Defoe's moral and theological intentions? Is repentance his metaphor for integration? Is integration our meta-phor for repentance?

Roxana's psychological strategy may be the essential artistic strategy of her creator. If we are led to wonder, even momentarily, in what sense Amy, the perfect friend, "exists" for Roxana, a greater crux arises when we consider the many "friends," those other-versions, of Defoe himself.

CHAPTER 4

• LOVELACE'S DREAM
•
•
•
•
•
•
•
•
•
•
•
•
•
•
•
•
•
•
•
•
•
•

One week after Clarissa has been drugged and raped, has fallen into madness and out of it, she begins to plot. She meditates an escape—from Mrs. Sinclair's brothel and from Lovelace. Her plot involves bribing Dorcas the servant with an offer of future rewards if she will help her get away. Dorcas, hypocritically agreeable, immediately informs Lovelace, who is put on his guard. The tricky servant confirms his maxim, repeated for Belford, that "the bond of wickedness is a stronger bond than the ties of virtue" (III, 247).[1] Yet the vision of his "charmer" "plotting" to escape lingers too in his imagination and excites him. So confident is he of his control over Clarissa he toys with the idea of letting her escape on purpose, simply in order to recapture her and thus demonstrate once more his ineluctable power over her. He half-hopes also to force her by this means into that marriage which he now claims, almost convincing himself, he wants with her. "I cannot live without intrigue," he writes to Belford. And of Clarissa he adds, with mock-portentousness, "She is now authorizing all my plots by her own example" (243).

At precisely this moment in the fiction Lovelace has a waking dream. In this daytime "reverie," which he describes to Belford in one of his June 20 letters, Clarissa does in fact escape him, or seem to. "Methought," he writes, "that a chariot with a dowager's arms upon the doors, and in it a grave matronly lady (not unlike Mother H. in the face; but in her heart, O how unlike!) stopped at a grocer's shop about ten doors on the other side of the way . . . and methought Dorcas, having been out to see if the coast was clear for her lady's flight, and if a coach were to be got near the place, espied this chariot . . . and this matronly lady" (248). Dorcas, he goes on, runs to the older woman and begs her to save her mistress, who, she says, has been kidnapped by a "wicked man" who is plotting to ruin her that night. Like a fairy godmother, the old dowager comes to Clarissa's rescue, saying "my house shall be her sanctuary" until Clarissa is able to contact her "rich and powerful friends" (249).

Together Clarissa and the matronly lady drive to a "sumptuous dwelling" in Lincoln's Inn Fields. (Lovelace, the dreamer, follows this flight from an inexplicable, unseen shifting vantage point: the effect is not unlike a tracking shot in film, with Lovelace as the invisible, moving "camera eye.") This house, oddly enough, is filled with "damsels, who wrought curiously in muslins, cambrics, and fine linen, and in every good work that industrious damsels love to be employed about" (249). Over dinner Clarissa tells her story, while the sympathetic old lady weeps and calls Lovelace a "plotting villain" and an "unchained Beezlebub." Suddenly, says Lovelace, "a strange metamorphosis" takes place. The kindly old lady is changed—in a moment, in a diabolical twinkling of an eye—into "Mother H.," the same Mother H. mentioned before, who we now learn is a brothel-keeper like Mrs. Sinclair and a crony of Lovelace's. This Mother H. is mysteriously "prevailed upon," Lovelace observes, "to assist me in my plot upon the young lady." She invites Clarissa, who is unaware of any change, to share her bed for the night and there continue telling her story. They remove to the bed, but Mother H. has a sudden colic and gets up for a "cordial," knocking over the candle in the process. The room is plunged into darkness, and when Mother H. returns to bed, Clarissa—to her "astonishment, grief, and surprise"—finds the old woman transformed into Lovelace himself. "What unaccountable things are dreams!" interjects Lovelace.

At this point Lovelace ceases to be merely a beholder of the action. Instead, with this bizarre piece of gender exchange, he is absorbed into the dreamscape. "A strange promiscuous huddle of adventures" ensues, he tells Belford, and his descriptive terms change accordingly, becoming auditory and tactile, as the action itself becomes more intimate: "Nothing heard from the lady but sighs, groans, exclamations, faintings, dyings, and from the gentleman, vows, promises, protestations, disclaimers of purposes pursued, and all the gentle and ungentle pressures of the lover's warfare" (250). With a final abrupt lurch, suggesting through ellipsis a jump in time, the dream switches to a scene of happy, if perverse domesticity: Clarissa has given birth to Lovelace's son, and together with Anna Howe (who has given birth to his daughter) the three live in a blissful *ménage à trois*. The two little babies, half-brother and half-sister, grow up and marry each other incestuously, for as Lovelace disingenuously concludes, "neither have dreams regard to *consanguinity.*"

Lovelace's remarkable dream unfortunately vanishes in most abridgements of *Clarissa,* including Sherburn's. This is something of a shame, because it offers ingenious readers much to comment on—indeed, almost too much. For modern readers Lovelace's dream will open itself inescapably, perhaps insipidly, to psychoanalytic glossing: by its sheer waywardness it invites us to connect it with the unconscious life of its driven, devious dreamer. One could, if one wished, use the dream to underwrite a devastating *exposé* of the Lovelacean psyche, for all those pathologies we tend across the fiction to associate with his character are if anything too insistently present here: his voyeurism, fantasies of dominance, incestuous wishes, fascination with faintly perverse female sexuality, and most disarmingly— in the bed-trick—what can only be described as latent transsexualism.

I do not wish to pursue this sort of reading, however, or treat this odd dream simply as a particularly byzantine efflorescence of the Lovelacean unconscious. As a species of wish-fulfillment, the dream seems transparent enough; its erotic content is indeed so overdetermined as to induce a certain *ennui,* or satiated feeling. Instead I want to use Lovelace's dream as an expression, as it were, of the "unconscious" of Richardson's fiction—as a revelation of certain ontological tendencies in *Clarissa* itself. I take my cue from that detail in the dream that stands out, almost like a freeze-frame, as singular, aberrant, unrelated to the relentless erotic business of the rest of the dream. I mean those unaccountable "weaving damsels" who embroider so "curiously" at the dowager's dream-mansion. Lovelace does not recognize them, but *Clarissa's* reader may; for these mysterious, magical spinsters seem nothing less than Fates, weavers of human destiny itself. Their presence—on the edge of the dream, seemingly peripheral—bespeaks certain complex and subtle affiliations.

Above all, these fabricators, these "plotters" of human event, hint at a connection between Lovelace's reverie and that enigmatic, multivalent notion one confronts at every turn in *Clarissa*—that of plot itself.[2] They remind us, subliminally, perhaps, but nonetheless compellingly, of those different "plots" at work in the fictional world—of which the villainous and the providential are but the most prominent. But beyond this, they call attention to another intimacy: between Lovelace's dream and that larger dream in which it is embedded, the plot of *Clarissa* itself. His dream, we find, is at once a crucial element in the actual plot of Richardson's fiction and an emblem of its transformational, recursive, hallucinatory structure. It functions both *within* the narrative, and in another sense to one side of it—as a commentary on plot, an allegory, a curiously worked insignia of the narrative itself. Lovelace's "weaving damsels" suggest a knot of relations—between dream and plot, plot and text, text and dream. But with these relations, the whole of Lovelace's peculiar vision has much to do.

Lovelace's dream is of course a "plot" itself—in all the ambiguous senses of the word. In describing his dream to Belford, Lovelace makes it into a narrative; it reads like a story, a literary plot in little. The dream is a ribald tale, almost a *fabliau.* And he recounts it with the enthusiasm of one telling an unusually good yarn. For his dream is above all a shapely narrative: it is structured by its own inevitable logic, what one could call classically "Lovelacean" logic—the logic of antithesis. The dream-story is governed by a single repeating function: the transformation of things into their opposites. Hence its giddy series of metamorphoses, of bizarre antithetical conversions. A jailer (Dorcas) becomes an accomplice in escape; a good old lady changes into a bad one; a woman turns into a man. Clarissa's imprisonment is transformed, for a moment, into freedom, only to be reconverted—according to the demonic logic of the dream—into imprisonment. The dream tells of a world incessantly turning inside-out.

But this, clearly, is precisely the sort of "plot" that enchants Lovelace most. He loves any tale of transformation—and the more manic the better. He is sufficiently inspired, in fact, to make the dream over into a plot of another sort: into an actual criminal design he will carry out against the heroine. His dream is his *donnée,* the seed for an intrigue, a magical script which only needs players to be realized. Thus he tells Belford he is attempting just this sort of *mise-en-scène:* he has arranged for Dorcas to pretend to help Clarissa get out of Sinclair's house, and has enlisted Mother H. to impersonate the "kindly old dowager" of the dream. He will stake out Clarissa from a distance, follow her and Mother H. in another coach, and when they arrive at Mother H.'s house, will exchange places with the bawd and insinuate himself—just as in the dream—into bed with Clarissa, where he will violate her once again. As he boasts to Belford, when his dream-plot is fulfilled, he will write an instructive book called *Lovelace's Reveries,* in which he will demonstrate the usefulness of dreams in providing "plots" for enterprising fellows, and cunning rakes in particular.

Lovelace treats his dream, only half-ironically, as a "prophecy" of the future, even though for it to come "true" he knows he must take elaborate steps. But for the real reader it is curiously retrospective. Lovelace's dream-scenario has an uncanny relationship to that intrigue in which we have by now been embroiled for some time: the plot of *Clarissa* itself. With a certain uneasiness we realize that his dream recapitulates in a somewhat transformed and displaced fashion a tale we already know too well—an ironical, appalling "History" in which a heroine's pathetic attempts at escape are converted into deeper imprisonment, a good mother is inexplicably replaced by a bad one, and the man one wants most to avoid is, nightmarishly, closer than anyone else in the world. This of course is the "plot" of Clarissa's entrapment and rape all over again. The incidental gothic apparatus of coaches, cordials, guttering candles, dark bedrooms, and mysterious female attendants reminds us, distressingly, of those diabolical props which have already figured in the scene of Clarissa's actual violation.

Lovelace's dream-plot repeats the narrative past and hints of a narrative future in which such repetitions are a matter of course. His dream—and the plan he extracts from it—raise the possibility of an infinite series of plot repetitions, rapes upon rapes, from which the reader, no less than Clarissa, is unable to escape. At this point the reader may fear a *Clarissa* that "tells," endlessly, cloyingly, of further plots on the heroine, further traps, further humiliations.[3]

But Lovelace's dream-plot leads, paradoxically, to something other than repetition. It leads in fact to a vast reversal, an unwinding of the spool, a turning inside-out—both of the respective fortunes of Clarissa and Lovelace, and of that larger plot in which Lovelace's little plots are woven, the plot of the fiction itself. In this sense the dream does become something of a portent, but an entirely ironic one. It prefigures nothing for Lovelace, rather the inversion of his hopes. It signals an abrupt, convulsive movement—the imminent unraveling of the Lovelacean plot, the sewing up of the Richardsonian. One might call this the "wit" of the dream—the way it knows something that Lovelace himself does not: that its manifold inversions, those playful, monstrous transformations on which its "plot" turns, are the sign of a coming turn in that other plot, *Clarissa's*—and, of course, Clarissa's.

The dream-plot is witty, as it were, because it fails. It fails abysmally, and in so doing—though no one is aware of it at the time—initiates a sequence of events that will result in Clarissa's *real* escape from Lovelace. The plot fails because Clarissa acts in a way not "predicted" by the dream—not articulated in advance in the Lovelacean script. Lovelace's plot of inversion has from the start depended on one stable element: the eminent naiveté of the heroine, her total, uneducable gullibility. But Clarissa here introduces novelty into the closed system of Lovelacean fantasy, and into the text of *Clarissa* itself. She behaves here in a way "unlike" herself—exactly opposite, in fact, to her usual manner. Where before she has been trusting, ingenuous, a naive interpreter of the "facts," she now metamorphoses into someone suspicious, streetwise, savvy. This is the one change that Lovelace— for all his talk of his charmer's "slyness," "penetration," and "plots"—does not anticipate. Thus when Mother H. arrives in the coach to "rescue" Clarissa, he watches in amazement as Clarissa refuses her, and calmly, voluntarily, walks back into her prison, Mrs. Sinclair's house.

The reader learns later from Clarissa's memorandum-book the depth of her new *savoir faire:* she has seen Dorcas and Lovelace whispering together and suspects a plan afoot between them; she thinks the arrival of the "rescue" coach all too fortuitous and improbable; she finds Dorcas's unerring deciphering of the heraldic arms on the coach indicative of a facility not usual "in a person of her station" (257). This last detail is a particularly ironic turnaround, for in the past Clarissa has been distinguished by her own persistent ineptitude at "reading" just this sort of sign system—the language of heraldic markings, liveries, shop signs, and the like. Lovelace has repeatedly exploited semiotic systems such as these precisely in order to play upon her naiveté and draw her further into his power.[4]

But Clarissa now applies, in effect, a Lovelacean logic to her situation. She treats each event, each phenomenon, as if it signified its opposite—which of course it does. Thus she reads "rescue" as "trap," "friend" as "enemy," and so on. Her violation, one might say, has had epiphanic consequences. She has mastered the hermeneutics of cynicism. And she beats Lovelace here at his own game, interpreting his "antithetical" signs antithetically. He, for his part, is utterly flummoxed by her non-participation in his scheme. He tells Belford in disgust that he is abandoning his "treatise of *dreams sleeping* and *dreams waking*," and will never more "depend upon those flying follies, those illusions of fancy depraved, and run mad" (255).

The collapse of the dream-plot, its total *débâcle*, marks the beginning of a role exchange which will become more intensely delineated in the remaining volumes of the fiction. For the first time Lovelace—who has so profoundly humiliated the heroine—is himself humiliated. His career as a successful "plotter" comes abruptly to a stop. Simultaneously Clarissa, the victim of countless plots (including, until now, the plot of *Clarissa* itself) emerges as a plotter in her own right, a maker of stratagems.[5]

This is not to say that her ascendancy—like everything in the novel—does not have its paradoxical aspects. As we have seen, it begins with a moment of apparent inaction, a refusal to "escape" into the waiting hands of Mother H. and Lovelace. Yet this temporary passivity is somehow in accordance too with the prevailing logic of inversion governing the fictional world. Earlier Clarissa's desperate attempts to elude her "fate" have functioned, morbidly, as flights into deeper confinement: witness her "escape" from the Harlowes into the snares of Lovelace, or that "escape" to Mrs. Moore's at Hampstead which only seems to intensify her persecutor's will toward violation. Escape in *Clarissa* has meant confinement; it follows that confinement should now mean escape. By accepting confinement Clarissa sets up the very conditions which allow ultimately for her real escape to Mrs. Smith's.

When it does come, the heroine's actual flight curiously recombines and inverts elements of Lovelace's dream. She gets away, we recollect, by offering some of her gowns as a gift to Mabel, Dorcas's young helper. Mabel takes off her own clothing and retires into a connecting room to try on the gowns in front of a glass. Clarissa quickly puts on Mabel's clothes, and, wearing the servant's hood over her head, runs out, gesturing silently to Will and Dorcas on the way. The escape parodies the dream-escape. Dorcas, in contrast to the dream, enacts her usual role of jailer (rather than "accomplice"), but Clarissa escapes anyway. A "kindly old lady" intervenes—not Mother H., however, but a *real* kindly old lady, Mrs. Smith. Most important, Clarissa is not cast here as the agonized dupe, but becomes the active designer of her flight. It is no small irony that in "plotting" this touch-and-go business Clarissa resorts to some of Lovelace's characteristic ploys: the bribery of gullible young women, hypocrisy, sartorial disguise, role-playing.

Clarissa's success as a "plotter" in the moment of her escape has its apparent corollaries later in the fiction. She employs stratagems to keep Lovelace away from her: that allegorical snare, the celebrated "Father's House" letter, is the most remarkable of these. But in the latter part of the fiction the heroine becomes a plotter in a larger, more dramatic sense too. Clarissa's elaborate preparations for death—the ornamented coffin, the writing of the will, her intense meditation on the "next" world—are themselves a sort of transcendent plotting, in that they suggest a purposiveness, an anticipation and manipulation of future events on Clarissa's part, unlike anything she has shown before. Her embellished, pious passage into death is a triumph of design, a work of "Art." Quite as much as any of Lovelace's artifices earlier, it seems conscious, managed, staged. Here at last the heroine seems to script the "plot" of her own future—and in a mysterious way too the plot of that fiction bearing her name.

On one level, then, Lovelace's dream stands out as a narrative marker of considerable significance. In a paradoxical way it is technically "responsible" for the fact that Clarissa ultimately makes a successful flight. Lovelace's ill-fated attempt to stage his dream results in confusion, dissension, paranoia, and increasing carelessness among his female accomplices—particularly Dorcas and Sinclair. Clarissa takes advantage of this disordered, fractious state of affairs when she makes her dash for freedom. But the dream is more than just one narrative link among many; it signals a profound twisting of the narrative thread—the convulsive turn Aristotle refers to as the *peripateia*, or "change by which the action veers round to its opposite" (*Poetics*, Book XI). For Lovelace's dream marks the point at which the plot of *Clarissa* flips over, turns inside-out.

Until the dream, one could say, the plot of the fiction has been utterly shaped by, indeed indistinguishable from, the Lovelacean "plot"—which has been no more or less than the plot of sexual entrapment. Yet at the moment the dream occurs, this Lovelacean plot is, so to speak, exhausted. Clarissa has undergone her "trial"—rape—once already; the Lovelacean plot can only prolong itself, speciously, through repetition. Looking back at the letter describing the dream-plot, one finds that even there Lovelace himself is half-aware of a certain exhaustion in his designs:

> What, as I have contemplated, is the enjoyment of the finest woman in the world, to the contrivance, the bustle, the surprises, and at last the happy conclusion of a well-laid plot? The charming *roundabouts*, to come the *nearest way home*; the doubts, the apprehensions, the heart-achings, the meditated triumphs—those are the joys that make the blessing dear. For all the rest, what is it? What but to find an angel in imagination dwindled down to a woman in fact? (248)

Lovelace knows only one plot, and by not-so-charming roundabouts, it has already come "home." His dream, which does little but rewrite the original rape, is tautological. And soon enough, the Lovelacean plot is eclipsed by a radically different one—Clarissa's "plot"—the plot of escape. At the moment of the dream, the plot of *Clarissa* becomes the plot of Clarissa.

If, as the formalists encourage us to do, we envisage the narrative as a rhetorical arrangement analogous to the sentence, it is structured, we find, like a chiasmus: the ordering of elements in the second part of the fiction, following the dream, reverses that of the first. In the first volumes Clarissa moves gradually deeper into confinement; in the latter volumes she moves by reverse stages out of it, likewise retracing the journey back to Harlowe-Place, where she began. Exile, humiliation, and violation are replaced, in inverse order, by their opposites: safety, vindication, reabsorption into her "Father's House," both earthly and celestial. The dream, rather than her rape itself, is that crossing-point, the X of the chiasmus, where everything changes. The X is bracketed by matching pairs of antithetical events. Two actions immediately precede it: Clarissa's abortive escape to Hampstead (failure of the plot of escape) and her rape by Lovelace (triumph of the plot of entrapment). Two actions immediately follow it: the collapse of Lovelace's dream-plot (failure of the plot of entrapment) and Clarissa's flight to Smith's (triumph of the plot of escape).

Having said all this, however, one makes everything of course much simpler than it is. I have suggested that Lovelace's dream functions purely ironically—that it is *not* prophetic, except in reverse—and that by backfiring it heralds Clarissa's now-imminent triumph. But nothing is ever purely anything in *Clarissa,* and Lovelace's phantasmatic, delirious reverie cannot be domesticated so easily. I would like to conclude here by obscuring—in fact inverting—what I have already said. This is not hard to do, because Lovelace's dream remains nothing if not problematic. In arguing here, I have already had to make several rhetorical elisions in order to suggest that the dream is devoid of proleptic elements. I avoided elaborating, for instance, on that part of the dream where Lovelace, in bed with Clarissa, hears from her "Nothing . . . but sighs, groans, exclamations, faintings, dyings." Yet what is this progression of nouns, one might ask, if not a suggestive "prophecy" of Clarissa's destiny? One might see it indeed as an appalling five-word *précis* of the plot of *Clarissa* itself, including, ominously, its tragic resolution. As if by accident, a slip of the tongue (that crucial word "dyings"), Lovelace has in fact prescribed—written in advance—the narrative future. In an apparent throwaway line, he articulates what is to come.

But the dream has even more troubling implications. These arise, again, from the ambiguities of the notion of "plot" itself, and its multiple range of reference. I have said that Clarissa emerges as a "plotter" just as Lovelace fails as one, in the collapse of his dream-plot, but again this is something of a simplification. For it is not altogether clear, from one perspective at least, that her successful escape *is* a plot. After Clarissa gets away Lovelace claims, half-seriously, that her seemingly clever flight was not "plotted" at all, but "accidental." "The Lady's plot to escape," he tells Belford, "appears to me no extraordinary one. There was much more luck than probability that it should do" (319). He denies Clarissa credit for designing her escape, and suggests instead it was in some sense a *random* event. One could dismiss this as Lovelace consoling himself for his own blunders were it not that Belford, the heroine's apologist, also suggests the "accidental" nature of her getaway. It succeeded, he informs Lovelace, not because Clarissa had thought everything out in advance, but because "it depended partly on the *weather*" (309). Clarissa was able to cover herself with Mabel's hood, and thus avoid detection, because it was "raining." Here, from a supposedly objective source, the same gloss: the heroine's escape has been brought about, not by her own efforts finally, but by an eminently unpredictable external agency, a bathetic "accident" of meteorology. This single detail confounds in a blow that neat symmetrical structure already formulated—the chiasmic balance between the Lovelacean "plot of entrapment" and Clarissa's "plot of escape"—for it problematizes the notion that Clarissa *is* in fact a true "plotter," at least in any rigorous sense. And if Clarissa is not designing her own destiny at this point, who is?

This last question abruptly calls our attention, however, to another "plotter," one outside the fictional world—Richardson himself. Someone obviously has "plotted" that rain should fall just as Clarissa gets hold of Mabel's hood—and who if not the mysterious perpetrator of *Clarissa* itself? We are suddenly conscious of *his* plot here, the literary plot. Yet as soon as Richardson is admitted into the discussion and his authorial agency acknowledged, one compromises utterly any transcendental notion of Clarissa's "escape." Though Clarissa escapes Lovelace's plot, it cannot be said that she escapes Richardson's. And ironically, it is her very flight from Lovelace that makes possible her final entrapment by Richardson. For he is now free to do with her what he has "plotted" all along—that is, transform her into his exemplary Christian heroine.

I spoke before of Clarissa's dying as something she plots—a premeditated leap from this world into the "next." But her death is more properly spoken of, perhaps, in relation to Richardson's plot. From our privileged place outside the fictional world we see it emerge—with an almost shocking translucency after a certain point—as part of Richardson's own grand "design." As he acknowledged himself, the dénouement of his fiction—the heroine's pious dying and beatification—was intended from the outset to be the most significant part of the text, the part which, by its exemplary power, would redeem any potentially questionable or overly "warm" scenes preceding it.[6] The incomparable vision of Clarissa on her deathbed—stilled, supine, purified, marvelous—was to crown his fiction, illuminate its Christian purpose, and, most important, work to effect the moral regeneration of readers. Richardson's own moral program demanded from the start that Clarissa die in the isolate, uninterrupted, revelatory way she ultimately does. Midway through the fiction, however, he needs a crucial scene change in order to create the noble final effect he wants. Clarissa's focused, meditative approach to death cannot take place, we see retrospectively, amid the din and outrages of Dover Street. Mrs. Sinclair's brothel is not the place for a Christian setpiece; Richardson has to "move" the heroine, as it were, to the neutral unblemished confines of Smith's. Clarissa's escape is therefore a necessary component in a larger symbolic moral scheme—that redemptive "plot" within which Richardson hopes to catch his reader.

Considered in the light of this Richardsonian design, Lovelace's dream— and the busy stratagem Lovelace extracts from it—function almost as a *deus ex machina,* a distraction, or elaborately paradoxical apparatus behind which Richardson can carry out the stagiest part of his own plot. The dream-plot prepares the reader psychologically for repetition; Clarissa's actual escape looks by contrast miraculous, uncontingent, "accidental." Yet in a way it is the most laboriously "plotted," artificial, and implausible event in the whole novel—a piece of sheer authorial wish-fulfillment. As Lovelace says, there is little "probability" in it. Common sense alone, gleaned perhaps from an age in which Yorkshire Rippers and Hillside Stranglers flourish, suggests that Clarissa's escape is stunningly improbable: women persecuted in the theatrical, obsessive, and ultimately necrophiliac manner that she is seldom—in reality—get out alive.[7] Before her flight, Clarissa herself fears she will be murdered at Sinclair's house and perhaps thrown "too deep for detection" into an ignominious pit in the "garden or cellar" (308). But such is not the fate her creator has in store for her. Richardson's great editor, the Marquis de Sade, recognized the sentimentality of this final turn in the Richardsonian plot, and by connecting the masculine plot of sexual entrapment with the plot of female torture and murder in *Justine* and *Juliette,* created histories at once more hideous and more realistic.

Leaping between levels, from"plots" within the fiction to "plots" without, we are forced to allow a certain prophetic tiding in Lovelace's dream after all. It has predicted that Clarissa, even as she seems to escape, will fall deeper into another plot. If the notion of plot is enlarged to include the Richardsonian plot as well as the Lovelacean, the dream comes at least "half" true. Clarissa, escaping, falls into that trap set by her own creator—one that decrees she may never escape her suffering except by exemplifying it: by serving as a personification of the sorrows of Christian womanhood.[8] Fleeing the villainous plot, she succumbs to the literary.

Lovelace's dream addresses us, then, with two mouths: it both lies and speaks the truth about the future of that narrative in which it is embedded. It admits of two contradictory propositions simultaneously: that it is both ironic and nonironic, that it fails to predict the outcome of plot in *Clarissa,* and at the same time, predicts it. It is both joke and allegory. This indeterminacy, what one might call the multivalent affect of the dream, is in accord of course with its own contradictory "plot" and the story *it* tells—of perverse exchanges, metamorphoses, and endless transformations of things into their opposites. Like all dreams, Lovelace's vision has to do most profoundly, not with the either/or, but with the both/and. On every level it subverts the notion of mutually exclusive possibilities and instead—dizzyingly, punningly—merges contraries, fuses opposites.

This perpetual doubleness in Lovelace's dream makes it, finally, a fitting epitome of *Clarissa* itself. For what is Richardson's fiction itself if not a great, dizzyingly recursive structure, where opposites mingle and the truth is always double? Lovelace's dream is paradoxical—"promiscuous" in structure and meaning, yet so too is *Clarissa*. Invariably, appallingly, antitheses collapse in the fictional world: escape and entrapment, life and death, body and soul, black and white, angels and women—all become curiously indistinguishable. A hallucinatory, shocking, almost anagrammatical sameness replaces difference; "Clarissa" and "Sinclair" mirror one another. And reading itself is transformed into a dream-like, recursive process: any proposition we make about the "plot" of *Clarissa* is instantly convertible into its opposite. Hence the endless series of antithetical readings the fiction generates.[9] What is needed in the end perhaps—and herein the witty hub of Lovelace's dream—is a new allegory for plot itself, one suited to this most monstrous and overdetermined of fictions. One suspects the apt emblem will not be Aristotle's extended piece of thread, with its single central twist, but an endlessly turning, endlessly twisting loop. In *Clarissa* the chiasmic "line" of plot becomes a Möbius strip, where two faces perpetually collapse into one, and vice versa. Said more mysteriously, the thread of plot is spun on a wheel, and the snake—even as it twists—takes its tail in its mouth.

CHAPTER 5

"MATTERS NOT FIT TO BE MENTIONED": FIELDING'S *THE FEMALE HUSBAND*

Befitting the festive, dangerous nature of its subject—sexual impersonation—Henry Fielding's *The Female Husband* has assumed a paradoxical place in English literary history. This small pamphlet, published anonymously in 1746, is the fictionalized report of the "Surprising History" of Mary Hamilton, alias "George," a female transvestite arrested and tried in that year at Wells for marrying another woman while in disguise. Fielding knew of the case through newspaper stories and—biographers suggest—wrote his own half-pious, half-prurient account for quick cash. As one might expect, given such scandalous content, the work sold out immediately and had to be reprinted. But again as one might expect, though Fielding's authorship has been acknowledged since the turn of this century, the pamphlet itself has been decorously ignored. Early on, Cross mentioned it as one of Fielding's "trifles," but did not describe its subject. F. Homes Dudden in turn called it a "mere piece of hackwork" and implied it was unworthy of its author. Pat Rogers is more charitable, but still treats *The Female Husband* only briefly, as a "sensational potboiler." Until very recently a guarded 1959 article by Sheridan Baker—concerned mainly with the stylistic attribution of the piece to Fielding—remained the longest critical discussion in print.[1] Like its phantasmagoric, impudent heroine, *The Female Husband* has existed, it seems, on a symbolic margin—at once present and absent, notorious and unmention-able, sublime and taboo.

This scholarly equivocation is interesting in itself, of course, particularly for anyone concerned with the sociology of literary criticism. One of the traditional projects of criticism, at least since the time of Samuel Johnson, has been the exhaustive taking note of all works by classic authors—even very minor pieces—on the theory that every writing may potentially manifest the signs of greatness or "genius." At the same time, however, literary scholars are obliged not to breach the prevailing decorum of critical discourse itself. Unlike literature, literary criticism is perceived as a form of polite writing, suitable for "mixed" company. It is a discourse heavily regulated by social constraints. *The Female Husband* clearly evokes conflicting critical imperatives. Freighted with authorial prestige, it seems to demand attention, yet it deals in the unmentionable—cross-dressing and lesbianism—subjects so charged they have conventionally seemed somehow both beneath and beyond discourse. The result has been a kind of embarrassed half-acknowledgment. Interestingly enough, the work has lately been rescued from its enforced oblivion—not by Fielding scholars, but by those most interested in expanding the subject matter of academic discourse: feminist critics, the new historians of sexuality.[2]

I do not make these observations randomly, for they are intimately bound up with the peculiar nature of *The Female Husband* itself—a narrative which at once describes and doesn't describe, tells and doesn't tell. As the semantic aberration of the title suggests, the text takes as its subject a metaphysical contradiction, a violation of categories. It sets out to represent a human paradox, that which shouldn't exist but does, a "monster" of perversity. Yet Fielding's project is itself contaminated by the perverse: his rhetorical task is precisely to mention the unmentionable, to speak decorously of a huge lapse in decorum (the sexual impersonator being always among the least decorous of figures), to address a "mixed" company of readers on the taboo subject of sexual mixtures. The task is utterly compromising, and *The Female Husband* is not surprisingly burdened with incoherencies, wild swings in tone, and moral and stylistic evasions. It is a deeply confused, even crude piece of writing.

But despite this confusion—indeed, I think, because of it—*The Female Husband* deserves another look. The work undeniably takes its place among Fielding's satiric writings: Mary Hamilton's usurpation of masculine sartorial and sexual privilege (and the two indiscretions are profoundly related) makes her a target not only for his general critique of dissimulation and hypocrisy, but also for some of his more revealing antifeminist sentiment. Because she disturbs the "natural" hierarchy of male-female relations so radically, Hamilton becomes for Fielding a version of what Susan Gubar has called the "female monster" of Augustan satire—an offense to the great chain of being.[3] She is quite literally a mock hero, and Fielding characteristically tries to put her back in her place through the use of the mock heroic.

Yet the satire is never easy, never straightforward. The very power the fantastical shape-shifting Hamilton exerts over Fielding's imagination suggests a more complex emblematic force. She embodies matters which preoccupy him in his plays and fiction: the hypnotic power and subversiveness of the masquerade, the ambiguous relation between sexual identity and the "trappings" of sex, the conundrum of gender and gender boundaries. And those mixed reactions she elicits—recoil and fascination, fear and attraction, the desire to deny and the desire to commemorate—are a sign of a larger ideological tension in Fielding: between his wish for "natural" distinctions between the sexes—a theology of gender—and his countervailing, often enchanted awareness of the theatricality and artifice of human sexual roles. One could say that in *The Female Husband* the satirist—conservative in values, committed to maintaining boundaries and preserving through irony an ideal typology of pure forms—comes into conflict with the theatrical *entrepreneur* (which Fielding also was): radical at heart, given to suspending boundaries and creating illusory, mutable, impure forms. The contradictions of the work are thus Fielding's own. Mary Hamilton is his symbol of the perverse, yet she also personifies some of his own paradoxes—the unmentionable possibility he is compelled to mention.

II

A word first about the real Mary Hamilton. Fielding indeed has few words for her: despite his claim that her story is "Taken From Her Own Mouth" it is unlikely he ever met her or studied her case firsthand. The original "female husband"—Sheridan Baker has discovered from trial records—was born in Somerset and lived afterwards in Scotland. At fourteen she left home dressed in her brother's clothes and became a travelling quack doctor. In May 1746 she returned to Somerset and took up lodgings at Wells under the name of "Dr. Charles Hamilton." Hamilton married Mary Price, the niece of her landlady, in July. After three months of marriage, apparently including sexual relations, Mary Price realized the fraud and had Hamilton arrested. The law being somewhat at a loss to find a precedent for her "uncommon notorious cheat," Hamilton was convicted on a clause in the vagrancy act. She was sentenced to public whippings in four Somerset towns and six months in Bridewell. After her sentencing, she disappears from the record.[4]

Though Fielding's lawyer cousin Henry Gould was consulted in the case, it is most likely that Fielding knew of Hamilton only through a short account appearing first in Boddely's *Bath Journal:*

> We hear from Taunton, that at a General Quarter Sessions of the Peace . . . *Mary Hamilton,* otherwise *George,* otherwise *Charles Hamilton,* was try'd for a very singular and notorious Offence: Mr. Gold, Council·for the King, open'd to the Court, That the said *Mary, &c.* pretending herself a Man, had married fourteen Wives, the

last of which Number was one Mary Price, who appeared in Court, and deposed, that she was married to the Prisoner, some little Time since, at the Parish Church of St. Cuthbert's in Wells, and that they were Bedded as Man and Wife, and lived as such for about a Quarter of a Year, during which Time, she, the said Price, thought the Prisoner a Man, owing to the Prisoner's using certain vile and deceitful Practices, not fit to be mentioned.[5]

In the classic manner of the criminal biographer Fielding transformed these few facts to create his own version of lesbian picaresque. As Baker found, *The Female Husband* is for the most part pure (or impure) fabrication. Throughout his text Fielding changed names and places for ludicrous or symbolic effect (Hamilton's birthplace becomes the "Isle of Man"), filled out her story with made-up adventures and new characters (including several other wives before Price), added snatches of dialogue and bits and pieces of comic detail—recast the whole, in fact, as Fieldingesque narrative. His fictional touches are everywhere. The woman who first seduces Mary Hamilton into "unnatural pollutions," Anne Johnson, is a Methodist—one of Fielding's favorite comic butts—and has previously practiced such impurity "at *Bristol* with her methodistical sisters" (31). The old widow whom Fielding has Hamilton marry before Mary Price, Mrs. Rushford (or "Rush-for-it"), is one of those sexually overwrought older women, like Lady Booby or Mrs. Slipslop or Lady Trap of *Love in Several Masques*, that he is so fond of caricaturing; and the stereotype is imagined here with a similar bland cruelty. Likewise, Mary Price, the woman who in reality turned Hamilton in, is transformed into an unmistakable Fielding ingenue—romantically enthralled by the dashing, designing impostor, and so astoundingly naive that even at the trial she is unwilling to believe her husband anything "other" than a man.

The many inventions of *The Female Husband*, Fielding's blithe lack of interest in recording the "real" life of his subject, suggest that—as with similar writings of Defoe—we must treat the work as a literary rather than a journalistic event. Despite Fielding's claim to historicity, we are in the sphere of fiction here, not reportage—phantasm, not history. *The Female Husband's* sociohistorical significance is consequently limited. This is something of a shame, for the real Mary Hamilton—described by the *Bath Journal* as being, even after her confinement, "very gay, with Perriwig, Ruffles, and Breeches"—sounds interesting in herself, and one would like to know more about her.[6]

As social historians have recently begun to acknowledge, female transvestism was a far more common phenomenon in the eighteenth and nineteenth centuries than has previously been suspected. Reasons for this are not hard to seek. Cross-dressing was a direct if risky way for a woman to escape those constraints—physical, economic, and psychological—imposed by rigid sex roles and the graphic demarcation of masculine and feminine spheres. In eighteenth-century English society, where female prerogatives were so drastically circumscribed, male disguise offered women otherwise impossible freedoms. A disguised woman, first of all, could travel alone and with greater safety. (Through the account of the difficult unescorted peregrinations of Sophie Western and Mrs. Waters, Fielding's own *Tom Jones* reminds us of course that ordinary women travelling alone constantly risked loss of reputation, harassment, or sexual assault.) Disguise meant a certain primary mobility. But it also allowed women to take on work or social functions otherwise denied them, particularly in times of economic depression. In an odd compendium entitled *Eighteenth-Century Waifs*, the Victorian antiquarian John Ashton described a number of "Eighteenth-Century Amazons"—women who joined the military and fought in battles while disguised—and twentieth-century historians have added to the list.[7] Criminal careers were another possibility. Female highwaymen were not unknown in the eighteenth century: chapbooks and broadsides of the period record many disreputable characters like "Miss Davis, Commonly Called the Beauty in Disguise." The latter, a Moll Flanders-like personage, robbed a man with whom she was sharing a room in an inn of a thousand pounds while disguised as a boy.[8] Finally, as the lives of Mary Hamilton, Fielding's theatrical associate Charlotte Charke, and several others suggest, male costume allowed women to make unobserved and hence unimpugned erotic contacts with other women. The full history of eighteenth-century homosexuality—its formal permutations, the subterranean cultural dream it embodies—has yet to be written, though a few historians and critics have begun to make a start.[9]

Fielding, however, is not interested in realizing Hamilton's charade from the "inside." He makes no attempt to imagine what complex motive might have led her to her act of impersonation, or how she herself might have described the meaning of her behavior. Psychological and political leaps, even of the rudimentary sort found in Defoe, are lacking in *The Female Husband*. And again, despite Fielding's claim that his tale comes from his subject's own "Mouth," it is precisely Mary Hamilton's own voice, the female voice, which is absent from the work. The real woman, her aspirations and desires, simply does not figure. What is figured is a symbolic woman, a trope for female iniquity. We know Mary Hamilton through her metaphysical affect alone—and this as Fielding perceives it. He treats her, never in her specificity, but as an allegory of transgression. By her sartorial imposture she transgresses against the code of feminine modesty, by her homoeroticism against the code of "nature" itself. The real woman is transformed into an occasion for an effusion of masculine rhetoric. At the outset then, one might claim that *The Female Husband* says more of Fielding himself—and certain characteristic projections of eighteenth-century masculine fantasy—than of its ostensible female "subject."

There is irony, as well as a troubling moral problem, in the fact that Fielding's would-be exposure of fraud (Hamilton is convicted of "having by false and deceitful practices endeavoured to impose on some of his Majesty's subjects") is itself something of a fraud. To borrow a word from *Tom Jones*, it is a "Rhodomontade"—a shapely lie, fable dressed up as history. But this very factitiousness suggests right away something of the peculiarly paradoxical nature of the work. For the desire to elaborate the "real" life in fictional terms—to subject the anecdotal to the formulae of art and thereby both alter its nature and extend its symbolic range—is often psychologically problematic. One might claim that Fielding here simply follows the conventions of a popular genre, the criminal biography, which traditionally bypassed truth in favor of legendary, sensational, and schematic incident. This observation, however, simply restates the question: why the tradition of false embellishment at all?

In the case of *The Female Husband*, the work of fictionalization, of rendering "literary," seems especially to bespeak conflicting underlying impulses. On the one hand, Fielding's attribution of made-up exploits to Mary Hamilton, his rejection of objective transcription and leap into cheeky invention (which all the while poses as negative exemplum), may reflect a wish, perhaps on an unconscious level, to de-actualize her profoundly subversive career. Making Hamilton over into a "fictive" personage is a way of transferring the troubling historical facts of female transvestism and homosexuality into the safe realm of literature. *The Female Husband's* epigraph from Book 12 of *Metamorphoses*, describing Neptune's transformation of a young woman, Caenis, into a man, indeed suggests as much: it invites us to connect its subject with the world of Ovidian fable and the "marvelous," where sex changes result from divine tampering rather than the threatening, bubbling extrusion, on the human level, of "unnatural lusts."[10]

At the same time, however, the shift into the fictional may express a quite contradictory wish. Fictionalizing allows one to stay with one's subject for longer than might otherwise be possible. In contrast to the historian, the fabulist is free to elaborate more than the facts warrant, to play out to excess, to deliquesce—to *dwell*, in short, on his or her topos. And this of course is exactly what Fielding does. From a paragraph's worth of fact he spins pages, multiplying his heroine's "vile impostures," filling out her life history with thick and fast (and false) comic detail. At the end of *The Female Husband*, when, as in the moment of *cognitio* in Roman comedy, Hamilton's scam is at last exposed, one has the feeling that Fielding is almost sorry the game is up. On one level, he is afraid of her and what she represents; on another, he delights in *speaking* of her.

This tension—between uneasiness and delight, suppression and expansion —pervades *The Female Husband* and conditions its several types of ambiguity. This ambiguity occurs across different levels—most grossly perhaps on the level of the paragraph. Sections of lubricious, wholly imaginary erotic happenstance are followed by sections of lumpy didactic piety, and vice versa. Typically, Fielding encloses descriptions of lesbian *galanterie* within moralistic "parentheses," but the effect remains one of confusion and bad faith.

Thus in the first paragraph of the pamphlet, he warns readers against the "monstrous" acts human beings are capable of when they ignore the "prudent and secure guides of virtue and religion" (29). And in the last (which follows a grisly word-picture describing Hamilton's "lovely" skin "scarified with rods, in such a manner that her back was almost flead" after her floggings) he repeats the message, hoping that "this example will be sufficient to deter all others from the commission of any such foul and unnatural crimes." Fielding concludes by asserting the suitability of his text for perusal by female readers—those, one assumes, who need most to be alerted to impostors like Mary Hamilton:

> In order to caution therefore that lovely sex, which, while they preserve their natural innocence and purity, will still look most lovely in the eyes of men, the above pages have been written, which, that they might be worthy of their perusal, such strict regard hath been had to the utmost decency, that notwithstanding the subject of this narrative be of a nature so difficult to be handled inoffensively, not a single word occurs through the whole, which might shock the most delicate ear, or give offence to the purest chastity. (51)

In between these "pure" parentheses, however, he indulges in moments of comically distended, one could even say theatrical, suggestiveness. One love scene, in which the elderly, infatuated Mrs. Rushford pounces on her quack husband, is a characteristic mixture of the coy and the lewd:

> One of our English poets remarks in the case of a more able husband than Mrs. *Hamilton* was, when his wife grew amorous in an unseasonable time,
>
> > *The doctor understood the call,*
> > *But had not always the wherewithal.*
>
> So it happened to our poor bridegroom, who having not at that time *the wherewithal* about her, was obliged to remain meerly passive, under all this torrent of kindness from his wife, but this did not discourage her, who was an experienced woman, and thought she had a cure for this coldness in her husband, the efficacy of which, she might perhaps have essayed formerly. Saying therefore with a tender smile to her husband, I believe you are a woman, her hands began to move in such a direction, that the discovery would absolutely have been made, had not the arrival of dinner, at that very instant, prevented it. (39)

The "accidental" arrival of dinner—a classic Fielding flourish—here functions to maintain the technical purity of his narrative, just as it maintains Hamilton's fraud for a little while longer. A certain precarious decency is in fact preserved, yet one may ask whether it really is, as Fielding claims it is, decency of the "utmost" sort.

Hamilton's dildo—for that is what one must assume is signified by the none-too-mysterious "wherewithal" in the foregoing passage—reappears later on as that "something of too vile, wicked, and scandalous a nature" discovered in her "trunk" and produced in evidence against her. The use of euphemism is symptomatic. It is everywhere in *The Female Husband*. And again, euphemism bespeaks ambivalence, here on the level of the sentence, It is a figure commonly associated with paradoxical rhetorical intentions—a way of simultaneously telling and not telling, censoring and not censoring. To speak periphrastically is to refer without naming, to point to the taboo without mentioning the taboo. Along with the ellipsis, which serves a similar function, it is Fielding's favored mode of (non-)description in *The Female Husband*. Thus he tells us that between Hamilton and her first lover, the "methodistical" Anne Johnson, passed "transactions not fit to be mention'd." When Mrs. Rushford boasts to a woman friend of her satisfaction with her new bridegroom, and the friend, noting Hamilton's peculiar "effeminacy," expresses skepticism, a discussion ensues between them "not proper to be repeated, if I knew every particular." At Wells, where Hamilton's impostures are at last unveiled, a mob of clownish townspeople revile her with "terms of reproach not fit to be commemorated." And again, the "means" the insouciant Hamilton uses to deceive the innocent is "something," the narrator explains, "decency forbids me even to mention." One could say that Fielding's circumlocutions have a certain charm—not unlike those in *Fanny Hill*—and that indeed they work rather neatly to recapitulate on the textual level those "disguises" which occupy him thematically. The euphemism—a "pure" term which stands in for one less pure, less decorous—is analogous in this sense to Hamilton herself, a member of the "fair sex," who is also a stand-in for the perennially indecorous phallicized male. The prose of *The Female Husband* is bowdlerized, "emasculated"; and Hamilton herself, the subject of this prose, is an emblem of emasculation. The simpler purpose of the euphemism also holds, however: it is a way of mediating the unspeakable, of presenting that which is in every way unpresentable. Euphemism suggests psychic tension, between impulses of denial and acknowledgment. Fielding tries at once to take note of Hamilton's doings, and pretend that he doesn't know what she has done. The effect is alternately campy and unpleasant.

For the most complex form of ambiguity in *The Female Husband*, however—and the most complex sign of Fielding's ambivalence about his subject—one must look to the mock heroic, that form into which the work so often lapses. The mock heroic is appropriate for a piece of antifeminist propaganda, which *The Female Husband* of course is. Mary Hamilton affects a sartorial and sexual prestige which is not by "nature" hers, but belongs to a higher set of beings (men). Her pretensions are thus fittingly burlesqued through mock elevation—an elevation intended to take advantage of the "surprising absurdity" which, as Fielding says in the Preface to *Joseph Andrews*, occurs when a writer "appropriates the manners of the highest to the lowest."[11] In classic mock-heroic texts, diction befitting an exalted subject is incongruously applied to a "low" one: the intent of such dislocation is to intensify our sense of the normal hierarchy, of things as they *should* be, of the proper relationship between "high" and "low." In *The Female Husband*, Fielding's persistent ironic use of the pronoun "he" for Hamilton (often together with "she" in the same sentence to heighten the reader's sense of sexual and semantic confusion) might be counted as a kind of minimalist mock heroic, at the most basic referential level. The little "he's" dotting the narrative are a constant comic reminder to the reader of the central feature of Hamilton's unacceptability: her "unnatural" and arrogant assumption of masculine rights. More typical, however, is Fielding's use of epic terms to describe her acts of spurious *machismo*. After receiving affectionate "hints" from Mrs. Rushford, for instance, the "female gallant" "very gladly embraced the opportunity, and advancing with great warmth of love to the attack, in which she was received almost with open arms, by the tottering citadel, which presently offered to throw open the gates, and surrender at discretion" (37). Again, describing a memorable tryst between Hamilton and Mary Price, the narrator notes, "if any corner of *Molly's* heart remain'd untaken, it was now totally subdued" (46). The mixing up of realms here—the application of the terms of Homeric conflict to rather perverse amorous exchanges—is an entirely fitting commentary on one (Hamilton) who mixes things up so profoundly, beginning with the sexes themselves. Fielding's rhetorical misappropriations work here in the way that those in *Jonathan Wild* do—only more so. The criminal Wild is ironically treated as a "Great Man" who is not at all great. Not only is Mary Hamilton not great, she is not even a man.

There is, however, a way in which such persiflage invariably imposes a latent textual uncertainty. The mock-heroic element in *The Female Husband* expresses the same psychological paradox characteristic of the mock heroic in general: it grants power to its target at the same time that it tries to minimize it. To elevate, even for the purposes of burlesque, is still always to elevate. Hamilton remains for Fielding a "heroine in iniquity"—a specimen of power dubiously achieved and dubiously expressed, but powerful nonetheless. His very defensiveness suggests her glamorous pull. Caricature and burlesque are reactive forms: they bespeak the original authority or psychic challenge posed by that which is satirized. Thus when Fielding comically displaces Hamilton's unconventional exploits into the realm of epic action—which we note is also the realm of *male* action—he may be engaged in what Freud in *Jokes and Their Relation to the Unconscious* saw as one of the prime objects of the "wit-work": defense against that which is acknowledged to be powerful. We are back here at the paradox I have been suggesting all along—that Fielding is both repulsed and attracted to his heroine, concerned to distance himself from her morally, but also unconsciously drawn to her. Indeed his mock heroics seem at times hardly mocking at all, but rather, curiously affectionate. For Fielding's Mary Hamilton *is* attractive—charming and energetic, as well as seductive. Women fall for her at the drop of a hat. In this magical success with women, this sheer amiability, she is not a little like another of his favored creations, Tom Jones himself. At the same time, like her inventor, Hamilton is also something of a wit, and shows an appealing élan in tight situations. One recollects with amusement her gallant comeback when, after being accidentally discovered a woman, she tells one of her discombobulated brides that she may now have "all the pleasures of marriage without the inconveniences" (42).

III

What to do then with the vagaries of *The Female Husband?* Some of its confusion, first of all, may simply result from Fielding's unprecedented attempt to address readers of both sexes on a subject—lesbianism—which had traditionally been thought suitable for only one: men. Lesbianism has had a long history as a *topos* in pornographic literature, and was never a more popular theme perhaps than in the eighteenth century. Cleland introduced a lesbian episode into *Fanny Hill,* as did the writer William King in his satirical poem of 1736, *The Toast.* Robert James, the friend of Johnson, included an inflaming passage on female homosexuality in his *Medicinal Dictionary* of 1745, and later in the century Diderot and Mairobert exploited lesbianism for pornographic purposes in *La Religieuse* and *L'Espion Anglois.* Pornography, however, has always been a segregated form of cultural discourse, one reflecting the double standard for men and women in sexual matters. (Indeed, pornography may perhaps be most adequately defined, not by any intrinsic content but by its distribution—its invariable appeal to a limited audience of "men only.") Fielding often seems tempted in *The Female Husband* to swell out Mary Hamilton's adventures in the direction of the pornographic, one assumes for the titillation of his male readers. At the same time, however, he seems also to respond to an intermittent yet inhibiting awareness of female readers— readers who must be regulated, lest, like Hamilton herself, they "prostitute and debase" all womanly modesty. Those very specifics which make for male enjoyment unfortunately provide women readers with too many insights into the techniques of vice, something Fielding does not want to appear to do. The result is unsatisfactory either way: he achieves neither a full unbuttoned pornographic elaboration, nor does he strike quite the right tone of ominous obfuscation characteristic of homiletic writing which sets out to warn women or adolescents of "sexual abomination."[12]

But the intellectual and moral precariousness of *The Female Husband* may be explained another way, I think—not just reductively in terms of audience, but as a reflection of Fielding's own much more complicated imaginative response to Mary Hamilton's charade. One could say she awakens in him both moral and aesthetic responses. The two types of response are here profoundly incompatible. He is torn between her criminality and her androgynous appeal, and the effect is chaotic.

Crucial to this chaos is the notion of masquerade—a subject about which Fielding had distinctly mixed feelings. The motif of the masquerade occurs frequently in Fielding's writings, and not just in the novels, though of course it makes important appearances there.[13] He is often concerned with the general moral symbolism of masquerade, and with the problematic distance disguise sets up between outward sign and inner reality, appearance and essence. In explicitly didactic pieces such as "An Essay on the Knowledge of the Characters of Men," sartorial disguise is linked with duplicity. The masque is Fielding's metaphor there for moral dissimulation and chicanery, the "*Art of Thriving*" through deception. The hypocrite imposes on others, he suggests, by affecting the "garments" of innocence: "while the crafty and designing Part of Mankind, consulting only their own separate Advantage, endeavour to maintain one constant Imposition on others, the whole World becomes a vast Masquerade, where the greatest Part appear disguised under false Vizors and Habits; a very few only shewing their own Faces who become, by so doing, the Astonishment and Ridicule of all the rest."[14] Mary Hamilton is a masquerader in this general negative sense—one who wears "false Vizor and Habit" in order to prey on the innocent. Her person embodies the displacement of truth by ornament, embroidery, design. Hers is the profoundly misleading surface.

But her masquerade is also of a very specific kind—sexual disguise. Hamilton willfully subverts gender, the most basic of "essential" human qualities. Masculine threads veil the signs of femininity; sexual motley conceals a sexual personality which is itself motley. "True" gender is here replaced by the "trappings" of gender. In his satiric writing Fielding makes repeated attacks on precisely this sort of deception. Female drag in particular seems to elicit an especially virulent and charged reaction from him. This reaction is as much ideological as psychological. In the early poem "The Masquerade," for instance—a satire on Count Heidegger's promotion of fashionable public masques at the Haymarket— Fielding links women's adoption of male garb to their revolt against patriarchal control, and blames both on the effeminacy of men in the present age. When the poet and his mysterious female guide at the masquerade discuss the subject of fops, she warns him that male dandyism leads to the masculinization of women, and will result in women establishing their own hegemony:

> Your empire shortly will be ended;
> Breeches our brawny thighs shall grace,
> (Another Amazonian race).
> For when men women turn—why then
> May women not be chang'd to men?[15] (128–132)

Similarly, in Fielding's imitation of Juvenal's Sixth Satire, included in the *Miscellanies,* female transvestism is a recurring trope for the perversity of women and their potential for rebellion. Unruly modern women, complains the satirist, follow the lead of actresses who take "breeches parts" (i.e., male roles) at Charles Fleetwood's Drury Lane, and

> themselves turn Players,
> with *Clive* and *Woffington's* gay Airs
> Paint their Faces out like Witches,
> And cram their Thighs in *Fle—w—d's* Breeches.[16] (107–110)

The hapless husband who tries to get rid of his wife by auctioning her off is mortified to hear, listed among the contents of his lady's closet, "those superb *fine*

Horseman's Suits,/And those magnificent *Jack-Boots*" (382-83). Unlike their docile "Great Grandmothers," contemporary Amazons brazenly intrude into the realm of male action. Their accoutrements are the visible sign of their overweening and unnatural ambition:

> Yet see, through *Hide-Park* how they ride!
> How masculine! almost astride!
> Their Hats fierce cock'd up with Cockades,
> Resembling Dragoons more than Maids. (388-391)

The female warrior—often shown in contrast to a man seated at the distaff— is a conventional image on those "world upside down" prints popular in England in the seventeenth and eighteenth centuries. She is an emblem of inversion, of normal hierarchies turned topsy-turvy. Historians disagree on whether such popular images were intended to conserve or subvert established sexual hierarchies; at least one, Natalie Zemon Davis, has suggested their connection with early popular movements and social change.[17] It is clear, however, that Fielding invokes the image negatively, as a way of ridiculing female aspiration. Disturbed by the sight of "Dragoon"-like women, the poet is concerned to reestablish firm boundaries between the sexes and return women to a quintessentially "feminine" sphere. What one could call the patriarchal intent of these passages is obvious: Fielding attacks sartorial ambiguity because sexual hierarchy (and the maintenance of masculine domination) depend on the sexes being distinguishable. (The "cock'd up"/"Cockade" play, with its hint of bawdy, suggests that much of the suppressed hysteria of these passages has to do with masculine fears of lesbianism, and the threat *it* poses to male phallic bravado.) The satire here, one might add, is closely related to Fielding's characteristic fictional attacks on "Amazonian" females, women who usurp masculine privilege in less spectacular ways. In *Tom Jones,* the "Amazon" charge is leveled at several women characters in succession: Molly Seagrim, who engages in the unladylike art of self-defense; Mrs. Western, who assumes masculine intellectual prerogatives, even daring to comment on politics; Lady Bellaston, who lives a life of sexual self-gratification more properly suited to male libertines.

Mary Hamilton would seem to rank among these guilty women: her career is an outrage against patriarchy. But as I have suggested, things are not quite so clear. And indeed, when we consider *Fielding's* career, we realize just how unclear they are. For the irony is that Fielding's complaints against masquerade, even sexual masquerade, are profoundly compromised by his own intimacy with the world of "false appearances" and illusion, pretence and *trompe l'oeil*—the world, in short, of art. Fiction is one form of linguistic masquerade—falsehood disguised as truth—and Fielding the novelist is one kind of masquer. But one need not be so metaphorical: Fielding's theatrical career is clue enough to that ambivalence he seems to feel for Mary Hamilton. His extensive theatrical activity in the 1730s meant, first of all, that he was utterly familiar with the conventions of stage transvestism. Since the introduction of actresses in the Restoration period, women had taken male roles on stage—those "breeches parts" Fielding mentions in the Juvenal imitation. In addition, many plays performed in the early and middle eighteenth century—all of which Fielding knew well—exploited women in male disguise as a comic plot device: Wycherley's *The Plain Dealer* and *The Country Wife*, Shadwell's *The Woman Captain* (rewritten and performed again in the thirties by Odell as *The Prodigal*), Farquhar's *The Recruiting Officer*, not to mention those Shakespearean comedies which are now the best-known examples of the phenomenon: *As You Like It, Twelfth Night, Cymbeline*.[18] Certain actresses played male roles as a matter of course. That masterpiece of inversion, *The Beggar's Opera*, was sometimes performed with a woman in the role of Macheath; a later staging in 1781, described by the *St. James Chronicle* as "ludicrous" entertainment, had all sexual roles reversed.[19] Likewise, as Peter Ackroyd notes, the eighteenth-century harlequinade, reflecting its origin in *commedia dell'arte*, also exploited the comic possibilities of cross-dressing by employing actresses in men's or boys' roles.[20]

Most important, however, is the fact that Fielding himself promoted such stage impersonations. The criticism he makes in the Juvenal imitation of actresses in breeches (and of the women who mimic them in real life) is transparently compromised by the fact that on several occasions as manager of the Little Theatre he encouraged the "strange abomination" of women in drag. He produced several of those plays involving women in disguise, and supported the career of Charlotte Charke, an actress who specialized in breeches parts. This last may have a particular bearing on Fielding's composition of *The Female Husband*. For Charke, renegade daughter of Colley Cibber, was also one of the most famous offstage male impersonators of the age, and later wrote a memoir describing, among other things, her many "mad pranks" in male garb. These included, as in the case of Mary Hamilton, sexual interludes with other women, and in one instance, a proposal of marriage from a "lady of fashion." Charke apparently passed undetected as a man for long periods, despite a fondness for an ostentatiously large "silver-laced hat." By the time Fielding cast her, in 1736–37, in male parts in his own plays *Pasquin, Eurydice Hiss'd,* and *The Historical Register,* she had already made a name for herself, as much for her escapades on the town as for her stage appearances as Macheath (in Roman dress), Lillo's George Barnwell, and Lothario in *The Fair Penitent*. Pat Rogers has speculated that Charlotte Charke may have been in Fielding's mind when he wrote *The Female Husband* in 1746, and indeed the similarities between Charke and Hamilton are striking.[21]

One may only guess at this point, but in the odd contrast between Fielding the satirist and Fielding the man of the theater, we may find an explanation, or part of one, for his paradoxical reaction to Mary Hamilton. That Fielding was always torn between moral impulses and playful impulses—between a desire for law and a desire for mischief—is certainly not a new idea.[22] His biography, the strange combination of the roles of magistrate and creative artist, suggests as much. And likewise, the tension in his fiction between moral vision and amusement at human villainies bespeaks the same conflict. But in *The Female Husband* this conflict seems particularly acute. Fielding oscillates here between the static moral universe of satire—and its implicit longing for the "world turned right side up"—and the fluid realm of stage comedy—with its joyful, potentially anarchical representations of the "world turned upside down." Hamilton is indeed a figure guaranteed to produce anxiety in typical male egos: she challenges the sexual order in the most basic ways. Yet, as Fielding realizes, she is also a marvel of theatricality—theatricality transferred into the mundane realm of everyday life. On several occasions he notes that she "acts her part" (as a man) so well that all succumb to it. She is a successful perpetrator of illusion, an expert at creative escapism. She embodies theatrical values in her own person—the hallucinatory primacy of costume over "identity," the suspension of so-called "natural" categories, sexual release, the notion that anything is possible. One need hardly reiterate at this point that Fielding was himself drawn to these values, and indeed preserved always a heightened sense of the theatricality of human experience. The narrator's famous comparison of life and stage in *Tom Jones* reminds us of Fielding's pervasive awareness of the fluidity, the artificiality, of so much of what passes for immutable human nature. "Some have considered the larger Part of Mankind in the Light of Actors, as personating Characters no more their own, and to which, in Fact, they have no better Title, than the Player hath to be in Earnest thought the King or Emperor whom he represents."[23] Such play-acting in the world of human affairs, he continues, undercuts essentialist notions of good and bad, for "it is often the same Person who represents the Villain and the Heroe; and he who engages your Admiration Today, will probably attract your Contempt To-morrow."

In one sense Mary Hamilton simply represents an excessively flamboyant version of human possibility. She is a player who reminds us of our own capacity for play—a sublime artificer. Her charade is so radical precisely because it subverts the most "natural" of all human distinctions, gender itself. The ideological burdens of masculinity and femininity are, in one carnival gesture, cast off. Through costume one can be either male or female: art triumphs over nature. The power Hamilton exerts, finally, is magical, numinous. For she is not unlike those double-sexed, marvelous figures that have fascinated the human imagination since the Greeks. She brings to mind Aristophanes' speech in *The Symposium,* where Plato acknowledges the universal desire for androgyny—a state unmarred by sexual differentiation and the limitation it implies: "So ancient is the desire of one another which is implanted in us, reuniting our original nature, seeking to make one of two, and heal the state of man. Each of us when separated, having one side only, like a flat fish, is but the tally-half of a man, and he is always looking for his other half."[24] Hamilton's theatricality, as Fielding seems half to realize, may allude ultimately to deeper human aspirations toward transcendence.

Michel Foucault has remarked that the figure of the transvestite haunts the eighteenth century. The point is suggestive—we think of Charlotte Charke, the Chevalier d'Éon, as well as of the intricate androgynous fantasy of eighteenth-century costume itself. One can be sure, however, that Fielding felt something of this haunting pull. The complex rhythm of attraction and recoil that orders (and disorders) *The Female Husband* reflects the disorderly nature of its heroine. It is a textual allegory for her disarmingly mutable nature. But it also reflects Fielding's own ambivalence regarding nature and theater, and his troubled absorption in the world of "false" appearance. In *The Female Husband,* the *persona* of the satirist— conservative, misogynist, concerned with boundary and purity—struggles with that of the theatrical entertainer—whose illusions subvert boundary and flirt with the impure. The peculiar rhetorical tension of the work, between avoidance and revelation, denial and celebration, bespeaks a greater imaginative tension. The polymorphous perversity of the narrative—its weird fluctuations from homily to satire to lyrical picaresque—mirrors a polymorphous response to its subject. Mary Hamilton is indeed both "Villain" and "Heroe" for Fielding; she is the object of both "Contempt" and "Admiration." From one part of him, she elicits anxiety, but from another, she draws engagement and identification—for the purity of her daring, the beauty of her sham. Ruffled and periwigged, the "female husband" awakens classic masculine fears of the Amazon, the woman who is more than woman. But at the same time, unnervingly, she awakens an equally classic *human* fascination—for that which is potentially both woman and man, or neither.

CHAPTER 6

THE CULTURE
OF TRAVESTY:
SEXUALITY AND
MASQUERADE
IN EIGHTEENTH-CENTURY
ENGLAND

When the eighteenth-century moralist wished to decry the cheating and whorishness of contemporary life, he found a potent image close at hand. So ubiquitous were chicanery and vice, wrote Fielding in 1743 in his "Essay on the Knowledge of the Characters of Men," the world was nothing more than "a vast Masquerade," where "the greatest Part appear disguised under false Vizors and Habits." Owen Sedgewick, in the same decade, entitled a lascivious compendium of modern evils *The Universal Masquerade; or, The World Turn'd Inside Out,* and later, in a *Rambler* essay describing the corruptions of wealth (No. 75), Samuel Johnson asserted that the rich and powerful "live in a perpetual masquerade, in which all about them wear borrowed characters." "The world's a masquerade!" wrote Goldsmith in his epilogue to Charlotte Lennox's *The Sister* (1762), and "the masquers, you, you, you."[1]

The rebarbative tone is ageless. The metaphor, however, places us at once in the hallucinatory lost world of eighteenth-century urban culture. For, moralism aside, each man was right in the literal sense: eighteenth-century English society was indeed a world of masqueraders and artificers, self-alienation and phantasmagoria. We are familiar of course with the many shape-shifters who inhabit the fiction and folklore of the period; Moll Flanders, Jonathan Wild, the female soldiers and masked highwaymen of contemporary balladry—these are among the archetypes of an age. But eighteenth-century culture as a whole might also be termed, without exaggeration, a culture of travesty. Especially in London, the manipulation of appearances was both a private strategy and a social institution. Readers of Boswell's journals will doubtless remember the occasions on which the future biographer adopted the guise of soldier or ruffian in order to search for clandestine sexual adventure in the London streets. But travesties took place on a larger, more public scale too. Whether practiced in assembly-rooms, theatres, brothels, public gardens, or at the masquerade itself (which flourished in London from the 1720s on), collective sartorial transformation offered a cathartic escape from the self and a suggestive revision of ordinary experience. The Protean life of the city found expression in a persistent popular urge toward disguise and metamorphosis.[2]

The historian of sexuality will find much to ponder in the exemplary diversions of the eighteenth century. For travesty, of course, is never innocent; it is often a peculiarly expressive, if paradoxical, revelation of hidden needs. In *The Masquerade* (1728), Fielding observed that to "masque the face" was "t'unmasque the mind." Likewise, Addison, in *The Spectator*, noted that contemporary masqueraders invariably dressed as what they "had a Mind to be."[3] For Boswell and others, one might argue, disguise provided a much-desired emotional access to new sensual and ethical realms.

Yet travesty had an even more subversive function in eighteenth-century life. It posed an intimate challenge to the ordering patterns of culture itself. Michel Foucault speaks, as I noted in the preceding chapter, of the haunting power of the transvestite in the eighteenth-century imagination.[4] In fashionable *équivoque* figures like the fop and amazon, moralizing contemporaries were quick to see a profound affront to "Nature" and the order of things. "In every country," a writer in the *Universal Spectator* observed in 1728, "Decency requires that the Sexes should be differenc'd by *Dress,* in order to prevent Multitudes of Irregularities which otherwise would continually be occasion'd."[5] Nonetheless, sexual impersonation remained one of the subtle obsessions of the age. From the notorious actress Charlotte Charke, who recorded her many "mad pranks" in male garb in a famous autobiography in 1755, to the hapless Chevalier d'Éon, with his sensational attempts at transvestite espionage in the 1770s and 1780s, a host of sexual shape-shifters throughout the century parodied and charmed away the hieratic fixities of gender. Even as the eighteenth century condemned such artifices, it also found in them an intimation of a quintessential modern truth: that culture itself was an affront to "nature"—non-transcendental in origin, shaped by convention, the ultimate product of fashion. In the carnivalesque figure of the transvestite, eighteenth-century society began to explore something of its own eminently secular and artifactual nature.

In examining the role of travesty in eighteenth-century life, I shall focus here on the public masquerade—the most expansive and controversial vehicle for the shape-shifting impulse in the period. I will touch, as a matter of course, on the masquerade's contemporary association with libertinism, and its place in the history of actual sexual practices such as homosexuality. But my main object is to present the masquerade as a representative institution—a magic lantern, as it were, in which we may see illuminated the new erotic self-consciousness of the age. For the masquerade indeed provided the eighteenth century with a novel imagery of sexual possibility. Its manifold displacements and enigmas were also heuristic—registering for the first time that ironic resistance to the purely instinctual which has increasingly come to characterize the erotic life of the West since the eighteenth century. In particular, through its stylized assault on gender boundaries, the masquerade played an interesting part in the creation of the modern "polymorphous" subject—perverse by definition, sexually ambidextrous, and potentially unlimited in the range of its desires.

The charismatic institution known as the "Midnight Masquerade" originated in England in the second decade of the eighteenth century. Similar events, to be sure, had taken place earlier; the impulse toward travesty had its historic roots in English culture. Popular religious rituals and seasonal festivities of the Middle Ages and Renaissance had often required the donning of costumes; the hobby-horse games and morris dances of rural England, in which men disguised themselves as women and animals, survived into the eighteenth century and beyond.[6] The court also had its early versions of the masquerade. Masked parties and entertainments, at times directly modelled on traditional festivals, had played an important part in the life of the English aristocracy at least since the time of Henry VIII. In the seventeenth century the masque was a lavish variation on the travesty theme: here nobility disguised themselves as gods and goddesses and acted out fantastic allegories of court life. During the Restoration period, as the Earl of Rochester's psychologically complex impersonations suggest, the court of Charles II offered a rich domain for sartorial play and self-estrangement.[7]

But only in the first decades of the century did the masquerade in the modern sense arise—as a form of large-scale commercial public entertainment, urban and non-exclusive in nature, cutting across historic lines of rank and privilege. Masquerades owed their sudden popularity in part to foreign influences; more travel abroad meant that more and more English people witnessed the traditional carnivals and fêtes of the Continent. The Venetian carnival in particular attracted large numbers of English tourists in the eighteenth century.[8] Foreign entrepreneurs, including the famous masquerade impresario John James Heidegger (the self-described "Swiss Count") and the Venetian-born Theresa Cornelys, settled in London in the first half of the century and introduced the middle-class English public to the sophisticated masked balls and ridottos of the Continent. Walpole reports that the Jubilee masquerade at Ranelagh in 1749 was advertised as being "in the Venetian manner." Masquerades throughout the century were described as "mock-carnivals."[9] Beneath the denatured trappings of urban society,

Figure 6.1. Italian masqueraders. *The Ridotto* by Giuseppe de Gobbis, mid-eighteenth century. Courtesy of the Fine Arts Gallery of San Diego, San Diego Museum of Art.

however, one might also discover nostalgic longings for the popular traditions of the English rural past. Like the fairs, processions and other crowd spectacles of the city, the masquerade revivified the festive life of earlier centuries in a new capitalistic and modern form.[10]

The first important public masquerades in London were those organized by Heidegger in 1717 at the Haymarket Theatre.[11] (Heidegger, who makes a memorable appearance in *The Dunciad,* also produced the first Handel operas in England.) The new venture was an instant scandal—and an instant success. In the 1720s and 1730s, Heidegger's "Midnight Masquerades" drew between seven and eight hundred people a week. Tickets were sold at White's coffee-house and the Haymarket itself, and no one entered the theatre without ticket and disguise. The event, which began at nine or ten, frequently lasted until early the next morning. In Swift's "The Progress of Marriage" (1721–22) an errant wife returns from a masquerade: "At five the footmen make a din, / Her ladyship is just come in."[12] Heidegger continued to hold masquerades at the Haymarket until his death in 1749.

The occasion had its pretensions to exclusivity: George II and the Prince of Wales are both reputed to have attended public masquerades.[13] But its real appeal lay in its heterogeneous and carnival-like atmosphere. It drew on all social ranks equally, and permitted high and low to mingle in a single "promiscuous" round.

"All state and ceremony are laid aside," wrote one witness in the *Weekly Journal* (25 January 1724), "since the *Peer* and the *Apprentice,* the *Punk* and the *Duchess* are, for so long a time, upon an equal Foot." Costume reinscribed the theme of class confusion. As Christopher Pitt wrote in "On the Masquerades" (1727):

> Valets adorned with coronets appear,
> Lacquies of state and footmen with a star,
> Sailors of quality with judges mix,—
> And chimney-sweepers drive their coach-and six.[14]

Not all observers were pleased with the masquerade's "strange Medley" of persons. "It is possible," wrote Mary Singleton in *The Old Maid,* "the confused mixture of different ranks and conditions, which is unavoidable at a masquerade, may well be agreeable to the dregs of the people, who are fond, even at every price, of gaining admittance into a place where they may insult their superiors with impunity."[15]

Given the liberating anonymity of the scene, collective behavior was unrestrained. Drinking, dancing, gaming, and intrigue flourished, ordinary decorum was overturned, and a spirit of saturnalia reigned. Not surprisingly, the masquerade quickly came under attack from moralists and divines. A host of anti-masquerade satires and pamphlets were published in the 1720s and continued to appear into the 1780s. Civil authorities made periodic attempts to suppress masquerades, particularly during times of social unrest, but these efforts were never very successful. For most of the century the masquerade retained a raffish and seductive hold on the public imagination. Large masquerades were held at Ranelagh Gardens and Marylebone in the 1740s and 1750s, and again at Carlisle House in Soho Square, the Pantheon and Almack's in the 1760s and 1770s. *Town and Country Magazine* for May 1770 reported a masquerade at the Pantheon attended by "near two thousand persons." Only after the French Revolution did the masquerade lose something of its subversive appeal, though occasional masquerades continued to be held in London well into the nineteenth century.[16]

Though public in nature, the masquerade had the reputation—and *frisson*—of an underground phenomenon. From the start it was felt to epitomize the clandestine sexual life of the city. This "libidinous Assembly," wrote Addison in the *Spectator,* was perfectly contrived for the "Advancement of Cuckoldom," being nothing more than a scene of "Assignations and Intrigues."[17] In his satiric *Masquerade Ticket* of 1727, as I noted in Chapter 2, Hogarth highlighted the erotic nature of the event by depicting Haymarket masqueraders cavorting beneath statues of Venus and Priapus and two large "Lecherometers"—fanciful devices for measuring sexual excitement. Masquerade debauchery was a popular theme in eighteenth-century fiction. In the novels of Defoe, Fielding, Richardson, and Smollett, the masquerade was a conventional setting for seduction and adultery. Other writers regularly linked it with scenarios of defloration, rape, and perversion.[18] "To carry on an Intrigue with an Air of Secrecy" or "debauch a Citizen's

Figure 6.2. An engraving by Remigius Parr commemorating the Royal Jubilee masquerade at Ranelagh Gardens, April 26, 1749. Courtesy of the Guildhall Library, Corporation of London.

Wife," exclaimed a character in Benjamin Griffin's *The Masquerade* (1717), "what Contrivance in the World so proper as a Masquerade?"[19] The anonymous writer of the *Short Remarks upon the Original and Pernicious Consequences of Masquerades* of 1721 was less sanguine: the masquerade, he wrote, was nothing more than a *"Congress to an unclean end."*[20]

Underlying such complaints was a sense of the moral scandal implicit in costume itself. "The being in disguise," wrote the author of *Guardian* 142, "takes away the usual checks and restraints of modesty; and consequently the beaux do not blush to talk wantonly, nor the belles to listen; the one as greedily sucks in the poison, as the other industriously infuses it."[21] Travesty eroticized the world. Not only was one freed of one's inhibitions, one might also experience, hypothetically at least, a new body and its pleasures. The exchange of garments was also an exchange of desires. The result was a flight from the "natural"—from all that was culturally preordained—into new realms of voluptuous disorder.

By all accounts, the masquerade was indeed a scene of unusual erotic stimulation. Many disguises, first of all, had an undeniably fetishistic power. Masks were considered notorious aphrodisiacs, associated with prostitutes (as in Hogarth's *Harlot's Progress*) and the perverse heightening of passion. "A Woman mask'd," Wycherley's uncouth Pinchwife had observed in *The Country Wife* (1675), "is like a cover'd Dish, gives a man a curiosity, and appetite, when, it may be, uncover'd 'twould turn his stomack."[22] But the mask also released its wearer from ordinary moral controls. Women, it was felt, were particularly freed from constraint. "The mask secures the Ladies from Detraction, and encourages a Liberty, the Guilt of which their Blushes would betray when barefac'd, till by Degrees they are innur'd to that which is out of their Vertue to restrain."[23] Combined with the mysterious black domino, the mask remained for the century the veritable icon of transgressive desire.

But costumes themselves were often highly suggestive and provided a rich symbolic lexicon of libidinous possibility. Granted, not every disguise of the century was meant to titillate; almost all masquerades had their requisite Turks and conjurers, Harlequins and shepherdesses, hussars and Pierrots, orange-girls and Punches. Eighteenth-century masquerade costumes were sometimes merely playful, exotic, or picturesque. Casanova himself appeared as a relatively innocuous Pierrot at an Italian masquerade.[24] But given the premium on voyeurism and self-display, visual scandal held a special place. Where else, indeed, might one find "a *Nobleman* [dressed] like a *Cynder-Wench*," or "*a Lady of Quality* in *Dutch Trowsers*, and a *Woman of the Town* in a *Ruff* and *Farthingale?*"[25]

Transvestite costume was perhaps the most common offense against decorum. Woman strutted in jack-boots and breeches, while men primped in furbelows and flounces. Horace Walpole describes passing "for a good mask" as an old woman at a masquerade in 1742. Other male masqueraders disguised themselves as witches, bawds, nursery-maids and shepherdesses.[26] At a Richmond masquerade, *Gentleman's Magazine* reported in April, 1776, "a gentleman appeared in woman's clothes with a head-dress four feet high, composed of greens and garden stuff, and crowned with tufts of endive nicely blanched." "The force of the ridicule," the account continued, "was felt by some of the ladies." At Almack's in 1773, one man appeared as a "procuress" and another as "Mother Cole," the matronly bawd in Cleland's *Memoirs of a Woman of Pleasure.*[27] Female masqueraders in turn metamorphosed into hussars, sailors, cardinals, or Mozartian boys. The Duchess of Bolton, Elizabeth Inchbald and Judith Milbanke, among others, appeared in male costumes at masquerades at one time or another during the century.[28] In Griffin's *The Masquerade,* the heroine attends as "a kind of Hermaphroditical Mixture; half Man, half Woman; a Coat, Wig, Hat, and Feather, with all the Ornaments requisite." Costumes representing the "Amazonian" goddess Diana (popular throughout the century) were likewise androgynous in nature.[29] The anti-masquerade writers, not surprisingly, found cross-dressing a palpable sign of masquerade depravity. The author of the *Short Remarks* complained that the confounding of garments had ever "been used by Wantons, to favour their lascivious Designs." This "artifice of the old Serpent," he wrote, was clearly intended to "regale and heighten the Temptation." Eighteenth-century masqueraders may not, indeed, have been oblivious to such imperatives. Judith Milbanke, who appeared along with her sister as "two smart Beaux" in 1778, complacently observed that she had made by far "the prettiest Fellow of the two,"[30] and the scandalous Harriette Wilson, recollecting a masquerade at which she and a female friend dressed as an "Italian or Austrian peasant-boy and girl," carefully recorded in her memoirs the various risqué comments they received from bystanders.[31]

But other costume types were also designed to inflame. The *parodia sacra,* or ecclesiastical parody, offered an opportunity to play upon themes of celibacy and forbidden desire. A classic vestige of carnival tradition, ecclesiastical disguises featured prominently in contemporary costume catalogues such as Thomas Jefferys' *Dresses of Different Nations* (1757) and remained fashionable throughout the century. Wayward nuns and priests, perversely amorous "Devotees," and licentious Capuchins are a staple in contemporary masquerade stories and illustrations. "I will be a Prude, a religious Prude," exclaims the flirtatious Lady Frances in Charles Johnson's *The Masquerade* (1719); "I will appear in all the gloomy inaccessible Charms of a young Devotee; there is something in this Character so sweet and forbidden."[32] By a predictable symbolic inversion, prostitutes were thought particularly likely to assume pious vestments. A writer in the *Weekly Journal* (25 January 1724) described meeting a pretty nun at a masquerade who "rapt out an Oath" and made it known "that she was of the Sisterhood, and belonged to a certain Convent, of which Mother N[eedham] is Lady *Abbess.*" In Henry Robert Morland's painting *The Fair Nun Unmasked* (1769), a simpering mock-*religieuse* is shown removing her mask and suggestively exposing the jewelled crucifix on her bosom.

Still other disguises were profane from the start. Miss Chudleigh, later the Duchess of Kingston, shocked onlookers by appearing at the Jubilee masquerade in 1749 as a bare-breasted Iphigenia—"so naked," Mrs. Montagu remarked, "that the high priest might easily inspect the entrails of the victim."[33] Several semi-pornographic prints commemorated her exploit. In 1755 the writer of *The Connoisseur* for 6 February described a gallant who went to a masked "Frolick" with "no breeches under his domino." In 1768 Miss Pelham appeared at a masquerade as a "blackamoor" with her legs exposed to the thighs,[34] and in 1770 a man went to one of Mrs. Cornelys's masquerades in Soho Square as Adam, in a flesh-colored silk body stocking complete with "an apron of fig leaves worked in it, fitting the body to the utmost nicety." The result, according to *Gentleman's Magazine,* was a certain "unavoidable indelicacy."[35]

This paradoxical connection between masquerading and nakedness, it is worth noting, was a joke that recurred in various forms throughout the century. Popular wisdom held that there was a causal relation between masquerading and (subsequent) states of undress: those who "dressed up" for the masquerade would undoubtedly bare themselves later—when they retired to brothels or bagnios to consummate their secret liaisons. Such a sequence is implicit in Plate 5 of Hogarth's *Marriage à la Mode,* in which an adulterous wife and her lover have retreated to a bagnio for sex after a masquerade. At other times, less logically, the masquerade itself was associated with images of naked excess. In *Guardian* 142

Figure 6.3. Anonymous print commemorating Elizabeth Chudleigh's semi-nude appearance at the Jubilee masquerade in 1749 in the costume of Iphigenia. Courtesy of the British Museum.

(24 August 1713), Steele linked an attack on masquerades ("the devil first addressed himself to Eve in a mask") with a parody of the "Evites," an imaginary cult of fashionable women who wore only fig-leaves. In 1755 Miss Chudleigh's scandalous appearance as Iphigenia prompted a satiric scheme for a "Naked Masquerade." At this "alfresco" event, described in *The Connoisseur* (1 May 1755), female masqueraders were to disport themselves as *"Water-Nymphs* and *Graces,"* and

male masqueraders in "the half-brutal forms of *Satyres, Pans, Fauns, and Centaurs.*" "The *Pantheon of the Heathen Gods, Ovid's Metamorphoses,* and *Titian's Prints,*" the author argued, would supply "a sufficient variety of undrest characters." In the resulting orgy, bucks might run mad with their mistresses "like the Priests and Priestesses of *Bacchus* celebrating the *Bacchanalian* mysteries."

To what extent was the Dionysian promise in masquerade spectacle fulfilled? Certainly, if all masquerades were disreputable, some were less reputable than others. Acts of outright sexual intercourse (if they occurred at all) took place, one suspects, only at the most clandestine and subfusc affairs, and certainly not at events like Heidegger's "Midnight Masquerade" or Mrs. Cornelys's public subscription balls. The sexual subculture, for instance, had its own more or less unbuttoned versions of the masquerade. In her scandalous memoirs of 1797, the courtesan Margaret Leeson described a private masquerade at which a couple performed love feats "buff to buff," and, later, another masquerade given by "Moll Hall" which degenerated into an orgy.[36] The author of the piece on the "Naked Masquerade" noted in passing that he modelled his entertainment on an actual event that had taken place the year before at Pimlico "among the lowest of the people." The participants, he observed, had been sent to Bridewell, but "the same act, which at the *Green Lamps* or *Pimlico* appears low and criminal, may be extremely polite and commendable in the *Haymarket* or at *Ranelagh.*" Similarly, in one of the numerous popular histories of Jonathan Wild, there is a description of a secret homosexual masquerade party attended by Wild, which featured a group of "He-Whores," "rigg'd in Gowns, Petticoats, Head cloths, fine lac'd Shoes, Furbelow Scarves, and Masks," all "tickling and feeling each other, as if they were a mixture of wanton Males and Females." This licentious gathering has been identified as the notorious "Sodomitish Academy" run by "Mother Clap" in Field Lane, Holborn.[37]

The public masquerade was nominally more restrained, in that the shift into overt sexual behaviour was seldom possible. This is not to say, however, that the masquerade's bacchanalian reputation was undeserved. The occasion was indisputably a catalyst for certain kinds of behavior, and functioned throughout the century—along with brothels, bagnios, and the London piazzas and parks—as an acknowledged public setting in which illicit sexual contacts might be made. Of course, evidence regarding actual behavior at masquerades must be primarily circumstantial; the scandal associated with the occasion meant that few participants recorded incriminating escapades directly. Often one must rely on journalistic accounts, literary descriptions, and the sometimes exaggerated comments of the masquerade's detractors. Still, eighteenth-century observers agreed (and common sense confirms) that the masquerade was indeed a "Country of Liberty"—a realm where transgressive liaisons were easily formed, precisely because they might remain anonymous.[38]

The Haymarket masquerade had its quota of prostitutes, first of all, owing in part to its location in the heart of London's prostitution district. Disguise permitted the prostitute, like the sharper, to ply her precarious trade in relative safety. The "Sisterhood of Drury" appear frequently in masquerade accounts throughout the century. On the night of a recent ball, wrote an observer in the *Weekly Journal* (25 January 1724), "all about the Hundreds of *Drury*, there was not a *Fille de Joie* to be had that Night, for Love nor Money, being all engaged at the Masquerade; and several Men of Pleasure receiv'd Favours from Ladies who were too modest to shew their Faces, and many of them still feel the Effects of the amorous Flame which they received from the unknown Fairs." The author of *A Seasonable Apology for Mr. H——g—r,* one of many anti-masquerade satires from the 1720s, ironically dedicated his work to the infamous bawd Mother Needham, whose many minions, he observed, exploited the "Mask of artificial Maidenhead" in addition to the ordinary mask of disguise.[39] In Addison's satire in *Guardian* 154, a nun makes an assignation with a "heathen god" at a masquerade, and then agrees to meet him nearby in "the Little Piazza in Covent-garden," the famous haunt of London's "trading dames."

Few eighteenth-century commentators acknowledged the economic necessity which drove prostitutes to masquerades; the popular theme of the whore-in-disguise was used merely to underwrite the moral assault on the event itself. Yet, amid a conventional attack in *The Masquerade* ("Thus Fortune sends the gamesters luck, Venus her votary a —"), Fielding offered the following unintentionally sympathetic vignette:

> Below stairs hungry whores are picking
> The bones of wild-fowl, and of chicken;
> And into pockets some convey
> Provisions for another day.

The lines may serve as a stark reminder that prostitutes constituted, after all, the most wretchedly exploited underclass in eighteenth-century London, and that some were undoubtedly driven to the masquerade out of more than simple concupiscence.

It was not just the "Punk", however, who found a special range at masquerades. Women in general assumed unprecedented liberties. The misogynist view of the age, of course, was that any woman who attended a masquerade did so, like the harlot, in order to seek unlawful sexual pleasure. The taboo against unescorted women and girls going to masquerades remained in force throughout the century.[40] It mattered little whether a woman was a virgin or not; any woman, it was assumed, fell into sexual danger at masquerades. In a salacious story in the *Weekly Journal* (8 February 1724) entitled "The Balls, a Tale," a wayward young woman persuades her mother to let her go to a masquerade.

> Virgins to Midnight Masques would go,
> And not a Mother durst say, No;
> She pass'd for unpolite and rude,
> and Miss would cry, *Mamma's a Prude.*

Needless to say, she quickly gives up her maidenhood to a sly domino named Roger. A few weeks later the same newspaper offered the following maxim: "Fishes are caught with Hooks, Birds are ensnar'd with Nets, but Virgins with Masquerades."[41] In turn, in married women the masquerade was thought to prompt adulterous longings. The occasion was perfect for cuckoldry, wrote Addison, because "the Women either come by themselves or are introduced by Friends, who are obliged to quit them upon their first Entrance."[42] Lady Bellaston, who seduces Tom Jones at the Haymarket while disguised as the "Queen of the Fairies," is a stereotypical eighteenth-century version of the older female masquerade libertine. In the satirical pamphlet *A Seasonable Apology for Mr. H——g—r* (1724), the comical "Countess of Clingfast" and her "Committee of Matrons" likewise relieve themselves of frigidity, green-sickness and "obstructions" by attending masquerades.

We need not mimic the pervasive misogyny of contemporary moralists (or the relentlessly anti-sexual ideology they endorsed) to recognize the element of truth in their animadversions. The critics were right to link masquerading with female sexual emancipation; the masquerade indeed provided eighteenth-century women with an unusual sense of erotic freedom. Disguise obviated a host of cultural proscriptions and taboos. A woman in masquerade might approach strangers, initiate conversation, touch and embrace those whom she did not know, speak coarsely—in short, violate all the cherished imperatives of ordinary feminine sexual decorum. Of course, only the boldest might openly acknowledge such pleasures. "I love a masquerade," wrote the brazen Harriette Wilson, "because a female can never enjoy the same liberty anywhere else."[43] In an account of a Pantheon masquerade in 1773, *Lady's Magazine* offered similar sentiments, purportedly through the voice of an anonymous female participant: "Indeed a masquerade is one of the most entertaining diversions that ever was imported; you may hear and see, and do every thing in the world, without the least reserve—and liberty, liberty, my dear, you know, is the very joy of my heart."[44]

Most important, masquerading granted women the essential masculine privilege of erotic object-choice. "It is delightful to me," Wilson wrote, only half-facetiously, "to be able to wander about in a crowd, making my observations, and conversing with whomsoever I please, without being liable to be stared at or remarked upon, and to speak to whom I please, and run away from them the moment I have discovered their stupidity."[45] Elsewhere in her memoir, she described meeting several lovers at masquerades. It would going too far, perhaps, to call the masquerade a feminist counterpart to the brothel; eighteenth-century culture, unremittingly patriarchal in structure, was never so Utopian in its sexual arrangements. Nonetheless, the masquerade offered contemporary women a subversive—if temporary—simulacrum of sexual autonomy. Besides obvious demi-mondaine figures like Wilson and Margaret Leeson, such distinguished women as Mary Wortley Montagu, Fanny Burney, and Elizabeth Inchbald acknowledged a fondness for masquerade privileges.[46] But unknown women too, one

LADY BETTY BUSTLE and her MAID LUCY preparing for the MASQUERADE at the PANTHEON.

Figure 6.4. Anonymous engraving, "Lady Betty Bustle with her maid Lucy, preparing for a masquerade at the Pantheon," 1772. Courtesy of the British Museum.

may assume, experienced unprecedented sensual release in the comic displacements of the night.

Likewise, homosexuals may have found a similar latitude at public masquerades. So much seems clear, at least, from contemporary attacks on the masquerade, which frequently called attention to "unnatural" liaisons struck up there. The sensational *Short Remarks upon the Original and Pernicious Consequences of Masquerades,* for example, was in large part a barely concealed assault on homosexual practices at the masquerade. Masquerade transvestism, charged its author, had led its proponents toward "Excesses, which otherwise they durst scarce have thought of" and was making the nation a veritable "*Sodom* for Lewdness." Citing infamous cross-dressers and bisexuals of antiquity—Sporus, Caligula, Heliogabalus and so forth—he warned that such men had been "branded in History as Monsters of Nature, the Scum, and Scandal, and Shame of Mankind." Modern masqueraders merely imitated the vice-ridden "Corybantes" and "dancing priests" of the past; the pagan "*Festum Kalendarium,*" scene of travesty, perversion and blasphemy, was "the black Original we transcribe in our Masquerades."

Fielding adopted a somewhat less dire tone in *The Masquerade,* but likewise condemned the masquerade as a world of enveloping sexual chaos, in which any kind of wrongful connection was possible. Complaining of the effeminate men ("little apish butterflies") everywhere to be seen at the masquerade, the poet's Muse cries:

> And if the breed been't quickly mended;
> Your empire shortly will be ended:
> Breeches our brawny thighs shall grace,
> (Another Amazonian race).
> For when men women turn—why then
> May women not be chang'd to men?

That Fielding connected transvestism with active homosexuality is obvious, as I suggested in the previous chapter, from his later anti-lesbian satire, *The Female Husband* (1746). This semi-prurient work (based on an actual case tried by Fielding's cousin) described how a woman named Mary Hamilton disguised herself as a man and tricked several women into marriage precisely in order to satisfy "unnatural" carnal urges.[47] As if to illustrate Fielding's vision of ensuing sexual disorder, a suggestive satiric engraving from the first half of the century, "The Masquerade Dance," depicted an all-male group of masqueraders performing a wild hornpipe to the music of a piping devil.

Yet the presence of homosexuals at masquerades can be deduced in other ways too. The Haymarket, as I have mentioned, was near to Covent Garden and Spring Gardens, both important sites for male as well as female prostitution. Along with molly-clubs and similar underground sexual establishments, masquerade rooms featured in the clandestine erotic topography of the new male homosexual subculture that was gradually coming into being in eighteenth-century London.[48] Even in supposedly "decent" or non-pornographic accounts, the masquerade is an acknowledged setting for acts of real or ostensible homoerotic flirtation. At a masquerade described in *Guardian* 154, for example, the male narrator, disguised as Lucifer, is accosted by a "Presbyterian Parson" who calls him a "pretty fellow" and offers to meet him in Spring Gardens. Later in the same piece, the narrator finds himself strangely attracted to an "Indian King" who, admittedly, turns out to be a woman in disguise. Similar errors are recorded elsewhere. According to her biographer, Mrs. Inchbald, who appeared as a man at a masquerade in the 1780s, unwittingly "captivated the affections" of her own sex as a result.[49] The *Weekly Journal* in 1724 had an account of a man who went to the Haymarket dressed as a female Quaker and was mistakenly almost "ravished" there by a young male domino.[50] And, in a particularly lascivious episode in Smollett's *Peregrine Pickle* (1751), a character dressed in women's clothes at a masquerade is forced, "in consequence of the Champaign he had so liberally swallowed that afternoon," to micturate in front of a group of fascinated male masqueraders. He is subsequently accosted by a Frenchman who compliments him on his "happy pisse" and fondles him, though the Frenchman later denies knowing his true sex.[51]

But eighteenth-century pornographic writing, as one might expect, confirms the presence of outright same-sex solicitation at masquerades. In Cleland's *Memoirs of a Women of Pleasure* (1749), Fanny Hill's fellow prostitute Emily, disguised as a boy, is approached by a "handsome domino" at a public masquerade. His courtship, she finds, is "dash'd with a certain oddity," but she attributes this to the "humour" of her disguise and not to any misunderstanding about her sex. His intentions are clearly homosexual, however; he has taken her for a "smock-fac'd boy," tries to sodomize her in a nearby bagnio and, in a moment of lubricious crisis, must be redirected "down the right road." While clearly obscene in design, the episode also points towards the underlying sociological reality; that Cleland (himself reputed to be a "sodomite" by several contemporaries) took for granted the association between the masquerade and homosexual seduction is clear, and, as with other realistic details in the novel, reflects more than mere pornographic convenience.[52]

For those hedged round by the implicit and explicit taboos of eighteenth-century sexual morality, therefore, the masquerade offered unprecedented pleasures and opportunities. Borrowing a term from the sociologist, we might call it a "backstage" area in eighteenth-century urban life—a setting in which ordinarily proscribed impulses might safely be indulged.[53] The irony was that to go "backstage" was to go "on stage," to adopt a new self, to play a new role, through the hallucinatory derangements of costume. Throughout the century, the masquerade mediated in a paradoxical fashion between public and private spheres. Behind the mask, one preserved the essential moral and psychological privileges of privacy, while participating at the same time in the spontaneous exchanges of the group. Disguise was the crucial means towards such mediation—the gesture which at once licensed collective exchange and infused the occasion with its secretive, compelling aura.

Yet, to identify the masquerade as a privileged space for the morally unconventional does not entirely explain its powerful hold on eighteenth-century English culture. I have argued that some people may have self-consciously sought its freedoms—prostitutes, libertines, feminists, the sexual avant-garde. The masquerade had much to do, certainly, with the subterranean liberalization of erotic life in eighteenth-century London,[54] but in speaking of a "culture of travesty" I have made large claims, admittedly, for something that remained in one sense a local phenomenon. Thousands attended masquerades during the century, but what of those who never ventured to the Haymarket, Ranelagh, or Soho Square? How did the carnivalesque exploits of an urban minority impinge upon the imaginative life of society as a whole?

We cannot underestimate the power that the idea of the "Midnight Masquerade" held in eighteenth-century discourse. Indeed, we might speak of the masquerade as one of the defining *topoi* of eighteenth-century cultural rhetoric. The numerous literary and artistic transformations of the masquerade were at least as significant, in some sense, as the institution itself. Whether or not they attended, the majority of English people knew about the masquerades. As witnessed by a host of novels, stories, poems, pamphlets, squibs and engravings, the event remained a subject of fascination throughout the century.[55]

And, in a way, masquerade liberty was as much a common imaginative property—part of the fantasy-life of the age—as it was the privilege of the masquerade crowd. The appeal of the mask, as we have seen, was that it permitted an escape from self; internalized moral and psychological constraints disappeared—for how could one be held responsible when one was not oneself? The logic of ordinary moral agency was suspended; whatever one did, whatever ensued, might be attributed to "someone else" or assimilated to the supposedly innocent realm of "accidents." Yet similar psychological fictions operated in the masquerade fantasies of the century. In stories of masquerade seduction and adultery, the timid reader might safely identify with an "other"—seducer or victim, adulterer or adulteress—without risk, obviously, to his or her consciously held scruples. Heavy didacticism added a comfortable (if spurious) protective moral layering to these powerfully charged sexual narratives. Like the related genre of the criminal biography, the masquerade tale typically gratified prurient or subversive interests while parading as "instructive" commentary. And just as the criminal biography, with its implicit glorification of the miscreant, reflected a growing popular revolt against traditional religious values (or so John Richetti has argued in *Popular Fiction before Richardson*), so the sensational masquerade tale may have articulated a new subliminal collective hostility toward age-old sexual prohibitions and taboos.[56]

One might go so far as to say that masquerade fantasy operated as a conceptual tool—a symbolic mechanism through which suppressed forms of behavior found representation. Virtually any form of perverse or proscribed sexual contact might be depicted in masquerade literature, so long as it was made to seem unintentional—an accidental function of the chaos and anonymity of the scene. The "mistake" was the crucial covering fiction. Innocent men thus couple unwit-

Figure 6.5. Charles White, *Masquerade Scene at the Pantheon*, 1773. Courtesy of the Guildhall Library, Corporation of London.

tingly with prostitutes in a host of masquerade stories: in *Spectator* No. 8, for example, an unfortunate Templar mistakes "a *Cloud* for a *Juno*" and discovers his *faux pas* too late. In still other accounts, virginal young women and loyal wives are ruined as a result of tragic masquerade errors—usually when they confuse a rapist with a fiancé or husband. In a sensational tale by Eliza Haywood in *The Female Spectator* (1746), the heroine Erminia allows herself to be escorted home from the masquerade by a man she takes to be her fiancé and is forcibly undone by him. In an "Affecting Masquerade Adventure" from 1754, a similar fate awaits Matilda, who is seduced after a masquerade by a mysterious domino she believes to be her husband.[57]

Other fanciful consummations were even more lurid. I have already mentioned cases of accidental homosexuality at the masquerade; accidental incest was another popular motif. The writer of the *Short Remarks* described an unfortunate gentleman who "debauch'd his own Daughter" by mistake at a masquerade and died of horror at the discovery. In the play *The Masquerade; or, The Devil's Nursery* (1732), a "Virtuous Wife" is "an Incestuous Mother made" after another tragic masquerade mix-up.[58] "By thee," the author of *A Seasonable Apology for Mr. H——g—r* wrote of the masquerade, "Sons aspire to the Wombs from whence they sprung; and Daughters wantonly embrace the Loyns that begot them."

While typically presented as proofs of the masquerade's diabolical nature, these narratives of accidental union also provided readers with a new and highly specific grammar of the illicit. In adumbrating their shocking tales of unwitting prostitution, adultery, homosexuality and incest, masquerade writers also gave unprecedented centrality to previously unmentionable desires—all the myriad taboo forms, in short, of non-marital, non-procreative sexuality. Their scenarios covertly dramatized new modes of intimacy, enacted outside the traditional framing institutions of marriage and the law. Like the mask, the fiction of accident was in the end, one suspects, nothing more than an enabling device, the psychological means by which subversive sexual themes found utterance. Concealed in the popular moralistic inventory of "accidental" masquerade attachments was an unprecedented imagery of transgressive pleasures.

The destabilizing power of the masquerade was expressed as much in its representations as in its own intrinsic disorders. We cannot separate the real and the fictive masquerade, for both were a part, ultimately, of a larger imaginative experiment in violation. Jean Starobinski has written that the most profound discovery of the eighteenth century was its "invention of liberty"—the intense evocation, as least in fantasy, of the freedom of the individual.[59] Granted, it would be foolish to speak of eighteenth-century Western European society as sexually permissive in the modern late twentieth-century sense. But one may still speak of the general liberalizing and individualistic tendency in eighteenth-century thought. (In England, the intellectual history of feminism from Astell to Wollstonecraft lends power to such a generalization.) In the realm of sexual ideology, the movement toward individualism manifested itself variously—in a growing resistance to traditional moral authority, in self-conscious attempts to redefine the controlling institutions of marriage and the family, in the various calls for the emancipation of women, and, increasingly, in the new and controversial perception of sexual freedom as one of the privileges of civilization. For sexual radicals such as the Marquis de Sade, erotic individualism culminated, quite predictably, in an assault on the bastion of heterosexuality itself.

Western culture over the past two centuries has largely internalized (if not always officially sanctioned) this historic idealization of sexual freedom. In the twentieth century, the unconstrained nature of desire—and the need of human beings to pursue diverse objects of gratification—has become a psychological if not a political commonplace. We need not be orthodox Freudians to accept the idea of the polymorphousness of the modern subject, for whom, in theory at least, all avenues of sexual pleasure stand open. Dryden's verse, "Love variously doth various minds inspire," has been echoed most recently by Michel Foucault, who argues that through its relentless "eroticization of the body," modern Western culture has animated new objects of desire and defined forms of erotic subjectivity unknown to our forebears.[60]

Yet it is impossible to separate these important intellectual developments, finally, from the "structures of everyday life" that gave rise to them. The great theme of sexual liberty inevitably germinated in the fertile ground of eighteenth-century social practice. The real function of the masquerade may ultimately have been a heuristic one. Even while it posed as frivolity, the masquerade was also a living catalyst for reflection—a mechanism for conceptualizing, as it were, the Protean future of desire. Its "studied Devices of Pageantry and Disguise," as Benjamin Griffin called them in 1717, were also rehearsals for future transgression: theatrical experiments in the carnivalization of sexual life itself. To its voluptuous confusions, we owe—at least in part—our modern (perhaps sentimental) image of the boundlessness, freedom, and incorrigibility of Eros.

The masquerade introduced a new moral irony into sexual relations. Masquerade travesty was a mark of the profane; the inversion of sacred categories. Yet, once acknowledged, the urge toward desacralization spread outwards into society at large. In the culture of travesty, a historic new self-consciousness invaded the silent pleasure-world of the body. The flight from the "natural" had begun; the modern challenge to traditional moral and psychic structures was inaugurated. To be sure, the eighteenth-century poet of masquerade railed against the "lewd joys" of the fantastic scene:

> New ways and means to pleasure we devise,
> Since pleasure looks the lovelier in disguise.
> The stealth and frolic give a smarter gust,
> Add wit to vice, and elegance to lust.[61]

Yet even as he turned, sardonically, from the "enormities" of the occasion, he preserved them, in the shape of an anthology—which was also a blueprint—for a universal masquerade.

CHAPTER 7

THE CARNIVALIZATION
OF EIGHTEENTH-CENTURY
ENGLISH NARRATIVE

"The secret history of a carnival," wrote Addison in his 1718 *Remarks on Italy*, "would make a collection of very diverting novels." One might take such a comment simply as part of the ingenuous discourse of eighteenth-century tourism: like Mary Wortley Montagu, Horace Mann, and many other English visitors, Addison delighted in the masked balls and carnivals of Venice, Rome, and Florence and celebrated the "great diversion" (as he put it) of dressing "as a false personage."[1] But one might also take his remark, paradoxically, as bearing a certain proleptic relation to English literary history itself. Addison offers what could be called an advertisement for a theme—a theme that the eighteenth-century English novel was subsequently to provide. With the spectacular rise of carnivalesque activity in England in the second and third decades of the eighteenth century—marked by the institutionalization of the public, or subscription, masquerade—the novel took a cue from popular culture: the carnival set piece, or masquerade scene, became a standard, though highly problematic, fictional topos. To the degree that writers incorporated the novel institution of the masquerade into an existing world of representation, the masquerade became an institution of the novel, making the multifarious body of eighteenth-century English fiction a "secret history of a carnival" indeed.

One need only recollect some of the eighteenth-century novels in which a masquerade occurs to appreciate the ubiquitousness of the scene: *Roxana, Tom Jones, Amelia, Pamela*, part 2, *Sir Charles Grandison, The Adventures of Peregrine Pickle, Fanny Hill*, Burney's *Cecilia*, Inchbald's *A Simple Story*, and Edgeworth's *Belinda*. In addition one can find significant allusions to the world of masquerade and public travesty in *Roderick Random, The Vicar of Wakefield, Evelina*, and a host of minor works of the period.[2] Critics have tended to discount masquerade scenes—in part, one suspects, because such episodes may seem deceptively inconsequential in the novels themselves. Authors like Richardson and Fielding typically try to bracket the masquerade scene—to set it off as merely a brief interlude in some more serious project of mimetic or didactic elucidation—disguising it as a narrative, as well as an existential, "diversion." This attempt at circumscription often occurs, oddly enough, while the characters themselves comment on the masquerade's powerful sensuous éclat. Nonetheless, one may still be deceived by a superficial aura of extraneousness or marginality.

But we are inclined to bypass fictional representations of the carnivalesque for deeper reasons too, reasons having to do with our notions of eighteenth-century English fiction itself. True to the masquerade's symbolic role as the exemplary site of mutability, incongruity, and mystery, the episode is often a strangely unrecuperable textual event. It may strike us as uncanny, or as discontinuous with those patterns of didactic or ideological meaning that characterize the work elsewhere. Though subliminally compelling, it may also have a mystifying or chimerical narrative impact. And since the scene often marks a moment in contemporary narrative when otherwise lucid character types, like the adepts of psychosis, suddenly seem to behave conspicuously unlike themselves, as though contaminated by the prevailing instability of the occasion in which they participate, the figure of the masquerade seems subtly linked to the violation of certain cherished critical paradigms—notably, the commonplace that early English fiction is distinguished by its new sense of the integrity of individual psychology and its coherent representation of character over time. The scene is almost invariably an affront to *Bildung:* it offends against those structures of consistency and logical development that we try, consciously or unconsciously, to impose on the classic eighteenth-century text.[3]

In what follows, however, I argue that the masquerade episode is not in fact inconsequential—either for the novel in which it appears or for the theory of eighteenth-century narrative in general. If the role of the masquerade is masked, so to speak, behind a textual facade of moralism and ideological decorum, it is powerfully subversive nonetheless. In particular I am concerned here with the peculiar intimacy between topos and plot, with the ways in which the masquerade, the emblem of universal transformation, is linked to the pleasurable processes of narrative transformation—to intrigue and the working out of larger, often comic fictional destinies. Besides being a symbolic epitome of plot—the embedded imago of a world of metamorphosis and fluidity—the masquerade is typically a perpetrator too: a dense kernel of human relations out of which are born the myriad transactions of the narrative. This plot-engendering function frequently undermines whatever explicit negative didactic or allegorical significance the occasion carries elsewhere—for instance, its conventional inscription as the archetype of a corrupt and hypocritical "Town." The scene may thus be considered a master trope of semantic destabilization in eighteenth-century fiction, in that it characteristically precipitates an entire range of thematic as well as narrative changes and discontinuities. Itself a problematic rhetorical event—its own ideological status remains finally unclear—the masquerade episode introduces a curious instability into the would-be orderly cosmos of the eighteenth-century English novel. Its moral indeterminacy is paradigmatic; its saturnalian assault on taxonomies and hierarchies—established "fixities" of every sort—is the prerequisite, often enough, to a general collapse of decorum in the fictional world.

As Bakhtin has memorably demonstrated, it is possible to make an analogy between the role of the carnivalesque in literary works and its role in culture.[4] Whether rhetorical or actual, the carnivalesque occasion—like the masquerade—is always provocative: it intimates an alternative view of the "nature of things" and embodies a liberating escape from the status quo. At the end of this essay I return to the comparison between the function of the masquerade in English fiction and that of the institution of masquerade in culture. First, however, a few words are necessary about the diversion itself.

The masked assembly became a popular form of urban entertainment in the mid-teens and early twenties of the eighteenth century, when the first public masquerades were organized in London at the Haymarket under the direction of the Swiss entrepreneur "Count" John James Heidegger. A nocturnal affair, held in brilliantly illuminated rooms, the "promiscuous Assembly" (as the *Spectator* called it) was open to anyone who could afford the price of ticket and costume. In many respects the occasion was modeled on the traditional public carnivals of the Continent. Thanks to the general anonymity of the scene, collective behavior was unrestrained: eating, drinking, dancing, and gaming were enjoyed to excess. Costumes were often spectacular and phantasmagoric. Besides the classic black mask and domino, popular masquerade disguises included foreign or exotic "fancy dress," transvestite costumes, ecclesiastical parodies (of nuns or priests), picturesque occupational costumes (of shepherds, milkmaids, and the like), as well as costumes representing animals, supernatural beings, and literary, historical, and allegorical personages.[5] The fantastic multiplicity and incongruity of the visual spectacle were to a large degree replicated in the disparate composition of the masquerade crowd itself, which drew on both sexes equally and on all ranks of contemporary English society. Only there, remarked a character in Griffin's 1717 comedy *The Masquerade*, could one meet "a *Nobleman* [dressed] like a *Cynder-Wench*, a *Colonel of Dragoons* like a *Country Rat-Catcher*, a *Lady of Quality* in *Dutch Trowsers*, and a *Woman of the Town* in a *Ruff* and *Farthingale*."[6] Both aesthetically and sociologically the scene was indeed a carnivalesque hodgepodge of promiscuous elements.

From the start, the masquerade occupied a paradoxical place in the symbolic order of eighteenth-century English culture. On the one hand, the new entertainment provoked a cacophony of public criticism—a sizable antimasquerade "complaint." Throughout the century, writers of satiric poems, sermons, squibs, and pamphlets, as well as visual artists like Hogarth, reiterated the exemplary dangers of the masquerade: it was an emblem of luxury and excess; it introduced a foreign element of theatricality and vice into English public life; it promoted a potentially inflammatory sense of social equality by allowing the "lower orders" to consort with their betters. Above all, the masked assembly was seen as the site par excellence for sexual transgression: women—again thanks to disguise—shared the sensual "freedom" of men; voyeurism and exhibitionism were pervasive; erotic taboos were broken. Adultery, prostitution, homosexuality, incest, and the defloration of virgins were all themes associated with the masquerade: the event became a cultural sign of libertinage itself.[7]

On the other hand, despite this explosion of negative discourse, the masquerade flourished. From the 1720s to the 1780s it was an irrepressible feature of urban public life—not just one among many popular diversions but the emblem of modernity itself, the very signature of fashion, spectacle, and surreptitious excitement. Heidegger's assemblies drew between seven hundred and one thousand persons weekly during the 1720s, while later in the century elaborate subscription masquerades, like those sponsored by Mrs. Cornelys at Carlisle House in the 1760s and 1770s, attracted up to two thousand costumed participants. The spasmodic efforts of civil and religious authorities to put an end to masquerading were generally unsuccessful; for the greater part of the century the masquerade had indeed the status of an established cultural institution, however intense the criticism it inspired.

For all the vociferousness of the opposition, the masked assembly apparently satisfied certain underlying impulses in the culture. Since participants typically adopted the costumes of beings whose natures were antithetical to their own—of a different culture, sex, or sphere of existence—one could conclude that individual masqueraders were acting out repressed fantasies of alterity, symbolically embracing otherness. But the same dialectic applies collectively too. By allowing manifold breaches of decorum, the carnivalization of social roles, and parodic symbolic reversals, the masquerade offered eighteenth-century culture an anti-image of itself: a kind of licensed topsy-turvydom, or *Spielraum,* in which the very principles of order and distinction might be challenged. In a rigidly taxonomic, conceptually polarized society, it opened up a temporary space of transformation, mutability, and fluidity. It embodied, one might say, a gratifying fantasy of change in a world that sanctioned few changes—metaphysical or otherwise.

I call attention here to the conflicting responses evoked by the masquerade because the same contradictions inform fictional representation. Eighteenth-century English culture inscribed the masquerade simultaneously in a code of danger and in a code of pleasure: though preeminently distinguished by its "pernicious" consequences (in the phrase of one critic), it was also a scene of ecstasy and euphoria—a site of atavistic "liberties" and golden-age delights. It was at once part of the topography of vice—a place where no one should go—and part of the topography of enjoyment—a place where everyone went.[8]

In the eighteenth-century masquerade novel, too, the masked assembly is a place where everyone goes—eventually. Which is not to say—at the outset at least—that it is not also part of a (textual) code of danger. The occasion figures notably in a larger theme of initiation: "going to the masquerade" is an exemplary part of the charged confrontation with urbanity, or "introduction to the Town," conventionally dramatized in eighteenth-century English novels. Yet initially the masquerade novel characteristically registers, as it were, an "official" resistance to its own carnivalesque topos—as though it wished to domesticate, or neutralize in advance, the very scene it will later represent. Some form of embedded negative comment or warning almost always precedes that problematic event, serving as a kind of anticipatory didactic gloss, usually by a character already invested in the fictional world with a certain moral prestige or authority. With such prefacing—a not so subtle attempt to shape the reader's subsequent interpretation of the episode—the writers signal the superficial didactic orthodoxy of their histories, even as these histories turn, ineluctably, toward this least orthodox of diversions.

The modes of stylized resistance are surprisingly uniform. In particular, the masquerade's association with sexual impurity—and consequent danger to heroines—is almost always enunciated. In *Pamela*, part 2, for example, when Richardson's paragon hears that Mr. B. plans to take her to a masked assembly, she expresses her distaste for such entertainments, condemns the "freedoms" taken with women at these events, and wishes she didn't have to go.[9] Similarly, despite claiming that she "never had any notion of Masquerades," Harriet Byron, in Richardson's *Sir Charles Grandison*, admits to her friend Miss Selby that she wishes the night of the masquerade were over, adding, somewhat ominously, that she fears the evening's party will be "the last diversion of this kind I shall ever be at."[10] In Inchbald's *A Simple Story*, Miss Milner's honorable guardian, Mr. Dorriforth, objects to the loose morals of the masked assembly and implicitly forbids her to go.[11] Even Defoe's *Roxana*, in which the didactic pattern is unstable from the outset, contains hints of the classic encoded warning: when the heroine hears that some "Gentlemen in Masquerade" are to visit her apartments, she immediately fears a "Disturbance" and balks at receiving them. She has to be assured that "a Party of Guards" will prevent any "Rudeness" of the sort found at the Haymarket masquerade.[12]

And finally—befitting the author of one of the first and most virulent poetic satires against the masquerade, *The Masquerade* (1728)—Fielding's novels offer striking examples of the embedded antimasquerade gloss. In book 13 of *Tom Jones,* after Tom offers to take Mrs. Miller and her daughter to a masquerade, his landlady animadverts on the danger of such "extravagant Diversions," particularly for innocent young women. When Mr. Nightingale disagrees, she reminds him that when her daughter went to the Haymarket with him the year before, "it almost turned her Head; and she did not return to herself, or to her Needle, in a month afterwards."[13] But it is in *Amelia,* the most complex of masquerade novels, that one finds the most severe strictures—an initial chorus of warnings so intense as to suggest that a masquerade is not to figure in the heroine's destiny at all. When the sinister Noble Peer presents Amelia with masquerade tickets, his gesture elicits a flood of preventive discourse. Booth fears aloud "what a wicked and voluptuous man, resolved to sacrifice every thing to the gratification of a sensual appetite, with the most delicious repast" might attempt on such an occasion and forbids his wife to go, while Amelia's friend, the wan Mrs. Bennet, is moved to divulge her own horrific experiences at the masked assembly.[14] She too has gone with the Peer to a masquerade, and with catastrophic consequences: after being overcome by the hallucinatory "intoxications" of the place, she tells Amelia, she unwittingly allowed herself to be drugged and raped by him. The "fatal masquerade" indeed seems to have been that: Mrs. Bennet subsequently causes the death of her husband by infecting him with the Peer's venereal disease, and her child succumbs to a mysteriously related "fever." This exemplary tale recounted, Amelia promptly rejects the gift of tickets, leaving the reader to conclude, logically enough, that a masquerade will play no part, except in this displaced form, in Fielding's novel.

Such embedded commentary seems intended, obviously, to limit the symbolic range of the masquerade to that of the moral emblem. Even before the event occurs, we are invited to comprehend it as a transparent epitome of vice, as part of the moralized topography of the corrupt "Town." The masquerade itself masquerades, the gloss warns: ostensibly the scene of pleasure, it is actually the scene of "snares"—a region of manipulation, disequilibrium, and sexual threat. It disguises itself as exquisite delight, yet degrades all who enter its estranging spaces. This initial treatment of the masquerade topos almost always coincides, not surprisingly, with a larger critique of a deceptive or hypocritical human society. Besides being the icon of a debauched world of "Fashion," the allegory of urban disorder, as in Fielding and Richardson, the diversion often seems to intimate a kind of global dysphoria—a universal inauthenticity, obfuscation, and brutality. Thus the internalized attack on the masquerade confirms the didactic pretensions of the larger fiction and establishes—for a time at least—the stereotypically "virtuous" persona of the novelist, the unmasker of vice.

Yet it is precisely this kind of emblematic transparency that is obscured by the actual representation of masquerade. For despite the encoded resistance, the event, if mentioned at all, always does seem to take place. Indeed, one may take it as a rule that if the possibility of attending a masquerade arises in an eighteenth-century English novel, at some point the characters will go, as though under a peculiar narrative compulsion. This turn toward the carnival world often violates didactic economy, since the "perniciousness" of the occasion has already been sufficiently established, and the textual switch into saturnalia frequently seems strangely unmotivated or irrational. In the sequel to *Pamela,* one cannot quite grasp, for instance, why a reformed B. should force his pregnant wife (she gives birth a day or two later) to attend this scene of riot against her will, but he does. Similarly in *Amelia,* though Booth strenuously opposes Amelia's accepting masquerade tickets from the Peer, he later insists, surprisingly, that she accept a set of tickets from the equally lustful and devious Colonel James. And in *A Simple Story,* Miss Milner's decision to thwart her fiancé, Dorriforth, and venture out to a masquerade is likewise baffling—a seemingly perverse affront to the emotional bond that she has earlier worked so passionately to establish. Thus this crucial spatial shift from domestic salon to assembly room, from the predictable scenery of "everyday" life to the estranging réalm of the carnivalesque, is almost always accompanied by a certain logical discontinuity, an incursion of irrationalism into the ordered cosmos of eighteenth-century psychologistic, as well as topographic, representation.

With the "entry" into the masquerade scene itself—for the characters a literal entry into a novel space of estrangement and moral instability—the sense of discontinuity and paradox may be intensified to a hallucinatory degree. However brief the scene and however much the novelist may try to circumscribe its problematic features, it remains a charged textual occasion, productive of unexampled pleasures for characters and readers alike. I do not mean merely the pleasures of local color, though the representation of the carnivalesque obviously entails supplemental interest of this sort, particularly for twentieth-century readers. To be sure, the typical masquerade episode contains some allusion to the spectacular delights of the scene: some rendering of masquerade *adynata*—the marvelous visual incongruities embodied in the costumed crowd itself. The representation of the carnivalesque "diversion" conventionally diverts in this way: it adds an element of spectacle, in the ancient sense, to the ordinarily quotidian landscape of the realistic novel. Thus in Burney's *Cecilia,* the reader may take vicarious pleasure in the manifold and dreamlike aspects of the entertainment depicted there, where men turn into "Spaniards, chimneysweepers, Turks, watchmen, conjurers, and old women" and women into "shepherdesses, orange girls, Circassians, gipseys, haymakers, and sultanas."[15]

But the masquerade diverts in a more important sense too. The verbal allusion to a rich and variegated phenomenological realm—a world of endless, enchanting metamorphosis—coincides always with an even more gratifying pattern of transformation: a proliferation of intrigue. Besides thematizing mutability through image, the masquerade episode serves as a nodal point for narrative transformation—the privileged site of plot. Above all, the masquerade represents that place in the novel at which significant events take place—a classic locale out of which the requisite mysteries of "story" may be elaborated.

This plot-developing function follows from the very nature of the diversion. In life as in fiction, the eighteenth-century masked assembly was a cultural "locus of intimacy." There persons otherwise rigidly segregated by class and sex distinctions might come together in unprecedented, sometimes disruptive combinations. Satiric references, like Addison's, to the "promiscuity" of the masquerade suggested not only the characteristic sensual excess of the scene but also the scandalous heterogeneity of the community temporarily constituted within its confines.[16] Constantly confronting "strangers" (with the mask the quintessential visual emblem of estrangement) was part of the masquerade's appeal: it substituted randomness and novelty—prerequisites of imbroglio—for the familiar, highly stylized patterns of contemporary public and private exchange.

This open-endedness, one realizes, is perfectly adapted to the elaboration of plot, the existence of which depends, as Todorov has pointed out, on an initial destabilization of the ordinary, a disequilibrium at the heart of things. In his study of the fantastic, Todorov defines the minimum requirement for narrative—that "nucleus without which we cannot say there is any narrative at all"—as "a movement between two equilibriums which are similar but not identical."[17] In the genre of the fantastic—including fantastic eighteenth-century tales like *The Castle of Otranto* and *Vathek*—that which precipitates "movement," the necessary catalyst for narrative, is usually the supernatural intervention, a mysterious or extralogical incursion that radically disrupts the stable modes of ordinary fictional existence. "Habitually linked to the narrative of an action," writes Todorov, the marvelous element "proves to be the narrative raw material which best fills this specific function: to afford a modification of the preceding situation, and to break the established equilibrium" of the fantastic text. Social and literary operations here coincide, for "in both cases, we are concerned with a transgression of the law." "Whether it is in social life or in narrative," he concludes, "the intervention of the supernatural element always constitutes a break in the system of pre-established rules, and in so doing finds its justification."[18]

An analogy might be made, however, between the role of the supernatural in fantastic literature and that of the masquerade in certain putatively "realistic" or secularized eighteenth-century narratives. The carnivalesque episode likewise transgresses the law, though not a transcendental one; it deranges the orderly world of human relations elsewhere intimated in classic eighteenth-century fiction, introducing an imbalance, a fundamental strangeness. The masquerade typically engenders a series of problematic *liaisons dangereuses* by throwing characters into proximity who, if an exhaustive cosmological decorum were truly the goal, would never meet: the high and the low, the virtuous and the vicious, the attached and the unattached. But by the same token, the episode may also bring about, for a time at least, the alienation of characters who *should* be together by virtue of established conjugal or familial ties: husbands and wives, parents and children, guardians and wards. Out of the masquerade's surplus of scandalous dialectical transactions, a multitude of intrigues develop. These localized complications characteristically infiltrate the larger fiction, shaping—either implicitly or explicitly—the remainder of the story. As a transgressive agent, the carnivalesque episode also provides that necessary mimetic disequilibrium on which plot depends.

The atavistic textual association between the masquerade episode and supernatural agency is typically inscribed in the imagery of costume: the characters often either disguise themselves as supernatural beings or meet others dressed in such costumes. In Inchbald's *A Simple Story,* for example, Miss Milner chooses the costume of the goddess Diana—somewhat ironically, it turns out, for the masquerade is subsequently instrumental in bringing about her marriage to Dorriforth. In *Tom Jones,* Lady Bellaston disguises herself as the queen of the fairies, while in *Cecilia,* the heroine's problematic suitor, Mr. Monckton, dresses as a fiend. Since each of these characters is a perpetrator of masquerade intrigue and an instrument in later plot developments, the sartorial hints of supernatural power might be taken as symbolic of his or her *narrative* influence.

The reader, to be sure, may enjoy the hyperelaboration of incident. The immediate puzzles of the masquerade episode (who is talking to whom? who wears what costume? what do the mystifying encounters signify?) are nicely calculated to promote the reader's engagement, and they soon lead to others. The masquerade scene almost always intimates a host of further plot developments and mysteries to be solved. But—and this is perhaps its most paradoxical function in eighteenth-century English narrative—the carnivalesque topos is often peculiarly implicated in the pleasure of characters as well as of readers. Often the masquerade is the instrument not just of plot but of a comic plot in particular. It characteristically precipitates a larger euphoric, or "rewarding," pattern of narrative transformation —even for those characters, like the beleaguered heroines, whom one would not expect to benefit from its disarming travesties. This subterranean comic agency is seldom if ever acknowledged; indeed, the narrator or the characters, like Richardson's Pamela, may describe the masquerade, before and after the fact, as the exemplary site of moral danger. Yet the association with a comic telos, a range of ultimately happy "consequences," is subtly insistent nonetheless. Instead of destroying, the masquerade seems finally to reward those who enter its chaotic midnight spaces.

The paradox is worth noting because, as we shall see in a moment, it suggests much about the contradictory and often compromising imaginative role played by the carnivalesque, not just in eighteenth-century fiction, but in eighteenth-century society itself. Granted, the beneficent instrumentality of the occasion may not seem immediately obvious: the narrative repercussions of masquerade can appear sinister, sometimes in highly melodramatic ways. But frequently these seemingly disastrous "consequences" are in fact a necessary prelude to something else: the ameliorization of a central character's fortunes, the "Providential" rewarding of the heroine. Like the Fortunate Fall (with which the carnivalesque has strong symbolic resonances), the masquerade episode typically stands out in the narrative as an indispensable event, as that temporary plunge into difficulty and enigma without which the characters could not realize their comic destinies.

Thus in *Sir Charles Grandison*—to take a schematic instance of the pattern—the "cursed masquerade" bears all the conventional hallmarks of an evil narrative agency: Harriet Byron is there abducted by the odious Sir Hargrave, and everyone fears that her sexual ruin is inevitable. On hearing the "fatal news" of Harriet's kidnapping, her distraught Uncle Selby exclaims that while he formerly believed public masquerades "more silly than wicked" he is now convinced that they are "the most profligate of all diversions."[19] But one soon learns that Harriet has not been ruined; rather, the paragon Sir Charles, fortuitously riding past the coach in which she is held after the masquerade, hears her muffled screams for help and, in "a glorious action," liberates her from her abductor. Such is the happy accidental meeting on which Richardson's heterosexual romance depends, for of course Harriet and Charles later fall in love and marry. Yet one might argue that it is Harriet's initial movement into the world of sexual danger, represented by the masked assembly, that diverts her toward her ultimate sexual reward: for without the masquerade, she would neither have entered the beatific Grandison household (which takes her in after her ordeal) nor have come to know her "god-like" benefactor intimately. The masquerade excursion is perversely responsible for all her subsequent happiness and the essential erotic comedy of Richardson's novel. Again, the fiction obscures this almost magical plot function: Harriet's relieved relations afterward revile the occasion that caused such "barbarous" suffering. But the disguised blessing is inscribed subliminally, in comments like Mr. Reeves' remark that Harriet's experience represents "a common case" heightened into "the marvelous."[20] Harriet too has the sense of supernatural agency: "How shall I bear this goodness!"—she exclaims after her adventure—"This is indeed bringing good out of evil! Did I not say, my cousin, that I was fallen into the company of angels?"[21]

One might multiply cases in which the heroine's masquerade venture affirms or reconstitutes the comic plot of heterosexual romance. Roxana meets her most powerful financial and erotic patron, the "Duke of M——," at the masquerade, attracting him with her lubricious "Turkish dance." Likewise, though in a somewhat more sedate manner, Burney's Cecilia attracts a lover at the masquerade—Delvile, the man who will become her husband. In *A Simple Story,* though the masquerade episode at first appears to estrange Miss Milner and Dorriforth, it actually sets up an ecstatic reconciliation and their subsequent marriage. And in the sequel to *Pamela,* Mr. B.'s masquerade flirtation with the Countess is not the disaster for the heroine it seems to be: it too produces a transporting moment of "éclaircissement," when B. renounces the Countess, begs his wife's forgiveness, and "redoubles" his love for her.

The masquerade episode, then, is not only a narrative crux; it is characteristically implicated in the larger comic patterns of eighteenth-century English fiction. Without it, many apparently "Providential" turns in contemporary narratives are difficult to imagine. Yet such instrumentality, one may notice, also undermines the conventional moral significance of the topos and threatens the didactic coherence of the work as a whole. By its very comic agency the carnivalesque episode contradicts its superficial negative inscription within the text, revealing itself instead as part of the paradoxical machinery of narrative pleasure. It ceases to be merely an emblem—of hypocrisy or anything else—at the moment that it facilitates, like a covert deus ex machina, the ultimate reward of character and reader alike.

This "scrambling" of emblematic significance, it turns out, is often paradigmatic; it can signal a collapse of didactic accountability in the fictional world. The masquerade scene typically leaves in its wake what might be called a world upside down. That is, it marks a moment in the narrative at which ordinarily sanctioned social or metaphysical hierarchies may suddenly weaken or show signs of being overthrown altogether. Following the representation of masquerade intrigue, the reader may experience a sense of ideological topsy-turvydom—as though the dramatic transformations in the narrative had somehow precipitated thematic changes too. To use Bakhtin's term, one might say that the fictional world itself suddenly appears "carnivalized."

Something of this effect is already obvious in the association just educed between the scene and the comic destiny of heroines. The masquerade frequently coincides with a peculiar reversal of those conventional male-female power relations encoded elsewhere in eighteenth-century fiction. Male characters may abruptly lose their authority following the masquerade, while female characters acquire unprecedented intellectual and emotional influence over them. As the symbolic theater of female power (women masqueraders, we recollect, usurped not only the costumes but the social and behavioral "freedoms" of the opposite sex), the assembly room engenders patterns of sexual reversal that subsequently pervade, as it were, the rest of the novel. Thus the heroine typically eludes her immediate masquerade persecutors—witness Harriet in *Sir Charles Grandison* or Mrs. Atkinson in *Amelia,* who outwits the evil Noble Peer at the masked conclave in that novel. But often she also derives more lasting powers of sexual control from the occasion. She is particularly likely, as we have seen, to gain psychological sway here over a future lover or husband. A parodic example occurs in *Tom Jones,* when Lady Bellaston, disguised as the queen of the fairies (her very dress a blazon of female authority), seduces Tom at the Haymarket masquerade and thus establishes a brief erotic and economic ascendancy over him. Even here, however, the effect of ideological destabilization remains potent: though Tom later escapes Bellaston's lascivious influence, the masquerade scene introduces an important thematic disturbance into Fielding's otherwise highly conservative fiction—one that both threatens the novel's patriarchal logic and temporarily subverts its normative vision of male-female relations.[22]

While the masquerade precipitates controversy in sexual relations—and is particularly linked to scenarios of female desire and authority—it is also associated with the disruption of class relations. (The two forms of inversion sometimes overlap in interesting structural and thematic ways.) Again it may seem as though the saturnalian reversals of the masked assembly—where "low" becomes "high" and vice versa—somehow work their way into the larger fiction. Just as women characters achieve a carnivalesque hegemony following the invocation of masquerade, so "low" characters may gain new status or importance from this powerful textual event.

Sometimes a directly subversive narrative causation is at work. In *Amelia*, for example, when Amelia's masquerade surrogate, Mrs. Atkinson, tricks the Noble Peer (who has mistaken her for the heroine) into granting her husband an officer's commission, she brings about a radical and lasting sociological change in Fielding's rigidly hierarchical fictional world. Through her ruse, which elegantly exploits the masquerade's requisite sartorial confusions, a carnivalesque transformation, from low into high, becomes permanent. The "humble" Sergeant Atkinson, who before has served as Booth's valet, indeed receives his commission a few days after the masquerade, thus abruptly rising to Booth's own rank and achieving the coveted status of gentleman.[23] Once again, one might say, the masquerade episode has permitted a breach in the social order and in the underlying ideological structure of Fielding's novel.

But the scandalous consequences of masquerade may occur at a symbolic remove too, as in the second part of *Pamela*. There, a seemingly sinister masquerade adventure—during which B. becomes estranged from the heroine and begins his "Platonick" affair with the Countess—ultimately produces a scene of ecstatic repetition, in which Pamela symbolically reenacts her own highly transgressive history. This reenactment is implicit in the language of emotion: when B. belatedly expresses his remorse and reaffirms his love for his wife, Pamela—who has taken to dressing again in the plain garments of a servant and asserting that she is not a true "lady" like the Countess—blissfully declares herself "lifted up" once more. B.'s transporting demonstration, she tells Lady Davers, has "exalted" her, and she reassumes her rich garments and her place by his side.[24] Yet in this "happy turn," the melodramatic climax of Richardson's narrative, one recognizes a displaced recapitulation of precisely that problematic change recorded in *Pamela*, part 1: the heroine's original (and revolutionary) "exaltation" from humble to genteel status. By precipitating this charged repetition, the masquerade episode again betrays its subliminal thematic link with fantasies of mutability and with the subversion of class and sexual distinctions.

Finally, the patterns of ideological destabilization associated with the masquerade are microcosmically reinscribed on the level of character. Just as the personae of eighteenth-century English fiction are likely to transcend supposedly "given" social or sexual categories following the representation of masquerade, so they are likely to display certain unaccountable moral or emotional traits, as though temporarily estranged, or "different" from themselves in basic psychological ways. The gesture of self-alienation implicit in the act of masquerading—where one indeed "becomes" the other—would seem to be exemplary. It heralds additional, more intimate transformations and an incursion of instability into the realm of human nature itself.

The phenomenon is particularly noticeable, as one might expect, in novels like Fielding's, where the allegorical representation of character predominates and the fictional world is ordinarily composed of fixed, even caricatured moral types. Here, true to its antitaxonomic function, the masquerade scene disrupts stereotypical distinctions, such as those between paragons and knaves, the virtuous and the vicious. Supposedly lucid moral types may suddenly behave like their opposites, intensifying the reader's sense of didactic confusion. In *Tom Jones*, for example, the masquerade in book 13 marks the point at which the hero seems, to many readers, to behave in ways notably unlike himself—displaying a venality and opportunism, manifest in his somewhat sordid dealings with Lady Bellaston, not previously associated with his usually open and good-natured character. It is as though, by donning the mask and domino supplied by his secret patron, he temporarily diverges also from a stereotypical mode of being. The schematic code of character structuring Fielding's novel—with its underlying essentialist distinction between good and evil natures—is suddenly thrown into question. Though Tom later recollects himself and becomes the same transparent, even banal moral type he was before, his peculiar opacity and inconsistency on this occasion have troubled *Tom Jones*'s critics. Likewise, the masquerade sequence as a whole has sometimes been educed as an "unsuccessful" or incongruous element in Fielding's larger artistic and thematic design.[25]

In *Amelia*, too, the masquerade episode marks enigmatic psychological as well as narrative transformations. The crude emblematic dichotomy established early in the fiction between paragons and hypocrites here tends to dissolve, even as Fielding's narrative pattern itself becomes more intricate and mysterious. Antithetical moral types merge in disarming ways. In particular, Amelia herself—elsewhere a model of uncomplicated virtue—reveals new and problematic depths to her character. Her ruse on the night of the masquerade, when she allows Mrs. Atkinson to take her place, unbeknownst to Booth or anyone else, is symptomatic: her complicity is technically a kind of hypocrisy, linking her with the role players

and double-dealers vilified earlier by Fielding's moralizing narrator. Though perhaps justifiable on the grounds of prudence, Amelia's gesture is still a compromising one, and for the first time her supposedly immaculate character is shaded with
a subtle admixture of deviousness and theatricality. But there are other puzzling
shifts in behavior following the masquerade: Amelia is not the only paragon to
show signs of lapsing from moral uniformity. Sergeant Atkinson, for example,
turns out to harbor an adulterous passion for the heroine, and confesses to the
theft of her "lost" miniature, while the villains of the novel, the Noble Peer and
Colonel James among them, are somewhat mystifyingly rehabilitated. Despite
having been tricked into granting the sergeant an officer's commission, the Peer
charitably permits him to retain it, and both the Peer and James inexplicably cease
their lustful machinations against Amelia. The masquerade scene is not only a
crux in Fielding's extremely convoluted plot, it marks a chiasmus on the level of
character: Fielding's implicit moral typology itself is, for a time at least, turned
upside down. With this confusion of types, *Amelia* loses much of its allegorical
legibility. To be sure, it becomes in many ways a more compelling fiction at this
point, but it is hardly any longer the simplistic didactic exemplum Fielding seems
to have conceived it to be.[26]

Thus, to speak of the "carnivalization" of eighteenth-century fiction is to
speak of a multifaceted textual phenomenon. Though the process may begin with
a localized, or strictly anecdotal, representation of masquerade—the discrete scene
or set piece—it does not end there. The invocation of the masquerade almost
invariably coincides with an elaboration of plot, in particular with comic plots of
sexual consummation and social mutability. Yet this transgressive narrative agency,
the masquerade's privileged relation to intrigue itself, offends against the prevailing
didactic economy of eighteenth-century English fiction. The pleasurable consequences of masquerade negate its superficial textual inscription as an emblem of
vice, inauthenticity, and corrupt urbanity. The topos cannot be recuperated simply
as a version of the *carnaval moralisé;* it conditions powerful transformations in the
fictional world.

One may describe these transformations in thematic as well as narrative
terms. As we have seen, the allusion to the scandals of masquerade typically
engenders, as though by contagion, a larger ideological scandal in the fiction—the
subversion of existing distinctions, the reversal of normative moral and social
hierarchies. By injecting an enigmatic, destabilizing energy into the orderly cosmos
of the eighteenth-century English novel, the carnivalesque episode alters the literary artifact itself, which seldom retains its claim to didactic purity following the
representation of this least purifying of diversions. Its imaginative structure may
suddenly appear contradictory or hybrid—"double" in potential significance,
unrecuperable according to any straightforward didactic logic. Though it may have
advertised itself as allegory, it ceases here to be merely that. With the turn toward
the irrationality of masquerade, one might say, the novel itself becomes unlike

itself; it diverges from its putative moral project and reshapes itself as phantasmagoria and dream.

Implicit in my argument here, of course, is Bakhtin's notion of "carnivalization," which means not just the invocation of a thematic but also a process of generic destabilization. The carnivalized work, Bakhtin suggests, resists generic classification and instead combines, like Rabelais's *Pantagruel*, a multiplicity of literary modes in a single increasingly "promiscuous" form. Interestingly enough, eighteenth-century English novels containing masquerade scenes often also display generic uncertainty. The masquerade may at times even seem to condition a formal "shifting" or ambiguity in the work. In *Amelia*, for example, the scene coincides with a general shift from satiric to mimetic modes: it marks the point at which Fielding's fiction lapses from a primarily "anatomizing" method—characterized by a ridiculing exposure of the "glaring evils" of society—and assumes more and more of the conventional features of realistic narrative. In Richardson's sequel to *Pamela*, the pattern of generic destabilization is even more obvious: after the masquerade intrigue in that novel, the work becomes a true hodgepodge of discourses—a mixture of embedded exempla, "table talk" (the symposia of the B. and Darnford households), and miscellaneous items, such as Pamela's lengthy commentary on Locke's treatise on education. Just as the masquerade episode precipitates transformation in the narrative, then, it appears to precipitate a transformation of the genre itself: it instigates a lapse in consistency on every textual stratum.

It may seem, at this point, that I have skirted an obvious epistemological problem by speaking elliptically of the manner in which the representation of masquerade engenders or precipitates a host of transformations in a novel. I have treated the carnivalesque episode as a kind of "ghost in the machine" in eighteenth-century English fiction—almost as a transcendental agency that provokes an irruption of narrative fluidity and didactic ambiguity. To identify the typical masquerade scene as a subversive textual crux is to sidestep larger matters of authorial intention and literary dynamics. Indeed, one might ask, what conditions the representation of masquerade itself?

The question returns us to the realm of cultural history and the role of the carnivalesque, not just in the literary imagination, but in eighteenth-century English society. Granted, it is always possible to treat the contradictory literary inscription of masquerade simply as a function of idiosyncratic authorial intentions. In Fielding and Richardson, for example, the complex invocation of the carnivalesque can always be seen as a symptom of individual imaginative ambivalence—as the outward sign of a deeper private debate on the questions of order and disorder, restraint and indulgence, decorum and transgression. I do not wish to imply that either Fielding or Richardson *consciously* manipulates the topos to build, as it were, a certain ideological paradox into his fiction—or that the thematic imbroglio precipitated by the masquerade scene is part of any explicitly premeditated design.

English novelists of the eighteenth century show little of that intentionally heuristic use of the carnivalesque that occurs later—say, in highly self-conscious writers like Flaubert.[27] Still, the masquerade episode does seem to satisfy diverse conscious and unconscious imperatives. It can express an underlying authorial ambivalence regarding the didactic project itself. For the eighteenth-century novelist, invoking the world of masquerade is typically a way of indulging in the scenery of transgression while seeming to maintain didactic probity. The occasion may be condemned in conventional terms, yet its very representation permits the novelist, like the characters, to assume a different role: to cast off the persona of the moralist and turn instead to the pleasures of intrigue. The writer may become at this point the purveyor of seductive fantasies rather than of staid instruction. In novelists like Fielding and Richardson, in whom the conflict between moralism and subversion is intense, the masquerade functions as a figure for ambiguous authorial intentions—the textual sign of an inward tension regarding the author's role.

But it is perhaps more compelling, as I suggested at the start, to make the larger argument: that the paradoxes implicit in the fictional allusion to masquerade mirrored paradoxes in the cultural response to the carnivalesque. The masked assembly institutionalized dreams of disorder not just for its literary adherents but for the real world. Even as eighteenth-century English society preserved, on the face of it, a host of distinctions and hierarchies, reinforced by repressive dictates of one sort or another, the masquerade, like a theater of doubt, dramatized the possibility of change. It expressed collective fantasies of metamorphosis; it intimated that prevailing moral, social, and metaphysical categories were mere artifacts. It may seem an obvious enough point to make, but the way the masquerade functions in eighteenth-century English narrative—as an episode at once diverting and threatening to the implicit taxonomies of the fictional world—is roughly analogous to the way it functioned in the culture: as a discontinuous, estranging, sometimes even hallucinatory event that nonetheless carried with it a powerfully cathartic and disruptive cognitive éclat.

The argument might be embellished in various ways. A proponent of Bakhtin's lyrical theory of carnival, for instance, might favor a historical interpretation of some of the contradictions in the literary masquerade, seeing them as symptomatic of that shift away from the carnivalesque spirit which, Bakhtin has suggested, characterizes the modern period. He claims that the great traditions of European carnival were already in decline by the eighteenth century—a fact he attributes to increasing secularization and the rise of philosophies of rational individualism. The traditional carnival, he argues—the masked fête, charivari, and sotie—celebrated a fluid metaphysics: an archaic popular belief in the underlying unity of opposites and the "organic" wholeness of experience. Folk spectacle emphasized union over separation, changing over "finished" forms, and the "ever incompleted character of being" itself.[28] With the development of modern notions of the subject, however—what Bakhtin calls the "completed atomized being" of rationalism—this popular metaphysics was superseded. A world of discrete individuals, without resemblance or dialectical connection to one another, took its place. Thus, in the eighteenth century one finds a "gradual narrowing down of the ritual, spectacle, and carnival forms of folk culture, which became small and trivial." Literature mirrors the change: while the themes and imagery of carnival are central to Rabelais and other writers of the Renaissance, they have become circumscribed and problematic in the literature of the Enlightenment.[29]

Of course the eighteenth-century masquerade itself might be described as a late or decadent form of the carnivalesque: particularly in England, where festive tradition was already far more attenuated than on the Continent, the masked assembly rapidly became an almost entirely secularized and commercial phenomenon.[30] Its philosophic dimension was somewhat paradoxical from the start, almost a vestigial effect. It is not surprising, therefore, that the contemporary novel of masquerade should also be peculiarly ambiguous. Even while the masquerade scene marks an atavistic incursion of mutability and flux into the symbolic world of representation, its moralistic bracketing—the suspicion and disavowal that surround the occasion—might be taken as the sign of a growing uneasiness and skepticism regarding the fluid epistemology of the older popular tradition. Seen in the elegiac Bakhtinian context, the masquerade novel of this period emerges as a penultimate moment in the literary history of the carnivalesque: it expresses larger philosophic and conceptual conflicts in an especially condensed and ambivalent way.

Certainly, with the exception of a few minor revivals in Regency literature, the masquerade set piece has all but vanished from the topography of the English novel by the late eighteenth century.[31] Yet this absence too reflected cultural reality: the public masquerade itself had virtually disappeared in England by the time of the French Revolution. To be sure, especially in the light of the growing moral and social conservatism of the upper classes in the last decades of the century, one might explain this disappearance politically as well as purely philosophically: in that period of pervasive rebellion and unrest, the utopian reversals of masquerade may have seemed altogether too inflammatory—too threatening to the somewhat precariously maintained balance of English society. During the unsettled 1770s and 1780s, the stylized chaos of the carnival world seemed everywhere to be giving way to unmediated scenarios of active political insurgency.

But the basic connection here—between the literary theme and the cultural institution—remains a compelling one. It may suggest something too, finally, about the history of the novel and about the genre's own complex negotiation with human realities. Tony Tanner has argued that the novel, since its beginnings, has been subliminally concerned with representing transgression, even while asserting itself as the embodiment of bourgeois values and vindicator of the moral and social status quo. It has harbored dreams of a world upside down while seeming to validate prevailing ideology.[32] For the English novelists of the eighteenth century, popular entertainments and diversions—the still extant realm of the carnivalesque—offered a convenient tropology of scandal, a way of figuring such dreams. The masquerade, one could say, was simply part of a larger preoccupation with disruption.

As society itself changed, however, so did the novel, and so did the characteristic scenery of transgression. The carnival topos may be typical of the novel in its infancy, the period when proponents of the genre are concerned most intensely with establishing the novel's claim to didactic authority. So powerful is the overt moralistic imperative in early fiction that the transgressive element appears, as it were, by accident; it is figured more or less unself-consciously. The particular appeal of the masquerade scene, as we have seen, was that it allowed for just such a "naive" elaboration of the transgressive plot, while permitting the novelist to maintain the appearance of moral orthodoxy. Presumably the writer could justify the episode, however logically discontinuous, by prefacing it with an explicit negative commentary. In contrast—it is tempting to speculate—novelists of the late eighteenth and nineteenth centuries had little need for ambiguously mediating figures like the masquerade; as the impulse toward crude didacticism weakened and the writer's absorption in transgressive modes became more integrated and self-conscious, scandal—whether sexual, social, or political—could be represented more directly. Tanner suggests that the plot of private erotic transgression—for example, adultery—has a new moral neutrality and imaginative centrality in the novels of Rousseau, Goethe, and Flaubert; unlike Richardson and Fielding, these writers rely less and less on devices of ideological or psychological mediation, such as the carnivalesque intrigue, to set the story in motion. Similarly, collective transgression seems to be depicted in increasingly unmediated forms in the nineteenth-century novel, often through a representation of the politicized divagations of the crowd or mob. Just as the masquerade scene loses its currency as the primary fictional topos of collective disorder, the crowd scene, or scene of urban riot, seems to take its place: witness the complex use of such episodes in Scott, Hugo, Dickens, Eliot, Flaubert, and Zola. The nineteenth-century crowd scene serves many of the same narrative and thematic functions as the earlier masquerade scene, but it is usually far more integrated, in imaginative terms, into the mimetic and ideological structure in which it occurs. For the nineteenth-century novelist, unlike his or her eighteenth-century counterpart, transgression no longer has the shape of a discontinuous or naive diversion. One might indeed ask whether it has not become the central, self-conscious concern of the fictional enterprise itself.

The classic masquerade scene, then, is to some extent a temporary phenomenon in the history of the novel—and perhaps a somewhat primitive one at that. In contrast with the topoi of nineteenth-century fiction, the masquerade episode functions in a curiously automatic way; it has the aspect at times of a piece of unconscious or unintegrated textual machinery. Yet its importance in eighteenth-century English fiction, as I have tried to show, is indisputable. The scene is typically a crux; it engenders a host of pleasurable fictional transformations. One might even call the carnivalesque episode an epitome of the seductive power of narrative: it introduces a surprising and gratifying potentiality into the static world of eighteenth-century representation, giving shape to that fantasy of change which lies at the heart of contemporary narrative. That this potentiality conflicts with the emblematic meaning of the scene—its inscription within the conventional moral allegory of the "Town"—represents a contradiction, of course, yet one with which the eighteenth century itself was at home. By turning to the spectacular, secretive figures of carnival, the novelists of the period reenacted a larger collective flight into theatricality. The novel of masquerade is also, finally, an epitome of the culture in which it flourished—a mark of eighteenth-century England's own ambivalent escape from consistency, transparency, and the claims of an otherwise pervasive decorum.

CHAPTER 8

THE SPECTRALIZATION

OF THE OTHER IN

THE MYSTERIES

OF UDOLPHO

Friends came to be possessed like objects, while inanimate objects were desired like living beings.
Philippe Ariès, *The Hour of Our Death* (606)[1]

When it is not treated as a joke, Ann Radcliffe's *The Mysteries of Udolpho* (1794) is primarily remembered today for its most striking formal device—the much-maligned "explained supernatural." Scott, we may recall, was one of the first to blame Radcliffe for supplying anticlimatic "rational" explanations for the various eerie and uncanny events in her novels, and in *Lives of Eminent Novelists* (1824) chastized her for not "boldly avowing the use of supernatural machinery" in her greatest fiction.[2] Jane Austen's satiric depredations in *Northanger Abbey* are even better known.[3] But modern critics have been similarly put out—that is, when they have bothered to write about Radcliffe at all. "A stupid convention," says Montague Summers of her admittedly intrusive rationalizations. "The vice of her method," writes another. A few hapless defenders merely compound the damage: "the poor lady's romances," wrote Andrew Lang, "would have been excluded from families, if she had not provided normal explanations of her groans, moans, voices, lights, and wandering figures."[4] *Requiescat in pace.*

It has always been easy, of course, to patronize Ann Radcliffe. No English writer of such historic importance and diverse influence has been so often trivialized by her critics. Granted, we have the occasional arch excurses on selected

Radcliffean topoi—the Villain, the Fainting Heroine (with her much-vaunted Sensibility), the Scenery. But the point of such commentary is usually to demonstrate the superiority of the critic to this notoriously "silly" writer and to have done with Radcliffe as quickly as possible. Even among admirers of Gothic fiction, the clumsy device of the "explained supernatural" is often taken as the final proof of Radcliffe's irredeemable ineptitude and bathos. By way of a formula, the author herself is explained away.

Which is not to say that the formula is entirely misleading. Blatantly supernatural-seeming events *are* "explained" in *Udolpho,* and sometimes most awkwardly. Mysterious musical sounds, groans emanating from walls, the sudden movement of a supposedly dead body: however incredibly, rational explanations for such phenomena are inevitably forthcoming. At numerous points in the fiction, moreover, Radcliffe self-consciously condemns what she calls "superstition." Not for her those primitive ancestral spirits described by Nietzsche in *The Genealogy of Morals,* who come back to earth to terrify, cajole, or exact various pious sacrifices from the living. Nor, despite occasional hesitations, has she any residual faith in the more benign ghosts of popular Christianity. St. Aubert, the father of the heroine in *Udolpho,* admits at one point to a hope that "disembodied spirits watch over the friends they have loved" (67), but later in the novel, when the enlightened Count de Villefort argues against the reality of specters, Radcliffe resolutely endorses his position, noting that "the Count had much the superiority of the Baron in point of argument" (549).[5] In this denial of the traditional spirit-world, *The Mysteries of Udolpho,* like the Gothic in general, anticipates the thoroughly God-abandoned forms of modern literature.

Yet already we oversimplify perhaps, for the very concept of the "explained supernatural" depends upon a highly selective—indeed schematic—vision of the novel. We "read," it seems, only part of *The Mysteries of Udolpho:* the famous part. As any survey of *Udolpho* scholarship will show, modern critics devote themselves almost without exception solely to those episodes in the novel involving the villainous Montoni and the castle of Udolpho—even though these make up barely a third of the narrative. Of the dreamlike wanderings of Emily St. Aubert and her father through the Pyrenees (which alone take up nearly one hundred pages at the outset of the work), of St. Aubert's drawn-out death scene and Emily's sojourn in a convent, of Emily's bizarre relationship with her lover Valancourt, of the episodes with Madame Cheron at Tholouse and Venice, of the lengthy post-Udolpho sections involving Du Pont, Blanche, the Marchioness de Villeroi, and the Count de Villefort, we have heard little or nothing.

The crude focus on the so-called Gothic core of *The Mysteries of Udolpho* has been achieved by repressing, so to speak, the bulk of Radcliffe's narrative. Many modern critics implicitly treat the fictional world as though it were composed of two ontologically distinct realms—one extra-ordinary, irrational, irruptive, and charismatic (that of Montoni and Udolpho), the other ordinary, domestic, and

uninteresting (the supposedly more "familiar" frame-world of La Vallée and the
St. Aubert family). Emily, it is often argued, is temporarily caught up in the
irrational Udolpho-world, and there subjected to much emotional dislocation, but
returns safely to ordinary life in the end. Commentators differ, to be sure, over
what exactly the irrationalism of Udolpho consists in, some claiming that the castle
is in fact a violent realm of moral and political chaos, while others, more psychologically inclined, argue that its terrors are merely notional, the result of the
heroine's supercharged sensibility. The assertion that Emily develops and learns to
control her "hysteria" in the course of her ordeal is a common didactic embellishment in the latter sort of reading. Seldom at issue in any of these accounts,
however, is the two-world distinction itself (with its normal/abnormal, rational/
irrational, ordinary/extra-ordinary oppositions) or the implicit assumption that
certain parts of *Udolpho* are intrinsically more interesting and worthy of discussion
than others. This tendency toward bifurcation, it is worth noting, has reappeared
even in the otherwise revisionist readings of the novel recently offered by feminist
critics.[6]

But what happens if we reject such reductive impulses and try to read all of
the fiction before us? For one thing, the supposedly ordinary parts of *Udolpho* may
begin to look increasingly peculiar. Take, for example, the ostensibly normalizing
ending. Montoni is dead, the putative terrors of Udolpho past, and Emily St.
Aubert has been joyfully reunited with her lost lover Valancourt. Yet Radcliffe's
language here, as elsewhere, remains oddly preternatural. Emily and Valancourt
marry in an "enchanted palace," the Count de Villefort's castle at Chateau-le-
Blanc, under sumptuous banners "which had long slept in dust." So exquisite is
the ceremony Annette the servant is moved to exclaim that "the fairies themselves,
at their nightly revels in this old hall, could display nothing finer," while Dorothée,
the old housekeeper, observes wistfully that "the castle looked as it was wont to do
in the time of her youth." The newlyweds proceed, as though entranced, to
Emily's beloved childhood home at La Vallée. There, in the picturesque spot "so
long inhabited" by her deceased parents, Monsieur and Madame St. Aubert, "the
pleasant shades welcomed them with a thousand tender and affecting remembrances." Emily wanders through her parents' "favourite haunts" in pensive
slow motion, her happiness heightened "by considering, that it would have been
worthy of their approbation, could they have witnessed it." Bemused by souvenirs
of the past, she and her lover seat themselves beneath a plane tree on the terrace, in
a spot "sacred to the memory of St. Aubert," and vow to imitate his benevolence
(671).

The mood of hypnotic, sweetish melancholy carries over into the last sentence of the novel, where Radcliffe addresses an ideal reader, likewise haunted by
personal history:

> And, if the weak hand, that has recorded this tale, has, by its scenes beguiled the
> mourner of one hour of sorrow, or, by its moral, taught him to sustain it—the effort,
> however humble, has not been vain, nor is the writer unrewarded. (672)

Enchantments, shades, haunts, sacred spots, the revivification (through memory) of a dead father, a perpetually mourning reader: the scene is tremulous with hidden presences. Not, again, the vulgar apparitions of folk superstition—the ghosts entertained here are subjective, delicately emotional in origin, the subtle protrusions of a yearning heart. No egregiously Gothic scenery obtrudes; we are still ostensibly in the ordinary world. But the scene is haunted nonetheless, as Radcliffe's oddly hinting figures of speech suggest. Home itself has become uncanny, a realm of *apophrades*. To be "at home" is to be possessed by memory, to dwell with spirits of the dead.

These passages epitomize a phenomenon in Radcliffe we might call the supernaturalization of everyday life. Old-fashioned ghosts, it is true, have disappeared from the fictional world, but a new kind of apparition takes their place. To be a Radcliffean hero or heroine in one sense means just this: to be "haunted," to find oneself obsessed by spectral images of those one loves. One sees in the mind's eye those who are absent; one is befriended and consoled by phantoms of the beloved. Radcliffe makes it clear how such phantasmata arise. They are the products of refined sentiment, the characteristic projections of a feeling heart. To be haunted, according to the novel's romantic myth, is to display one's powers of sympathetic imagination; the cruel and the dull have no such hallucinations. Those who love, by definition, are open to the spirit of the other.

The "ghost" may be of someone living or dead. Mourners, not surprisingly, are particularly prone to such mental visions. Early in the novel, for instance, Emily's father, St. Aubert, is reluctant to leave his estate, even for his health, because the continuing "presence" of his dead wife has "sanctified every surrounding scene" (22). The old peasant La Voisin, likewise bereaved, can "sometimes almost fancy" he sees his dead wife "of a still moonlight, walking among these shades she loved so well" (67). After St. Aubert dies and Emily has held a vigil over his corpse, her fancy is "haunted" by his living image: "She thought she saw her father approaching her with a benign countenance; then, smiling mournfully and pointing upwards, his lips moved, but instead of words, she heard sweet music borne on the distant air, and presently saw his features glow with the mild rapture of a superior being" (83). Entering his room when she returns to La Vallée, "the idea of him rose so distinctly to her mind, that she almost fancied she saw him before her" (95). When she and Valancourt sit in the garden, she finds her father's image "in every landscape" (106).

But lovers—those who mourn, as it were, for the living—are subject to similar experiences. The orphaned Emily, about to be carried off by her aunt to Tholouse, having bid a sad farewell to Valancourt in the garden at La Vallée, senses a mysterious presence at large in the shades around her:

> As her eyes wandered over the landscape she thought she perceived a person emerge from the groves, and pass slowly along a moon-light alley that led between them; but the distance and the imperfect light would not suffer her to judge with any degree of certainty whether this was fancy or reality. (115)

A haunted lover can do nothing, it seems, but haunt the haunts of the other. To love in the novel is to become ghostly oneself. When Valancourt, defying Madame Montoni's prohibition against meeting Emily, finds his way back to her, he exclaims, "I do then see you once again, and hear again, the sound of that voice! I have haunted this place—these gardens, for many—many nights, with a faint, very faint hope of seeing you" (152). Near the end of the novel, after Emily rejects him for supposed debaucheries, he makes obsessive "mournful wanderings" around her fateful garden: "the vision he had seen [of Emily] haunted his mind; he became more wretched than before, and the only solace of his sorrow was to return in the silence of the night; to follow the paths which he believed her steps had pressed, during the day; and, to watch round the habitation where she reposed" (627).

Such porous lovers, to be sure, may sometimes be mistaken for the cruder, traditional kind of spectre. But the lover's ghostliness is somehow more febrile and insistent. Emotionally speaking, it is not susceptible to exorcism. When Emily's gallant suitor Du Pont, the Valancourt-surrogate who appears in the midsection of the novel, traverses the battlements at Udolpho in the hope of seeing her, he is immediately mistaken by the castle guards (who seem to have read *Hamlet*) for an authentic apparition. He obliges by making eerie sounds, and creates enough apprehension to continue his lovesick "hauntings" indefinitely (459). Similarly, at the end of the fiction, when Emily is brooding once again over the absent Valancourt, her servant Annette suddenly bursts in crying, "I have seen his ghost, madam, I have seen his ghost!" Hearing her garbled story about the arrival of a stranger, Emily, in an acute access of yearning, assumes the "ghost" must be Valancourt (629). It is in fact Ludovico, Annette's own lover, who disappeared earlier from a supposedly haunted room at Chateau-le-Blanc and is presumed dead. Annette's own joy at seeing him, we note, "could not have been more extravagant, had he arisen from the grave" (630). Whoever he is, wherever he is, the lover is always a *revenant*.

Already, given what we might call Radcliffe's persistently spectralized language, one cannot merely say with aplomb that the supernatural is "explained" in *The Mysteries of Udolpho*. To speak only of the rationalization of the Gothic mode is to miss one of Radcliffe's most provocative rhetorical gestures. The supernatural is not so much explained in *Udolpho* as it is displaced. It is diverted—rerouted, so to speak, into the realm of the everyday. Even as the old-time spirit world is demystified, the supposedly ordinary secular world is metaphorically suffused with a new spiritual aura.

II

Why this pattern of displacement? And why have modern readers so often been impervious to it? The questions are deceptively simple, yet they bear profoundly both on the reception of the novel and the history of Western consciousness. *The Mysteries of Udolpho* became one of the charismatic texts of late eighteenth-century European culture (a fact all too easily forgotten) not merely because it gratified a passing taste for things Gothic—many contemporary works did this—but because it articulated a new and momentous perception of human experience. Like Rousseau's *Julie ou la Nouvelle Héloïse* or Goethe's *Werther,* which shared a similar shaping influence on contemporary psychic life, the novel owed its vast popularity across Europe to its encompassing emotional power—its paradigmatic role in what one writer has called "the fabrication of romantic sensitivity."[7] *Udolpho* was more than simply fashionable; it encapsulated new structures of feeling, a new model of human relations, a new phenomenology of self and other.

We often sum up such developments, of course, with the phrase romantic individualism. In what follows I will argue that a crucial feature of the new sensibility of the late eighteenth century was, quite literally, a growing sense of the ghostliness of other people. In the moment of romantic self-absorption, the other was indeed reduced to a phantom—a purely mental effect, or image, as it were, on the screen of consciousness itself. The corporeality of the other—his or her actual life in the world—became strangely insubstantial and indistinct: what mattered was the mental picture, the ghost, the haunting image.

The twentieth century, I hope to show, has completely naturalized this historic shift toward the phantasmatic. We are used to the metaphor of the haunted consciousness—indeed hardly recognize it as metaphoric. Often enough, we speak colloquially of being haunted by memories or pursued by images of people inside our heads. In moments of solitude or distress, we may even seek out such "phantoms" for companionship and solace. Not coincidentally, the most influential of modern theories of the mind—psychoanalysis—has internalized the ghost-seeing metaphor: the Freudian account of psychic events, as I will suggest in my conclusion, is as suffused with crypto-supernaturalism as Radcliffe's. Yet this concern with so-called mental apparitions, and the sense we have come to share, thanks to Sigmund Freud, of their potentially demonic hold over us, is itself the historic product of late eighteenth-century romantic sensibility. Radcliffe's novel remains one of the first and greatest evocations of this new cognitive dispensation —of a new collective absorption in the increasingly vivid, if also hallucinatory, contents of the mind itself. We feel at home in Radcliffe's spectralized landscape, for its ghosts are our own—the symptomatic projections of modern psychic life.

How to recognize that which has become too much a part of us? A series of vignettes, extracted, again, from the supposedly banal parts of the novel, will help to focus our attention on the historical phenomenon I am calling the spectralization of the other: this new obsession with the internalized images of other people. I present these Radcliffean "souvenirs of the other" in a somewhat paradoxical form in order to bring out both the uncanniness of the fictional world and its oddly familiar emotional logic:

1. *To think of the other is to see him.* Whenever Emily St. Aubert thinks

about her lover, Valancourt, he suddenly appears. This is especially likely to occur even when she (and the reader) have been led to assume he is far away. After Emily's first engagement to Valancourt is broken off by Madame Cheron (later Madame Montoni), Emily is beset by a painful "remembrance of her lover" and fantasizes a clandestine reunion: "As she repeated the words—'should we ever meet again!'—she shrunk as if this was a circumstance, which had never before occurred to her, and tears came to her eyes, which she hastily dried, for she heard footsteps approaching, and the door of the pavilion open, and, on turning, she saw—Valancourt" (127). Later, after escaping from Udolpho, Emily walks in the woods at Chateau-le-Blanc and broods about the time when her father was alive and she had just met Valancourt. Then: "She thought she heard Valancourt speak! It was, indeed, he!" (501).

2. *The other is always present—especially when absent.* The familiar "objects of former times," pressing upon one's notice, writes Radcliffe, make departed loved ones "present" again in memory (92). Hats, books, chairs, rooms, pets, miniatures, gardens, mountains, graves—all possess this affecting metonymic power. Pieces of furniture in the study of the dead St. Aubert brings his "image" forcibly into his daughter's mind (94–98). Elsewhere at La Vallée, Emily finds that her parents seem "to live again" in the various objects in their rooms (591). Picturesque landscapes (La Vallée, the Pyrenees, Languedoc, Chateau-le-Blanc) provoke visions of the person with whom one first saw them (92, 97, 116, 163, 490). Valancourt, as he is about to leave Emily at one point, says to her that they will "meet . . . in thought" by gazing at the sunset at the same time of day (163). Similarly, by retracing a page in one of Valancourt's books, and "dwelling on the passages, which he had admired," Emily is able to summon her absent lover "to her presence" again (58). His "vacant chair" prompts an image of him sitting beside her (521), while the garden, with "the very plants, which Valancourt so carefully reared," supplies further remembrances (583). Graves and grave monuments are obviously the most fascinating and paradoxical relics of the other, for even as they officially confirm absence (and indeed take on all the displaced pathos of the corpse), they also evoke powerful "living" images of the person they memorialize. Forcing herself after an "hour of melancholy indulgence" to leave the site of St. Aubert's grave, Emily remains "attached" to the place in her thoughts, "and for the sacred spot, where her father's remains were interred, she seemed to feel all those tender affections which we conceive for home" (91).

3. *Every other looks like every other other.* Characters in *Udolpho* mirror, or blur into one another. Following the death of her father, Emily is comforted by a friar "whose mild benevolence of manners bore some resemblance to those of St. Aubert" (82). The Count de Villefort's benign presence recalls "most powerfully to her mind the idea of her late father" (492). Emily and Annette repeatedly confuse Du Pont with Valancourt (439–40); Valancourt and Montoni also get mixed up. In Italy Emily gazes at someone she believes to be Montoni who turns

out, on second glance, to be her lover (145). But even Emily herself looks like Valancourt. His countenance is the "mirror" in which she sees "her own emotions reflected" (127). She, in turn, also looks like the deceased Marchioness of Villeroi. Dorothée comments on Emily's resemblance to "the late Marchioness" (491). The dying nun Agnes is maddened by it: "it is her very self! Oh! there is all that fascination in her look, which proved my destruction!" (644). This persistent deindividuation of other people produces numerous dreamlike effects throughout the novel. Characters seem uncannily to resemble or to replace previous characters, sometimes in pairs. Even as they assume quasi-parental control over the heroine, M. and Mme. Montoni become, in the mind of the reader, strangely "like" a new and demonic version of M. and Mme. St. Aubert. The Count and Countess de Villefort are a later transformation of the Montoni pair—and of M. and Mme. St. Aubert. Du Pont, of course, is virtually indistinguishable from Valancourt for several chapters. Blanche de Villefort is a kind of replacement-Emily, and her relations with her father replicate those of the heroine and St. Aubert, just as the Chateau-le-Blanc episodes recombine elements from the La Vallée and Udolpho episodes, and so on. The principle of *déjà vu* dominates both the structure of human relations in *Udolpho* and the phenomenology of reading.

One is always free, of course, to describe such peculiarly overdetermined effects in purely formal terms. Tzvetan Todorov, for example, would undoubtedly treat this mass of anecdotal material as a series of generic cues—evidence of the fantastic nature of Radcliffe's text. The defining principle of the fantastic work, he posits in *The Fantastic*, is that "*the transition from mind to matter has become possible.*"[8] Ordinary distinctions between fantasy and reality, mind and matter, subject and object, break down. The boundary between psychic experience and the physical world collapses, and "the idea becomes a matter of perception." "The rational schema," he writes,

> represents the human being as a subject entering into relations with other persons or with things that remain external to him, and which have the status of objects. The literature of the fantastic disturbs this abrupt separation. We hear music, but there is no longer an instrument external to the hearer and producing sounds, on the one hand, and on the other the listener himself. . . . We look at an object—but there is no longer any frontier between the object, with its shapes and colors, and the observer. . . . For two people to understand one another, it is no longer necessary that they speak: each can become the other and know what the other is thinking.[9]

The fantastic universe, he concludes—with a nod to Jean Piaget—is like that of the newborn infant or psychotic. Self and other are not properly distinguished; everything merges—inside and outside, cause and effect, mind and universe—in a vertiginous scene of "cosmic fusion."[10]

Radcliffe's fictional world might be described as fantastic in this sense. The mysterious power of loved ones to arrive at the very moment one thinks of them or else to "appear" when one contemplates the objects with which they are associated—such events blur the line between objective and subjective experience. Magical reunion is possible. Thoughts shape reality. In such instances Radcliffe indeed creates a narrative simulacrum of that sense of omnipotence briefly experienced, according to D. W. Winnicott, in our infancy: wishes seem to come true; the hidden desires of the subject appear to take precedence over logic or natural probability.[11]

But the fantastic nature of Radcliffe's ontology is also manifest, one might argue, in the peculiar resemblances that obtain between characters in her novel. When everyone looks like everyone else, the limit between mind and world is again profoundly undermined, for such obsessive replication can only occur, we assume, in a universe dominated by phantasmatic imperatives. Mirroring occurs in a world already stylized, so to speak, by the unconscious. Freud makes this point in his famous essay "The 'Uncanny'" in which he takes the proliferation of doubles in E. T. A. Hoffman's "The Sandman" as proof that the reader is in fact experiencing events from the perspective of the deranged and hallucinating hero.[12] And once more, infantile psychic life provides the appropriate analogy. For we can indeed imagine, if not recollect, a stage in our early development at which we did not fully distinguish individuals from one another, or recognize other people as wholly separate beings. Our powers of physiognomic comparison must have once been quite crude, and our sense of the difference between the faces we observed somewhat precarious. Everybody *did* look like everybody else at one period in our lives. That various forms of literature, and the Gothic and romance in particular, atavistically dramatize this primal stage in human awareness, is an idea implicit, though not fully articulated, in the early work of Eve Kosofsky Sedgwick.[13]

The formalist description, however, can only go so far. As the psychoanalytic gloss already intimates, the Todorovian notion of ontological transgression—this breakdown of limits between mind and matter—invites historicization. By invoking Freud or Piaget, we add one kind of diachronic dimension: fantastic works like *Udolpho*, we imply, return us symbolically to an earlier stage of consciousness, a prior moment in the history of the individual psyche. But we still do not contend with larger shifts in human consciousness itself. Todorov himself makes only a few comments on the place of fantastic themes in the changing psychic history of the West.

For this kind of analysis we must turn elsewhere, though one of Todorov's own remarks will again prove suggestive. He cites the following passage from Freud—

> A young woman who was in love with her brother-in-law, and whose sister was dying, was horrified by the thought: "Now he is free and we can be married!" The instantaneous forgetting of this thought permitted the initiation of the process of repression which led to hysterical disturbances. Nonetheless it is interesting to see, in just such a case, how neurosis tends to resolve the conflict. It takes into account the change in reality by repressing the satisfaction of the impulse, in this case, the love for

the brother-in-law. A psychotic reaction would have denied the fact that the sister was dying.

And in the last sentence he uncovers one of the central themes of the fantastic: "To think that someone is not dead—to desire it on one hand, and to perceive this same fact in reality on the other—are two phases of one and the same movement, and the transition between them is achieved without difficulty."[14] Only the thinnest line separates the experience of wishing for (or fearing) the return of the dead and actually seeing them return. Fantastic works, he argues, repeatedly cross it. Here indeed is the ultimate fantasy of mind over matter.

Just such a fantasy—of a breakdown of the limit between life and death—lies at the heart of Radcliffe's novel and underwrites her vision of experience. To put it quite simply, there is an impinging confusion in *Udolpho* over who is dead and who is alive. The ambiguity is conveyed by the very language of the novel: in the moment of Radcliffean reverie, as we have seen, the dead seem to "live" again, while conversely, the living "haunt" the mind's eye in the manner of ghosts. Life and death—at least in the realm of the psyche—have become peculiarly indistinguishable. Yet it is precisely this essentially fantastic ambiguity that is most in need of historical analysis. Why should it be in a work of the late eighteenth century, especially, that the imaginative boundary between life and death should suddenly become so obscure?

III

The work of the French historian Philippe Ariès provides, to my mind, the most useful insight into this problem, for he, more than any other recent writer, has speculated on the complex symbolic relationship between life and death in the popular consciousness of recent centuries. Ariès's magisterial *L'Homme devant la mort,* published in 1977 and translated into English as *The Hour of Our Death* in 1981, is a study of changing attitudes toward death and dying in European culture since the Middle Ages. I cannot do justice here, obviously, to the grand scale of Ariès's project, or to his richly idiosyncratic, even lyrical response to this profound intellectual theme. Let me focus instead merely on one thread of his argument— his assertion that new and increasingly repressive emotional attitudes toward death in the late eighteenth century constituted a major "revolution in feeling" with far-reaching social and philosophic consequences (471). If Ariès is correct, Radcliffe's spectralized sense of the other may be understood as an aspect of a much larger cognitive revolution in Western culture.

In brief, Ariès's hypothesis is this—that in contrast with earlier periods such as the Middle Ages, when physical mortality was generally accepted as an organic, integral and centrally meaningful facet of human existence, late eighteenth-century Western culture was characterized by a growing dissociation from corporeal reality, and a new and unprecedented antipathy toward death in all its aspects. Changing affectional patterns, the breakdown of communal social life, and the increasingly individualistic and secular nature of modern experience played an important role, Ariès argues, in engendering this new spirit of alienation. The twentieth century, he claims, has inherited the post-Enlightenment attitude. Through a complex process of displacement, he claims, Western civilization has repressed the body and its exigencies; in the face of death, it retreats into anxious mystification and denial.

Ariès finds, in essence, a new spiritualization of human experience beginning in the late eighteenth century. His evidence for such a shift is twofold. A break with traditional patterns was first apparent, he suggests, in the practical sphere, in the period's obsession with what he calls the "beautiful death"—its concern with hiding or denying the physical signs of mortality and decay. Where death was once a public spectacle of considerable magnitude, it now became primarily a private event, witnessed only by one's closest relations. The cosmetic preservation of the corpse took on a new emotional urgency: the arts of embalming and even mummification (one thinks of Bentham's corpse) became common practices among all but the very lowest classes. Funerals were carried out more and more discreetly. And in contrast with the relaxed practice of earlier centuries, the dead were increasingly segregated from the living. Cemeteries were removed from their once-central locations in cities and towns to outlying areas, and their necrological functions obscured. The romantic "garden of remembrance," with its idealizing statuary, landscaped walks and prospects, was a quintessentially eighteenth-century invention.[15]

Just such an urge toward mystification, we note, may be allegorized at various points in *Udolpho*. It is interesting to find, for example, how many moments in the novel traditionally adduced by critics as classically "Radcliffean" have to do with supposed deaths that have not really taken place, or with corpses that turn out not to be corpses after all. Radcliffe often flirts with an image of physical dissolution, then undoes it. Thus Emily at Udolpho, thinking she has found the dead body of her aunt, follows a trail of blood toward a horrible "something" that turns out to be a pile of old clothes (323). An open grave in the castle crypt is empty (345). A body suddenly jerking under a pall on a bed in the abandoned apartments of the dead Marchioness of Villeroi is found to be a pirate who has hidden there and frightens off intruders in this manner (634). And most strikingly of course, the famous terrifying object under the black veil that Emily thinks is the "murdered body of the lady Laurentini" (248) is a piece of *trompe l'oeil:* an old wax effigy of a decomposing body "dressed in the habiliments of the grave," formerly used as a *memento mori* (662). While such moments provide an undeniable *frisson,* they also hint at new taboos. Uneasy fascination gives way before the comforting final illusion that there is no such thing as a real corpse. (Radcliffe delicately refers to the *memento mori* as an example of that "fierce severity, which monkish superstition has sometimes inflicted on mankind" [662]). If we are now inclined to recoil from Radcliffe's ambiguous thanatological artifacts, or indulge in nervous laughter over the "morbid" or "macabre" nature of Gothic literature in general, our responses, if Ariès is correct, merely indicate how much further the process of repression has advanced in our own day.[16]

But the most important sign of shifting sensibilities in the period, according to Ariès, is the emergence of a "romantic cult of the dead"—a growing subjective fascination with idealized images of the deceased. Older ideas of the afterlife—those of the Middle Ages, for example—had not typically emphasized the possibility of meeting one's family and friends after death. Death meant rupture, a falling asleep, or a falling away into "the peace that passeth understanding." In the era of romantic individualism, however, the theme of sentimental reunion became paramount. The coming together of husbands and wives, brothers and sisters, or parents and children after death, the blissful renewal of domestic life in a new "home" in the hereafter became staple images in late eighteenth and early nineteenth-century popular belief. Consolatory literature, grave inscriptions and monuments, and the keeping of mementos of the dead all bespoke the new fantasy of continuity, while a host of theories, not necessarily theological in origin, regarding the eternal life of disembodied spirits reinforced popular emotion. Death was no longer ugly or frightening, supposedly, because its physical separations were only temporary. Much of nineteenth-century spiritualism, Ariès argues, was simply an extenuation of the notion that the familiar souls of the dead continued to dwell in a nearby invisible realm, invited communication with the living, and awaited a happy future meeting with those who had mourned them in this life (432–60).

He attributes this new and fantastical mode of belief to changing patterns in family structure and the historic transformation of affectional relationships:

> The various beliefs in a future life or in the life of memory are in fact so many responses to the impossibility of accepting the death of a loved one. . . .
>
> In our former, traditional societies affectivity was distributed among a greater number of individuals rather than limited to the members of the conjugal family. It was extended to ever-widening circles, and diluted. Moreover, it was not wholly invested; people retained a residue of affectivity, which was released according to the accidents of life, either as affection or as its opposite, aggression.
>
> Beginning in the eighteenth century, however, affectivity was, from childhood, entirely concentrated on a few individuals, who became exceptional, irreplaceable, and inseparable. (472)

The underlying dream, of course, was that the precious dead were not really dead. He calls this hope the "great religious fact of the whole contemporary era" and notes its continued survival in the late twentieth century, despite all the incursions of "industrial rationalism." Even in the secular societies of the modern West, interviews with the dying and the recently bereaved reveal the same vestigial hope of an afterlife, "which is not so much the heavenly home as the earthly home saved from the menace of time, a home in which the expectations of eschatology are mingled with the realities of memory" (471). There, all shall be united "with those whom they have never ceased to love" (661).[17]

A poignant fantasy indeed—but what is perhaps most interesting here is not so much the emotional content per se, but the connection between this affective content and a new kind of introspection. What Ariès's work suggests, it seems to me, is not just a new response to death, but a new mode of thought altogether—a kind of thinking dominated by nostalgic mental images. The fear of death in the modern era prompts an obsessional return to the world of memory—where the dead continue to "live." But so gratifying are the mind's consoling inner pictures, one becomes more and more transfixed by them—lost, as it were, in contemplation itself. One enters a world of romantic reverie.

Certainly, returning to Radcliffe, we sense both a new anxiety about death, and a new reactive absorption in mental pictures. Radcliffe is fixated, first of all, on the idea of reunion, and dramatizes the romantic fantasy of futurity more explicitly than any previous novelist. Of course dreams of posthumous intimacy had appeared before in eighteenth-century fiction: in Richardson's *Clarissa*, Anna Howe's affirmation, while grieving over Clarissa's coffin, that they will "meet and rejoice together where no villainous *Lovelaces*, no hard-hearted *relations*, will ever shock our innocence, or ruffle our felicity!" anticipates the new sentimental model.[18]

What is new in Radcliffe, however, is the fervor with which the finality of death is denied. Continuity is all. Thus the dying St. Aubert discoursing on the afterlife with the noble peasant La Voisin:

> "But you believe, sir [says La Voisin], that we shall meet in another world the relations we have loved in this; I must believe this." "Then do believe it," replied St. Aubert, "severe, indeed, would be the pangs of separation, if we believed it to be eternal. Look up, my dear Emily, we shall meet again!" He lifted his eyes toward heaven, and a gleam of moonlight which fell upon his countenance, discovered peace and resignation, stealing on the lines of sorrow. (68)

Later, after her father dies, Emily is comforted by the thought that he indeed "lives" still, invisible yet otherwise unchanged, in a nearby spiritual realm: "'In the sight of God,' said Emily, 'my dear father now exists, as truly as he yesterday existed to me; it is to me only that he is dead; to God and to himself he yet lives!'" (82). Gazing on his corpse ("never till now seen otherwise than animated"), she fantasizes for a dizzying moment that she sees "the beloved countenance still susceptible," and soon after has the first of those uncanny mental images of her father's living form (83). His convent tomb rapidly becomes the inviting "home" to which she is repeatedly drawn, and La Vallée—the counter-Udolpho—the privileged site around which his presence seems palpably to linger.[19]

Nature itself becomes a mere screen—the sublime backdrop against which the potent fancies of mourning are played out. The vast peaks of the Pyrenees, the picturesque valleys of Gascony and Languedoc, even the rocky scenes around Udolpho—all become part of the same elegiac landscape: the zone of reverie itself. Nature in *Udolpho* sets the stage for phantasmagoric dramas of memory (" 'There, too, is Gascony . . . O my father,—my mother!' " [580]) or falls away against a fantastic mental picture of the blissful life to come: "She . . . fixed her eyes on the heavens, whose blue unclouded concave was studded thick with stars, the worlds, perhaps, of spirits, unsphered of mortal mould. As her eyes wandered along the boundless aether, her thoughts rose, as before, toward the sublimity of the Deity, and to the contemplation of futurity" (72). In either case, the emptiness of the world is filled: "How often did she wish to express to him the new emotions which this astonishing scenery awakened, and that he could partake of them! Sometimes too she endeavoured to anticipate his remarks, and almost imagined him present" (163). One is put in mind here of that patient of Freud's, mentioned in the case history of Schreber, who having "lost his father at a very early age, was always seeking to rediscover him in what was grand and sublime in nature."[20]

IV

What Radcliffe articulates so powerfully, as our detour through Ariès helps us to see, is not just the late eighteenth century's growing fear of death, but the way in which this fear was bound up with a new, all-consuming and increasingly irrational cognitive practice. In the Radcliffean thanatopia, immediate sensory experience gives way, necessarily, to an absorption in illusion—an obsessional concentration on nostalgic images of the dead. Yet these recollected "presences," it turns out, are paradoxically more real, more palpable-seeming, than any object of sense. No external scene, not even the most horrid or riotous, can undermine this absorbing faith in the phantasmatic. Even the castle of Udolpho, where every hallway is plunged in gore, is but the deceptive "vision of a necromancer" and yields before the mind's "fairy scenes of unfading happiness" (444). Unpleasant realities cannot compete with the marvelous projections of memory, love, and desire.

Which is not to say that people in previous epochs had been unaware of, or uninterested in, the mysterious "images" and "pictures" of the mind. Aristotle spoke of *phantasmata*, and Aquinas of the "corporeal similitudes" present to the memory.[21] In the Middle Ages and Renaissance, mental imagery played an important part in the devotional practices of Christianity. Employing the traditional mnemonic techniques known as the "arts of memory," for example, one might contemplate a certain complex mental image—a house, say, with many adjoining rooms—as a way of remembering an associated sequence of spiritual disciplines or sacred themes.[22] And needless to say, though in a somewhat different register, poets and mythographers had invoked the "shapes of fancy" for centuries before *The Mysteries of Udolpho*.

What emerges so distinctively with Radcliffe in the late eighteenth century, however, is an unprecedented sense of the subjective importance—the ontological weight, if you will—of these phantasmatic inner "pictures." In earlier times, mental simulacra, especially images of other people, had been clearly distinguished as such—as fanciful, nostalgic, or unreal. (An exception, of course, were the ambiguous visionary phenomena known as ghosts or specters. These uncanny entities were felt to exist outside the self, as real—if not material—objects of sense.)[23] At the end of the eighteenth century, however, through a complex process of historical change, phantasmatic objects had come to seem increasingly real: even more real at times than the material world from which they presumably derived. Powerful new fears prompted this valorization of illusion. Above all, as Ariès suggests, a growing cultural anxiety regarding the fate of the body after death conditioned an unprecedented collective flight into fantastic ideation.

Early eighteenth-century popular epistemology, to be sure, had prepared the ground for this conceptual shift. John Locke, interestingly enough, had hinted at the uncanny "life" of mental images in *An Essay Concerning Human Understanding*. In the section "Of Retention" (II.x), we may recall, he set out to describe in mechanistic terms the mind's curious ability to bring back into view those sensory impressions "which, after imprinting, have disappeared, or have been, as it were, laid out of sight." Locke's would-be scientific description of the memory is everywhere confused, however, by an imagery of supernatural reanimation. The mind, he asserts several times, has the power to "revive" its old impressions—that is, to give back life to the dead. Revived ideas reappear in the mind like *revenants*:

> This further it is to be observed, concerning ideas lodged in the memory, and upon occasion revived by the mind, that they are not only (as the word *revive* imports) none of them new ones, but also that the mind takes notice of them as of a former impression, and renews its acquaintance with them, as with ideas it had known before.

These strangely "lively" images are in turn bound up with the life of the mind itself. A sad contingency, Locke is forced to admit, is that our ideas can "decay" in times of illness, and crumble like forgotten monuments: "the flames of a fever in a few days calcine all those images to dust and confusion, which seemed to be as lasting as if graved in marble." But elsewhere he celebrates the mind as a kind of magical *daemon* or demiurge—one that infuses life, brings back the dead, paints "anew on itself" things that are "actually nowhere."[24]

Writers on the imagination—Burke, Hartley, Baillie, and Blair (and after them Wordsworth, Blake, and Coleridge)—took up the transcendental implications of Lockean theory in various programmatic ways throughout the century.[25] But it was Radcliffe, without question, who gave the supernaturalized model of mental experience its most charismatic popular brief. She injected the Lockean metaphor of mental reanimation with a rapturous emotional reality. In the ardent, delirious world of *Udolpho,* the "soaring mind" indeed makes dead things live again, including dead people. Like a new and potent deity, it turns absence into presence, rupture into reunion, sorrow into bliss—aspiring in the end to "that Great First Cause, which pervades and governs all being" (114).

One can speculate, of course, on the wishful content in this new-style devotionalism: to undo the death of another by meditating on his visionary form is also a compelling way of negating one's own death. Romantic mourning gave pleasure, one suspects, precisely because it entailed a magical sense of the continuity and stability of the "I" that mourned. To "see" the dead live again is to know that one too will live forever. Thus at times Radcliffe hints at a peculiar satisfaction to be found in grief. The vision of life-in-death is so beautiful one wants to grieve forever. In the final paragraph of *Udolpho,* for example, when she hopes that her fiction will help the mourner to "sustain" his sorrow, the subtle ambiguity of the verb suggests the underlying appeal of the new immortalizing habit of thought. *Lugeo ergo sum:* I mourn, therefore, I am.[26]

That this supernaturalization of the mind should occur precisely when the traditional supernatural realm was elsewhere being explained away should not surprise us. According to the Freudian principle, what the mind rejects in one form may return to haunt it in another. A predictable inversion has taken place in *The Mysteries of Udolpho:* what once was real (the supernatural) has become unreal; what once was unreal (the imagery of the mind) has become real. In the very process of reversal, however, the two realms are confused; the archaic language of the supernatural contaminates the new language of mental experience. Ghosts and spectres retain their ambiguous grip on the human imagination; they simply migrate into the space of the mind.

The Radcliffean model of mourning nonetheless presents certain problems. The constant denial of physical death results, paradoxically, in an indifference toward life itself. Common sense suggests as much: if one engages in the kind of obsessional reflection that Radcliffe seems to advocate—a thinking dominated by a preoccupation with the notion that the dead are not really dead (because, after all, one can still "see" them)—the real distinction between life and death will ultimately become irrelevant. If the dead appear to be alive in the mind, how does one distinguish between them and one's mental images of the living? Is such a distinction necessary? For, if seeing the dead in visionary form is more comforting than seeing them in the flesh, doesn't it pay to think of the living in this way too? The emotional conviction that the dead "live" in the mind can easily grow into a sense that the living "live" there too—that is, that one's mental images of other people are more real in some sense, and far more satisfying, than any unmediated confrontation with them could ever be. One can control one's images of other people; their very stability and changelessness seem to offer a powerful antidote to fear. In the end one begins to mourn the living as well as the dead—to "see" them too—but only in this spectral and immutable form. Life and death merge in the static landscape of the mind.

I spoke at the outset of a new sense of the ghostliness of other people emerging in the late eighteenth century. I meant this in two senses. First, as we have seen, the "ghost" of the dead or absent person, conceived as a kind of visionary image or presence in the mind, takes on a new and compelling subjective reality. In the moment of romantic absorption, one is conscious of the other as a kind of mental phantom, an *idée fixe,* a source of sublime and life-sustaining emotion. But this subjective valorization of the phantasmatic has a profound effect on actual human relations. Real human beings become ghostly too—but in an antithetical sense, in the sense that they suddenly seem insubstantial and unreal.[27] The terrible irony—indeed the pathology—of the romantic vision is that even as other people come to hold a new and fascinating eminence in the mind, they cease to matter as individuals in the flesh. One no longer desires to experience flesh at all, for this is precisely what has become so problematic. The direct corporeal experience of other people, what Locke called "bare naked perception"—seeing, touching, smelling, tasting, hearing the other—has become emotionally intolerable, thanks to the new and overwhelming fear of loss and separation. Real people, needless to say, change, decay, and ultimately die before our eyes. The successful denial of mortality thus requires a new spectralized mode of perception, in which one sees through the real person, as it were, towards a perfect and unchanging spiritual essence. Safely subsumed in this ghostly form, the other can be appropriated, held close, and cherished forever in the ecstatic confines of the imagination.

We have seen certain consequences of this cognitive reorientation in the mummified emotional world of *Udolpho.* Absence is preferable to presence. (An absent loved one, after all, can be present in the mind. One is not distracted by his actual presence.) The dead are more interesting than the living. (If the dead are alive in *Udolpho,* the living might as well be dead.) Objects are more compelling than people. (Objects evoke memories; people disturb them.) But most unsettlingly perhaps, living individuals—as opposed to the visionary forms of the mind—are curiously inconsequential. A new indeterminacy enters into human relationships. Is so and so who he claims to be? He looks like St. Aubert. He makes me see the ghost of St. Aubert; I must really be with St. Aubert. Other people seem bizarrely amorphous—lacking in specificity. Anyone can summon up the image of another. Everyone reminds us of someone else.

It's an interesting question, of course, whether the habit of seeing those who aren't there, once firmly established, can ever be broken. No one, certainly, seems able to give it up in *Udolpho.* For Radcliffe's heroes and heroines, visionary experience of this kind has become indistinguishable from consciousness itself. The issue persists, however, as a historical problem. For once mental images have been linked with powerful subjective fantasies, such as the wish for immortality, can their strange hold on us ever be weakened? Put most bluntly, do we not continue to exhibit the fantastic, nostalgic, and deeply alienating absorption in phantasmatic objects dramatized in Radcliffe's novel?

That we take for granted the uncanny Radcliffean metaphor of the haunted consciousness is one proof, it seems to me, that the romantic habit of thought has not gone away. Indeed the preference for the phantasmatic may have strengthened its grip on Western consciousness over the past two centuries. Even more than Radcliffe and her contemporaries, we seek to deny our own corporeality and the corporeality of others; even more deeply than they, we have come to cherish the life of the mind over life itself. What *The Mysteries of Udolpho* shows so plainly—could we perhaps begin to acknowledge it—is the denatured state of our own awareness: our antipathy toward the body and its contingencies, our rejection of the present, our fixation on the past (or yearnings for an idealized future), our longing for simulacra and nostalgic fantasy. We are all in love with what isn't there.

The reader may object that the kind of illusionism that Radcliffe advocates is clearly an aberration: we all know that our mental fabrications are not "real," and have a name for what happens when we lose this knowledge: psychosis. Yet, as the history of attitudes toward death suggests, it is precisely the distinction between so-called normal and psychotic patterns of belief that has become increasingly confused since the eighteenth century. The everyday has come to seem fantastic; and the fantastic more and more real.

In a much longer study, it would be possible to document the growth of this psychic confusion in more detail. Nineteenth-century romanticism, for example, undoubtedly owes much to the new belief in the reality of mental objects. Indeed, the celebrated romantic concept of the creative imagination is itself a displaced affirmation of faith in the "life" of one's mental perceptions. Certain tendencies in nineteenth- and twentieth-century philosophical thought may likewise arise out of a similar emotional shift toward the phantasmatic. In particular the rise of modern skepticism—and the fact that we have come to speculate about the nature of reality with an urgency and insistence unknown to our forebears—may paradoxically have resulted from a subliminal faith in the reality of thoughts: for only when mental phenomena assume a powerful and disorienting emotional presence does the boundary between mind and world in turn become a pressing philosophical problem. Finally, any study of the spectralizing habit in modern times would have to take into consideration what might be called its technological embodiment: our compulsive need, since the mid-nineteenth century, to invent machines that mimic and reinforce the image-producing powers of consciousness. Only out of a deep preference for the phantoms of the mind, perhaps, have we felt impelled to find mechanical techniques for remaking the world itself in spectral form. Photography was the first great breakthrough—a way of possessing material objects in a strangely decorporealized yet also supernaturally vivid form. But still more bizarre forms of spectral representation have appeared in the twentieth century—the moving pictures of cinematography and television, and recently, the eerie, three-dimensional phantasmata of holography and virtual reality.[28]

V

In lieu of any such extended investigation, however, let me conclude with some remarks that may point up in a more suggestive way the preeminence of the spectralizing habit in modern Western consciousness. Apart from that of Ann Radcliffe, the most important ghost haunting this essay has perhaps been that of Sigmund Freud, whose description of psychic experience and the uncanny offers an interesting perspective on the theme of the supernatural in *The Mysteries of Udolpho*. And yet to think of Freud and the invention of psychoanalysis is to see what one might call the Radcliffean paradox inscribed in a new form. Freud, of course, like Radcliffe, often felt compelled to explain the supernatural. The following passage from *The Interpretation of Dreams* is as complacent (and amusing) a rationalization as anything to be found in *Udolpho:*

> Robbers, burglars, and ghosts, of whom some people feel frightened before going to bed, and who sometimes pursue their victims after they are asleep, all originate from one and the same class of infantile reminiscence. They are the nocturnal visitors who rouse children and take them up to prevent their wetting the bed, or lift the bedclothes to make sure where they have put their hands in their sleep. Analyses of some of these anxiety-dreams have made it possible for me to identify these nocturnal visitors more precisely. In every case the robbers stood for the sleeper's father, whereas the ghosts corresponded to female figures in white nightgowns.[29]

Ghosts, for Freud, have ceased to exist anywhere but in the mind: they are representatives (in white nightgowns) of "infantile reminiscence"—visitants from the realm of unconscious memory and fantasy. The psychoanalyst supposedly has the power to raise these troubling spectres—in a controlled fashion—and exorcise them. In the course of the therapeutic process, Freud observed, the analyst "conjures into existence a piece of real life," calling up those shapes from the "psychical underworld" that have begun to obsess or disturb the patient.[30] These figures carry with them all the frightening "power of hallucination," but can ultimately be laid to rest by the skillful clinician.[31]

Or can they? The crucial stage in Freudian analysis is the moment of transference—when the analyst himself suddenly appears before the patient as a ghost: "the return, the reincarnation, of some important figure out of his childhood or past."[32] At this stage the patient experiences a near-total "recoil from reality" and responds to the analyst as a "re-animated" form of the "infantile image."[33] It is up to the analyst to draw the patient out of his "menacing illusion" and show him that "what he takes to be real new life is a reflection of the past."[34]

There is a tremendous paradox, however, in the central Freudian notion that by calling up ghosts one will learn, so to speak, to let go of them. Psychoanalysis proposes that we dwell upon what isn't there, the life of fantasy, precisely as a way of freeing ourselves from it. Yet can such a liberation ever really take place? Freud himself, it turns out, was often strangely uncertain whether the process of transference could ever be completely resolved, and sometimes hinted that for certain patients the spectral forms of the past might continue to haunt them indefinitely.[35] In his most pessimistic statement on the matter, the essay "Analysis Terminable and Interminable," written late in his career, he even began to entertain the notion that the idea of a "natural end" to analysis might itself be an illusion and "the permanent settlement of an instinctual demand" an impossible task.[36]

The problem, of course, is that even as it tries to undo it, psychoanalysis recreates the habit of romantic spectralization in a new and intensified form. Freud's goal was to help his patients escape the sense of being "possessed" by the past—yet his very method involves an almost Radcliffean absorption in the phantasmatic. One denies ghosts by raising them up, frees oneself of one's memories by remembering, escapes the feeling of neurotic derealization by plunging into an unreal reverie. That such a paradoxical process should inspire mixed results should not surprise us. Seen in historical terms, as an offshoot of the radically introspective habit of mind initiated in the late eighteenth century, psychoanalysis seems both the most poignant critique of romantic consciousness to date, and its richest and most perverse elaboration.

It may be that any attempt to domesticate the demonic element in human life will inevitably result in its recurrence in a more intense and chronic form. Ann Radcliffe, as we have seen, dismissed at a blow the age-old vagaries of Western superstition, and sought, in *The Mysteries of Udolpho*, to create a new human landscape: one in which no primitive spirits harassed the unwary, and no horror— even that of death itself—could disrupt the rational pleasures of the soul. Yet, as would be the case with Freud later, this urge toward exorcism created its own recoil effect, a return of irrationality where it was least expected—in the midst of ordinary life itself. This effect, even now, is difficult to acknowledge. No wonder we prefer to reduce Radcliffe to banalities; to see the full depth of illusion in her work would be to acknowledge our own predicament. Ann Radcliffe explained many things, but she also saw ghosts, and in these we too, perhaps, continue to believe.

CHAPTER 9

•
•
•
•
•
•
•
•
•
•
•
•
•
•
•
•
•
•
•
•
•
•

PHANTASMAGORIA AND
THE METAPHORICS OF
MODERN REVERIE

What does it mean to speak of phantasmagoria? In his *French Revolution* Thomas Carlyle, we find, obsessively figures the bloody spectacle of civil insurrection as a kind of spectral drama—a nightmarish magic-lantern show playing on without respite in the feverish, ghostly confines of the "Historical Imagination." Witness, for example, his description of the storming of the Bastille, as seen through the eyes of the Jacobin leader Thuriot: "But outwards, behold, O Thuriot, how the multitude flows on, welling through every street: tocsin furiously pealing, all drums beating the *générale:* the Suburb Saint-Antoine rolling hitherward wholly, as one man! Such vision (spectral yet real) thou, O Thuriot, as from thy Mount of Vision, beholdest in this moment: prophetic of what other Phantasmagories, and loud-gibbering Spectral Realities, which thou yet beholdest not, but shalt!"[1] The same phantasmic imagery occurs again in the account of the September massacres. While the ghastly figure of Murder stalks though "murky-simmering Paris," her "snaky-sparkling head" raised in grim anticipation of the Terror, the narrator warns us that "the Reader, who looks earnestly through this dim Phantasmagory of the Pit, will discern few fixed certain objects" (FR, 3:22–24). "Most spectral, pandemonial!" he observes, describing a subsequent scene in which the Convention, led by the austere Jacobin faction, finally condemns Louis XVI to death: "Figures rise, like phantoms, pale in the dusky lamp-light; utter from this Tribune, only one word: Death. 'Tout est optique,' says Mercier, 'The world is all an optical shadow'" (FR, 3:88–89). And once again, as the frightful climax of the Terror draws near, the figures of phantom-show proliferate: Robespierre's "Feast of Pikes" is a "Scenic Phantasmagory unexampled" (FR, 3:155), while in the terrible days of Prairial, the red-shirted crown of condemned "flit" toward the guillotine—a "red baleful Phantasmagory, towards the land of Phantoms" (FR, 3:229).

A phantasmagoric effect indeed: the most delirious-sounding of English words has come to stand, in Carlyle's heightened, expressionistic rhetoric, for the delirium of history itself. But what does this fantastical word *phantasmagoria* really mean? We are familiar, of course, with its late romantic denotation, as in the third entry under the term in the *Oxford English Dictionary:* "a shifting series or succession of phantasms or imaginary figures, as seen in a dream or fevered condition, as called up by the imagination, or as created by literary description." But few people, I imagine, know the word's original technical application to the so-called ghost-shows of late eighteenth-century and early nineteenth-century Europe—illusionistic exhibitions and public entertainments in which "spectres" were produced through the use of a magic lantern. Hence the first OED entry: "A name invented for an exhibition of optical illusions produced chiefly by means of the magic lantern, first exhibited in London in 1802." An appended note continues: "In Philipstal's 'phantasmagoria' the figures were made to increase and decrease in size, to advance and retreat, dissolve, vanish, and pass into each other, in a manner then considered marvellous." These "dark rooms, where spectres from the dead they raise," wrote a poet in the pages of *Gentleman's Magazine* in June 1802—

> What's the Greek word for all this *Goblinstoria?*
> I have it pat—It is *Phantasmagoria*.[2]

Yet it is precisely this literal meaning—and the connection with post-Enlightenment technology and popular spectacle—that has been lost.

In what follows I would like to uncover part of this history, not just as an exercise in romantic etymology (or for the sake of a certain Carlylean local color) but as a way of approaching a larger topic, namely, the history of the imagination. For since its invention, the term *phantasmagoria*, like one of Freud's ambiguous primary words, has shifted meaning in an interesting way. From an initial connection with something external and public (an artificially produced "spectral" illusion), the word has now come to refer to something wholly internal or subjective: the phantasmic imagery of the mind. This metaphoric shift bespeaks, I think, a very significant transformation in human consciousness over the past two centuries—what I have called elsewhere the spectralization or "ghostifying" of

Figure 9.1. Frontispiece from *Phantasmagoria; or, The Development of Magical Deception* (1803). Reproduced courtesy of the University of Virginia Library, Sadleir-Black Gothic Novel Collection.

mental space. By spectralization (another nonce word!) I mean simply—as I suggested in my essay on Ann Radcliffe—the absorption of ghosts into the world of thought. Even as we have come to discount the spirit-world of our ancestors and to equate seeing ghosts and apparitions with having "too much" imagination, we have also come increasingly to believe, as if through a kind of epistemological recoil, in the spectral nature of our own thoughts—to figure imaginative activity itself, paradoxically, as a kind of ghost-seeing. Thus in everyday conversation we affirm that our brains are filled with ghostly shapes and images, that we "see" figures and scenes in our minds, that we are "haunted" by our thoughts, that our thoughts can, as it were, materialize before us, like phantoms, in moments of hallucination, waking dream, or reverie.

We consider such beliefs to be rational; and indeed in an important sense they provide a conceptual foundation for the rationalist point of view. Ghosts are of course only things "of the mind"—or so we learn at an early age. Whether or not we recall, each of us was once taught that to see things no one else could see, to envision monsters or phantoms or strange figures at the foot of the bed, was really but to *imagine*—to engage in a certain intensified form of thought itself. The rationalist attitude, it might be argued, inevitably depends on this primal internalization of the spectral. For as long as the external world is populated by spirits—whether benign or maleficent—the mind remains unconscious of itself, focused elsewhere, and unable to assert either its autonomy or its creative claim on the world.

What I would like to explore by examining the history of phantasmagoria, however, is the latent irrationalism haunting, so to speak, this rationalist conception of mind. How comprehensible is it, after all, to say that thoughts have a power to "haunt" us? The post-Enlightenment language of mental experience is suffused with a displaced supernaturalism that we seldom stop to examine. Ironically, it is precisely the modern attempt to annul the supernatural—to humanize the daemonic element in human life—that has produced this strange rhetorical recoil. In the very act of denying the spirit-world of our ancestors, we have been forced to relocate it in our theory of the imagination.

The ambiguity of the phantasmagoria captures the paradox neatly. The spectre-shows of the late eighteenth and early nineteenth centuries, we will find, mediated oddly between rational and irrational imperatives. Producers of phantasmagoria often claimed, somewhat disingenuously, that the new entertainment would serve the cause of public enlightenment by exposing the frauds of charlatans and supposed ghost-seers. Ancient superstition would be eradicated when everyone realized that so-called apparitions were in fact only optical illusions. The early magic-lantern shows developed as mock exercises in scientific demystification, complete with preliminary lectures on the fallacy of ghost-belief and the various cheats perpetrated by conjurers and necromancers over the centuries. But the pretense of pedagogy quickly gave way when the phantasmagoria itself began, for clever illusionists were careful never to reveal exactly how their own bizarre, sometimes frightening apparitions were produced. Everything was done, quite shamelessly, to intensify the supernatural effect. Plunged in darkness and assailed by unearthly sounds, spectators were subjected to an eerie, estranging, and ultimately baffling spectral parade. The illusion was apparently so convincing that surprised audience members sometimes tried to fend off the moving "phantoms" with their hands or fled the room in terror. Thus even as it supposedly explained apparitions away, the spectral technology of the phantasmagoria mysteriously re-created the emotional aura of the supernatural. One knew ghosts did not exist, yet one saw them anyway, without knowing precisely how.

Translated into a metaphor for the imagery produced by the mind, the phantasmagoria retained this paradoxical aspect. It was never a simple mechanistic model of the mind's workings. Technically speaking, of course, the image did fit nicely with post-Lockean notions of mental experience; nineteenth-century empir-icists frequently figured the mind as a kind of magic lantern, capable of projecting the image-traces of past sensation onto the internal "screen" or backcloth of the memory. But the word phantasmagoria, like the magic lantern itself, inevitably carried with it powerful atavistic associations with magic and the supernatural. To invoke the supposedly mechanistic analogy was subliminally to import the lan-guage of the uncanny into the realm of mental function. The mind became a phantom-zone—given over, at least potentially, to spectral presences and haunting obsessions. A new kind of daemonic possession became possible. And in the end, not so surprisingly, the original technological meaning of the term seemed to drop away altogether. "Je suis maître en fantasmagories," wrote Arthur Rimbaud in *Un Saison en enfer.*[3] By the end of the nineteenth century, ghosts had disappeared from everyday life, but as the poets intimated, human experience had become more ghost-ridden than ever. Through a strange process of rhetorical displace-ment, thought itself had become phantasmagorical.

II

How then, amid such metaphoric fantasia, do we recover the world of the "real" phantasmagoria? We need to return, interestingly enough, to the French Revolu-tion. In Germinal Year VI (March 1798) a Belgian inventor, physicist, and student of optics named Étienne-Gaspard Robertson presented what he called the first "fantasmagorie" at the Pavillon de l'Échiquier in Paris.[4] Robertson, whose long and unusual career reflects the excitement and instability of his epoch, was both a brilliant eccentric and a tireless self-promoter. He came first to public notice in 1796 when he proposed to the Directoire a scheme for burning up the British fleet with a gigantic *"miroir d'Archimède"*—an assemblage of mirrors designed to concentrate solar rays on a distant object until the object caught fire. This particu-lar plan was never put into action, but "Citoyen" Robertson carried out a number of other public-spirited ventures in the years that followed. He experimented with galvanism and gave popular demonstrations in physics and optics in the 1790s and early 1800s. He was best known, however, as a balloon aeronaut, setting an altitude record in a *montgolfière* in Hamburg in 1803. He later accompanied the Russian ambassador to China, where he demonstrated ballooning technique in the 1820s.

Figure 9.2. Two contemporary illustrations of Robertson's "Fantasmagorie." The first is reproduced from Paul Hammond, *Marvellous Méliès* (London, 1974); the second from Robertson's *Mémoires récréatifs*. Photos courtesy of Stanford Library.

Robertson's phantasmagoria grew out of an interest in magic, conjuring, and optical effects. As he recalled in his *Mémoires récréatifs, scientifiques et anecdotiques* of 1830–34, he had been fascinated in youth with the conjuring device known as the magic lantern, invented by Athanasius Kircher in the seventeenth century. Kircher's device, from which all of our modern instruments for slide and cinematic projection derive, consisted of a lantern containing a candle and a concave mirror. A tube with a convex lens at each end was fitted into an opening in the side of the lantern, while a groove in the middle of the tube held a small image painted on

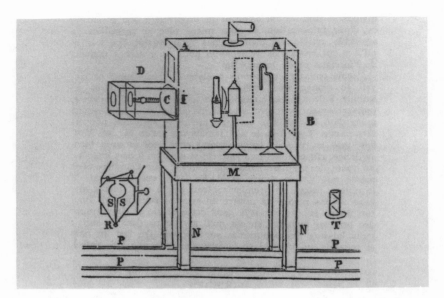

Figure 9.3. Illustration of magic lantern from Robertson's *Mémoires récréatifs*. Courtesy of Stanford Library.

glass. When candlelight was reflected by the concave mirror onto the first lens, the lens concentrated the light on the image on the glass slide. The second lens in turn magnified the illuminated image and projected it onto a wall or gauze screen. In darkness, with the screen itself invisible, images could be made to appear like fantastic luminous shapes, floating inexplicably in the air. In the 1770s a showman named François Séraphin produced what he called Shadow Plays, or "Ombres Chinoises," using a magic lantern at Versailles; another inventor, Guyot, demonstrated how apparitions might be projected onto smoke.[5] Robertson began experimenting in the 1780s with similar techniques for producing "fantômes artificiels." He soon devised several improvements for the magic lantern, including a method for increasing and decreasing the size of the projected image by setting the whole apparatus on rollers. Thus the "ghost" could be made to grow or shrink in front of the viewer's eyes.

Robertson recognized the uncanny illusionistic potential of the new technology and exploited the magic lantern's pseudonecromantic power with characteristic flamboyance. He staged his first "fantasmagorie" as a Gothic extravaganza, complete with fashionably Radcliffean decor. An observer described the scene at the Pavillon de l'Échiquier:

> The members of the public having been ushered into the most lugubrious of rooms, at the moment the spectacle is to begin, the lights are suddenly extinguished and one is plunged for an hour and a half into frightful and profound darkness; it's the nature

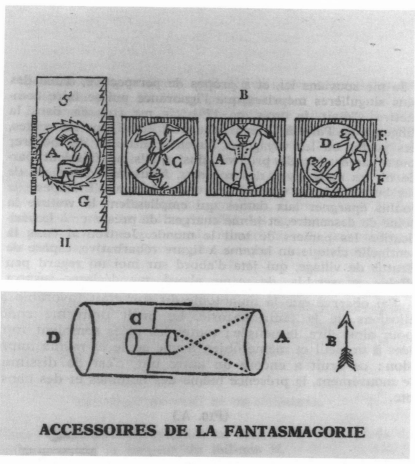

ACCESSOIRES DE LA FANTASMAGORIE

Figure 9.4. Phantasmagoria slides and lens apparatus from Robertson's *Mémoires récréatifs*. Courtesy of Stanford Library.

of the thing; one should not be able to make anything out in the imaginary region of the dead. In an instant, two turnings of a key lock the door: nothing could be more natural than that one should be deprived of one's liberty while seated in the tomb, or as in the hereafter of Acheron, among shadows. (M, 1:129)[6]

Robertson then emerged, spectrelike, from the gloom, and addressing the audience, offered to conjure up the spirits of their dead loved ones. A long newspaper account (cited in his memoirs) recorded the somewhat comical scenes that followed on one of these early occasions:

A moment of silence ensued; then an Arlesian-looking man in great disorder, with bristling hair and sad wild eyes, said: "Since I wasn't able . . . to reestablish the cult of Marat, I would at least like to see his face."

Then Robertson poured on a lighted brazier two glasses of blood, a bottle of vitriol, twelve drops of aqua fortis, and two numbers of the journal *Hommes-Libres*. Immediately, little by little, a small livid, hideous phantom in a red bonnet raised itself up, armed with a dagger. The man with the bristling hair recognized it as Marat; he wanted to embrace it, but the phantom made a frightful grimace and disappeared.

A young fop asked to see the apparition of a woman he had tenderly loved, and showed her portrait in miniature to the phantasmagorian, who threw on the brazier some sparrow feathers, a few grains of phosphorus and a dozen butterflies. Soon a woman became visible, with breast uncovered and floating hair, gazing upon her young friend with a sad and melancholy smile.

A grave man, seated next to me, cried out, raising his hand to his brow: "Heavens! I think that's my wife"; and ran off, not believing it a phantom anymore.

A Helvetian whom I took to be Colonel Laharpe asked to see the shade of William Tell. Robertson placed two old-fashioned arrows on the brazier, which he drew from a large hat . . .

Instantly, the shade of the founder of Swiss liberty showed itself with revolutionary fierceness and seemed to offer its hand to the colonel to whom Switzerland owes her regeneration. (M, 1:131–32)[7]

Robertson, it should be allowed, disclaimed the accuracy of this account and accused its author, Armand Poultier, of trying to get him in trouble with the authorities. This particular exhibition, Poultier had written, concluded with an old royalist in the audience importuning Robertson to raise the shade of Louis XVI: "To this indiscreet question, Robertson responded very wisely: I had a recipe for that, before the eighteenth of Fructidor, I have lost it since that time: it is probable I shall never find it again, and it will be impossible from now on to make kings return in France" (M, 1:133). This inflammatory story was false, Robertson complained in his memoirs, but nonetheless the police temporarily closed down the phantasmagoria and forced him to decamp for Bordeaux, where he remained for over a year.

When he returned to Paris he began producing even more elaborate and bizarre spectacles in the crypt of an abandoned Capuchin convent near the Place Vendôme. Here, amid ancient tombs and effigies, Robertson found the perfect setting for his optical spectre-show—a kind of sepulchral theatre, suffused with gloom, cut off from the surrounding city streets, and pervaded by (as he put it) the silent aura of "des mystères d'Isis." His memoirs, along with a surviving "Programme Instructif" from the early 1800s, provide a picture of a typical night in the charnel house. At seven o'clock in the evening spectators entered through the main rooms of the convent, where they were entertained with a preliminary show of optical illusions, trompe l'oeil effects, panorama scenes, and scientific oddities. After passing through the "Galerie de la Femme Invisible" (a ventriloquism and speaking-tube display orchestrated by Robertson's assistant "Citoyen Fitz-James"), one descended at last to the "Salle de la Fantasmagorie." Here, the single, guttering candle was quickly extinguished, and muffled sounds of wind and thunder (produced by "les sons lugubres de *Tamtam*") filled the crypt. Unearthly music emanated from an invisible glass harmonica. Robertson then began a somber, incoherent speech on death, immortality, and the unsettling power of superstition and fear to create terrifying illusions. He asked the audience to imagine the feelings of an ancient Egyptian maiden attempting to raise, through necromancy, the ghost of her dead lover in a ghastly catacomb: "There, surrounded by images of death, alone with the night and her imagination, she awaits the apparition of the object she cherishes. What must be the illusion for an imagination thus prepared!" (M, 1:163)[8] At last, when the mood of terror and apprehension had been raised to a pitch, the spectre-show itself began. One by one, out of the darkness, mysterious luminous shapes—some seemingly close enough to touch—began to surge and flit over the heads of the spectators.

In a "Petit Répertoire Fantasmagorique" Robertson listed some of the complex apparitions he produced on these occasions. Several, we notice, specifically involved a metamorphosis, or one shape rapidly changing into another—an effect easily achieved by doubling two glass slides in the tube of the magic lantern over one another in a quick, deft manner. Thus the image of "The Three Graces, turning into skeletons." But in a sense the entire phantasmagoria was founded on discontinuity and transformation. Ghostly vignettes followed upon one another in a crazy, rapid succession. The only links were thematic: each image bore some supernatural, exotic, or morbid association. In selecting his spectral program pieces Robertson drew frequently on the "graveyard" and Gothic iconography popular in the 1790s. Thus the apparition of "The Nightmare," adapted from Henry Fuseli, depicted a young woman dreaming amid fantastic tableaux; a demon pressing on her chest held a dagger suspended over her heart. In "The Death of Lord Lyttelton," the hapless peer was shown confronting his famous phantom and expiring. Other scenes included "Macbeth and the Ghost of Banquo," "The Bleeding Nun," "A Witches' Sabbath," "Young Interring his Daughter," "Proserpine and Pluto on their Throne," "The Witch of Endor," "The Head of Medusa," "A Gravedigger," "The Agony of Ugolino," "The Opening of Pandora's Box." Interspersed among these were single apparitions familiar from the earlier phantasmagoria shows—often the bloody "revolutionary" spectres of Rousseau, Voltaire, Robespierre, and Marat. Robertson concluded his shows with a parting speech and a macabre coup de théâtre. "I have shown you the most occult things natural philosophy has to offer, effects that seemed supernatural to the ages of credulity," he told the audience; "but now see the only real horror . . . see what is in store for all of you, what each of you will become one day: remember the phantasmagoria." And with that, he relit the torch in the crypt, suddenly illuminating the skeleton of a young woman on a pedestal (M, 1:165).

I shall return in a moment to the symbolic aspects of the phantasmagoria and the various philosophical and psychological themes with which it quickly became associated. It is enough to note here that the show itself was an immediate, overwhelming success. Robertson himself continued to produce spectre-shows for six years and acknowledged later that they had made his fortune. But he soon had imitators at home and abroad. In the course of a lawsuit in 1799 against two former assistants who had started their own "fantasmagorie," Robertson was forced to reveal many of his technical secrets to the public. From then on, he recalled afterwards, magic-lantern exhibitions sprang up everywhere. So popular were such shows, he wrote, Paris itself came to resemble the Elysian Fields: "It only took a slightly metaphorical imagination to transform the Seine into the river Lethe; because the phantasmagoria were principally located on its banks, there was not one quai . . . which did not offer you a little phantom at the end of a dark corridor or at the top of a tortuous staircase" (M, 1:183).

The phantasmagoria soon travelled across the Channel, where it met with— if possible—an even more enthusiastic reception. Given the indigenous mania for things Gothic, England indeed seemed the natural home for phantasmagoria. A Parisian showman, Paul de Philipstal, offered extremely successful spectre-shows on the Robertsonian model at the Lyceum Theatre in London in late 1801 and 1802, and later took the phantasmagoria on tour (with his partner Madame Tussaud) to Edinburgh and Dublin.[9] William Nicholson described one of his shows in February 1802:

> All the lights of the small theatre of exhibition were removed, except one hanging lamp, which could be drawn up so that its flame should be perfectly enveloped in a cylindrical chimney, or opake shade. In this gloomy and wavering light the curtain was drawn up, and presented to the spectator a cave or place exhibiting skeletons, and other figures of terror, in relief, and painted on the sides or walls. After a short interval the lamp was drawn up, and the audience were in total darkness, succeeded by thunder and lightning; which last appearance was formed by the magic lanthorn upon a thin cloth or screen, let down after the disappearance of the light, and consequently unknown to most of the spectators. These appearances were followed by figures of departed men, ghosts, skeletons, transmutations, &c. produced on the screen by the magic lanthorn on the other side, and moving their eyes, mouth, &c. by the well known contrivance of two or more sliders.

Philipstal's most startling illusions, according to Nicholson, were "the head of Dr. Franklin being converted into a skull" and a display of "various terrific figures, which instead of seeming to recede and then vanish, were (by enlargement) made suddenly to advance; to the surprize and astonishment of the audience, and then disappear by seeming to sink into the ground."[10]

Phantasmagoria shows rapidly became a staple of London popular entertainment. Mark Lonsdale presented a "Spectrographia" at the Lyceum in 1802; Meeson offered a phantasmagoria modeled on Philipstal's at Bartholomew Fair in 1803.[11] A series of "Optical eidothaumata" featuring "some surprising Capnophoric Phantoms" materialized at the Lyceum in 1804. In the same year the German conjurer Moritz opened a phantasmagoria and magic show at the King's

Arms in Change Alley, Cornhill, and in the following year, again at the Lyceum, the famous comedian and harlequin Jack Bologna exhibited his "Phantoscopia." Two "Professors of Physic," Schirmer and Scholl, quickly followed suit with an "Ergascopia."[12] In 1807, Moritz opened another phantasmagoria show at the Temple of Apollo in the Strand, this one featuring a representation of the raising of Samuel by the Witch of Endor, the ghost scene from *Hamlet,* and the transformation of Louis XVI into a skeleton.[13] In 1812 Henry Crabb Robinson saw a "gratifying" show of spectres—their "eyes &c" all moving—at the Royal Mechanical and Optical Exhibition in Catherine Street.[14] In De Berar's "Optikali Illusio," displayed at Bartholomew Fair in 1833, Death appeared on a pale horse accompanied by a luminous skeleton.[15]

How realistic were the "ghosts"? Strange as it now seems, most contemporary observers stressed the convincing nature of phantasmagoric apparitions and their power to surprise the unwary. Robertson described a man striking at one of his phantoms with a stick; a contributor to the *Ami des Lois* worried that pregnant women might be so frightened by the phantasmagoria they would miscarry (M, 1:129).[16] One should not underestimate, by any means, the powerful effect of magic-lantern illusionism on eyes untrained by photography and cinematography. Still, not everybody was satisfied. As early as 1802 Nicholson had complained of the "poorly drawn" figures on Philipstal's lantern slides, and the scientist Sir David Brewster, in his *Letters on Natural Magic* from 1833, observed that "even Michael Angelo would have failed in executing a figure an inch long with transparent varnishes, when all its imperfections were to be magnified."[17] Better images and a more complex technology were required. Brewster's own solution was the "catadioptrical phantasmagoria"—an apparatus of mirrors and lenses capable of projecting the illuminated image of a living human being. "In place of chalky ill-drawn figures, mimicking humanity by the most absurd gesticulations," he wrote, "we shall have phantasms of the most perfect delineation, clothed in real drapery, and displaying all the movements of life."[18] In the renowned show of "Pepper's Ghost," exhibited at the Royal Polytechnic Institution in London in the 1860s, just such an apparatus was used to great effect. Wraithlike actors and actresses, reflected from below the stage, mingled with onstage counterparts in a phantasmagorical version of Dickens' "The Haunted Man" on Christmas Eve, 1862. "The apparitions," wrote Thomas Frost, "not only moved about the stage, looking as tangible as the actors who passed through them, and from whose proffered embrace or threatened attack they vanished in an instant, but spoke or sang with voices of unmistakable reality."[19]

But the desire for more compelling illusions also produced momentous changes in the magic lantern itself. Lime ball, hydrogen, and magnesium gaslight replaced the candle inside the apparatus, thus giving a more powerful illumination to the phantasmagoric image. Photographic transparencies—as in the modern slide projector—gradually took the place of painted glass slides. Ultimately,

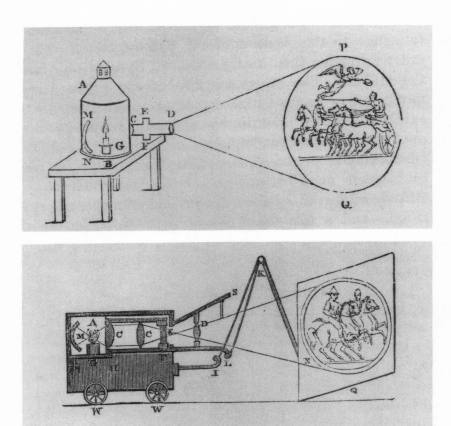

Figure 9.5. Magic-lantern illusions illustrated in Sir David Brewster's *Letters on Natural Magic* (1883). Courtesy of Stanford Library.

Figure 9.6. Optical illusion from Robertson's *Mémoires récréatifs*. Courtesy of Stanford Library.

Figure 9.7. Two contemporary illustrations of the "Pepper's Ghost" illusion exhibited at the Royal Polytechnic Institution, London, 1860s. Reproduced from *Apparatus: Cinematographic Apparatus: Selected Writings,* ed. Theresa Hak Kyung Cha (New York, 1980).

of course, the technology of phantasmagoric illusion, like that of the panorama, the bioscope, stereoscopic projection, and related nineteenth-century image-reproduction techniques, provided the inspiration for early cinematography. A desire to give lifelike movement to the ghostly images of the magic lantern prompted Eadweard Muybridge, for example, to construct a "Zoopraxiscope," which projected some of the world's first moving pictures in 1882.[20] In the end the phantasmagoria gave way to new kinds of mechanical representation. Yet amid all the technological breakthroughs and the refinements in cinematic technique, the ghost-connection, interestingly enough, never entirely disappeared. Well into the twentieth century motion-picture shows continued to be advertised in the manner of the old ghost-shows, and many early films, such as Georges Méliès's, featured explicitly phantasmagorical illusions. In various ways the new medium of motion pictures continued to acknowledge and reflect on its "spectral" nature and origins.[21]

We cannot conclude this brief history of the phantasmagoria without noting one final development—the popularization of do-it-yourself magic-lantern shows in the later decades of the nineteenth century. At the same time that staged phantasmagoria became more and more elaborate, the basic technology of the magic lantern became increasingly accessible to ordinary people. Middle-class Victorians began purchasing magic lanterns as toys and tabletop curiosities in the middle part of the century; books like *The Magic Lantern: How to Buy and How to Use It,* by "A Mere Phantom" (1866), containing a section on "How to Raise a Ghost," offered simple instructions for making "Parlour or Drawing-Room Phantasmagoria."[22] Promoters liked to argue that the device "charmed away" the monotony of home life and brought parents and children together. "How delightful," wrote "A Mere Phantom," "is one of those gatherings! where youth, infancy, and maturity are, for different reasons, equally interested in the mimic scenes so vividly presented; infancy charmed with the rapid change of form and colour and grotesque fun, and its infectious laughter echoed by young and old."[23] A less sentimental—and more evocative—response to the new technology appears, however, in the opening pages of *À la recherche du temps perdu:*

> At Combray, as every afternoon ended, long before the time when I should have to go to bed and lie there, unsleeping, far from my mother and grandmother, my bedroom became the fixed point on which my melancholy and anxious thoughts were centered. Someone had indeed had the happy idea of giving me, to distract me on evenings when I seemed abnormally wretched, a magic lantern, which used to be set on top of my lamp while we waited for dinner-time to come; and, after the fashion of the master-builders and glass-painters of gothic days, it substituted for the opaqueness of my walls an impalpable iridescence, supernatural phenomena of many colours, in which legends were depicted as on a shifting and transitory window. But my sorrows were only increased thereby, because this mere change of lighting was enough to destroy the familiar impression I had of my room, thanks to which, save for the torture of going to bed, it had become quite endurable. Now I no longer

recognised it, and felt uneasy in it, as in a room in some hotel or chalet, in a place
where I had just arrived by train for the first time. . . . The anaesthetic effect of habit
being destroyed, I would begin to think—and to feel—such melancholy things.[24]

Here, ironically, the magic lantern produces nothing but estrangement—by
plunging the child Marcel into a world of solitary reverie. Under its flickering,
uncanny influence, he becomes obsessed, as it were, with the "supernatural phenomena" of his own mind. What the Proustian anecdote encapsulates, while also
infusing with pathos, is the classic nineteenth-century connection between phantasmagoria and the alienating power of the imagination. To this complex metaphoric formulation we may now turn.

III

From the start phantasmagorical spectacle had seemed fraught with symbolic
potential. The bizarre, claustrophobic surroundings, the mood of Gothic strangeness and terror, the rapid phantom-train of images, the disorientation and powerlessness of the spectator—every aspect of the occasion seemed rich in metaphoric
possibility. Given its sensational nature, it is not surprising the phantasmagoria
should become a kind of master trope in nineteenth-century romantic writing. This
is not to say that every contemporary use of the term was elaborately figurative: in
many nineteenth-century writings the simple referential power of the word is still
very much present—as in Honoré de Balzac's description of one of his characters
disappearing with "une rapidité fantasmagorique," or Victor Hugo's image, in
Notre-Dame de Paris, of wavering objects on the Seine at night making "une sorte de
fantasmagorie."[25] In the spectral context of *The Vision of Judgment* (1822), Byron's
comic description of the ghostly George III as "a phantasmagoria in himself" seems
hardly metaphorical at all:

> The more intently the ghosts gazed, the less
>   Could they distinguish whose the features were;
> The Devil himself seem'd puzzled even to guess;
>   They varied like a dream—now here, now there;
> And several people swore from out the press,
>   They knew him perfectly; and one could swear
> He was his father; upon which another
>   Was sure he was his mother's cousin's brother:
>
> Another, that he was a duke, or knight,
>   An orator, a lawyer, or a priest,
> A nabob, a man-midwife; but the wight
>   Mysterious changed his countenance at least
> As oft as they their minds: though in full sight
>   He stood, the puzzle was only increased;
> The man was a phantasmagoria in
>   Himself—he was so volatile and thin![26]

The term also made a number of straightforward, if anachronistic appearances in contemporary writings on ancient necromancy and magical deception. Sir Walter Scott, in his *Letters on Demonology and Witchcraft* (1830), described the mysterious apparition raised by the Witch of Endor in the Book of Samuel as a "phantasmagoria"; and Eusèbe Salverte, in *Sciences occultes* (1837), spoke of the spirit-illusions manufactured by ancient Egyptian and Mesopotamian magicians as "similar to those exhibited in the modern Dioramas and Phantasmagorias."[27] William Gell, in *Pompeiana* (1832), described the various "machines by which phantasmagoria and oracular prestiges were played off" in the temples of Pompeii.[28] Bulwer-Lytton, we find, applies the term to the sinister magic-lantern effects produced by the sorcerer Arbaces in *The Last Days of Pompeii* (1834). In one scene in that novel, the "sensual Egyptian" tries to seduce the innocent Ione by showing her—through an aperture behind an altar—a weird image of his spectral form beseeching hers:

> A new actor appeared; he was clothed from head to foot in a dark robe—his face was concealed—he knelt at the feet of the shadowy Ione—he clasped her hand—he pointed to the throne, as if to invite her to ascend it.
>   The Neapolitan's heart beat violently. "Shall the shadow disclose itself?" whispered a voice beside her—the voice of Arbaces.
>   "Ah, yes!" answered Ione, softly.
>   Arbaces raised his hand—the spectre seemed to drop the mantle that concealed its form—and Ione shrieked—it was Arbaces himself that thus knelt before her.
>   "This is, indeed, thy fate!" whispered again the Egyptian's voice in her ear. "And thou are destined to be the bride of Arbaces."
>   Ione started—the black curtain closed over the phantasmagoria: and Arbaces himself—the real, the living Arbaces—was at her feet.[29]

But the general tendency in nineteenth-century writing was toward metaphoric displacement. The crucial connection between phantasmagoria and the so-called ghosts of the mind seems to have been made very early on. Even before Robertson's first spectre-shows opened in Paris, Goethe, for example, anticipated the paradoxical imagery of the nineteenth century in several influential passages in *The Sorrows of Young Werther* (1774). "Wilhelm," exclaims Werther at one point, "what would the world mean to our hearts without love! What is a magic lantern without its lamp! As soon as you insert the little lamp, then the most colorful pictures are thrown on your white wall. And even though they are nothing but fleeting phantoms, they make us happy as we stand before them like little boys, delighted at the miraculous visions."[30] Desire, like Kircher's amazing invention, produces marvelous "phantoms" in the mind's eye. Thus Werther, overwhelmed by his passion for Lotte, speaks of seeing her inside his head—"in my forehead, at the focus of my inner vision"—like a kind of apparition: "How her image haunts me!" (S, 124). Compared with the impressive *noumena* of the imagination, the everyday world looks, ironically, like a mere "optical illusion" (S, 84).

Other late eighteenth-century writers borrowed the Goethean magic-lantern image. When the heroine of Mary Wollstonecraft's *Maria; or, The Wrongs of Woman* (1798) falls in love with a prisoner in the madhouse in which she is incarcerated, she too, like Werther, delights in imagining her lover obsessively: "a magic lamp now seemed to be suspended in Maria's prison, and fairy landscapes flitted round the gloomy walls, late so blank."[31]

The first writer to offer a metaphoric gloss on the actual phantasmagoria itself, however, seems to have been Henry Lemoine, the editor and bookseller, who published a poem called "Phantasmagoria" in *Gentleman's Magazine* in June 1802, undoubtedly to capitalize on the popularity of Philipstal's recently installed exhibition at the Lyceum.[32] Lemoine turned his poetic account of the new spectacle into a meditation on the delusional nature of reverie. The poem begins with an Addisonian reflection, reminiscent of *Spectator* no. 12, on the power of darkness and imagination to create terrifying illusions, even in the minds of brave men:

> How sweep the forms which magic fears impart,
> Dismay and trembling to the doubtful heart!
> Ah! e'en to those whom Death could ne'er appall,
> Before the polish'd steel or cannon ball.
> Nocturnal fear, we know, has cowards made
> Of heroes that no dread had e'er betrayed.

Similar forms, he continues, rise up at the spectre-show, where hideous demons "swim in array and crowd the pictur'd plain" and sepulchral figures hover in the gloom:

> Down from her head the mournful shroud depends,
> Beneath her feet the winding garment ends;
> Her lucid form a ghastly paleness wears,
> Her trembling hand a livid taper bears. . . .

Yet such "mimic scenes" merely remind us, he concludes, that supposedly real ghosts and apparitions are but the "motley visions" of an overwrought imagination. Only by despising such "wild fantastic forms" can one avoid the fate of the "lonely dame" who nods "delirious o'er the expiring flame" and "faints with the haunted notions of her mind."

Lemoine's poem preserves the facetious tone of eighteenth-century satire, but nonetheless makes a powerful protoromantic discovery: the true "Phantasmagoria" is the human brain itself. By the second decade of the nineteenth century this notion had become a poetic and philosophical commonplace. Thus Byron in *Don Juan* (1819) could speak of fears and nightmares spreading "their loathsome phantasmagoria o'er the Mind."[33] Similarly, Thomas De Quincey, in *Confessions of an English Opium-Eater* (1822), described the multifarious "phantasmagoria" playing in the brain of the philosophical opium-fiend.[34] "We sit as in a boundless Phantasmagoria and Dream-grotto," Carlyle affirmed in *Sartor Resar-*

tus (1833–34); the phenomenal world is but "the reflex of our own inward Force, the 'phantasy of our Dream.'"[35] And later in the century Matthew Arnold made a classic use of the figure when he spoke of the exotic philosophical traditions influencing early Christianity in *Literature and Dogma* (1873): "The phantasmagories of more prodigal and wild imaginations have mingled with the work of Israel's austere spirit; Babylon, Persia, Egypt, even Greece, have left their trace there."[36]

The emotional valence of the metaphor fluctuated. Some writers, to be sure, used the phantasmagorical image fairly lightheartedly, to evoke pleasurable or whimsical states of imaginative experience. Thus Washington Irving, in *Newstead Abbey* (1835), described the "boyish fancies" of knights and ladies inspired in him by a sunlit forest near Byron's ancestral home—"Such was the phantasmagoria that presented itself for a moment to my imagination, peopling the silent place before me with empty shadows of the past."[37] In the preface to *The Blithedale Romance* (1852), Nathaniel Hawthorne associated the image with the charming poetic freedom of the romance. His purpose in describing the fanciful community of Blithedale, he wrote, was "to establish a theatre, a little removed from the highway of ordinary travel, where the creatures of [my] brain may play their phantasmagorical antics, without exposing them to too close a comparison with the actual events of real lives."[38]

More common, however, was the application of the word to disturbing and frightening mental phenomena—states of delirium and psychic alienation, hallucination, the sensation of being pursued or possessed by horrifying thoughts—as in Bulwer-Lytton's melodramatic novel of mesmeric possession, *A Strange Story* (1862). The narrator is obsessed with the mysterious figure of Margrave, a young man who seems to have diabolical powers: "To my astonishment now succeeded shame and indignation—shame that I, who had scoffed at the possibility of the comparatively credible influences of mesmeric action, should have been so helpless a puppet under the hand of the slight fellow-man beside me, and so morbidly impressed by phantasmagorical illusions; indignation that, by some fumes which had special potency over the brain, I had thus been, as it were, conjured out of my senses."[39] He has dreadful visions of Margrave surrounded by snakes and scorpions: "the phantasmagoria of the naturalist's collection revived" (SS, 162). Still later Margrave's "Luminous Shadow" seems to lead him in his sleep to a ruined mausoleum. But the whole excursion is strangely hallucinatory: "How I got into my own room I can remember not—I know not; I have a vague reminiscence of some intervening wanderings, of giant trees, of shroud-like moonlight, of the Shining Shadow and its angry aspect, of the blind walls and the iron door of the House of the Dead, of spectral images—a confused and dreary phantasmagoria" (SS, 263–64).

J. H. Shorthouse gave a similarly unsettling cast to the metaphor in his

popular historical fiction *John Inglesant* (1881). After his brother is murdered in
Italy, the hero suffers a febrile mental derangement:

> Every new object seemed burnt into [his brain] by the sultry outward heat, and by
> his own fiery thoughts. The livid scorched plains, with the dark foliage, the hot
> piazzas and the highways, seemed to him thronged with ghastly phantoms, all
> occupied more or less in some evil or fruitless work. . . . A sense of oppression and
> confusion rested upon him mentally and physically, so that he could see no objects
> steadily and clearly; but without was a phantasmagoria of terrible bright colours, and
> within a mental chaos and disorder without a clue.[40]

This association with delirium, loss of control, the terrifying yet sublime
overthrow of ordinary experience, made the phantasmagoria a perfect emblem,
obviously, of the nineteenth-century poetic imagination. Especially among the later
romantic and symbolist writers—Poe, Baudelaire, Rimbaud, the Goncourt brothers, Loti, Lautréamont, Nerval, and later still, Yeats, Pound, Apollinaire, Eliot, and
Artaud—the phantasmagoria was a favorite metaphor for the heightened sensitivities and often-tormented awareness of the romantic visionary. It conveyed
exquisitely the notion of the *bouleversement de tous les sens:* that state of neur-
asthenic excitement in which images whirled chaotically before the inward eye,
impressing on the seer an overwhelming sense of their vividness and spiritual
truth. As Yeats put it, "there is always a phantasmagoria" in the mind of the poet.[41]
The word has persisted in this context in critical writing to this day.[42]

IV

The figure of the inward spectre-show was not, however, as straightforward, conceptually speaking, as its popular exploitation might lead us to assume. Indeed, it
concealed a profound epistemological confusion. The confusion derived from the
ambiguous notion of the ghost. What did it mean, after all, to "see ghosts"? Were
ghosts themselves real or illusory? Inside the mind or outside it? Actual phantasmagoric spectacle, we recall, had enforced on it audience a peculiar kind of split
consciousness on exactly this point. Promoters like Robertson and Philipstal pref-
aced their shows with popular rationalist arguments: real spectres did not exist,
they said; supposed apparitions were merely "l'effet bizarre de l'imagination" (M,
1:162). Nonetheless, the phantoms they subsequently produced had a strangely
objective presence. They floated before the eye just like real ghosts. And in a crazy
way they *were* real ghosts. That is to say, they were not mere effects of imagination:
they were indisputably there; one saw them as clearly as any other object of sense.
The subliminal power of the phantasmagoria lay in the fact that it induced in the
spectator a kind of maddening, contradictory perception: one might believe ghosts
to be illusions, present "in the mind's eye" alone, but one experienced them here

as real entities, existing outside the boundary of the psyche. The overall effect was unsettling—like seeing a real ghost.

Some nineteenth-century writers, to be sure, sensed an epistemological abyss at the heart of the metaphor. Edgar Allan Poe, for example, in his supernatural tales, used the phantasmagoria figure precisely as a way of destabilizing the ordinary boundaries between inside and outside, mind and world, illusion and reality. Poe was well aware, of course, of the technical meaning of *phantasmagoria*. He often uses the word near the beginning of a tale specifically to describe an eerie optical effect—as in "The Fall of the House of Usher," when the narrator returns to the ancestral hall of his friend Roderick Usher and finds himself strangely disturbed by the once familiar surroundings: "the carvings of the ceilings, the sombre tapestries of the walls, the ebon blackness of the floors, and the phantasmagoric armorial trophies which rattled as I strode."[43] Similarly in "Ligeia," the word first appears in a description of the bizarre chamber filled with Egyptian carvings, rugs in "Bedlam patterns," and "gorgeous and fantastic draperies" in which the narrator lives with his bride Rowena: "The phantasmagoric effect was vastly heightened by the artificial introduction of a strong continual current of wind behind the draperies—giving a hideous and uneasy animation to the whole" (CW, 2:321–22).

But Poe's references, predictably enough, soon become psychological in nature. The narrator of "The Fall of the House of Usher" learns that his sickly friend Usher suffers from "phantasmagoric conceptions" (CW, 2:405) and is obsessed, to the point of madness, with thoughts of phantoms and apparitions, Rowena, in "Ligeia," gives way to the "phantasmagoric influences" of the cryptlike chamber and falls victim to terrifying fancies:

> She partly arose, and spoke, in an earnest low whisper, of sounds which she *then* heard, but which I could not hear—of motions which she *then* saw, but which I could not perceive. The wind was rushing hurriedly behind the tapestries, and I wished to show her (what, let me confess it, I could not *all* believe) that those almost inarticulate breathings, and those very gentle variations of the figures upon the wall, were but the natural effects of that customary rushing of the wind. But a deadly pallor, over-spreading her face, had proved to me that my exertions to reassure her would be fruitless. (CW, 2:324–25)

In such passages Poe seems to evoke a simple environmental determinism: to dwell in "phantasmagoric space" (the decaying House of Usher, the tomblike chamber) is to become vulnerable to the maddering "phantoms" of the mind. The familiar metaphor enforces a pervasive sense of the *illusory:* just as we take artificially produced effects of light and shadow for apparitions, or see figures in moving draperies, Poe implies, so we mistake the images in our heads for realities.

Disturbing this relatively coherent structure of meaning, however, is the uncanny horror at the end of each story. In "Usher" one of Roderick Usher's most powerfully "phantasmagoric" notions—his belief that his dead sister is really alive—far from being illusory, is grotesquely realized when Madeline Usher indeed returns, spectrelike, from the crypt in which she has been interred. A similar fantasy is realized in "Ligeia." After the death of Rowena (who has yielded to her insanity), the narrator has "passionate waking visions" over her corpse (CW, 2:327). Gazing with "unquiet eye" on "the varying figures of the drapery," he begins to think obsessively of his first love, the dead Lady Ligeia (CW, 2:326). And gruesomely enough, each time he imagines her, the corpse of Rowena seems to shift under its shroud. This "hideous drama of revivification" (CW, 2:328) reaches its terrible climax when Rowena's corpse slowly rises from its bier, and letting its "ghastly cerements" fall away, reveals itself—as the Lady Ligeia herself (CW, 2:330).

In each case a mental image appears to come to life, fantastically, *in the flesh.* The phantom becomes a reality. Granted, hints of illusionism remain: Madeline Usher's "lofty and enshrouded figure" comes through a doorway in a "rushing gust" of air (CW, 2:416), like one of Robertson's luminous deceptions; the corpse of Rowena seems to grow "taller" than itself, even as the narrator gazes at it, like a spectrum projected from a moving magic lantern. The entire Rowena/Ligeia transformation is very much like the phantasmagorical effect known as the trans-mutation, achieved by shifting two magic-lantern slides together. But even as we recognize these signs of artifice, we also succumb—along with the narrator in each tale—to the incontrovertible reality of that which is *seen.* It is the real Madeline Usher, we are led to believe, who returns from the crypt; the real Lady Ligeia who rises from the bier.[44]

How to account for this uncanny movement from mental image to spectral reality? To answer this we need to gain some historical distance—to relate the ambiguous metaphor of the phantasmagoria to the larger problem of ghost belief in post-Enlightenment Western culture. In particular we need to look at the powerful modern theme of demystification and the highly paradoxical arguments by which scientists and philosophers in the late eighteenth and early nineteenth centuries attempted to do away with the old theological world of apparitions and gave voice to a new and explicitly psychological theory of supernatural phenomena. What we find, it seems to me, is that the demystifying project was peculiarly compromised from the start. The rationalists did not so much negate the tradition-al spirit world as displace it into the realm of psychology. Ghosts were not exorcized—only internalized and reinterpreted as hallucinatory thoughts. Yet this internalization of apparitions introduced a latent irrationalism into the realm of mental experience. If ghosts were thoughts, then thoughts themselves took on—at least notionally—the haunting reality of ghosts. The mind became subject to spectral presences. The epistemologically unstable, potentially fantastic metaphor of the phantasmagoria simply condensed the historical paradox: by relocating the world of ghosts in the closed space of the imagination, one ended up super-naturalizing the mind itself.

V

The phantasmagoria was invented, it turns out, at a crucial epoch in the history of Western ghost belief—at precisely that moment when traditional credulity had begun to give way, more or less definitively, to the arguments of scientific rationalism. This is not to say that ghost belief simply vanished at the end of the eighteenth century: orthodox religious opinion had always supported the idea of a transcendental spirit world, and popular faith in apparitions weakened only gradually.[45] In England, for example, spectacular episodes like the Cock Lane Ghost in the 1760s, Lord Lyttelton's Ghost in 1779, and the Hammersmith Ghost of 1804 testified to the vestigial power of traditional beliefs.[46] But the forces of secularization had also been at work for some time. Renaissance skepticism had called into question the nature of many supposedly supernatural phenomena, and the successes of Enlightenment science reinforced the rationalist view. In 1751 the writers of the *Encyclopédie* ridiculed "les esprits timides & crédules" who mistook everything they saw for apparitions. By 1800 similar attitudes had more or less triumphed among the educated classes across Western Europe. When Scott, quoting Crabbe, mockingly described the belief in spirits as "'the last lingering fiction of the brain,'" he illustrated how profoundly received opinion had altered since the days of Lavater, Glanvill, Baxter, Beaumont, Mather and other renowned defenders of the "invisible world."[47]

How had such a remarkable cognitive reorientation come about? Without attempting to speculate here on ultimate causes, we can nonetheless characterize the basic shift in thought. The age-old philosophical problem had always been how to account for the many sightings of ghosts reported by reputable witnesses throughout the centuries. Rather than resort to the theological notion of a spirit world, the rationalists proposed two new modes of explanation. The first line of argument held that apparitions were the result of simple deception. Writers since Reginald Scot had argued that many apparitions were in fact the products of legerdemain or trickery—conjurers' illusions (like the Witch of Endor's famous "raising" of Samuel in the Bible, or Cagliostro's fake crystal-ball apparitions) or simple cheats perpetrated by those out to intimidate or manipulate the credulous. The spread of popular scientific knowledge in the eighteenth century supported this kind of explanation; recent developments in optics, the new technology of mirrors and lenses, and the refinement of inventions like the magic lantern itself gave would-be skeptics a technical language with which to debunk, retroactively, many reported spectral appearances, including the notorious spirit-raisings performed by ancient pythonesses and necromancers.[48]

But the second line of argument (not always in perfect accord with the first) ultimately came to dominate modern thinking on the apparition problem. According to this hypothesis, spectres came somehow from within, originating in the disordered brain or sensorium of the ghost-seer himself or herself. Earlier writers, again, had propounded a crude version of the idea. Those suffering from a surplus of melancholy humours, wrote Robert Burton in his *Anatomy of Melancholy*, were especially likely to see spectres.[49] Thomas Hobbes, in *Leviathan* (1651), argued that it was not God's doing, but the "distemper of some of the inward parts of the Body" that brought on dreams and apparitions.[50] At the end of the eighteenth century, however, thanks to the emergence of the new scientific theory of mind, the projective argument took on a conceptual sophistication and an ideological urgency unmatched in previous epochs.

A host of polemical treatises on apparitions appeared in England, France, and Germany beginning around 1800.[51] The authors were usually medical men, concerned to eradicate superstition and place all seemingly supernatural phenomena on a solid psychological footing. Their arguments were resolutely Lockean and mechanistic in nature. Thus, in one of the first and most influential of such works, *An Essay Towards a Theory of Apparitions* (1813), the Manchester physician John Ferriar invoked the new mentalist concept of the hallucination to explain spectral occurrences.[52] Poor digestion, a diseased state of the nerves, irregular circulation, or some other "peculiar condition of the sensorium," he argued, all served to enflame the brain and "renew" visual or auditory impressions imprinted in the past. A "renewed" impression then manifested itself upon the brain as if it were an external object—to the surprise or terror of the perceiver. The images most likely to be revived in this delusional way, Ferriar deduced, were precisely those originally accompanied by a strong sense of fear or horror: thus the prevalence of corpses and bloody sights and other grotesque images in popular ghost visions. Religious mania, poetic frenzy, or an overburdening sense of guilt, he added, might intensify the power of the spectral illusion.[53]

Something of Ferriar's influence can be felt in a comic essay in *Blackwood's Magazine* from 1818 (significantly entitled "Phantasmagoriana"), which celebrated the "decisive victory of the genius of physiology over the Prince of Darkness." Thanks to *"ferriarism,"* its author averred, one no longer had to cross a dark churchyard with "any *worse* apprehension than that of mere mortal rheumatism or asthma"—all phantom-fear having been annihilated by the new "principle of *hallucination."*[54] But other important debunking texts quickly followed: Joseph Taylor's *Apparitions; or, The Mystery of Ghosts, Hobgoblins, and Haunted Houses, Developed* (1815), Samuel Hibbert's *Philosophy of Apparitions* (1825), John Abercrombie's *Inquiries Concerning the Intellectual Powers* (1830), William Newnham's *Essay on Superstition* (1830), Brewster's *Letters on Natural Magic* (1833), Walter Cooper Dendy's *The Philosophy of Mystery* (1841), and Charles Ollier's *The Fallacy of Ghosts, Dreams, and Omens* (1848). In France the most significant book on the subject (and indeed one of the most influential works of nineteenth-century psychology before Freud) was undoubtedly Alexandre Brierre de Boismont's *Des Hallucinations: ou, Histoire raisonnée des apparitions, des visions, des songes, de l'extase, des rêves, du magnétisme et du somnambulisme* (1845), translated into English in 1850.

Allowing for certain variations in emphasis, the basic argument in each of these works was the same: spectres were products of the imagination. Yet herein lay an unforeseen epistemological pitfall. The paradoxical effect of the psychological argument was to subvert the boundary between ghost-seeing and ordinary thought. Of course some apparitions could be attributed, quite simply, to specific pathological causes—fevers, head injuries, inhaling or imbibing stimulants. But the rationalists, at the same time, could not forebear reaching after a seemingly more universal or totalizing explanation: that thought itself was a spectral process, and, as such, easily modulated into hallucination. Ferriar led the way by confusing the distinction between simple recollection and the "faculty of spectral representation." "From recalling images by an art of memory," he wrote, "the transition is direct to beholding spectral objects, which have been floating in the imagination."[55] But others soon enlarged on the spectral nature of contemplation. It was possible for the mind to become so absorbed by an idea, wrote William Newnham, that the idea "then haunts its waking and its sleeping moments."[56] "The objects of mental contemplation," Samuel Hibbert observed, "may be seen as distinctly as external objects."[57] Describing "Ghosts of the Mind's Eye, or Phantasma" in his philosophical dialogue *The Philosophy of Mystery*, Walter Cooper Dendy, senior surgeon at the Royal Infirmary for Children, concluded that a ghost was "nothing more than an *intense idea*" and that seeing a phantom was "an act of thinking." Yet if ghosts were thoughts, it was not far to go, through a kind of symbolic recoil, to a perception that thoughts were ghosts:

> It is as easy to believe the power of mind in conjuring up a spectre as in entertaining a simple thought; it is not strange that this thought may appear *embodied*, especially if the external senses be shut: if we think of a distant friend, do we not *see* a form in our mind's eye, and if this idea be intensely defined, does it not become a phantom?

Between an idea and a phantom, wrote Dendy, "there is only a difference in degree; their essence is the same as between the simple and transient thought of a child, and the intense and beautiful ideas of a Shakespeare, a Milton, or a Dante."[58]

In the end, it seemed, one could no longer distinguish between the specialized psychic act of seeing a ghost and the everyday business of remembering or imagining. Brierre de Boismont made this indeterminacy strikingly obvious when he argued for the existence of what he called "normal hallucinations"—the "delirious conceptions . . . forever flitting around man, similar to those insects that are seen whirling around by thousands on a fine summer evening" (HD, 354, 359).[59] And in a crucial passage on the etiology of illusion, he found an even more suggestive metaphor:

> Sufficient attention has not been bestowed on this misty phantasmagoria in which we live. Those undecided forms, which approach and retire unceasingly, with a thousand tantalizing smiles, and after which we run with so much ardor, travel through our brains, emerge from their clouds, and become clearer and clearer; then the

moral or physical point is reached; thought revived, colored, and represented, suddenly appears in a material form, and is transformed into an hallucination. (HD, 287)

What such statements articulated, at bottom, was a new conception of the daemonic or irrational nature of thought. There was now a potential danger in the act of reflection—a danger in paying too much attention to mental images or in "thinking too hard." One's inmost thoughts might at any moment assume the strangely externalized shape of phantoms. The antiapparition writers often attacked the activity they referred to as reverie—the habit of indulging in erotic or poetic fancies, dwelling too long on things one had read, or brooding over obscure intellectual problems. Like a supernatural impulsion, reverie had the power to lead one out of oneself into madness. Given the spectral nature of thought, anyone theoretically could become like that "monomaniac of a cultivated and ardent mind," mentioned by Brierre de Boismont, who, through too great a delight in the creations of his imagination, saw waking dreams as realities:

> One day . . . we found him with eyes fixed, a smiling mouth, and in the act of clapping his hands in sign of applause. He did not hear us open the door of his room. To our question: "What does this mean? What are you doing?" "I am," he replied, "like the fool that Horace speaks of: I am seeing an imaginary play. I was wearied by my fireside; I am fond of the beauties of the opera, and have been playing to myself the ballet of *The Sylphide;* and when you touched me on the shoulder, I was applauding Taglioni, with whose graceful and noble dancing I had never before been so much charmed." (HD, 369)

We can see how the metaphor of the phantasmagoria mediated perfectly between the two contradictory perceptions inherent in the rationalist position. Ghosts were unreal, according to the skeptics, in the sense that they were artificial—the product of certain internal mechanistic processes. The magic lantern was the obvious mechanical analogue of the human brain, in that it "made" illusionary forms and projected them outward. But in another highly paradoxical sense, ghosts now seemed *more real than ever before*—in that they now occupied (indeed preoccupied) the intimate space of the mind itself. The paradox was exactly like that achieved at the real phantasmagoria: ghosts did not exist, but one saw them anyway. Indeed, one could hardly escape them, for they were one's own thoughts bizarrely externalized.

The reader may object here that I have been hedging, wildly, on an obscure yet crucial issue—namely, whether the phantasmagoria figure was merely a rhetorical device, a way of speaking, or if real people, beginning in the nineteenth century, actually came to experience the so-called ghosts inside their heads *as such.* When Carlyle spoke of the "boundless Phantasmagoria" of everyday life, or Rimbaud described himself as a "maître en fantasmagories," did these writers mean to imply that they indeed "saw" things in the manner of the ghost-seers of old? The question is perhaps imponderable. Still, it seems conceivable that if one holds to

Figure 9.8. Spirit photograph by Edouard Buguet (c. 1870). Courtesy of the Bibliothèque Nationale.

the romantic belief in the haunting nature of thoughts (or alternatively, to the idea that ghosts exist inside the head), one will be especially likely to experience one's own thoughts in an uncanny, involuntary, oddly embodied way—as a kind of bizarre, alienating spectacle imposed from without. Certainly many people in the nineteenth century spoke of the "phantoms of the brain" as though they came from outside—as if there were, at the very heart of subjectivity itself, something foreign and fantastic, a spiritual presence from elsewhere, a spectre-show of unaccountable origin. By the time of Freud, the rhetorical pattern had resolved, as it were, into a cultural pathology: everyone felt "haunted." That is to say, the mind itself now seemed a kind of supernatural space, filled with intrusive spectral presences—incursions from past or future, ready to terrify, pursue, or disable the harried subject. Freud struggled with the paradoxes of spectralization, largely by attempting to define a cognitive practice—psychoanalysis—which would exorcize these "ghostly presences" once and for all. But as I will argue in the next chapter, his project was compromised by the classic rationalist paradox. Even as he attempted to demystify the uncanny forces of the psyche, he could not help reinventing in the very theory of the unconscious itself an essentially daemonic conception of thought. Despite heroic efforts, Freud never fully escaped the pervasive crypto-supernaturalism of early nineteenth-century psychology.[60]

Rather than contend further, however, with such ultimately elusive matters, let me conclude with a suitably ambiguous emblem of my theme. This is a so-called spirit photograph from the 1860s taken by Edouard Buguet, showing the diaphanous form of a young woman floating obliquely over the head of a young man deep in contemplation. Or is she "inside" his head? The image is truly phantasmagorical—and not only in the sense that the camera, like a magic lantern, has realized the phantom-woman in a curiously literal way. From one perspective this carefully staged double exposure (if that is what it is) is a kind of self-reflexive commentary on the uncanny nature of photography, the ultimate ghost-producing technology of the nineteenth century. But the image is phantasmagorical in another sense, in that it is also a representation of reverie itself—a fantastically exalted picture of what one "sees" when one thinks. It strikes us as comical, perhaps, because it makes the spectral drama of psychic life almost too obvious; it borders on *kitsch*. Yet, in this very theatricality, it also evokes something unmistakably familiar—something both inside and outside, real and unreal, the luminous figure of thought itself.

CHAPTER 10

SPECTRAL POLITICS: APPARITION BELIEF AND THE ROMANTIC IMAGINATION

Where are the soules that swarmed in times past? Where are the spirits? Who heareth their noises? Who seeth their visions?
Reginald Scot, *The Discoverie of Witchcraft*, 1584[1]

hy do we no longer believe in ghosts? In his nostalgic celebration *The Book of Dreams and Ghosts* (1897), Andrew Lang blamed the skeptical eighteenth century: "the cock-sure common-sense of the years from 1650 to 1850, or so, regarded everyone who had an experience of a hallucination as a dupe, a lunatic, or a liar."[2] Enlightenment thinking—to put it bluntly—made spirits obsolete. Keith Thomas takes up a similar theme in *Religion and the Decline of Magic* (1971), but develops it rather more ingeniously. Men and women of the eighteenth century "stopped seeing ghosts," he asserts, not so much because ghosts came to seem "intellectually impossible" (though this was certainly the case) but because ghosts gradually lost their "social relevance."[3] In traditional English society, he suggests, the belief in apparitions performed a powerful community function. The idea that spirits of the dead might come back to haunt murderers, locate stolen objects, enforce the terms of legacies, expose adulterers, and so on, functioned as a kind of implicit social control—a restraint on aggression and a "useful sanction for social norms."[4] With the emergence after 1700 of new and bureaucratic forms of surveillance—with the rise of an organized police force, grand juries, insurance companies, and other information-gathering bodies—the need for a spectral monitoring agency, composed of ethereal headless

Figure 10.1. Seeing a "real" ghost. Anonymous print showing Lord Lyttelton being warned of his coming death by a female spectre, 1779. The prediction—that Lyttelton would die within three days—came true. Courtesy of Mary Evans Picture Library.

ladies, morose figures in shrouds, and other supernatural busybodies, gradually began to fade.[5]

Like most functionalist arguments, Thomas's hypothesis has an attractive economy. It also makes a kind of intuitive sense, offering a larger explanation, perhaps, for one's inmost feelings of paranoia. As the author of a nineteenth-century text on hallucinations and mental delusions put it, "our brains are no longer . . . ballrooms for devils to dance in, but fear has taken other forms; and is manifested in dread of the police, of enemies, etc."[6] Yet Thomas himself shies away from the psychological aspects of his subject:

> The belief in ghosts, and, even more, the belief of particular individuals that they had actually seen such ghosts, present many interesting psychological problems. But it is no part of our purpose here to consider just how it was that these hallucinations could convince witnesses of undoubted integrity. The social historian should be ready to concede that mental and perceptual processes can be extensively conditioned by the cultural content of the society in which men live: [in the seventeenth century] contemporaries were taught that ghosts or similar apparitions existed; they were therefore more likely to see them. But in the present state of knowledge the investigation of these mental and perceptual processes must be left to the psychologist and the psychic researcher.[7]

The irony here is that Thomas's own sociological argument itself depends on an unacknowledged psychological assumption: ghosts are really "hallucinations." Mysterious "mental and perceptual processes" make people think they see apparitions. But where, one might ask, does the modern conception of the hallucination come from? And how does it really differ, if at all, from the older conception of the supernatural agent? It is precisely the historian's own psychological language, intruding quietly in the very passage in which he renounces psychology, that requires some historical investigation.

The belief that ghosts and spectres are only products of imagination—that they come from within the mind itself—is in fact, as I suggested in the coda to "Phantasmagoria," a relatively recent notion, one that has emerged in a definitive form in Western Europe only over the past two hundred and fifty years. In earlier times popular thinking held that most apparitions were supernatural in origin: messengers from an invisible world of spirits—either angels or demons in human guise, or, more frighteningly and atavistically, the wandering souls of the dead. After 1700, however, with the breakup of traditional communities, the growing challenge to religious orthodoxy, and the popularization of new scientific attitudes, a more skeptical and mechanistic view gradually came to prevail: that ghostly apparitions were "things of the mind"—figments, or phantasmata, produced by a disordered or overwrought brain.

Which isn't to say, I hasten to add, that men and women in earlier periods either failed to recognize or denied the delusion-making powers of the imagination. Plato and Aristotle had both spoken of the mind's capacity for producing eidetic images and projecting them outward: that the fancy, or "mind's eye," could produce realistic-seeming "phantoms" was a common enough theme in medieval and Renaissance writing. In the seventeenth century Robert Burton argued in *The Anatomy of Melancholy* that certain apparitions could be attributed to a surplus of melancholy humors. What is new in the eighteenth century—and particularly the second half of the eighteenth century—is the peculiar sense of urgency that begins to attach to such psychological speculation. Because traditional beliefs regarding the "Invisible World" no longer seemed plausible—the ancient belief in spirits and demons, Enlightenment rationalists like to argue, had been utterly exploded —apparitions had to be reinterpreted as coming from within. The pneumatological gave way to the phantasmatic. We tend to take this relocation of the spectral for granted. Yet what I would like to argue in what follows is that the act of internalization—the uncanny absorption of ghosts and apparitions into the world of thought—was actually a momentous event in the history of Western consciousness, with paradoxical consequences for the modern theory of the imagination.

The rationalist assault on ghosts and spirits had begun in the sixteenth and seventeenth century, inspired by the anti-witchcraft writings of Reginald Scot and John Webster and the skeptical theorizing of Hobbes, Spinoza, and Descartes. Despite the often fiery animadversions of the orthodox, debunking arguments continued to gain support in the first half of the eighteenth century. Christian divines such as Joseph Glanvill, Richard Baxter, Cotton Mather, and later John Wesley warned—with considerable prescience—that giving up the doctrine of spirits would ultimately undermine other articles of religious faith, including the belief in the Resurrection and the immortality of the soul.[8] Nonetheless by the 1750s, the authors of the *Encyclopédie* felt free to satirize "les esprits timides & crédules" who mistook every pale or shadowy object they saw for an apparition.[9] In England, especially after the memorable Cock Lane hoax of the 1760s—in which the inhabitants of a house in Cock Lane, Smithfield, briefly convinced several distinguished investigators (including Samuel Johnson) that the house was infested with spirits—it became increasingly acceptable to scoff at popular credulity. Satiric attacks on ghosts and ghost believers appeared frequently in literary works of the later eighteenth century—as in Charles Churchill's poem *The Ghost* (1764), for example, and the novels of Smollett, Burney, Radcliffe, Edgeworth, and Maturin.

As I noted in "Phantasmagoria," this skeptical assault on traditional beliefs culminated in the 1790s and early decades of the nineteenth century with a remarkable cluster of scientific and philosophical anti-apparition writings, beginning with Christoph Friedrich Nicolai's influential "Memoir on the Appearance of Spectres or Phantoms occasioned by Disease, with Psychological Remarks," presented to the Royal Society of Berlin in 1799 and translated into English in 1803. Similar works quickly followed—of which John Ferriar's *An Essay Towards A Theory of Apparitions* (1813), Samuel Hibbert's *Philosophy of Apparitions* (1825), David

Figure 10.2. Two plates from George Woodward's "The Effect of Imagination" (1797) showing how ordinary objects can be mistaken for apparitions by superstitious individuals. Courtesy of the Houghton Library, Harvard University.

Brewster's *Letters on Natural Magic* (1832) and Alexandre Brierre de Boismont's *Des Hallucinations* (1845) are perhaps the most interesting and instructive for the modern reader.

The great problem the skeptics faced was how to explain the numerous spirit-sightings reported by reputable witnesses down through the centuries. Some of these apparitions, it was argued, were the result of simple acts of deception: the notorious shade of Samuel supposedly raised in the Old Testament by the Witch

of Endor, for example, the crystal-ball apparitions of Cagliostro, or the illusions produced by ancient necromancers and pythonesses with the aid of mirrors and magic lanterns.[10] Other reported "ghosts," such as those believed to inhabit gloomy country houses, were reclassified as optical illusions: aberrations of light and shadow. (Sir Walter Scott's famous example of the spectral effect produced by a moonbeam striking shawls and cloaks hanging on a screen—given life in George Woodward's comic print "The Effect of Imagination" from 1797—is a classic instance of the new "optical" argument.)[11] Still other apparitions might be referred to gross physiological causes: head injuries, fevers, imbibing or inhaling stimulants. But a large class of phantoms, those attested to by reliable witnesses under seemingly normal circumstances, still required explanation. What was necessary was a kind of totalizing theory—an epistemology of apparitions—that might explain even the most enigmatic cases. The hallucination theory developed in response to this need. The vast majority of apparitions, the skeptics concluded, were simply *mental* images which, for one reason or another, had manifested themselves externally, with the disturbing vividness of real objects. They were thoughts, so to speak, that had become estranged from the thinker. Thus Coleridge, when asked in 1818 by a female aquaintance whether he believed in ghosts, could reply: "No, Madam! I have seen far too many myself."[12]

Eighteenth- and nineteenth-century spirit-debunkers figured the new theory of the spectre-producing imagination as a triumphant escape from superstition—a view most modern readers are likely to share. Mary Weightman, author of *The Friendly Monitor: or, dialogues for youth against the Fear of Ghosts, and other Irrational Apprehensions, with Reflections on the Power of the Imagination and the Folly of Superstition* (1791), couched her attack on ghost belief, for example, in the invigorating language of political liberation. Her spokeswoman is an adolescent skeptic named Caroline who has herself escaped from "the most abject slavery of mind to the tyrant Fear." She longs to unbind the "slavish fetters" of her susceptible friends Matilda and Henrietta, and lead them from the Bastille of ghost-terror in which they have been immured: "You have raised a horrid buiding [in your minds]," she tells them, "and laid many a trembling foundation."[13] Proceeding in the manner of a modern psychotherapist, Caroline then advances a number of arguments designed to show them that the "impressions of horror" from which they suffer are only "chimerical representations" produced by the imagination. Breaking the mental "chains of association" that provoke fear, the individual is free at last of "the tormenting sybil" of superstition."[14]

But at the same time that it challenged superstition, the psychological paradigm also created the possibility of new and more insidious kind of enslavement: to the haunting forms of the imagination itself. Once an apparition-producing faculty was introduced into the human psyche, the psyche became (potentially) a world of apparitions. Human beings continued to see ghosts, only the ghosts were now inside, not outside. This view of the mind as a phantom-scene, or spectropia, I have elsewhere suggested, deeply influenced early romantic writing. Coleridge's description of the mind as a "phantom-world so fair" or Wordsworth's conception of the creative imagination as an "awful Power" rising spectre-like "from the mind's abyss," were only two of the many secondary poetic formations inspired by the late eighteenth-century apparition debate. The familiarity—indeed the banality—of romantic metaphors should not blind us to their somewhat uncanny implication: that here was now an alienating force within subjectivity itself—a kind of crypto-supernatural agency implicit in the very act of thinking. One could now be "possessed" by the phantoms of one's own thought—terrorized, entranced, *taken over* by mental images—just as in earlier centuries people had suffered the visitations of real spirits and demons.

To prevent thoughts from turning into ghosts, the act of thinking had to be regulated. The rationalists of the last eighteenth and nineteenth century developed a host of prescriptions designed to ward off the new kind of inwardly generated phantom. Too much study, brooding over obscure intellectual problems, reading into the night, excessive mourning, and, especially, overindulgence in poetic or erotic fancies—all prompted the appearance of spectral forms. The anti-apparition writers warned of the dangers of reverie—the obsessional solipsistic replay of mental images in "the mind's eye." The inward process of ghost-seeing all too easily modulated into actual ghost-seeing, the eruption of the hallucinatory. The political metaphor resurfaced, only in a new repressive context: the imagination itself was now figured as a capricious tyrant, always threatening to overthrow the frail authority of reason. Thus John Abercrombie, echoing Samuel Johnson's *Rasselas*, wrote in his *Intellectual Powers of Man* (1830), that once the mind "riots in delights which nature and fortune, with all their bounty, cannot bestow," the reign of fancy is confirmed: "she grows first imperious, and in time despotic. Then fictions begin to operate as realities, false opinions fasten upon the mind, and life passes in dreams of rapture or of anguish."[15]

The displacement of ghosts into the realm of psychology had far-reaching intellectual consequences. In particular, the new explanation of apparitions and the resulting anxiety about the mind's "spectralizing" capacities had a shaping influence, as I will suggest in my conclusion, on the most prestigious theory of thought regulation to emerge in the nineteenth century: namely, Freudian psycho-analysis. Freud's barely metaphoric conception of ghosts lurking in the unconscious —the phantoms of repressed desire—develops directly out of the tradition of spirit-debunking rhetoric of the late eighteenth century, recapitulating, in a pseudo-scientific form, the Enlightenment rationalists' essentially supernaturalistic view of mental experience. Likewise, Freud's effort to free patients such as the Rat Man of obsessional thoughts through the analytic work recalls earlier prescriptive attempts to control the "haunting" effect of the hallucination-producing imagination. To draw out this historical connection in more detail, however, let us return to some of the eighteenth- and early nineteenth-century apparition writings and trace the steps by which the new and explicitly supernaturalized conception of the imagination emerged.

We might take Daniel Defoe's *Essay on the History and Reality of Apparitions* (1727) as an interesting transitional work—one that both evokes the traditional spirit-world of pneumatology and anticipates certain aspects of the modern psychological argument. Defoe was on the whole a believer in the supernatural nature of apparitions, and devoted much of his book to describing their reasons for

Figure 10.3. Apparitions and eros. George Woodward's "A Monkish Vision," 1797. Courtesy of the Houghton Library, Harvard University.

appearing, and how one should behave in their presence.[16] The *Essay* includes a number of exemplary tales. Some of these, such as the story of a man on his way to engage in "a Secret and Criminal Conversation with a certain Lady" who is intercepted by the reproachful apparition of his mother ("the Look was a Lash"), connect Defoe's writing with the moralizing works of earlier religious apologists such as Glanvill and Baxter, and lend support to Keith Thomas's view of the normative function of the ghost story in earlier times. At the same time, however, Defoe exhibits an intermittent yet powerful skepticism. "I believe we form as many Apparitions in our Fancies," he observes, "as we see really with our Eyes" (2).[17] In his concluding chapters he turns briefly to "Sham Apparitions," the effects of fraud, and what he calls "Imaginary Apparitions"—"the Apparitions of Fancy, Vapours, waking Dreams, delirious Heads, and the Hyppo."

For Defoe, some false apparitions are merely the "Vapour of the Brain, a sick delirious fume of Smoke in the Hypochondria; forming it self in such and such Figure to the Eye-sight of the Mind . . . which all look'd upon with a calm Revision, would appear, as it really is, nothing but a Nothing, a Skeleton of the Brain, a Whymsy, and no more" (390). But other supposed ghosts come about for more compelling reasons. He posits a phantom-producing faculty within the brain, a psychic mechanism which (as Nietzsche would later) he labels the "Conscience." "This thing called Conscience is a strange bold Disturber," writes Defoe; "it works upon the Imagination with an invincible Force; like Faith, it makes a Man view things that are not, as if they were; feel things that are not to be felt, see things that are not to be seen, and hear things that are not to be heard" (113). (One thinks of his novelistic rendering of the "Hag-ridden" frights of the guilty Roxana.) Under its influence, "the Murderer sees the murther'd Innocent as plainly before his Eyes, as if he was actually sent back from his Place to charge him" (101). Yet, Defoe assures his reader, it is not a real ghost, only a "Picture of the Crime in Apparition" that haunts the guilty one. He concludes with a paradoxical conceit: "CONSCIENCE, indeed, is a frightful Apparition itself, and I make no Question but it oftentimes haunts an oppressing Criminal into Restitution, and is a ghost to him sleeping or waking" (100).

Despite this modern-sounding argument, however, Defoe remains a transitional figure because he is ultimately bound to a traditional religious determinism. Conscience might appear to be an inward force—mysteriously working "on" the imagination—but it is of course a divine instrument: that "Drummer in the Soul" placed there by God to call the evildoer to repentance (100). Instead of sending supernatural agents directly to earth to convey spiritual warnings, Providence now works at one remove, through the medium of individual psychology, but the end result is the same: apparitions are still meaningful in the familiar moral and theological sense.

This kind of recuperative Christian argument, interestingly enough, would occasionally be revived by nineteenth-century scientific skeptics anxious to avoid charges of downright atheism. Thus Sir Walter Scott, otherwise a staunch disbeliever in modern spirit manifestations, wrote in his *Letters on Demonology and Witchcraft* that "under the direction of Heaven," superstitious terror "may be the appointed means of bringing the criminal to repentance for his own sake, and to punishment for the advantage of society."[18] In general, however, later writers moved dramatically away from the idea of an unseen Providential influence on

Figure 10.4 Ghosts in the brain. Sir Joseph Noel Paton's "Dante Meditating the Episode of Francesca da Rimini and Paolo Malatesta," 1852. Courtesy of the Bury Art Gallery.

human psychology. Instead, the apparition-producing faculty increasingly came to seem a self-activating and irrational force within the mind—the "ghost in the machine," so to speak, that produced spectres unpredictably and often for no apparent reason.

True, the later skeptics attributed some apparitions to objective physical causes—more or less plausibly. As I suggested in Chapter 9, the delusion-inducing effects of opium, alcohol, nitrous oxide, and other intoxicating substances had been well documented by the turn of the century. (In a famous set of experiments with nitrous oxide performed in 1800, the chemist Sir Humphrey

Davy used the poet Coleridge as one of his human guinea pigs.)[19] In 1813 the Manchester physician John Ferriar asserted that the appearance of a ghost was invariably a symptom of "bodily distemper" or of some "peculiar condition of the sensorium." Such events should be of as little concern to the sufferer, he wrote reassuringly, as "the head-ache and shivering attending a common catarrh."[20] A few decades later, in his curiously illustrated *Spectropia* (1864), J. H. Brown declared that the vast majority of such visions resulted from simple retinal fatigue. The pictures in *Spectropia* itself—showing various dark-hued "spirits" against a white background—could be used to demonstrate the phenomenon experimentally, Brown argued: if one stared hard at one of the images for a minute or two, then looked away into a darkened room, one would see a luminous afterimage of the same figure "floating" before one's eyes.[21] Other would-be debunkers turned to the new art of photography for technical analogies: according to the anonymous author of an 1872 article on "Spectral Illusions" in *Chambers' Miscellany*, "the mind, as it were, daguerreotypes [the spectral image]—the flash of thought—on the retina, or mirror of the eye, where it is recognized by the powers of perception." The retina was simply a photographic plate on which the ghostly "flashes of thought" were captured.[22]

At the same time, however, even the most scientifically minded could not help grasping after rather more problematic sorts of explanation. It became popular to argue, for example, that merely hearing stories about ghosts, or seeing them represented in some compelling aesthetic form, could lead one to see one. Locke had warned that nursemaids who told ghost stories predisposed their infant charges toward hallucinations later in life.[23] And in *The Philosophy of Apparitions*, the physician Samuel Hibbert described a similar process of mediation: "from the imagination of ecclesiastical writers; from the stone or carved images of saints and angels which have adorned the walls of religious edifices; or from emblematical pictures or portraits, which might have otherwise met with a popular diffusion, the sensible forms assumed by apparitions . . . have been derived."[24] One of his own hallucinating patients, he added, saw spectral figures "exactly like the forms he had recently seen exhibited on the stage in the popular drama of Don Giovanni."[25] A woman mentioned by John Ferriar in his *Essay Towards a Theory of Apparitions* described seeing apparitions exactly like "the imps of our terrific modern romances," while another woman, mentioned in "Spectral Illusions," was assailed by phantoms after an unfortunate trip to the opera:

> She went, not very wisely, to see that banquet of demonology, *Der Freischütz;* and of course, for some time afterwards, the *dramatis personae* of that edifying piece, not excepting his Satanic majesty in person, were her nightly visitors.[26]

Perhaps the most paradoxical case of such ghost-seeing by suggestion was that of "Mrs. A.," mentioned by Sir David Brewster in his *Letters on Natural Magic*, who,

Figure 10.5. Reverie as spectralization. "A Boy's Dream of the Coming Christmas" by Adrian Marie, from *The Graphic*, 1889. Courtesy of Stanford Library.

despite being an avid reader of debunking literature and a confirmed skeptic, found herself pursued by a frightening crowd of apparitions shortly after reading Samuel Hibbert's ultra-skeptical *Philosophy of Apparitions*.[27]

The fear that thinking too much about ghosts might make one see one—for that is the anxiety expressed, I think, in the foregoing examples—resolved very quickly into a deeper fear: that thinking too much, period, led to ghost-seeing. For ordinary thought, the scientific skeptics affirmed, was itself a kind of spectral envisioning. Thus Ferriar, propounding his theory of hallucinations in 1813, described the working of the memory as a process of "spectral representation." "From recalling images by an art of memory," he maintained, "the transition is direct to beholding spectral objects, which have been floating in the imagination."[28] Sir David Brewster argued that certain "objects of mental contemplation" could be seen "as distinctly as external objects." In an unhealthy state of mind, these inward spectra simply "overpowered" the impressions of external objects, resulting in hallucinations.[29] At such moments, wrote John Netten Radcliffe in *Fiends, Ghosts, and Sprites: Including an Account of the Origin and Nature of Belief in the Supernatural* (1854), "the mental image is liable to excite sensations, and to be portrayed with a distinctness and 'outness' which approximates to, or equals, that of a real object, and it is regarded as such."[30]

Yet by blurring the distinction between ghost-seeing and the seemingly ordinary processes of contemplation or recollection, the apparition-debunking writers of the early nineteenth century had introduced a dizzying problem into rationalist epistemology. What prevented the mental image, visible to the mind's eye, from turning into an outright hallucination? If all thinking was a kind of spectralization —a mysterious process by which mental phantoms took on an uncanny "life" in the mind—what was to stop one, while engaged in some intense or prolonged contemplation, from dissociating from the real world altogether? Even the most ardent materialists—such as Ferriar and Hibbert—were troubled by the idea that "squadrons of phantastical chimeras" could conceivably invade ordinary subjectivity at a moment's notice. "Profound preoccupation and prolonged concentration of thought on a single object," wrote Brierre de Boismont in 1845, "are eminently favorable to the production of hallucinations." During such hynogogic states,

> a single impression, a single image, appears sometimes to remain long in the thought, and hold it, as it were, in a state of siege; then our understanding acts only by intuition. Entire scenes, pictures, complete or in part, succeed to the interior sense, now slowly, now with rapidity. We think we see, and truly see, that which we have never seen. Indeed, these are real phantoms that are imagination, by its sole power, gathers around us, happy or unhappy beneath the charm of its sorcery.[31]

The much-cited case of the German skeptical philosopher and publisher Christoph Friedrich Nicolai aroused particular anxiety. In a celebrated address delivered to the Royal Society of Berlin in 1799, Nicolai had described being harassed for several months by hundreds of apparitions after a period of prolonged solitary reflection. Beginning in February 1791, after several months of brooding over "incidents of a very disagreeable nature," he had seen the spectre of a "deceased person" in his study. This was quickly followed by "human figures of both sexes" parading through his rooms "like people at a fair, where all is bustle."

Figure 10.6. Sir Frank Dicksee, "A Reverie," mid-nineteenth century. Widower listening to daughter playing the piano imagines dead wife, whose spectral image appears far left. Courtesy of Walker Art Gallery, Liverpool.

> Once or twice I saw amongst them persons on horseback, and dogs and birds; these figures all appeared to me in their natural size, as distinctly as if they had existed in real life, with the several tints on the uncovered parts of the body, and with all the different kinds and colours of clothes. But I think, however, that the colours were somewhat *paler* than they are in nature.

The crowd of phantasmata was only routed, Nicolai claimed, when he underwent a dramatic blood-letting operation, complete with an "application of leeches to the anus."[32]

Yet equally alarming were cases like that of the introspective "Miss S. L."—described by the Scottish physician Robert Macnish in his *Philosophy of Sleep* of 1834—who, while preparing for bed one night, saw "a *stream* of spectres, persons' faces, limbs, in the most shocking confusion . . . pour into her room from the window, in the manner of a cascade." ("Although the cascade continued, apparently, in rapid descending motion," wrote Macnish, "there was no accumulation of figures in the room, the supply unaccountably vanishing after having formed the cascade.")[33] The unfortunate "White Lady," memorialized by Washington Irving in his description of Lord Byron's ancestral home, *Newstead Abbey* (1835), suffered similar visitations. This "poor enthusiast," a passionate admirer of Byron's poetry, had taken up residence in the woods outside the abbey so that she might dwell continually among scenes associated with her idol. "Cut off, as it were, from all human society," she told a curious visitor, "I have been compelled to live in a world of my own, and certainly with the beings with which my world is peopled I am at no loss to converse." Lost in these visionary encounters, she "spread an ideal world around her in which she moved and existed as in a dream, forgetful at times of the real miseries which beset her in her mortal state." This pathetic monomania ended in death; she was killed by a runaway cart, Irving tells us, after failing to heed the frantic warning cries of the driver.[34]

Haunted by the problem of the thought-turned-ghost, late eighteenth- and early nineteenth-century rationalists felt obliged to issue warnings about the dangers of thinking too much. Indulging in reveries, wrote Alexander Crichton in his *Inquiry into Mental Derangement* (1798) was a dangerous mental activity that often led to "an incurable habit of inattention."[35] Indeed, the compulsive image-making of the reverie-prone individual—the constant meditation on imaginary objects and scenes—resulted directly in the unleashing of spectres. "The belief in the reality of the phantoms of the imagination," he warned, arose when images of the mind "acquired such a degree of force from frequent repetitions, as to be superior in their effect to those derived *ab externo*."[36] According to William Newnham, author of *An Essay on Superstition* from 1830, "the bad habit of indulging the love of mental wandering, without guidance, or fixed rule, or definite object," produced a "brainular irritation," which in turn led to apparition-seeing. In an overactive or brooding state, he thought, even the healthiest mind could fall victim to such "incipient derangement."[37]

Reading became dangerous because it prompted obsessional thoughts. The "sickly taste for light and desultory reading," as one writer called it, led to visions from which one could not always escape. Books were "seducers"; one could easily become lost in their dizzying "mazes" of fantasy."[38] Even the works of esteemed authors could prompt spectral reveries. In his *Zoonomia* of 1794 Erasmus Darwin described the case of a young woman suffering from hallucination who "conversed aloud with imaginary persons with her eyes open, and could not be brought to attend to the stimulus of external objects by any kind of violence." Her somnambulistic states were characterized from the start by a tendency to recite "whole pages from the English poets." In repeating some lines from Pope, she forgot one word, and continued to say the passage over and over, stopping each time at the missing word. Her medical attendants began to shout the word aloud in her ear each time she halted, but to no avail. This scene of collective frenzy ceased only when she "regained" the word herself and went on with her bizarre recitation.[39]

But other kinds of behavior promoted the new disease of reverie. Too much solitude, sitting in gaudily decorated churches, walking in gardens and terraces (as opposed to along the seashore), opium chewing, corpulence, the "debility subsequent to a debauch," even drumming with one's fingers on tabletops, according to one writer, were all dangerous reverie-inducers. He prescribed a number of countermeasures. Frequent exercise in a bracing atmosphere, the study of mathematics, intercourse with the learned and refined, hanging pictures of worthies in one's study, reading Scripture, and nailbiting (to encourage practical thinking) were sometimes effective in "dissolving the spell of reveries, into which evil thoughts are apt to enter."[40]

The rationalist attack on the "effeminizing" habit of reverie had powerful buried connections, of course, with the medical attack on masturbation waged in the same period: the "criminal reveries" of the vicious and sensual, it was suggested, easily modulated into "the pampering of . . . base appetite."[41] "There is certainly no power of the mind that requires more cautious management and stern control," wrote Abercrombie, "and the proper regulation of it cannot be too strongly impressed upon the young."[42] Like masturbation, reverie was a self-indulgent, repetitive activity resulting in a debilitating psychic "discharge": the discharge of hallucination. It was a demonic force at loose in the world of thought, to be fought at every turn. "Reverie resembles the enemy of mankind," one writer affirmed; "resist it, and it will flee from you."[43]

The same metaphors and the same superstitious fear of haunting thoughts carried over, with little modification, into modern psychoanalysis. Freud was aware of several of the earlier theoretical writings on reverie and hallucination and interested in the traditional problem of apparitions.[44] Perusing nineteenth-century debunking works on apparitions, one often finds uncanny anticipations of Freud's theories. Hibbert's 1825 assertion, for example, that apparitions were simply "unconscious ideas" returning in an "insulated manner," so that one could no longer directly trace the original chain of associations giving rise to them, is more than a little reminiscent of later Freudian formulations. Elsewhere Hibbert sounds positively Viennese: "the force of the sexual and parental ties will often be indicated by the subject of these visions."[45] Most unsettlingly, however, Freud's writings exhibit the same rhetorical and epistemological paradoxes troubling the works of the Enlightenment rationalists. He inherited both their crypto-supernatural language and their sense of the psyche as a vulnerable domain subject to frightening spectral intrusions. Thus for Freud, as for the debunking writers generally, thoughts have a curious tendency to take on a "phantom" life of their own. Unconscious ideas are precisely those haunting figments—apparitions out of the past—with the power to estrange the subject from reality. The analyst's task is to intervene, as it were, in the reverie-world of the subject and lay these haunting forces to rest. At the same time, however, precisely because they are ghostly in nature, the products of the unconscious also stand outside any purely human control. They preserve a vestigial magical force and a terrifying, irrational persistence in the life of the mind. The repressed anxiety at the heart of psychoanalysis is that no purely analytic technique, no merely secular process of thought-control or self-monitoring—however "scientific"—can finally eradicate this numinous potential for return.

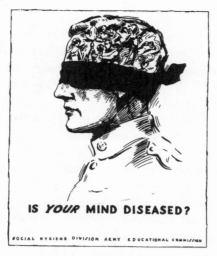

Figure 10.7 Monitoring reverie. The dangers of spectralization represented in two twentieth-century posters. Courtesy of Wilber Landesman.

The texts of psychoanalysis are haunted by the possibility of supernatural possession. Which is not to say that Freud did not claim, most of the time, an official, quasi-secretarial power over the ghosts of the unconscious. Psychoanalysis was in a sense the bureaucratic realization—the institutionalization—of the anti-reverie prescriptions of the nineteenth-century apparition writers. From the start it had a hidden sociopolitical dimension: it was a way of recuperating—for the benefit of bourgeois society—the potentially anarchical and phantasmagoric inner life of the subject. Freud's hysterical patients were the alienated victims of reverie in a new guise. Each one had to be resocialized, reeducated, drawn out of his or her solipsistic and immobilizing involvement with phantoms. The "talking cure" was itself the first step in this process of resocialization: a conversation with a human being instead of a spectre.

We can see the continuity most clearly, perhaps, in the case of the Rat Man, whose symptoms are in many ways a throwback to the pathology of 1800. The Rat Man is a slave, of course, to fanciful thoughts—most notably, to the recurrent mental image of his fiancée undergoing a horrible rat torture practiced "in the East." But other fantasies assail him: while working late at night, for example, he repeatedly imagines that his dead father is still alive and about to enter his study. Freud explicitly connected these repetitive thoughts with the Rat Man's habits of reading and his compulsive masturbation. An erotic scene in Goethe's *Dichtung und Wahrheit,* the Rat Man recalls, prompted one of his most memorable onanistic episodes. Yet "the problem of onanism," Freud is led to theorize, "becomes insoluble if we attempt to treat it as a clinical unit, and forget that it can represent the discharge of every variety of sexual component and of every sort of phantasy to which such components can give rise" (340).[46] In the famous conclusion to the case history he explains the Rat Man's particular mental fixations as a function of an unconscious desire to be sexually penetrated by his father. In cases of obsessional neurosis, Freud writes, the act of thinking itself, the compulsive recall of certain mental images, takes on an onanistic quality and becomes a substitute for the repressed erotic idea: "the thought process itself becomes sexualized, for the sexual pleasure which is normally attached to the content of thought becomes shifted onto the act of thinking itself, and the gratification derived from reaching the conclusion of a line of thought is experienced as a *sexual* gratification" (380). A typically startling and brilliant Freudian deduction, on the face of it. Viewed in its historical context, however, this diagnosis is merely an updating of the late eighteenth- and early nineteenth-century correlation of reverie with self-abuse. The Rat Man, like a new young Werther, both thinks too much and masturbates too much, but the two problems are really one: the mark of an overinvolvement with phantoms.

A more important ghost haunts the Rat Man case history, however—the spectre of supernaturalism itself. Freud doesn't hesitate, of course, to disparage the Rat Man for being "to a high degree superstitious" and a somewhat pathetic believer in the "miraculous apparitions" of his own thought (365–66). Yet consider Freud's own oddly superstitious turn in the following passage. He is describing his patient's "favourite phantasy that his father was still alive and might any moment reappear."

He used to arrange that his working hours should be as late as possible in the night. Between twelve and one o'clock he would interrupt his work, and open the front door of the flat as though his father were standing outside it; then, coming back into the hall, he would take out his penis and look at it in the looking-glass. This crazy conduct becomes intelligible if we suppose that he was acting as though he expected a visit from his father at the hour when ghosts are abroad. He had on the whole been idle at his work during his father's lifetime, and this had often been a cause of annoyance to his father. And now that he was returning as a ghost, he was to be delighted at finding his son hard at work. (342)

The ghost here, we notice, is Freud's interpolation, not the Rat Man's. For the Rat Man simply imagines his father "still alive"; it is Freud who transforms him into the more ambiguous figure of a spectre, complete with the obligatory nocturnal visiting hours. Later Freud will speak of this "ghost" as an established fact of the Rat Man's case, and as a "spectre" that had to be "laid" (358–59).

The romantic transformation of the Rat Man's Oedipal wish into a scene of haunting—almost a scene out of Radcliffe or Poe—suggests, it seems to me, Freud's own deeply ambivalent vision of the contents of the unconscious. On the one hand, Freud invariably tried to rationalize the mind's "shadowy forms." The repressed connection between obsessive ideas and unconscious thoughts, he explains at one point, "appears to persist in some kind of shadowy form (which I have elsewhere compared to an entoptic perception), and they are thus transferred, by a process of projection, into the external world, where they bear witness to what has been effaced from consciousness" (367). On the other hand, the very invocation of spectral forms subtly undermines any reassuring clinical message. The "shadowy forms" can only be figured—can only be known—in externalized form, as daemonic beings, separate from the subject, with a power to pursue and enthrall. In the ambiguous language of the case history, they "force their way into consciousness," "make their appearance openly," "dart" into view, even "speak" to the sufferer. "During the process of a psychoanalysis," writes Freud, "it is not only the patient who plucks up courage, but his disease as well; it grows bold enough to speak more plainly than before" (359).

Listening to the speech of the ghost, Freud argues, gives one a power over it. A successful analysis, ostensibly, is a kind of exorcism—forces the ghost to flee. "Dropping the metaphor," Freud concludes, "what happens is that the patient, who has hitherto turned his eyes away in terror from his own pathological productions, begins to attend to them and obtains a clearer and more detailed view of them" (359). But in a deeper sense, the metaphor of the ghost is not dropped—either here, in the very passage in which Freud claims to drop it, or indeed anywhere else in his writing. The profound counterstrain of pessimism in Freudian theory, visible most distinctly perhaps in the late essay "Analysis Terminable and Interminable," seems to grow directly out of this poetic impasse: if unconscious thoughts are in fact spectral in nature, what is to keep them from recurring forever?

"A large part of the mythological view of the world," Freud wrote in a famous passage in *The Psychopathology of Everyday Life,*

Figure 10.8 Spectralization as kitsch. Romantic wedding photo, c. 1987. Courtesy of Karen Cuff.

is nothing but psychology projected into the external world. The obscure recognition (the endopsychic perception, as it were) of psychical factors and relations in the unconscious is mirrored—it is difficult to express it in other terms, and here the analogy with paranoia must come to our aid—in the construction of a *supernatural reality,* which is destined to be changed back once more by science into the *psychology of the unconscious.* One could venture to explain in this way the myths of paradise and the fall of man, of God, of good and evil, of immortality, and so on, and to transform *metaphysics* into *metapsychology.*[47]

The problem with displacing the supernatural "back" into the realm of psychology, however, is that it remains precisely that: only a displacement. The unearthliness, the charisma, the devastating *noumenon* of the supernatural is conserved. One cannot speak in the end, it seems to me, of a "decline of magic" in post-Enlightenment Western culture, only perhaps of its relocation within the new empire of subjectivity itself. The apparition writers in the decades around 1800 took on the traditional world of spirits, and like sorcerers' apprentices performed on them the very act of magical metamorphosis that Freud would later celebrate— the transformation of metaphysics into metapsychology. But the effect was to demonize the world of thought. We have yet to explore very deeply the social, intellectual, and existential implications of the act of demonization. Instead we continue to speak—innocently perhaps but also with subtle anxiety—of being "haunted" by our thoughts and pursued by "ghosts" inside our heads. We fear (and legislate against) the madness of the phantom-world within. Until it is possible to speak of the ghost inhabiting, as it were, the mind of rationalism itself, this sense of being haunted is likely to remain—far more than any nervous fear of the police—the distinctive paranoia of modern life.

CHAPTER 11

CONTAGIOUS FOLLY:

AN ADVENTURE

AND ITS SKEPTICS

What to make of someone who sees a ghost? In his 1830 attack on superstition, *Letters on Demonology and Witchcraft*, Sir Walter Scott was forthright: anyone who claimed to see an apparition was either mad or on the way to becoming so. Since ghosts, according to Scott, did not exist, to maintain that one had seen one was to be pathetically unbalanced—the victim of some "lively dream, a waking reverie, the excitation of a powerful imagination, or the misrepresentation of a diseased organ of sight." The skeptic was not to be deceived by the air of apparent reasonableness with which the ghost-seer typically described his or her visions: in the case of every such person he had met with, Scott wrote, "shades of mental aberration have afterwards occurred, which sufficiently accounted for the supposed apparitions, and will incline me always to feel alarmed in behalf of the continued health of a friend, who should conceive himself to have witnessed such a visitation."[1]

But what if *two* people claim to see a ghost? If spectres are indeed to be understood, as Scott thought, psychologically—as hallucinatory products of an abnormally excited or "diseased" imagination—how then to account for an apparition seen by two people at once? Are we to conclude that hallucinations can be shared? Or that spectral delusions, like the germs of a virus, can somehow be transmitted from the brain of one person to another? What sort of psychical mechanism would explain such a strangely infectious brand of folly? Scott himself avoids the issue by refusing to allow that simultaneous sightings ever occur. Yet the omission is clearly tactical: for to acknowledge such a possibility, let alone debunk it, the resolute skeptic would have to work twice as hard, if only to remain half-convincing.

The question of the so-called collective hallucination (as it has come to be known to psychical researchers) is neither as arcane nor as irrelevant to everyday life as it might first appear. On the contrary, it illuminates a much larger philosophical issue. In *Group Psychology and the Analysis of the Ego*, his 1921 book devoted to the relationship between individual and group psychology, Sigmund Freud lamented that there was still "no explanation of the nature of suggestion, that is, of the conditions under which influence without adequate logical foundation takes place."[2] What the science of psychology lacked, in other words, was an understanding of ideological transference—the process by which one individual imposed his or her beliefs and convictions on another. How did an idea spread, so to speak, from one person to the next, resulting in the formation of a group consciousness? The phenomenon of the collective hallucination puts the issue starkly—if ambiguously—in relief. If a ghost or apparition can be said to represent, in Freud's terms, an idea "without adequate logical foundation," a *delusion*, then the process by which two people convince each other that they have seen one—and in turn attempt to convince others—might be taken to epitomize the formation of ideology itself.

In what follows I shall examine a case of collective hallucination—certainly the most notorious and well documented in the annals of modern psychical research—precisely as a way of spotlighting this larger problem. My goal in so doing is not so much to expose the folly of people who claim to see ghosts (though the notion of folly will play a crucial part in what I have to say) but the difficulty that inevitably besets anyone who attempts to debunk such claims on supposedly rationalist grounds. For in the absence of any satisfying explanation of how such "folly" spreads—how a private delusion becomes a *folie à deux* (or *trois* or *quatre*)—the labors of the skeptic are doomed to result only in a peculiar rhetorical and epistemological impasse.

The case I wish to resurrect—at some risk, I realize, of exciting readerly mirth—is that of the "Ghosts of Versailles." The case dates from 1911. In that year two eminent English women academics, Charlotte Anne Moberly and Eleanor Jourdain, the principal and vice-principal, respectively, of St. Hugh's College, Oxford, published under the pseudonyms "Miss Morison" and "Miss Lamont" a book entitled *An Adventure* in which they asserted that while on a sightseeing tour of the gardens of the Petit Trianon near Versailles on 10 August 1901, they had encountered the apparitions of Marie Antoinette and several members of her court precisely as they had existed in the year 1789. After jointly researching the matter for nearly ten years in the French national archives, Moberly and Jourdain wrote,

Figure 11.1. Charlotte Anne Moberly (1846–1937). Courtesy of St. Hugh's College, Oxford.

they had been forced to conclude that they had traveled backwards in time—perhaps by entering telepathically into "an act of memory" performed by Marie Antoinette herself during her incarceration following the sacking of the Tuileries. In the central chapters of *An Adventure* (which quickly became a best-seller) they laid out this bizarre theory in detail, along with a mass of so-called historical and topographical evidence supposedly confirming it.

What prompted Moberly and Jourdain—the respectable daughters of clergymen both—to make such a fantastic claim? The story behind *An Adventure*, though a convoluted one, is worth relating in some detail. At the time of their fateful trip to Versailles in the summer of 1901, Miss Moberly and Miss Jourdain, who were subsequently to live and work together for twenty-three years, were only slightly acquainted. Charlotte Anne Moberly (1846–1937), the older and better connected of the two (her father was the bishop of Salisbury), had been principal of the small Oxford women's college, St. Hugh's, since its founding in 1886. Eleanor Jourdain (1864–1924) was an Oxford graduate in history and the head-mistress of a girls' school in Watford. When Jourdain was recommended for the vacant post of vice-principal at St. Hugh's, Moberly agreed to meet with her in Paris (where Jourdain was staying) to see if the two of them could work together compatibly. The trip to Versailles, a place neither woman had visited before, came at the end of several days of sightseeing together in the French capital.[3]

As the two recount it in the opening chapter of *An Adventure*, they set off by train for Versailles on 10 August. After touring the main palace (which left them unimpressed) they decided to venture out into the grounds in search of the Petit

Figure 11.2. Eleanor Jourdain (1864–1924). Courtesy of Stanford Library.

Trianon. At the time—or so they claimed—neither one of them knew much about French history, or indeed about the Trianon itself, except that it had been the favorite retreat of the ill-fated queen, Marie Antoinette, before the French Revolution. The day was pleasant, however, and both were in the mood for a walk. Soon after passing an imposing building at the bottom of the Long Water—the Grand Trianon—the two women got lost. They wandered for a while at random, passing a deserted farmhouse where Jourdain noticed a peculiar-looking old plough and began to feel (as she put it later) as if "something were wrong."[4] Moberly was surprised that Jourdain did not ask the way from a woman shaking a cloth out the window of one of the outbuildings, but concluded that her companion knew where she was going. Turning down a lane, they espied two men dressed in "long greyish-green coats with small three-cornered hats." Moberly remembered seeing "a wheelbarrow of some kind close by" and assumed that the men were gardeners, or else "dignified officials" of some sort (A, 4). Here Miss Jourdain did ask the way, and they were instructed to go down a path in front of them. As they began to walk forward, Jourdain saw a cottage on her right in front of which a woman and a girl were standing. Both were dressed unusually, with "white kerchiefs tucked into the bodice." The woman handed the girl a jug, and for a moment they seemed to pause, like figures "in a *tableau vivant*" (A, 17, 18n).

As they continued down the path, Moberly and Jourdain next came upon something resembling a garden kiosk, shaded by trees. A man was sitting nearby. Moberly was instantly overtaken by an "extraordinary" sensation of depression.

"Everything suddenly looked unnatural, therefore unpleasant; even the trees behind the building seemed to have become flat and lifeless, *like a wood worked in tapestry*. There were no effects of light and shade, and no wind stirred the trees. It was all intensely still" (A, 4, 5). Jourdain had similar sensations—she had a feeling of "heavy dreaminess" as if she were walking in her sleep—but neither woman shared her forebodings with the other at the time. These feelings of distress intensified when the man by the kiosk looked up at them. According to Moberly he was "repulsive" in appearance: his complexion was "dark and rough," and despite the heat, he wore a heavy black cloak and a slouch hat (A, 5). Jourdain remembered him as "dark" with an "evil and yet unseeing" expression: she thought his face had been pitted by smallpox (A, 18). Both were relieved when a "red-faced" man wearing "buckled shoes" suddenly rushed up behind them, warned them (in oddly accented French) that they were going the wrong way, and then ran off in another direction.

Quickly they set off after him, crossed over a small bridge with a stream under it, and at last came in view of what they presumed to be the Petit Trianon. At this point Moberly saw a fair-haired woman sitting on a stool with her back to the house, apparently sketching. The woman wore a large white summer hat and a curiously old-fashioned dress "arranged on her shoulders in handkerchief fashion" (A, 8). The dress, which Moberly thought unusual at the time, was covered with a pale green fichu. As she and Jourdain went up the steps of the terrace to the house, Moberly, looking back at the sketching woman, had once again an unaccountable feeling of gloom. Suddenly a young man dressed like a footman came out of a second building opening out onto the terrace. Slamming a door behind him, he hurried toward them with a "peculiar smile" and told them that the main entrance was on the other side of the house (A, 20). Accordingly, they went around to the front of the house where a French wedding party was waiting to tour the rooms. Recovering their spirits, Moberly and Jourdain attached themselves to the happy group and the rest of the day passed off uneventfully. They returned to Paris that evening.

For a week neither woman alluded to the afternoon at the Trianon. One day, however, as Miss Moberly began to write about it in a letter to her sister, her uneasiness returned:

> As the scenes came back one by one, the same sensation of dreamy unnatural oppression came over me so strongly that I stopped writing, and said to Miss Lamont [Jourdain], "Do you think that the Petit Trianon is haunted?" Her answer was prompt, "Yes, I do." I asked her where she felt it, and she said, "In the garden where we met the two men, but not only there." She then described her feeling of depression and anxiety which began at the same point as it did with me, and how she tried not to let me know it. [A, 11–12]

There the matter rested, however, until both returned to England. That November, three months after their visit, Miss Jourdain (who in the meantime had accepted Moberly's offer of the St. Hugh's vice-principalship) came to stay with her new friend and the two took up the subject again. In the course of their conversation Moberly referred in passing to the "sketching lady" and was shocked to discover that Jourdain had not seen her. "I exclaimed that it was impossible that she should not have seen the individual; for we were walking side by side and went straight up to her, passed her and looked down upon her from the terrace." Having uncovered this new "element of mystery" (A, 13), each resolved to write a separate, detailed account of what she had seen, to be shown to the other later. Moberly completed her account on 25 November; Jourdain hers on 28 November.

Comparing narratives, the two soon noticed more eerie discrepancies. Besides the sketching lady, Miss Moberly had seen a woman shaking a cloth out of a window—Miss Jourdain had seen neither. Moberly in turn had not seen Jourdain's "woman and girl with a jug," even though, according to Jourdain, they had walked right past them. But this was not all: Jourdain had also discovered two startling pieces of information. While turning over a set of school lessons on the French Revolution, she had suddenly realized that the day on which they had visited the Trianon, 10 August, was the anniversary of the sacking of the Tuileries. On that day in 1792, Louis XVI and Marie Antoinette had witnessed the massacre of their Swiss Guards and been imprisoned in the Hall of the Assembly. Struck by this ominous coincidence, Jourdain immediately asked a French friend if she had ever heard anything about the Petit Trianon being haunted. To her amazement the friend confirmed that indeed, "on a certain day in August," Marie Antoinette was regularly seen in the Trianon garden, wearing a light flapping hat and a pink dress. The queen's servants and courtiers also appeared in the vicinity, reenacting their distinctive "occupations and amusements" for a day and a night (A, 22).

At once they started to wonder (in Moberly's words)

> whether we had inadvertently entered within an act of the Queen's memory when alive, and whether this explained our curious sensation of being completely shut in and oppressed. What more likely, we thought, than that during those hours in the Hall of the Assembly, or in the Conciergerie, she had gone back in such vivid memory to other Augusts spent at Trianon that some impress of it was imparted to the place? (A, 23–24)

They began reading up on the life of Marie Antoinette—with thrilling results. Leafing through Gustave Desjardins's *Petit Trianon* (1885), Moberly found a portrait of the doomed queen by Wertmüller in which, astonishingly, she recognized the face of the sketching lady. The clothes were also identical. Could the lady, Jourdain asked her friend, have been an apparition of the queen herself? Conjecture turned to conviction after Jourdain made a second visit to Versailles in January 1902. Not only was she unable to retrace their steps, all the grounds around the Trianon seemed mysteriously altered. (Nowhere, for example, could she find the strange "kiosk," or the bridge with the stream under it.)[5] She did gather, however, another crucial bit of information: on her last day at the Trianon—

Figure 11.3. Miss Moberly in youth and middle age. Reproduced from Lucille Iremonger, *The Ghosts of Versailles.*

supposedly 5 October 1789—Marie Antoinette had been sitting in her garden when a page ran toward her with a message that a mob from Paris would be at the gates in an hour's time. Suddenly, the two women realized, it all made sense. While imprisoned in the Hall of the Assembly in 1792, Marie Antoinette must undoubtedly have thought back to that day in 1789 when she first heard the awful news that her crown was in danger. This would indeed explain the terrible "depression" both of them had experienced in the grounds. The "red-faced" man who had run past them in such a hurry near the kiosk, they concluded, was probably the very messenger running to the queen with the news: they had literally stepped "into" her memory.

Exalted by their discovery, Moberly and Jourdain sent a letter to the Society for Psychical Research asserting that the Trianon was haunted and including their written accounts from 1901 as evidence. To their chagrin the accounts were returned as unworthy of investigation. They realized they would have to put their case more compellingly. What better way to do so, they surmised, than to demonstrate that everything they had seen at the Trianon—from the moment they found themselves lost to the moment they joined the wedding party—had in fact *only* existed in the year 1789? Accordingly, they set out to do just this. For the next nine years, in libraries, historical archives, and at the Trianon itself, they carried out an elaborate, if not obsessional, search for evidence. In 1911, convinced they had found just the proofs they needed, they published the fruits of their research in the pages of *An Adventure.*

In their central chapter—"Summary of Results of Research"—the two laid

Figure 11.4. Miss Jourdain in youth and middle age. Reproduced from Lucille Iremonger, *The Ghosts of Versailles*.

out this "proof" in surreal detail. They began with the first object they had seen, the peculiar-looking plough noticed by Miss Jourdain just after they had lost their way. Questioning a gardener at the Trianon in 1905, they reported, they had learned that no ploughs had been kept there in 1901, there being "no need of one" (A, 41). Some time later, in 1908, another gardener told them that the shape of ploughs had "entirely altered in character since the Revolution" (A, 41–42) and that the one seen by Miss Jourdain was definitely of an "old type" no longer found anywhere in France. True, they conceded, on a document they had uncovered in "the Archives Nationales" listing all the gardening tools bought for the Trianon between 1780 and 1789, there had been no mention of a plough. But as they had learned "from Desjardins's book," during the reign of Louis XVI, "an old plough used in his predecessor's reign had been preserved at the Petit Trianon and sold with the king's other properties during the Revolution" (A, 42). The implication was obvious: Miss Jourdain had seen a plough that could only have emanated from the eighteenth century.

Other objects received similar glosses. The cottage, for example, in front of which Jourdain had seen the woman and the girl with the jug, they argued, most closely resembled a structure "not now in existence" shown on an old map from 1783 found in the Trianon archives in 1907 (A, 47). The mysterious kiosk—nowhere to be seen in the present garden—was identical, they had discovered, to a lost "ruine" pictured on another old eighteenth-century plan (A, 48). As for the little bridge with a stream under it, this corresponded to an obscure "*'pont rustique'*" mentioned by the Comte D'Hezecques in his *Souvenirs d'un page de la cour de Louis XVI* (1873)—also no longer in existence. It was definitely *not*, they asserted, the more famous (and obvious) Rocher Bridge, which, according to calculations they had carried out on the spot, was "too high above the lakes" to be the same one they had crossed (A, 67). Most eerily perhaps, the door they thought they had heard slamming as they went up the steps of the Trianon terrace—the door from which the footman with the "peculiar smile" had emerged—led only to a ruined chapel that had never been used, according to a guide, "since it was used by the Court." Indeed, when Miss Jourdain attempted to open the door from the inside, some time in 1906, she found it "bolted, barred, and cobwebbed over from age and disuse" (A, 81).

Their evidence relating to people, however, was no less extensive. The two men in "greenish-grey coats" to whom they had first spoken, they contended, were members of Marie Antoinette's famed *gardes Suisses:* only royal bodyguards from the 1780s, they had learned, ever wore liveries of this color at the Trianon. Indeed, they had concluded, they were probably "two of the three Bersy brothers," said to have been on duty on the fateful day of 5 October 1789 (A, 46). The woman and the girl with the jug were identified as the wife and daughter of one of Marie Antoinette's undergardeners: the girl was the same age as "Marion," a gardener's child they had read about in Julie Lavergne's 1879 *Légendes de Trianon* (A, 54). The sinister pockmarked "kiosk man," in turn, was none other than the wicked Comte de Vaudreuil, who had acted "an enemy's part" toward the queen by encouraging her to permit a performance of Beaumarchais's politically dangerous play *Le Mariage de Figaro* in 1784. Vaudreuil was a Creole and marked by smallpox: this explained the kiosk man's "dark and rough" complexion. The fact that the latter wore a large slouch hat and heavy black cloak on a hot summer's day confirmed the identification: according to Pierre de Nolhac's *La Reine Marie-Antoinette* (1890), they noted, Vaudreuil had himself once taken the role of Count Almaviva in Beaumarchais's drama, dressing for it in "a large dark cloak and Spanish hat," and often wore his costume on other occasions (A, 52). In a similar fashion, the "running man" was identified as Marie Antoinette's page De Bretagne (his Breton origins supposedly explained his unusual French accent), and the "chapel man" as a footman named Lagrange, who in 1789 had had rooms near the Trianon terrace (A, 65, 85).[6]

But Moberly and Jourdain's crowning proofs, not surprisingly, had to do with the sketching lady seen by Miss Moberly. The Wertmüller portrait had made them suspect from the start of course that the lady might be the queen herself: the features were identical, they confirmed, right down to the short nose and somewhat "square" face (A, 74). This particular portrait, moreover, had always been considered, they had found, the truest likeness of the queen. But their clinching piece of evidence once again was sartorial. In 1908, looking into the journals of Madame Éloffe, Marie Antoinette's *modiste,* they had discovered to their amazement that in July and September of 1789 Madame Éloffe had made for the queen "two green

Figure 11.5. The Petit Trianon, west front, showing the terrace from which Miss Moberly espied the "sketching lady." Courtesy of Stanford Library.

silk bodices" and several "white fichus." This information "agreed exactly" with the dress worn by the sketching lady in 1901. What Miss Moberly remembered as the lady's unusual-looking "pale green fichu," they realized triumphantly, was actually one of Madame Éloffe's green bodices, with a light-colored "muslin, or gauze" fichu over it (A, 75–76). The lady was none other than Marie Antoinette herself.

After completing these demonstrations, all of which were supplemented with numerous scholarly footnotes, appendices, and diagrams, Moberly and Jourdain concluded with something they called, rather more lyrically, "A Rêverie." Subtitled, "A Possible Historical Clue," "A Rêverie" was actually an imaginary account—composed in a suitably pathetic, pseudo-Carlylian manner—of the supposed meditations of Marie Antoinette during her imprisonment with Louis XVI and the Dauphin following the sacking of the Tuileries on 10 August 1792. In the course of this florid narration (which Moberly and Jourdain clearly intended as a kind of royalist apologia as well as an explanatory coda to their "adventure" itself) the much-abused queen, worn out by her sufferings at the hands of the revolutionary mob, is depicted sinking into a trancelike state in which she sees a series of phantom images of her beloved Trianon: an "old plough" from her husband's boyhood, two of her loyal bodyguards, the Bersy brothers, in "long green coats," the "rustic cottage" where the gardener's daughter Marion and her mother lived, the Comte de Vaudreuil in his "Spanish" costume, and so on. What she hallucinates, in short, is everything seen by Moberly and Jourdain in 1901— with one significant addition. Thinking back to her last day at the Trianon, and how she sat sketching on the lawn, she suddenly remembers "the two strangers"

Figure 11.6. The Wertmüller portrait of Marie Antoinette, 1785. Courtesy of the National Swedish Art Museum.

who walked past her "onto the terrace." Thus did Moberly and Jourdain, imagining the doomed queen imagining them, seek to lend telepathic credibility to their own richly phantasmagorical vision.[7]

Dare one call *An Adventure* preposterous? Certainly most people who read the book in 1911 thought so. From the start *An Adventure* provoked both extraor-

Figure 11.7. A plate from the journal of Madame Éloffe, dressmaker to Marie Antoinette, showing a transparent fichu worn over a bodice, as described by Moberly. Courtesy of Stanford Library.

dinary public interest (11,000 copies had been sold by 1913) and an extraordinary number of skeptical attacks. The first and most wounding of these assaults was unquestionably the review published in the *Proceedings of the Society for Psychical Research* by Mrs. Henry Sidgwick, the wife of the Society's president, late in 1911. Not only did she find Moberly and Jourdain's voluminous "evidence" ridiculous, Mrs. Sidgwick (who was the sister of Lord Balfour) took a distinctly satirical attitude toward the ladies themselves. Citing one "M. Sage," a French associate of the society who had walked over the Trianon gardens with *An Adventure* in hand, she maintained that Moberly and Jourdain ("who at best do not seem to be very good at topography") had simply gotten lost in the grounds and then misidentified what they had seen—after the fact. What they encountered there, she argued, were merely "real persons and things" from 1901, which they had subsequently "decked out by tricks of memory (and after the idea of haunting had occurred to them) with some additional details of costume suitable to the times of Marie Antoinette."[8] Her factotum M. Sage provided examples: Moberly and Jourdain's two "Swiss guards," for instance, were undoubtedly ordinary Trianon gardeners; the latter wore little caps, or *képis*, which could easily be mistaken for parts of a uniform. Likewise, all the buildings and objects they had seen could be correlated with existing structures in the Trianon grounds—the Temple of Love, the Belvédère, the Rocher bridge, and so forth.

But other attacks soon followed. In a chapter on apparitions in his book *Psychical Research,* also from 1911, W. F. Barrett, a physicist and Fellow of the Royal Society, declared that Moberly and Jourdain's visions were the result of "lively imagination stimulated by expectancy" and lacked "any real evidential value."[9] Interestingly, he wondered whether the two had been influenced by a 1907 account in the *Journal of the Society for Psychical Research* of a young woman who claimed to have been in communication with the spirit of Marie Antoinette since girlhood. He also reminded his readers of another recent case of Marie Antoinette-obsession: that of the celebrated medium Hélène Smith, who believed herself to be a reincarnation of the queen. Smith's bizarre accomplishments, which included being able to produce bits of automatic writing in Marie Antoinette's hand, had been exhaustively documented in a book published in 1900 by the Swiss psychologist Theodore Flournoy.[10]

Meanwhile Moberly and Jourdain were not silent. In 1913 they issued a revised edition of *An Adventure* including a section called "Answers to Questions We Have Been Asked," designed to deflect such assaults. Here they reiterated their belief that they had indeed seen people from the eighteenth century—and not unusually dressed gardeners, tourists, or people in masquerade costume, as Sidgwick and others had suggested. No "historical fetes" had taken place at the Trianon on 10 August 1901, they had discovered, nor had any "cinematographs" in which costumed actors might have appeared been filmed on the grounds that day (see A, 111–17). Responding to Barrett's insinuation that they had been influenced by stories of other apparitions, the two denied any morbid interest in spiritualism or the occult ("we are the daughters of English clergymen, and heartily hold and teach the faith of our fathers") and stoutly reaffirmed their native good sense (A, 101). Finally, by way of rejoinder to those who thought the whole thing a hoax, they now reproduced the "original" accounts each had written—supposedly independently—in November 1901, along with two "fuller" accounts, composed a few weeks later for the benefit of readers "unfamiliar" with the Trianon grounds.11

Yet these gambits seemed merely to inflame the skeptics further. For the next sixty years, in fact, books and articles disputing the claims of *An Adventure* (which itself went through three more editions) continued to appear. Neither the death of Jourdain in 1924, nor that of Moberly in 1937, did anything to stop the flow: indeed, the posthumous revelation that the pseudonymous "Miss Morison" and "Miss Lamont" were in fact two distinguished Oxford lady dons only intensified popular fascination with the case.12 J. R. Sturge-Whiting published a book-length study *The Mystery of Versailles* in 1938, shortly after the death of Moberly; David Landale Johnston's *The Trianon Case, A Review of the Evidence* appeared in 1945. In 1950 W. H. Salter's detailed examination of the supposedly "original" 1901 accounts—"'An Adventure': A Note on the Evidence"—was published in the *Journal of the Society for Psychical Research,* followed in 1952 by the first French article on the subject, Léon Rey's "Promenade hors du temps" in the *Revue de Paris.* (An annotated French translation of *An Adventure,* complete with sardonic preface by Jean Cocteau, appeared in 1959.)13 Perhaps the most damning as well as most exhaustive assault on the book came in 1957—in the shape of Lucille Iremonger's 300-page *ad feminam* attack, *The Ghosts of Versailles: Miss Moberly and Miss Jourdain and Their Adventure.* But even twenty years later the Trianon case was still arousing controversy: seventy-five years after Moberly and Jourdain's first encounter with the "sketching lady" and her ilk, Joan Evans, Eleanor Jourdain's literary executor and holder of the copyright to *An Adventure,* put forth her own debunking explanation of the Trianon apparitions in an essay entitled "An End to *An Adventure:* Solving the Mystery of the Trianon" in *Encounter* in 1976.14

Few of Moberly and Jourdain's numerous critics, to be sure, explicated the Trianon "ghosts" in precisely the same way. Most were convinced, certainly, that there had to be some commonplace explanation for what the two women had seen—the likeliest being that Moberly and Jourdain had simply mistaken ordinary people and objects from 1901 for those of the ancient régime. But given the intricacies of the case, there was little agreement on specific details—whether the kiosk was "really" the Temple of Love or "really" the Belvédère, whether the men in greenish coats were gardeners or officials, and so on. Certain features of the case became much-debated cruxes—the mysterious "chapel door," for instance, to which Sturge-Whiting (whose on-the-spot investigations became as tireless as Moberly and Jourdain's own) devoted an entire chapter of *The Mystery of Versailles.*15

Opinion was also divided on the subject of Moberly and Jourdain themselves.

The chivalrous Sturge-Whiting, writing in the '1930s, was inclined to see the authors of *An Adventure* in relatively flattering terms, as a pair of eccentric spinsters, harmlessly caught up in a sentimental flight of fancy. Though their claim to have encountered Marie Antoinette was nothing more—in his view—than a "pathetic illusion," they had elaborated it, he thought, in perfectly good faith: he saw no reason to question their integrity. Far from intending to deceive anyone, the "brave ladies," he gallantly intoned, had simply been swept away by a conception of the greatest "beauty and pathos."[16]

Others were less sure. Salter, writing in 1950, suspected—as Mrs. Sidgwick had done earlier—that Moberly and Jourdain had in fact tampered with the "evidence" in order to make their time-travel story more convincing. Salter was particularly dubious about the two sets of "original" accounts—supposedly written in November and December of 1901—printed in the 1913 edition of *An Adventure*. How reliable could such eyewitness accounts be, he asked, when they had been produced almost three months after the events described? What proof was there that Moberly and Jourdain had not collaborated on them? Most damagingly, he presented evidence, gleaned from the abortive correspondence between Moberly and Jourdain and the Society for Psychical Research in 1902, that the second, "fuller," or more elaborate set of accounts—which Moberly and Jourdain claimed to have composed only a week or two after the first set—had not been written in 1901 at all, but possibly as late as 1906.[17] Since a number of crucial details in Moberly and Jourdain's story—that the chapel door had been "slammed," for example—only appeared in the longer accounts, much of the so-called proof for their identifications suddenly became suspect. To claim in 1901 that they had heard the door slam was one thing: it made the subsequent discovery, several years later, that the chapel door had been "barred and bolted" all the more exciting and remarkable. But if the slamming sound was a superaddition from 1906, after they had already gone back and *seen* the door, then it began to look as though Moberly and Jourdain had been embellishing—for dramatic effect—all along.

Still even Salter was reluctant to say anything directly incriminating about two long-deceased and "much respected" ladies. No such scruples inhibited Iremonger, author of *The Ghosts of Versailles* (1957). Iremonger had been a student at St. Hugh's, where memories of Moberly and Jourdain loomed large. She was also a descendant of the Comte de Vaudreuil—the "repulsive-looking" kiosk man—and may have wished to vindicate her unprepossessing ancestor, for her book is without question the most gossipy attack on *An Adventure*, being largely devoted to compromising rumors and anecdotes about its authors' private lives. Among Iremonger's more provocative findings was that despite their protestations to the contrary, both Moberly and Jourdain had had paranormal experiences before and after the Trianon visit, and that Moberly in particular was prone to aural and visual hallucinations. As a child she had heard the words "PIN-

NACLED REALITY" as she stared at the spires of Winchester Cathedral; on the day her father, the bishop, died in 1885, she had seen two strange birds with dazzling white feathers and immense wings fly over the cathedral into the west. In Cambridge in 1913 she saw a procession of medieval monks; and at the Louvre the following year, she saw a man "six or seven feet high" in a crown and togalike dress whom she at first took to be Charlemagne, but later decided was an apparition of the Roman emperor Constantine (GV, 40–45).

But Iremonger's most sensational revelations had to do with Moberly and Jourdain's relationship itself. That the two were lesbians, and hence morally and psychologically suspect, was one of Iremonger's barely concealed assumptions. After they had "joined forces" following their experience at Versailles (GV, 89), she declared, their relationship was that of "'husband and wife.'" In the beginning Miss Moberly—the older, shyer, and plainer of the two—was the "husband" and Miss Jourdain the "wife":

> The shy woman liked the sociable one; the rugged woman liked the smooth one; the plain unfeminine creature warmed to the little charmer, flowery hats, silken ankles and all. The clumsy Miss Moberly fell for the airs and graces of 'French' Miss Jourdain. (GV, 86)

Very quickly, however, the roles reversed. Jourdain was the more powerful personality, according to Iremonger, and over the years came to dominate her friend more and more, especially after 1915, when Moberly retired and Jourdain succeeded her as principal. Jourdain ruled over Moberly and St. Hugh's in equally peremptory fashion, becoming increasingly subject to paranoid delusions. During the war she became convinced a German spy was hiding somewhere in the college; later, in a fit of megalomaniac pique, she accused several members of the St. Hugh's faculty of plotting against her and Moberly. She dropped dead of a heart attack—literally—during the resulting scandal, and Moberly was left to mourn her for the next thirteen years. Given such pathological goings-on, Iremonger insinuated, it was not hard to see the Trianon ghost story as symptomatic—of the "unhealthy" emotional tie that existed between its perpetrators.[18]

Iremonger's exposé prompted a rebuttal; reviewing the literature surrounding the *Adventure* case in 1976, Joan Evans—who as a child had known both Moberly and Jourdain and was herself a distinguished don of English literature—censured Iremonger for being indiscreet and "less than generous to Miss Jourdain" ("E," 42n). Evans's own explanation of the Trianon mystery was in part a not-so-subtle attempt to defend Moberly and Jourdain against the suggestions of double-dealing and sexual deviance. Evidence had come to light, she wrote, that, while failing to substantiate the time-travel thesis, nonetheless "vindicated" the two women and confirmed "the accuracy of their observations" ("E," 45). What this "evidence" turned out to be was a 1965 biography of Robert de Montesquiou (1855–1921), the wealthy dandy and aesthete on whom Marcel Proust modeled his character of the Baron de Charlus, in which it was alleged that Montesquiou had at one time lived in a house at Versailles and held fancy-dress parties there.[19] Though it was not clear in what year Montesquiou's parties had taken place, or whether he had ever held one near the Trianon, this did not stop Evans from indulging in a fairly elaborate fantasy of her own. Moberly and Jourdain had inadvertently wandered into a "rehearsal" for a kind of homosexual garden fete, she maintained, in which Montesquiou, his young lover Gabriel Yturri (formerly "a salesman in a smart tie shop") and various male friends were "trying out" their costumes. The two men in "greenish coats" were probably Montesquiou and Yturri; the others were probably members of the Montesquiou clique. The "sketching lady" was most likely a transvestite: "the well-bred Miss Moberly," Evans noted, had thought "she showed 'a good deal of leg.'" Evans was not exactly sure who the repulsive "kiosk man" was, but she was confident that Moberly and Jourdain's discomfort in his presence was "a credit to their morals and their breeding" ("E," 46). Neither woman had any previous knowledge of "the more decadent aspects of the aristocratic, plutocratic and artistic classes in 'la belle époque,'" nor of "the London world of Oscar Wilde and Aubrey Beardsley"; hence the disgust they felt toward the kiosk man, Evans concluded, "may well have arisen from the instinctive reaction of a decent woman to a pervert" ("E," 45, 47).

What to make of these theories and countertheories? To the reader confronting them for the first time, the controversies surrounding *An Adventure* are likely to seem as bizarre as *An Adventure* itself. For in their own way the skeptics were as bewitched by the Trianon apparitions as Moberly and Jourdain were. The task of proving Moberly and Jourdain wrong became for many of them a compulsion—a kind of ruling passion. In a revealing aside in *The Ghosts of Versailles*, Iremonger warned of the *"Adventure-manie"* that so often overtook those (like herself) who began delving too deeply into the details of the case. "There have been many enthusiastic amateurs," she wrote,

> who, coming to it often as believers in *An Adventure,* but unable to overlook its weaknesses, have permitted themselves what Nietzsche called the luxury of scepticism, and have submerged themselves in its intricacies almost to the abandonment of a sense of proportion. No doubt many more will do so in the future, for interest in this story can grow first into an absorbing hobby and then into a real *Adventure-manie.* (GV, 298)

The prime symptom of *Adventure*-mania was a passion for invoking "evidence"— often of a strikingly dubious sort.[20] Yet in this Moberly and Jourdain's critics simply followed in the footsteps of the ladies themselves. If Moberly and Jourdain, rummaging through archives, had fallen victims to a kind of hermeneutic *folie*—a befuddling obsession with proving themselves right at any cost—it was precisely this obsession which, like an infection, they succeeded in transmitting to their critics.

At the same time the skeptics were strangely oblivious to what now seems the most intriguing psychological aspect of the case. The peculiar fervor, the near-hysteric nature of the response generated by *An Adventure* can only be explained, it seems to me, by the fact that the book was the work of *two* authors—and two women at that. The "united front" presented by Moberly and Jourdain, their openly collaborative intellectual and emotional relationship, served without question as a subliminal goad to their critics. As female dons, Moberly and Jourdain represented a new and hitherto unprecedented generation of independent educated women; as single women living their lives together (in however enigmatic a dyad) they stood as a threat to conventional sexual arrangements as well. In a society in which masculine prestige was under assault on a number of fronts, the spectacle of two eminent women speaking, uncannily, "as one"—even on so fantastical a theme—must have seemed unusually disturbing to those concerned with upholding patriarchal values. To prove such women wrong—to show them up as victims of the most comical and exquisite folly—was also to validate reactionary sexual and intellectual hierarchies.[21]

And yet it was precisely this "conglomerate" aspect of *An Adventure* that the skeptics seemed unprepared—or unable—to elucidate. There was, if not exactly a logical flaw, what one might call a theoretical absence at the heart of the skeptical point of view. If it were true (as even hostile critics such as Iremonger allowed) that Moberly and Jourdain were women of at least some dignity and intelligence, then why had neither one of them ever once questioned the judgment of the other? If it were possible (barely) to imagine one of them inventing the Marie Antoinette fantasy, how had the other one gotten sucked into it too? How to explain the bizarre mutuality of their conviction, the intense, self-perpetuating, seemingly symbiotic exchange of illusion that must have taken place between them for nearly twenty-five years? While obsessed with what they regarded as Moberly and Jourdain's "folly," what the skeptics failed to explain, paradoxically, was its most curious feature—its spectacularly collaborative nature.

At this point a brief authorial confession is in order. When I first began to think of writing about *An Adventure* I was convinced—perhaps as a result of my own creeping "*Adventure*-mania"—that I could in fact clarify this most bewildering aspect of the Trianon case.[22] What, I asked myself, was the partnership of Moberly and Jourdain—so intimate and yet so bizarre—if not but an instance of the psychological phenomenon know as *folie à deux?* Wasn't a *folie à deux* precisely a kind of "double" or "shared" delusion? But even as I invoked the concept, doubts assailed me: I realized I had only the vaguest notion of how a *folie à deux* actually worked, and no idea at all when the term itself originated. My ignorance led me to a perusal of the psychoanalytic writing on the subject—with problematic results. For if here indeed was a theory of collective folly, it was hardly one to resolve the enigmas of *An Adventure*. On the contrary, far from "explaining" Moberly and Jourdain, the concept of the *folie à deux* merely reinstated the theoretical problem in a new way.

What is a *folie à deux?* The term, which literally means "psychosis of two," was coined in the late nineteenth century by two French psychiatrists, Charles Lasègue and J. Falret, whose 1877 paper, "La Folie à deux (ou folie communiquée)," is still regarded as the classic clinical description of the phenomenon.[23] Clinicians in the early part of the century had been much puzzled by something they usually referred to, for want of a better term, as "infectious insanity," or "insanity by contagion": the apparent transmission of delusional ideas between two persons. Heredity alone, it seemed, was not sufficient to explain such cases: though two family members were sometimes involved, numerous instances of shared insanity had been documented between persons who were unrelated to one another.[24] Lasègue and Falret were the first writers to explain "contagious insanity" as a function of interpersonal dynamics. Of course, as they were quick to point out, under ordinary circumstances insanity was *not* contagious; nurses in asylums, after all, seldom contracted lunatic ideas from their patients. But under pathological conditions, they warned, "delusional conceptions" could in fact spread— exactly like an infectious disease—from one person to another, resulting in the syndrome of *folie à deux*.

A *folie à deux*, wrote Lasègue and Falret, necessarily involved an active and a passive partner.[25] The active partner—that is, the one "carrying," or initiating the delusion—typically suffered from some sort of hereditary insanity. The passive partner, though not insane in a social or legal sense, was usually a person of somewhat "low intelligence, better disposed to passive docility than to independence" ("F," 4). Close proximity over a long period of time was essential for the delusional conception to spread from one partner to the other: the two almost always lived together in relative isolation, away from other friends or family. In isolation, the passive partner gradually yielded to the unremitting "moral pressure" applied by the actively insane partner. Women who lived alone together (often sisters or mothers and daughters) were especially prone to *folie à deux*, though the syndrome was known to affect married couples as well.

Crucial to Lasègue and Falret's analysis was that the delusion itself be of what they called a "moderate" or semi-plausible nature. Grossly lunatic fancies were not easily transmissible, they thought, only those that had a certain probability inherent in them already. "The less preposterous the insanity," they noted, "the easier it becomes communicable." Typically, the delusion related to some past or future event and thus was difficult to disprove on evidentiary grounds:

> If the insane person gives persuasive and lengthy details about these events, it is difficult to prove either to him or to one's self that this event has not taken place. The deluded person has developed his ideas so consistently and logically that no gaps are apparent. His topical memory excludes everything except his morbid ideas. He is never caught at fault, whatever the date of the event he describes, and the more monotonous and circumscribed his persuasive description becomes, the more likely that his listener will be convinced. ("F," 4)

The delusion had also to strike a "sentimental" chord in the passive partner, reinforcing existing hopes or fears. Delusions regarding lost legacies, or persecu-

Figure 11.8. The twins, "Marie and Maria," suffering from *folie à deux,* 1950s. From *Psychiatric Quarterly* 37 (July 1963). Courtesy of the editors.

tion by hidden enemies, were common. Among the case histories related by Lasègue and Falret was one involving a poverty-stricken mother and daughter who moved to Paris under the delusion (initiated by the daughter) that they were about to inherit a huge legacy; another involved an elderly spinster who persuaded her orphaned niece that someone was attempting to poison them. In the case of the twin sisters, "Joséphine" and "Lucille," Joséphine's conviction that police were threatening to "expose" her and her sister for living together resulted in a joint suicide attempt.[26] Admittedly, wrote Lasègue and Falret, the passive partner sometimes resisted, yet this initial resistance only prompted the active partner to modify the delusion so as to make it more plausible to his or her associate. The passive partner gave way by gradual stages, "fighting at first, giving in little by little, and finally identifying himself completely with the conceptions that he has slowly assimilated" ("F," 8). At that point, after countless rehearsals and much discussion of "evidence," the delusion became their "common cause," to be repeated to all in an almost identical fashion." The only therapeutic indication in such cases was to separate the partners, in the hope that at least one of them might recover, especially the passive partner, who would be thereby "cut off from his source of delusions" ("F," 18).

Subsequent studies of *folie à deux* seemed to confirm Lasègue and Falret's clinical observations. Though Freud did not write about the phenomenon of *folie à deux,* several of his protégés, including A. A. Brill, C. P. Oberndorf, and Helene Deutsch, did.[27] Deutsch, in a 1938 article, was the first to connect the syndrome explicitly with homosexuality, especially between women. The paranoid nature of most shared delusions could almost always be attributed, she thought, to strong homosexual bonds between the two partners, and offered two case histories—one involving a mother and daughter, and the other, a pair of sisters—to demonstrate the point.[28] Reviewing the clinical literature on *folie à deux* in 1942, Alexander Gralnick reiterated the connection: not only did most reported cases of *folie à deux* involve female couples, "the impression one gets from reading the cases in the literature is that homosexual drives are often present in a marked degree." "If the Freudian-minded are correct," he wrote, "homosexuality must be a large element in these cases, because persecutory ideas are so prominent."[29]

With a little imagination, much here obviously could be made to apply to Moberly and Jourdain. If we take the Trianon story to be the sign of a *folie à deux,* then the "active" partner, it seems clear, would have had to have been Jourdain: she was the first to introduce the all-important figure of Marie Antoinette into the discussions of the Versailles events; she was the first to make the crucial connection between 10 August 1901 and 10 August 1789; she was the more enthusiastic of the two in the subsequent search for "evidence." Moreover throughout her adult life—at least according to the muckraking Iremonger—she seems to have suffered from increasingly vehement paranoid fantasies.[30] Jourdain's sister, the furniture historian Margaret Jourdain, always referred to the Trianon case as "my sister's folly"; the novelist Ivy Compton-Burnett, Margaret Jourdain's companion for over thirty years, said she could not think of anyone more likely than Eleanor "to delude herself into believing *An Adventure.*"[31]

But much about the Trianon story itself—quite apart from the obsessional manner in which Moberly and Jourdain defended it—also suggests the classic *folie.* If we accept, in however etiolated a form, the rumor that Moberly and Jourdain were lesbians, then the Trianon "delusion," with its incriminating admixture of romantic and paranoid elements, seems almost too good to be true. How else, one might ask, might two repressed female homosexuals express their relationship than through such a story? Whether or not Moberly and Jourdain were aware of the lingering rumors regarding Marie Antoinette's own lesbianism (rumors that persisted well into the early twentieth century), the choice of Marie Antoinette—a sentimental emblem both of female sexuality and unjust persecution—seems inspired.[32] Indeed the whole Trianon "adventure" might be read as a sexual allegory—a kind of Freudian dream quest—symbolizing, through the imagery of the queen and her court, the formation of a female-female erotic bond. The wandering through mysterious wooded glades, the two male guides (would-be suitors?) who give wrong directions, the encounter with, and subsequent flight from, the repulsive-looking man, the revelatory vision of the sketching lady, the final meeting up with the joyful wedding party (celebrating Moberly and

Jourdain's own symbolic marriage?) outside the gynocentric pavilion of the Petit Trianon itself—all suggest a turning away from masculine sexuality toward a world of female-female love and ritual.[33] It is worth noting, perhaps, that the Wertmüller portrait of Marie Antoinette, in which Moberly and Jourdain took such an interest, depicts the queen with her two children—combining the themes of maternal love and erotic triangulation. For Moberly and Jourdain to have triangulated their relationship with one another, so to speak, through the figure of the dead queen does not seem so improbable when one considers other similarly "spiritualizing" triangles between women in the period, such as that between Radclyffe Hall, her lover Lady Una Troubridge, and Hall's deceased ex-lover, "Ladye," Mabel Batten, with whom she and Troubridge communicated regularly through a spirit medium for over twenty years.[34]

And yet how much does the diagnosis of *folie à deux* really tell us? As even its earliest formulators seemed to realize, the concept is something of an ambiguous one. Lasègue and Falret, for example, were clearly troubled by the clinical difficulties involved in identifying the syndrome at all—so deceptively "probable" were the stories often told by their patients. "How often the doctor, even an experienced one," they wrote, "asks himself whether the original fact reported has not really happened rather than being imaginary, and hesitates between an exaggeration and an emotional aberration" ("F," 4). Precisely because *folie à deux* was a form of mental alienation "sitting," as they put it, "between reason and confirmed insanity," the clinician often found himself in the position of the passive partner—on the verge of being persuaded himself of the supposedly "lunatic" idea ("F," 9).

In several telling passages Lasègue and Falret associated the delusions of *folie à deux* with the seductive fantasies of literature. The case histories of *folie à deux*, they wrote, were "intimate tragedies" of a sort "familiar to physicians, unknown to novelists" ("F," 16). (Their own case histories, replete with quasi-novelistic details of life in the less salubrious environs of late nineteenth-century Paris, often recall the novels of Émile Zola.) Couples suffering from shared delusions typically elaborated their tales with "the apparent sincerity with which one relates the events of a romantic novel" ("F," 10). The clinician was put into the role of literary critic: on the lookout for those palpably "imaginative" touches by which the maddened pair revealed their joint alienation. The danger, of course, was that he might fall under the narrative spell himself, transforming the *folie à deux* into a *folie à trois*.

In an attempt to allay the problem (which was at bottom an epistemological one) later clinicians sought to clarify the interpsychic mechanism by which the so-called *folie* spread from one person to another. In her much-cited essay on the subject, Deutsch proposed that *folie à deux* was a pathological form of "identification" in which each partner sought through fantasy to reconstitute a "lost object" from his or her psychic past. The contagion metaphor was somewhat misleading, she thought: in cases of true *folie à deux*, it was not so much that one partner "infected" the other, but that "both already possessed in common, repressed psychic contents which broke out earlier in one and later in the other." "Close living together, apart from others," did not induce the *folie à deux;* it was merely the first expression of those "unconscious bonds" which later brought both parties to similar delusional ideas ("FD," 316).

But at the same time Deutsch's invocation of unconscious forces made the underlying diagnostic problem more glaring. The same process of identification at work in a *folie à deux,* she noted, "can also be found in a psychic state so universally human that its character of 'normality' cannot be denied: 'being in love.'" On a grander scale, at the level of mass psychology, the same process also explained the behavior of "large groups of men, entire nations and generations." It was necessary, she concluded, to

> distinguish here as with individuals between hysterical, libidinally determined mass influences, and schizophrenic ideas held in common; likewise between mass liberations of instincts under the guise of ideals, and paranoid projections, etc. Many things have their place in these *folies en masse* and the approval or disapproval of the surrounding world is often the sole criterion as to whether a particular action is deemed a heroic deed or an act of madness. ("FD," 318)

But how to distinguish them? If the psychic process behind *folie à deux* was identical to that behind supposedly "normal" phenomena—such as falling in love or sharing in some collective social ideal—what made the *folie à deux* pathological? Deutsch's cryptic final sentence gave it away: only the "approval or disapproval of the surrounding world."

Yet if society alone decided which shared beliefs were "normal" and which were not, it was not hard to see how the diagnosis of *folie à deux* might be exploited for social and political ends: to demonize relationships between persons in whom intellectual or emotional solidarity was suspect. It is not perhaps accidental that what might be called the "invention" of *folie à deux* coincided with the rise of a number of emancipation movements in Europe and the United States— notably the women's suffrage movement, the organized labor movement, and the incipient homosexual emancipation movement.[35] How better to discredit new and threatening political associations than by labeling their proponents—in advance—as prone to shared insanity? A number of early writers on *folie à deux* displayed their animating prejudices quite openly. In an essay on *folie à deux* in the *Journal of Mental Science* from 1910, for instance, the psychiatrist Arthur W. Wilcox took as his prime example of "contagious political insanity" the "unlawful and in every way extraordinary conduct of the suffragettes."[36] Later clinicians associated *folie à deux* not only with women and homosexuals—always the primary target groups—but also with other "dangerous" minorities, including the laboring poor, immigrants, and blacks.[37]

To be sure, in many of the cases related in the annals of *folie à deux* one is hard pressed to say what role social or political determinants may have played in the diagnosis, so patently "mad" do the beliefs involved seem to be. To read

Oberndorf's 1934 case history about a husband and wife, Mr. and Mrs. V., who refused to leave their house for two years because both experienced an uncontrollable sensation of "whirling" and "fear of slipping" when they did so, is to feel oneself in the presence of a deep-seated and ultimately obscure mental aberration. (This same couple, wrote Oberndorf, also practiced "an unusual sexual perversion—a compulsion which involved the plunging of Mrs. V. fully dressed into a bath tub of water.")[38] Yet in other cases, such as that of the famous "silent twins" June and Jennifer Gibbons—two black twins who grew up in an immigrant West Indian family in Wales in the 1970s, invented their own private language, wrote novels and stories together, and refused to communicate with adults—one senses that much of their so-called madness was in fact merely an adaptive response to intolerable social alienation and emotional deprivation.[39]

To invoke the concept of the *folie à deux* as a way of discrediting Moberly and Jourdain, therefore, is to involve oneself, at the very least, in rhetorical and epistemological difficulties. To dismiss "les dames d'Oxford" (as Cocteau called them) as crazy is clearly not enough: the challenge, as we have seen, is to explain how the two of them could have been "crazy" in exactly the same way. Yet the classic psychological explanation—that Moberly and Jourdain suffered from some kind of "contagious insanity" or psychosis by association—is fraught with ideological problems. From the start the theory of *folie à deux* reinscribed a host of late nineteenth-century cultural prejudices—that women were more "delusional" than men, that pairs of women were untrustworthy, that women exhibiting "morbid" sexual tendencies (lesbians, in other words) were the least trustworthy of all. Nor have modern-day psychiatrists and clinicians entirely dispensed with these problematical assumptions: most recent studies of *folie à deux* have continued to rely, uncritically, on the antiquated etiological principles established by Lasègue and Falret over a hundred years ago.[40]

Have we thus arrived at a backhanded vindication of the authors of *An Adventure?* After a fashion, perhaps. True, the skeptic will still object, it remains difficult to credit Moberly and Jourdain's most pressing claim—that on 10 August 1901 at the Petit Trianon, they "entered into an act of memory" and encountered Marie Antoinette and her court. The so-called evidence marshalled on behalf of this claim—the business of antique ploughs, footmens' liveries, unusually buckled shoes, pockmarked faces, garden kiosks, and green fichus—will remain for most of us, perhaps, eternally unconvincing: a testament to folly alone.

And yet skepticism too has its pitfalls. Skepticism is liable, as we have seen, to its own kind of folly—that debunking "mania," or compulsion to disprove, so ruefully acknowledged by Iremonger in *The Ghosts of Versailles.* To disbelieve—at least in the case of *An Adventure*—is to risk losing oneself in an alienating welter of evidence and counterevidence. But, more troublingly, skepticism is silent on what one might suppose to be the central issue of the case: how a belief ostensibly as "delusional" as Moberly and Jourdain's should have grown up between the two of them in the first place. Rationalism holds, above all, that delusions are a disease of subjectivity—that they come about, as Deutsch put it, when an individual fails to separate "inner content" from "perception." It is a complicated developmental process," she observes,

> to be able to distinguish inner content from perception. The simplest criterion is: perception is that which others accept as perception. A contact with the surrounding world is indispensable in applying this criterion. A psychotic individual has not only given up the differentiation of the inner world from the world of reality, but he has given up the need for confirmation from the latter by destroying the bridge between himself and other objects. The ego then takes its delusion for reality and professes it as truth. ("FD," 317)

Yet according to such logic, we notice, Moberly and Jourdain were not delusional. Neither one gave up her "contact" with the surrounding world; indeed, precisely in their contact with one another, each found the primordial confirmation that she needed.

Here, then, is the impasse into which skepticism leads: it becomes impossible to distinguish so-called normal collective convictions from pathological ones. If folly is contagious, paradoxically, then it can no longer be folly; for folly is defined by the very fact that it is *not* contagious. Indeed, at the collective level, one might argue, folly ceases to exist: it is transformed into ideology. Were Moberly and Jourdain the victims of *folie à deux* or the inventors of a new romantic ideology? Were they "insane" or were they "in love"? And how to dismiss them, or even to begin to dismiss them, without revealing one's own ideological presumptions and prejudices? As long as skepticism is unable to answer such questions—to make, in short, any coherent distinction between collective dogma and collective hallucination—*An Adventure* will remain what Moberly and Jourdain intended it to be: a rebuke to scoffers and a challenge to the incredulous.

NOTES

Chapter 1

1. Natalie Barney, *Adventures of the Mind*, trans. John Spalding Gatton (New York: New York University Press, 1992), p. 184.

2. See John Bender, "A New History of the Enlightenment," in Leo Damrosch, ed., *The Profession of Eighteenth-Century Literature* (Madison: University of Wisconsin Press, 1992), p. 77.

3. Sigmund Freud, "The 'Uncanny,'" in *The Standard Edition of the Complete Psychological Works of Sigmund Freud,* ed. and trans. James Strachey (London: Hogarth Press, 1955), XVII, p. 249. All further citations are from this edition; parenthetical notations refer to page numbers in the English text.

4. This uncanny "bringing to light" is figured within the story, one might argue, as that blinding illumination cast by the "bright glowing masses" of embers that the Coppelius/Sandman figure, early in the story, snatches out of the fire in Nathanael's father's study and thrusts in the direction of Nathanael's eyes. When Nathanael, who falls into a terrified faint, awakens later, he finds that the world has indeed become dark and indistinct. "I have only to relate to you the most terrible moment of my youth," he tells his friend Lothair, "for you to thoroughly understand that it must not be ascribed to the weakness of my eyesight if all that I see is colourless, but to the fact that a mysterious destiny has hung a dark veil of clouds about my life, which I shall perhaps only break through when I die." See E. T. A. Hoffman, *The Best Tales of Hoffmann,* ed. E. F. Bleiler (New York: Dover, 1966), p. 188.

5. See John Locke, *An Essay Concerning Human Understanding,* ed. A. D. Woozley (London: Collins, 1964), Book I, "Introduction," Sec. 7.

6. On the history of automata, see Richard D. Altick, *The Shows of London* (Cambridge, Mass.: Harvard University Press, 1978), pp. 64–76; and Jean-Claude Beaune, "The Classical Age of Automata: An Impressionistic Survey from the Sixteenth to the Nineteenth Century," in Michel Feher, ed., *Zone: Fragments for a History of the Human Body,* 3:1 (1989), 430–80.

7. Bleiler, "Introduction," *Best Tales of Hoffmann,* pp. xxi–xxii.

8. W. E. H. Lecky, *History of the Rise and Influence of the Spirit of Rationalism in Europe,* rev. ed. (New York: D. Appleton, 1919), I, pp. 27–28.

9. Lecky, *Rise of the Spirit of Rationalism,* I, p. 6.

10. Keith Thomas, *Religion and the Decline of Magic* (New York: Charles Scribner's Sons, 1971).

Chapter 2

1. An account of James Ayscough's career and a picture of one of his barometers may be found in Nicholas Goodison. *English Barometers, 1680–1860* (Woodbridge, Suffolk, 1977), 131.

2. See, for example, the following description in the *Village Voice* (11 December 1984) of the 1984 clerical workers' strike at Yale: "Yale is home to 10,000 students, 2100 professors and 1700 managerial and professional employees—the barometers by which both sides have been gauging their success" (17). A writer in another popular weekly recently referred to *The Phil Donahue Show* as "that unimpeachable barometer of the female psyche"; Jane Hall, "Sex and the Senior Girls: NBC's Golden Girls Are the Toast of TV with Their Mid-Life Miami Spice," *People*, 6 January 1986, 55.

3. See Bert Bolle, *Barometers* (London, 1984), for a concise history of early meteorological instruments. The standard technical works on the subject are W. E. Knowles Middleton, *A History of the Barometer* (Baltimore, 1964); and *A History of the Thermometer and Its Uses in Meteorology* (Baltimore, 1966). See also Goodison, *English Barometers*, chap. 1.

4. Goodison, *English Barometers*, 36–37.

5. Bolle, *Barometers*, 15.

6. Edward Saul, *An Historical and Philosophical Account of the Barometer, or Weather-Glass* (London, 1725), 11.

7. An illustration of a barometer decorated in this fashion appears on the first page of John Patrick's *A New Improvement of the Quicksilver Barometer* (London, c. 1700).

8. In the Middle Ages mercury was held to be one of the five principles out of which all material substances were composed. The element took its name from the Roman god Mercury, patron of traveling, roads, thieves, eloquence, and feats of skill, who was also the messenger of the gods and conductor of departed souls to the underworld. In medieval alchemy, mercury was an essential ingredient in the formation of the Exalted Matter or Philosopher's Stone, and it was linked with the mysterious figure of the androgyne. Over the centuries its medical and quasi-scientific uses have been numerous. In the eighteenth century mercurial powder was a popular purgative, as well as a treatment for venereal disease. On its various therapeutic and technological uses, see the entry in *Chambers' Cyclopaedia* (rev. ed., London, 1778). Generally speaking, quicksilver has always had associations with movement, change, and transformation. It is worth noting that in the sixteenth and seventeenth centuries the world *mercury* not only referred to quicksilver but was also used to signify a signpost or milestone ("mercurial stone"). In the eighteenth century, *mercury* became a standard title for a newspaper or journal, a usage that survives today. Through a particularly interesting metonymic transfer, the word could also refer to a female hawker of newspapers and pamphlets. See the *OED* and Margaret Hunt, "Hawkers, Bawlers, and Mercuries: Women and the London Press in the Early Enlightenment," in *Women and the Enlightenment*, ed. Phyllis Mack (New York, 1984), 41–68.

9. In the seventeenth century those born under the sign of Mercury were felt to have especially volatile, fantastical, and poetic temperaments. The "mercurialist," with his seemingly feminized nature, was often explicitly contrasted with the "martial" type, as in Thomas Urquhart's description in *The Jewel* (1634), "He speaks too well to be valiant; he is certainly more Mercurial than military"; *The Jewel* (Edinburgh, 1983), 130. Compare also Robert Burton's observation in *The Anatomy of Melancholy* (1628): "Mercurialists are solitary, much in contemplation, subtle, poets, philosophers, and musing most part about such matters" (London, 1932), 398. In *The Tatler*, no. 30 (18 June 1709), Richard Steele contrasted "Jack Careless," a "mercurial gay-humour'd Man," with the sober military man, "Colonel Constant."

10. In the *Philosophical Transactions* of the Royal Society for 1694 there is a reference to "a tender Weather-Glasse or Thermometer"; 18:205. Describing the thermograph constructed by Robert Hooke and Christopher Wren in 1664, Thomas Birch, author of *The History of the Royal Society of London*, 4 vols. (London, 1756), wrote that the society

subsequently tried to determine "whether this instrument were sensible and nice enough" (2:1–2). The author of the article on barometers in *Chambers' Cyclopaedia* spoke of the design of the "nicest barometer" and observed that variations in the barometric fluid were "more sensible" in northern regions than in the south. He added that changes in the height of the mercury might sometimes be attributed to a dispersal of the quicksilver particles known as "fretting."

11. Gustavus Parker, *An Account of a Portable Barometer, with Reasons and Rules for the Use of It* (London, 1710).

12. See Leo Spitzer, "Milieu and Ambiance: An Essay in Historical Semantics," *Philosophy and Phenomenological Research 3* (1942): 1–42, 169–218; reprinted in Spitzer, *Essays in Historical Semantics* (New York, 1947), 179–316; and Arden Reed, *Romantic Weather: The Climates of Coleridge and Baudelaire* (Hanover, N. H., 1983).

13. John Smith, *Horological Disquisitions* (London, 1694), 77.

14. George Adams, *A Short Dissertation on the Barometer, Thermometer, and Other Meteorological Instruments* (London, 1790), 48–49.

15. Sir John Suckling, *Brennoralt*, 2.3; in *The Works of John Suckling*, ed. L. A. Beaurline (Oxford, 1971), 203.

16. See Middleton, *History of the Thermometer*, 43–44.

17. John Dryden, *The Conquest of Granada*, 4.2; in *John Dryden: Three Plays*, ed. George Saintsbury (New York, 1957), 54.

18. Susannah Centlivre, *The Gamester* (London, 1723), 1.1.

19. Jonathan Swift, *A Discourse Concerning the Mechanical Operation of the Spirit*, in *The Prose Works of Jonathan Swift*, ed. Herbert Davis, 14 vols. (Oxford, 1939), 1:188.

20. Citations from *The Spectator* are from the four-volume Everyman edition, ed. G. Gregory Smith (London, 1945).

21. See the illustrations in Martin Friedman, *Hockney Paints the Stage* (New York, 1984), 103. In his commentaries on the *Enthusiasm* and *Credulity* plates in *Hogarth's Graphic Works*, 2 vols. (New Haven, 1965), 2:244-49, Ronald Paulson refers to Hogarth's instruments as thermometers. It is not clear, however, whether they are in fact thermometers or barometers—or both. The instrument in *Enthusiasm Delineated* resembles the common eighteenth-century thermometer/barometer combination, like the one depicted in Patrick's advertisement (Fig. 2.1), with the thermometer on the bottom and the barometer on the top. This would mean that the lower markings, "Prophecy" through "Revelation," and the upper ones, "Wrathful" to "Joyful," are, contrary to Paulson's implication, two separate scales—monitoring, perhaps, different aspects of the congregation's condition, or different individuals in the crowd. A major technical confusion is introduced, however, by the fact that the lower scale, which certainly measures heat, also measures changing "spirits," and has markings such as "settled grief"—in an obvious parody of contemporary discursive barometrical markings such as "settled fair." In *Credulity, Superstition, and Fanaticism*, the upper markings have been done away with, and the result is a simpler instrument—though one that is still, as Hogarth probably intended, highly ambiguous in nature.

22. Horace Walpole to Horace Mann, 24 June 1742, in *The Correspondence of Horace Walpole*, ed. W. S. Lewis, et al., 39 vols. (New Haven, 1937–79), 17:467.

23. John Arbuthnot, *The History of John Bull*, ed. Herman Teerink (Amsterdam, 1925), 140. Maynard Mack suggests that Pope may have had his friend Arbuthnot's description in mind when, during an illness, he wrote to John Caryll (21 December 1712) that his spirits "like those of a thermometer mount and fall thro' this delicate contexture just as the temper of air is more benign or inclement"; see Maynard Mack, *Alexander Pope: A Life* (New York, 1985), 848.

24. David Hume, *Political Discourses* (London, 1752), part 4, p. 73.

25. *The Observer* no. 97 described a "Thermometer of Merit" that measured literary inspiration by gauging "every author's altitude to a minute" and could be used for monitoring imaginative excesses. See *British Essayists,* ed. Alexander Chalmers, 38 vols. (London, 1823), 33:321. Also worth noting is Samuel Johnson's satiric "treatise of barometrical pneumatology" in *The Rambler* no. 117 (30 April 1751). Here, a certain "Hypertatus" analyzed the effect of "the various compressions of the ambient element" at differing altitudes on "the operations of the genius" and deduced that it was better to write in a garret than a cellar for one thus escaped "the pressure of a gross atmosphere"; *British Essayists,* 17:332–33.

26. Samuel Richardson, *Clarissa; or, The History of a Young Lady,* 4 vols. (London, 1932), 4:478.

27. Denis Diderot, *Sur les femmes* (Paris, 1919), 24; my translation.

28. Mary Wollstonecraft, *A Vindication of the Rights of Woman,* ed. Miriam Kramnick (New York, 1975), 180.

29. Spitzer, "Milieu and Ambiance," 260 and 294.

30. George Sinclair, *Observations Touching the Principles of Natural Motions; and Especially Touching Rarefaction and Condensation* (London, 1677), 51–52.

31. Early fever thermometers were placed in the hand, mouth, or armpit. It should be pointed out, however, that even though a clinical thermometer had been invented in the seventeenth century by Sanctorius, thermometers were rarely used for medical purposes until the end of the eighteenth century. James Currie (1756–1805) was one of the first to monitor the fevers of typhoid patients using thermometry. It was not until the appearance of Carl Wunderlich's classic *Das Verhalten der Eigenwarme in Krankheiten* (1868), published in English in 1871 under the title *On the Temperature in Diseases: A Manual of Medical Thermometry,* that taking temperatures became commonly established medical practice. See Charles Singer and E. Ashworth Underwood, *A Short History of Medicine* (Oxford, 1962), 116-17, 171, and 624–27; and Hugh A. McGuigan, "Medical Thermometry," *Annals of Medical History* 9 (1937):148–54.

32. On the famous apparitions of the Cock Lane Ghost and Tedworth Drummer, see Paulson's commentary in *Hogarth's Graphic Works,* 2:248. Eric Partridge records the use of *drumstick* as a bawdy term for the penis in *A Dictionary of Historical Slang* (New York, 1972), 282.

33. See Terry Eagleton's discussion of the "feminization of discourse" in *The Rape of Clarissa* (Minneapolis, 1982), 13ff. Of related interest is Anne Douglas, *The Feminization of American Culture* (New York, 1977), which documents similar changes in American sexual roles in the nineteenth century. On the complex feminine etiology of sensibility in the eighteenth century, see, among others, George S. Rousseau, "Nerves, Spirits and Fibres: Toward the Origins of Sensibility," in R. F. Brissenden and J. C. Eade, eds., *Studies in the Eighteenth Century,* vol. 3, Proceedings of the David Nichol Smith Conference (Canberra, Australia, 1976), 137–57; Janet Todd, *Sensibility: An Introduction* (London: Methuen, 1986); John Mullan, *Sentiment and Sociability: The Language of Feeling in The Eighteenth Century* (Oxford: Clarendon Press, 1988); G. J. Barker-Benfield, *The Culture of Sensibility: Sex and Society in Eighteenth-Century Britain* (Chicago: University of Chicago Press, 1992); and Ann Jessie Van Sant, *Eighteenth-Century Sensibility and the Novel* (New York: Cambridge University Press, 1993).

34. George Cheyne's influential work *The English Malady; or, A Treatise of Nervous Diseases of All Kinds* (1733) helped to popularize the new sensitive masculine subject. See Mullan, *Sentiment and Sociability,* on the rise of the spleen and other "masculine" hysterical illnesses in the eighteenth century.

35. *British Essayists,* 27:112–13.

36. See Mullan, *Sentiment and Sociability,* 205–6. Of special interest in this regard is Casanova's strange account of his brief religious conversion while under a mercury cure for a venereal infection: "I sincerely thanked God for having made use of Mercury to lead my mind, until then wrapped in darkness, to the light of truth. There is no doubt that this change in my method of reasoning proceeded from the mercury." He describes how he fell under the influence of a homosexual religious fanatic and recounts the long, pious tale the man told him in order to "put the finishing touch to his seduction of me." Here, through a complex psychosomatic association, Casanova connects the ingestion of mercury with his religious mania, the "weakening" of his mind, and his feminization at the hands of the dogmatist: "The mercury must have made a hollow in the region of my brain, in which enthusiasm had taken its seat." See Giacomo Casanova de Seingault, *History of My Life,* trans. Willard R. Trask, 12 vols. (New York, 1967), 3:82–85.

37. Jean-Jacques Rousseau, *Reveries of a Solitary Walker,* trans. Peter France (Harmondsworth, 1979), 33.

38. John Keats to John Taylor, 30 January 1818; see *The Complete Poetry and Selected Prose of John Keats,* ed. Harold E. Briggs (New York, 1951), 435.

39. Leigh Hunt, "A Rainy Day," in *Essays and Sketches,* ed. R. Brimley Johnson (London, n.d.), 348–49.

40. Sir Walter Scott, *The Abbot,* in *Waverley Novels,* 12 vols. (Edinburgh, 1844), 5:418.

41. Samuel Taylor Coleridge, *Biographia Literaria,* in *Selected Poetry and Prose,* ed. Donald A. Stauffer (New York, 1951), p. 116. Coleridge occasionally reverted to the more traditional *femme-machine,* as in his description of Dorothy Wordsworth from 1797: "But her manners are simple, ardent, impressive. In every motion her most innocent soul beams out so brightly, that who saw would say 'Guilt was a thing impossible in her.' Her information various. Her eye watchful in minutest observation of nature; and her taste a perfect electrometer. It bends, protrudes, and draws in, at subtlest beauties and most recondite faults"; cited by Helen Darbishire in her introduction to *The Journals of Dorothy Wordsworth,* 2nd ed. (London, 1971), x.

42. Sigmund Freud, "The 'Uncanny'" (1919), in *The Standard Edition of the Complete Psychological Works,* ed. and trans. James Strachey, 24 vols. (London, 1955), 17:218–52.

43. Freud's attribution of Nathanael's inward debilitation to the effects of the castration complex encourages the female identification. In one psychoanalytic reading, Nathanael's purchase of a perspective glass instead of the phallic weatherglass might be seen as an abdication from adult male sexual identity in favor of the passive "feminine" voyeurism of an earlier stage.

44. Charles Baudelaire, "Du vin et du hachisch, comparés comme moyens de multiplication de l'individualité," in *Les Paradis artificiels* (1851); my translation. See *Oeuvres complètes,* ed. Claude Pichois (Paris, 1975), 378.

45. John Coakley Lettsom (1744–1815), a noted Quaker physician and philanthropist, was the author of "On the Effects of Hard Drinking" (1791) and *Hints Designed to Promote Beneficence, Temperance, and Medical Science* (1801). His "moral and physical thermometer" is reproduced in *The Times Literary Supplement,* 2 November 1984.

46. I take issue here obviously with Roland Barthes's famous description of "le baromètre de Flaubert" as the classic case of "meaningless" detail in realistic writing. In "L'Effet de réal," in *Littérature et réalité* (Paris, 1982), 81–90, Barthes analyzes the barometer in "Un Coeur simple." The instrument in question stands next to some boxes on the piano in the Aubain drawing room. The piano itself, he observes, can be read as a symbol of its owners' bourgeois standing, and the miscellaneous boxes as "un signe de

désordre," but the barometer does not in any way participate in what he calls "l'ordre du *notable*." Its only purpose, he concludes, is to confer upon Flaubert's narrative the "reality effect" that is its hallmark. While Barthes's general account of realistic effects undoubtedly holds, his choice of illustrative object seems here—for so accomplished a Flaubertian— unusually unhappy.

47. Gustave Flaubert, *Madame Bovary,* trans. Mildred Marmur (New York, 1964), 157, 183.

48. Gustave Flaubert, *Bouvard and Pécuchet,* trans. A. J. Krailsheimer (New York, 1976), 32, 75.

49. Sigmund Freud, *Dora: An Analysis of a Case of Hysteria,* ed. Philip Rieff (New York, 1963), 72. One of Freud's modern followers, the neurologist Oliver Sacks, has offered a further refinement of the metaphor. "To pretend that the brain is a sort of barometer," he writes, "is to make a reduction of its real complexity":

> Jevons used to compare economic situations to weather, and we must use the same image here: the brain-weather or ontological weather [of Parkinsonian patients] becomes singularly complex, full of inordinate sensitivities and sudden changes, no longer susceptible to an item-by-item analysis, but requiring to be seen as a whole, as a *map.*

See *Awakenings* (rev. ed., New York, 1983), 227–28.

50. In 1886 Freud gave his controversial paper "On Male Hysteria," in which he corroborated Charcot's finding that hysterical symptoms might appear in men as well as women. Elsewhere he observed that "the borderline between the nervous, normal, and abnormal states is indistinct, and . . . we are all slightly nervous." See *The Psychopathology of Everyday Life* (New York, n. d.), 159. Freud's point was to demystify hysterical and neurotic symptoms, but in so doing he also confirmed their universal nature.

51. Virginia Woolf, *To the Lighthouse* (New York, 1927), 50.

52. Adrienne Rich, *Twenty-One Love Poems,* in *The Dream of a Common Language* (New York, 1978), 31. In another recent poem Peter Redgrove evokes semimystical states of altered consciousness through a complex play on the "spirits" in the (weather-)glass in an English pub:

> And the clouds, the air-fronts cresting,
> Heavy waves that grind your neck down
> To pray your nose into your glass, and the spirits
> And the barometers drop, the glass is falling,
> So the same again, please.

"To the Habitués," *The Times Literary Supplement,* 23 November 1984; rpt. in *The Mudlark Poems & Grand Buveur* (London, 1986), 41–42.

53. I borrow the title of Fernand Braudel's *The Structures of Everyday Life: The Limits of the Possible,* trans. Sian Reynolds, vol. 1 of *Civilization and Capitalism* (New York, 1981). Compare Marx's observation in *The German Ideology:* "The production of ideas, of conceptions, of consciousness, is at first directly interwoven with the material activity and the material intercourse of men, the language of real life"; in *The Marx-Engels Reader,* ed. Robert C. Tucker (New York, 1978), 154.

54. Patrick, *Quicksilver Barometer,* 1.

55. See, for example, two books on the subject that explicitly invoke the dynamic model: Roberto Mangabeira Unger, *Passion: An Essay on Personality* (London, 1984); and Richard Wollheim, *The Thread of Life* (Cambridge, 1984). The theme of modern psychic mutability also informs Karl Miller's *Doubles: Studies in Literary History* (London, 1985).

Chapter 3

1. Page references are to the Oxford edition of *Roxana*, Jane Jack, ed. (London: Oxford University Press, 1974).

2. Introduction, *Colonel Jack*, ed. Samuel H. Monk (London: Oxford University Press, 1965), p. xvii.

3. See Maximillian E. Novak, "Crime and Punishment in Defoe's *Roxana*," *JEGP*, 65 (1966), 445–65, and G. E. Starr, *Defoe and Spiritual Autobiography* (Princeton, N.J.: Princeton University Press, 1973), pp. 163–83.

4. John J. Richetti, *Defoe's Narratives: Situations and Structures* (Oxford: Clarendon Press, 1973), pp. 192–232.

5. In "Daniel Defoe and the Anxieties of Autobiography," *Genre* 6 (1973), 76–97, Leo Braudy suggests that Defoe's use of the double is his way of emphasizing "the inner complexity of human character in opposition to any unitary view, which believes evil, for example, to come from the outside" (92). Braudy's insights—likewise those of Everett Zimmerman in *Defoe and the Novel* (Berkeley: University of California Press, 1973), who also concentrates on the problematic nature of personal identity in Defoe's fictions—suggest an interesting general backdrop for the particular psychological reading I am advancing for *Roxana*. For an aggressively antipsychological interpretation of Defoe's novel, see Bram Dijkstra, *Defoe and Economics: The Fortunes of 'Roxana' in the History of Interpretation* (London: Macmillan, 1987). Dijkstra, mistakenly assuming me to be a man, accuses me of portraying Roxana—in the present essay—as a "mentally diseased incompetent" in order to allay what he imagines to be my fear of feminism and powerful women.

6. Northrop Frye, *Anatomy of Criticism* (Princeton: Princeton University Press, 1957), p. 365.

7. See Homer O. Brown, "The Displaced Self in the Novels of Daniel Defoe," *ELH*, 38 (1971), 562–90, for a different examination of Defoe's "dialectic between self and other" in *Roxana*. Brown suggests that Roxana, Amy and Susan form a significant pattern (581–82), yet does not particularize this pattern in terms of maternal relationships. His final remarks stress the indeterminacy of the fiction: "The book ends in the uncertainty of the unspeakable. It is either the most resolved of all the dialectical struggles between self and other in Defoe's fiction or the most unresolvable" (582).

8. Michael Shinagel, "The Maternal Paradox in *Moll Flanders*: Craft and Character," rpt. in *Moll Flanders* (Norton Critical Edition), ed. Edward Kelly (New York: W. W. Norton & Co., Inc., 1973), pp. 404–14.

9. Sigmund Freud, *Three Contributions to the Theory of Sex*, in *The Basic Writings of Sigmund Freud*, ed. A. A. Brill (New York: Random House, Inc., 1938), p. 582.

10. For recent biographical speculation on Defoe's complex psychological investment in acts of "narrative transvestism," see Paula R. Backscheider, *Daniel Defoe: His Life* (Baltimore: Johns Hopkins University Press, 1989) and Madeleine Kahn, *Narrative Transvestism: Rhetoric and Gender in the Eighteenth-Century English Novel* (Ithaca, N. Y.: Cornell University Press, 1991).

Chapter 4

1. Samuel Richardson, *Clarissa, or the History of a Young Lady*. All references are to the Everyman edition (New York: Dutton, 1979), 4 vols. For the sake of space, I have omitted the volume number in subsequent references; all quotations are from volume 3.

2. Lovelace's dream—at least not this dream—has received little critical attention.

(His *other* dream, later, in volume 4, of Clarissa ascending, like a baroque vision, into a cloud [Letter lvi], has by contrast attracted considerable notice. See, for example, Margaret Doody's commentary in *A Natural Passion: A Study of the Novels of Samuel Richardson* [Oxford: Clarendon Press, 1974], pp. 234–39.) Mark Kinkead-Weekes mentions the Mother H. dream briefly in *Samuel Richardson: Dramatic Novelist* (Ithaca: Cornell University Press, 1973), but only as a specimen of Lovelace's desire for "intrigue" and inability to "live in the real world" (p. 249). In "Underplotting, Overplotting, and Cor-respondence in *Clarissa*," (*Modern Language Studies*, 11 [Fall 1981], 61–71), Melinda Rabb quotes Lovelace's complaint after the failure of the dream-plot ("I almost hate the words *plot, contrivance, scheme*" [III, 298]), but is concerned with the general existential consequences of Lovelace's obsession with "overplotting" and does not discuss the dream itself. And in *The Rape of Clarissa* (Minneapolis: University of Minnesota Press, 1982) Terry Eagleton contents himself with a short aside on the dream's revelation of Lovelace's "polymorphous perversity" and "infantile sadism." While such comments on Lovelacean psychology are clearly apt, it has been my purpose here to show that one may treat his unusual dream as a textual as well as psychologistic allegory. At least as much as it suggests the ambivalent structure of Lovelacean fantasy, the dream also stands as an emblem of that text in which it appears—as a figure for the peculiarly ambivalent structure of *Clarissa* itself.

3. The dream, one might note, provides little in the way of reassuring narrative closure itself. Its ludicrous domestic coda, and the odd business of the children's incestuous marriage, suggest a future governed by endless perverse couplings, Lovelacean delinquency across the generations. For a discussion of his propensity, in particular, for cross-dressing and sexual disguise, see Madeleine Kahn, *Narrative Transvestism: Rhetoric and Gender in the Eighteenth-Century English Novel* (Ithaca: Cornell University Press, 1991), pp. 145–46.

4. I comment on the Lovelacean manipulation of conventional eighteenth-century iconographic codes elsewhere, in *Clarissa's Ciphers: Meaning and Disruption in Richardson's 'Clarissa'* (Ithaca: Cornell University Press, 1982), ch. 5.

5. Commentators who see in *Clarissa* an unambiguously symmetrical plot structure make much, obviously, of the apparent role exchange taking place here between Clarissa and Lovelace. See, for example, Frederick Hilles's "The Plan of *Clarissa*," in *Samuel Richardson: A Collection of Critical Essays*, ed. John Carroll (Englewood Cliffs, N. J.: Prentice Hall, 1969), pp. 80–91, or Elizabeth Napier's "Tremble and Reform: The Inversion of Power in Richardson's *Clarissa*," *ELH*, 42 (1975), 214–23. Melinda Rabb figures the exchange—part of what she sees as a larger thematicization of "dualism" in the fiction—specifically in terms of plot-making ability: in early letters, Clarissa is "inept at counterplotting," but later learns to manipulate Lovelace in many of the same ways he has previously manipulated her (p. 64). Such views have in turn been challenged by revisionist readings: in *Reading Clarissa: The Struggles of Interpretation* (New Haven: Yale University Press, 1979), William B. Warner, for example, maintains that Clarissa remains a dominating (and domineering) textual presence from start to finish. Her discourse itself, he suggests, constitutes an ongoing "powerful rhetorical system" whose effects are felt by everyone—including *Clarissa's* modern critics, who have unwittingly reproduced in their interpretations of the fiction Clarissa's own unchanging and (in Warner's view) oppressive ideological prescriptions.

6. Compare, for instance, Richardson's comments to Lady Bradshaigh, who had demanded that Clarissa be allowed to marry Lovelace at the conclusion of the fiction: "I intend another Sort of Happiness (founded on the Xn. System) for my Heroine . . . And to rescue her from a Rake, and give a Triumph to her, over not only him but over all her Oppressors, and the World beside, in a triumphant Death (as Death must have been her

Lot, had she been ever so prosperous) I thought as noble a View, as it was new" (cited in T. C. Duncan Eaves and Ben D. Kimpel, *Samuel Richardson: A Biography* [London: Oxford University Press, 1971], pp. 217–18). In *A Natural Passion* Margaret Doody suggests that Richardson's vision of Clarissa's "holy dying" owes much to eighteenth-century devotional manuals and contemporary depictions of the ideally meditative Christian death. See Doody, chapter 7, "Holy and Unholy Dying: The Deathbed Theme in *Clarissa*."

7. In *"Clarissa's* Debt to the Period" (presented at the Northeast American Society for Eighteenth-Century Studies, October 1981), Morris Golden suggests that several actual cases—reported in newspapers of the 1740s—in which young women were imprisoned and brutalized by violent men may have been in Richardson's mind during the composition of *Clarissa*. Interestingly, each of the contemporary cases Professor Golden cites ended with the woman's murder by her persecutor. *Old England* for 27 September 1746 reported, for example, that a woman kidnapped the week before and imprisoned in a lodging-house by a man claiming (according to witnesses) to be her husband had subsequently been found drowned in the Serpentine. She was "quite naked," the account somberly concluded; "her arm was broke, her wrists were tied together, and her ancles were also tied."

8. For another account of Clarissa's victimization by literary "plot" itself, see Nancy K. Miller's suggestive discussion of *Clarissa* in *The Heroine's Text: Readings in the French and English Novel 1722–1782* (New York: Columbia University Press, 1980).

9. The hermeneutic indeterminacy of Richardson's text—the way the fiction, by its very form, generates contradictory, seemingly mutually exclusive interpretations—has emerged as an important theme in Richardson criticism. See, for example, Leo Braudy's "Penetration and Impenetrability in *Clarissa*,," in *New Approaches to Eighteenth-Century Literature* (Selected Papers from the English Institute), ed. Phillip Harth (New York: Columbia University Press, 1974), Warner's *Reading Clarissa* and my study, *Clarissa's Ciphers*, for diverse accounts of the complex hermeneutic problem embodied by the fiction.

Chapter 5

1. Copies of the original pamphlet (which are scarce) exist in the British Museum, Huntington Library, and Bristol Public Library. The text here referred to is that of the English Reprints Series edition, *The Female Husband and Other Writings*, ed. Claude E. Jones (Liverpool: Liverpool University Press, 1960). For early bibliographic references to the work see Wilbur L. Cross, *The History of Henry Fielding*, 3 vols. (New Haven: Yale University Press, 1918) and F. Homes Dudden, *Henry Fielding: His Life, Works, and Times*, 2 vols. (London: Oxford University Press, 1952). Pat Rogers devotes a witty paragraph to the work in *Henry Fielding: A Biography* (London: Paul Elek, 1979), but by far the most extensive account is Sheridan Baker's "Henry Fielding's *The Female Husband:* Fact and Fiction," *PMLA*, 74 (1959), 213–224. I am indebted here to Baker's description of the factual elements of *The Female Husband*, and his reconstruction of Fielding's knowledge of the actual Hamilton case.

2. At the time I wrote this essay—over ten years ago—little scholarly commentary existed on *The Female Husband* or the related subjects of female transvestism and homosexuality. Vern L. Bullough had given a brief account of Fielding's pamphlet in *Sexual Variance in Society and History* (Chicago: University of Chicago Press, 1976)—as had Janet Todd in *Women's Friendship in Literature* (New York: Columbia University Press, 1980) and Lillian Faderman in her groundbreaking book on lesbianism, *Surpassing the Love of Men: Romantic*

Friendship and Love Between Women from the Renaissance to the Present (New York: William Morrow, 1981)—but Sheridan Baker's essay remained the only detailed discussion in print. Nor was there much in the way of related historical or theoretical speculation: Michel Foucault's introduction to the memoir of the nineteenth-century hermaphrodite Herculine Barbin (New York: Pantheon, 1980) offered a useful general approach for thinking about sexual identity, but was not historically oriented in the usual sense. Since 1981, however, a host of studies have added dramatically to our understanding both of Fielding's own work and its historical context. Martin Battestin's superb new biography, *Henry Fielding* (London: Routledge, 1989), fills out in intricate detail the personal and publishing history behind *The Female Husband*. In *Natural Masques: Gender and Identity in Fielding's Plays and Novels* (Stanford: Stanford University Press, 1995), Jill Campbell shows the centrality of the travesty theme in Fielding's artistic imagination and relates *The Female Husband* to his other writings of the 1730s and 1740s. Historians of sexuality have in turn shed new light on eighteenth-century female cross-dressers: see, for example, Lynn Friedli, "'Passing Women'—A Study of Gender Boundaries in the Eighteenth Century," in G. S. Rousseau and Roy Porter, eds., *Sexual Underworlds of the Enlightenment* (Manchester: Manchester University Press, 1987): 234–60; Rudolf M. Dekker and Lotte C. Van de Poll, *The Tradition of Female Transvestism in Early Modern Europe* (New York: St. Martin's Press, 1989); Julie Wheelwright, *Amazons and Military Maids* (London: Pandora, 1989); Randolph S. Trumbach, "London's Sapphists: From Three Sexes to Four Genders in the Making of Modern Culture," in Julia Epstein and Kristina Straub, eds., *Body Guards: The Cultural Politics of Gender Ambiguity* (New York and London: Routledge, 1991): 112–41; Marjorie Garber, *Vested Interests: Cross-Dressing and Cultural Anxiety* (New York: Routledge, 1992); and Emma Donoghue, *Passions Between Women: British Lesbian Culture 1668–1801* (London: Scarlet Press, 1993). Two other recent works are of related interest: Thomas Laqueur's *Making Sex: Body and Gender from the Greeks to Freud* (Cambridge: Harvard University Press, 1990), and my own literary-historical study of female homosexuality, *The Apparitional Lesbian: Female Homosexuality and Modern Culture* (New York: Columbia University Press, 1993).

3. Susan Gubar, "The Female Monster in Augustan Satire," *Signs: A Journal of Women in Culture and Society*, 3 (1977), 380–94.

4. Baker, pp. 219–20.

5. Baker, p. 222.

6. Baker, p. 221.

7. John Ashton, *Eighteenth-Century Waifs* (London: Hurst and Blackett, 1887), pp. 177–202. In *Amazons and Military Maids* Julie Wheelwright discusses the lives and careers of a number of eighteenth-century "Amazons," including Mrs. Christian Davies (commemorated by Defoe), and Deborah Sampson, the Revolutionary War heroine. One might note also the striking case of "James Barry," first Colonial Medical Officer in the British Navy and pioneer in the field of naval health improvements, who was discovered to be a woman after her death, when fellow naval officers performed an autopsy on her body. See June Rose, *The Perfect Gentleman: The Remarkable Life of James Miranda Barry* (London: B. Hutchinson, 1977). On the numerous male impersonators in eighteenth-century ballad tradition, see Dianne Dugaw, *Warrior Women and Popular Balladry 1650–1850* (Cambridge: Cambridge University Press, 1989).

8. John Ashton, *Chapbooks of the Eighteenth Century* (London, 1882; rpt. with introduction by Victor Neuburg, New York: Augustus M. Kelley, 1970), p. 449. The apparent success of female cross-dressing in earlier centuries (and the recorded cases suggest that many more disguised women must have passed undetected) strains modern

credulity at times. One should remember, however, that, historically speaking, gender may have revealed itself once through less subtle outward signs than it does now, in the age of unisex fashion. Writing in *Seeing Through Clothes* of historical changes in the interpretation of gender "through" clothing, Anne Hollander suggests—provocatively—that changes in perception itself may be responsible:

> In simpler days, as literature suggests, disguise was rather easy. When sex, age, and rank were all instantly conveyed through clothes, a fine lady could presumably dress as a barge captain and be taken for a barge captain. One important reason for this was that eyes were as yet untrained by photography, cinematography, and the revelations offered by electric light. It was evidently less easy to recognize distinctions of texture and line among details of gesture and posture. Perhaps people simply saw less clearly before cinematic close-ups and snapshot photography taught everyone to observe each other with sharper eyes than centuries of drawing, painting, and engraving had done.

This may be something of an oversimplification, but it does raise the possibility that, in perpetrating her sham, Mary Hamilton took advantage of perceptual conventions of the period, at the same time that she acted out, paradigmatically, certain underground tendencies in the collective life of eighteenth-century women. See Hollander, *Seeing Through Clothes* (New York: Viking, 1978), p. 346.

9. In addition to the works mentioned in note 2, see Randolph Trumbach's article, "London's Sodomites: Homosexual Behavior and Western Culture in the Eighteenth Century," *Journal of Social History*, 11 (1977), 1–33; Alan Bray, *Homosexuality in Renaissance England* (London: Gay Men's Press, 1982); and Rictor Norton, *Mother Clap's Molly House: The Gay Subculture in England 1700–1830* (London: Gay Men's Press, 1992). For a larger overview of the history of homosexuality in Western culture see John Boswell, *Christianity, Social Tolerance, and Homosexuality* (Chicago: University of Chicago Press, 1980); and Martin Duberman, Martha Vicinus, and George Chauncey, Jr., eds., *Hidden From History: Reclaiming the Gay and Lesbian Past* (New York: Meridian, 1990). On the history of lesbianism in particular, see also Louis Crompton, "The Myth of Lesbian Impunity: Capital Laws from 1270–1791," in Salvatore J. Licata and Robert P. Petersen, eds., *Historical Perspectives on Homosexuality* (New York: Haworth Press, 1981), pp. 11–25; Theo Van der Meer, "Tribades on Trial: Female Sex Offenders in Late Eighteenth-Century Amsterdam," *Journal of the History of Sexuality* 1 (January 1991), 424–44; and Martha Vicinus, "'They Wonder to Which Sex I Belong': The Historical Roots of the Modern Lesbian Identity," *Feminist Studies* 8 (Fall 1992), 602–28.

10. The epigraph reads, "Quoque id mirum magis esset in illo; / Femina natus erat. Monstri novitate moventur, / Quisquis adest: narretque rogant" ("'He . . . was famous / For all he did, but the strange thing about it / Is, he was born a woman.' All who listened / Clamored to hear the story" [Rolfe Humphries translation]). Ovid's hapless transsexual Caenis elicits a certain feminist sympathy: after Neptune rapes her on the seashore, she asks him to change her into a man, so that "I may never again be able to suffer so." Ovid, *Metamorphoses*, Book 12, ll. 168–209. Fielding, obviously, disregards the possibility that Mary Hamilton, like Caenis, may have transformed herself in order to escape the pressure of unwelcome male advances.

11. Fielding, Preface to *Joseph Andrews*, ed. Martin C. Battestin (Boston: Houghton Mifflin, 1961), p. 8.

12. Early American examples of religious and medical tracts warning against homosexual activity may be found in Jonathan Katz's *Gay American History* (New York: Thomas Y. Crowell, 1976), chapters I and II.

13. Masquerade and the "festive stance" inform Andrew Wright's reading of Fielding in *Henry Fielding: Mask and Feast* (London: Chatto and Windus, 1965). Grete Ek has

written on the motif of masquerade in Fielding's fiction in "Glory, Jest, and Riddle: The Masque of Tom Jones in London," *English Studies* 60 (1979), 148–58. For an account of Fielding's general absorption in comedic inversions and theatricality, see Ian Donaldson's *The World Upside-Down: Comedy from Jonson to Fielding* (Oxford: Clarendon Press, 1970), and Campbell (note 2).

14. Fielding, "An Essay on the Knowledge of the Characters of Men," in *Miscellanies*, ed. Henry Knight Miller (Oxford: Clarendon Press, 1972), I, 155.

15. Fielding, *The Masquerade*, in Jones, ed., *The Female Husband and Other Writings*.

16. *Juvenalis Satyra Sexta* in *Miscellanies*, I.

17. Natalie Z. Davis, "Women on Top: Symbolic Sexual Inversion and Political Disorder in Early Modern Europe," *Society and Culture in Early Modern France* (Stanford: Stanford University Press, 1975); rpt. in *The Reversible World: Symbolic Inversion in Art and Society*, ed. Barbara A. Babcock (Ithaca: Cornell University Press, 1978). See also David Kunzle's "World Upside Down: The Iconography of a European Broadsheet Type," also in the Babcock collection.

18. Nancy K. Hayles has written on male impersonation in Shakespeare in two pieces: "Sexual Disguise in *As You Like It* and *Twelfth Night*," *Shakespeare Survey*, 32 (1979), 63–72, and "Sexual Disguise in *Cymbeline*," *Modern Language Quarterly*, 41 (1980), 231–47. For reasons that remain enigmatic—though of course one may speculate—Fielding did not exploit the convention of female sexual disguise in the plots of any of his own comedies or farces. Similar comic effects were undoubtedly achieved, however, by Charke's drag appearances. Fielding's plays do, one might add, show male-to-female cross-dressing: both *The Universal Gallant* and *The Old Debauchees* have male characters who disguise themselves as women.

19. Peter Ackroyd, *Dressing Up—Transvestism and Drag: The History of an Obsession* (New York: Simon & Schuster, 1979), p. 98. See also Pat Rogers, "The Breeches Part," in Paul-Gabriel Boucé, ed., *Sexuality in Eighteenth-Century Britain* (Manchester: Manchester University Press, 1982), pp. 244–58; and Kristina Straub, "The Guilty Pleasures of Female Theatrical Cross-Dressing and the Autobiography of Charlotte Charke," in Epstein and Straub, pp. 142–66.

20. Ackroyd, p. 98.

21. Rogers, p. 149. Charlotte Charke's autobiography has been edited by Leonard Ashley. See *A Narrative of the Life of Mrs. Charlotte Charke* (Gainesville, Fla.: Scholar's Facsimiles and Reprints, 1969). For an annotated treatment of the autobiography see Fidelis Morgan, *The Well-Known Troublemaker: A Life of Charlotte Charke* (London: Faber & Faber, 1988).

22. Cf. Pat Rogers' commentary on Fielding's divided nature in *Henry Fielding*: "As we follow Fielding's career we . . . witness the contest between a roué and a scholar, a reformer and a prodigal, a classicist and a show-business huckster, an athlete and an aesthete" (*Henry Fielding*, p. 14).

23. *Tom Jones*, ed. Sheridan Baker (New York: W. W. Norton, 1973), p. 247.

24. Plato, *Symposium*, pp. 189–91. One might note that the real Aristophanes was in some sense the originator of the comic stage stereotype of the woman who adopts male dress in order to challenge masculine authority: the *Ecclesiazusae* presents Praxagora, leader of the rebel "women in parliament," wearing her husband's clothes. On the Greek stage, as on the Shakespearean, the parts of male-impersonating women characters would have been taken by boys or men, thus adding to the sexual confusion.

Chapter 6

1. Henry Fielding, "An Essay on the Knowledge of the Characters of Men," in *Miscellanies,* ed. Henry Knight Miller (Oxford: Clarendon Press, 1972), I, p. 155; Owen Sedgewick, *The Universal Masquerade: or The World Turn'd Inside Out* (London, 1742); Samuel Johnson, *The Rambler,* No. 75 (4 December 1750), in *British Essayists,* ed. Alexander Chalmers (Boston, 1856), XVII, p. 92; Oliver Goldsmith, *Works,* ed. Peter Cunningham (New York: G. P. Putnam's, 1908), I, p. 153.

2. On Boswell's impersonations, see Max Byrd, *London Transformed: Images of the City of the Eighteenth Century* (New Haven: Yale University Press, 1978), pp. 95–97.

3. Henry Fielding, *The Masquerade* (London, 1728), reprinted in *The Female Husband and Other Writings,* ed. Claude E. Jones, English Reprints Series (Liverpool: Liverpool University Press, 1960); Joseph Addison, *The Spectator,* No. 14 (16 March 1711). All citations from the *Spectator* are drawn from the Oxford edition, Donald F. Bond, ed. (Oxford: Clarendon Press, 1965), 5 vols.

4. Michel Foucault, Introduction, *Herculine Barbin,* trans. Richard McDougall (New York: Pantheon, 1980), p. xvii.

5. *Universal Spectator* (14 December 1728).

6. E. C. Cawte, *Ritual Animal Disguise* (Cambridge: D. S. Brewer, 1978), Ch. 3, esp. pp. 71 and 86.

7. On popular entertainments in the English Renaissance, see C. L. Barber, *Shakespeare's Festive Comedy: A Study of Dramatic Form and its Relation to Social Custom* (Princeton, N. J.: Princeton University Press, 1959), and Michael D. Bristol, *Carnival and Theatre: Plebian Culture and the Structure of Authority in Renaissance England* (London: Methuen, 1985). For a description of masquerading at the court of Charles II, see Gilbert Burnet, *History of His Own Times,* ed. Thomas Burnet (London, 1818), I, p. 292. Further anecdotal information on Restoration masquerades can be found in William Connor Sydney, *Social Life in England from the Restoration to the Revolution* (New York: Macmillan, 1892), pp. 367–72.

8. Peter Burke, *Popular Culture in Early Modern Europe* (New York: Harper and Row, 1978), p. 249. See also Joseph Spence, *Letters from the Grand Tour,* ed. Slava Klima (Montreal: McGill-Queens University Press, 1975), p. 95.

9. See, for example, the letter condemning "mock Carnivals at Ranelagh-house" in *Gentleman's Magazine* (May 1750).

10. On the commercialization of popular entertainment in eighteenth-century England, see Burke, *Popular Culture,* pp. 248–49, and J. H. Plumb's essay "Commercialisation and Society" in *The Birth of a Consumer Society: The Commercialisation of Eighteenth-Century England* (London: Europa, 1982), pp. 265–85.

11. See G. F. R. Barker's biographical essay, "John James Heidegger," *Dictionary of National Biography,* and Pat Rogers' "Masquerades and Operas: Hogarth, Heidegger and Others," in *Literature and Popular Culture in Eighteenth Century England* (Brighton: Harvester, 1985), pp. 40–70. Public masquerades had in fact been established a few years earlier in London: there were advertisements for public masquerades at Lambeth-Wells, Spring Gardens, and elsewhere in *The Spectator* as early as 1711 (see Bond's note in the Oxford edition, I, p. 36). Heidegger's Haymarket balls later in the decade, however, attracted far more public attention.

12. Jonathan Swift, *The Complete Poems,* ed. Pat Rogers (New Haven: Yale University Press, 1983), p. 245.

13. See "Heidegger," *DNB*, and J. Ireland and John Nichols, *Hogarth's Complete Works* (Edinburgh, 1883), pp. 229–30.

14. Christopher Pitt, "On the Masquerades," *Poems and Translations* (London, 1727), reprinted in Samuel Johnson, ed., *Poets of Great Britain* (London, 1807), XLVII, pp. 19–21.

15. Mary Singleton [Frances Brooke], *The Old Maid*, No. 11 (24 January 1756).

16. Pierce Egan depicts a Regency masquerade in *Life in London* (London, 1821), Book II, Ch. 3. Byron attended a masquerade at Burlington House in 1814. See Leslie A. Marchand, *Byron: A Portrait* (Chicago: University of Chicago Press, 1970), p. 171.

17. Addison, *Spectator*, No. 8 (9 March 1711).

18. Suggestive masquerade scenes occur in Defoe's *Roxana* (1724); Mary Davys' *The Accomplished Rake; or, The Modern Fine Gentleman* (1727); Richardson's *Pamela*, Part 2 (1741); Cleland's *Memoirs of a Woman of Pleasure* (1749); Fielding's *Amelia* (1751); Smollett's *Adventures of Peregrine Pickle* (1751), and a host of minor works of the period. A typically melodramatic shorter tale is the "Affecting Masquerade Adventure," published in *Gentleman's Magazine* (December 1754).

19. Benjamin Griffin, *The Masquerade; or, An Evening's Intrigue* (London, 1717).

20. *The Conduct of the Stage Consider'd, with Short Remarks upon the Original and Pernicious Consequences of Masquerades* (London, 1721). I refer to this work elsewhere as the *Short Remarks*.

21. Richard Steele, *The Guardian*, No. 142 (24 August 1713), in *British Essayists*, Vol. XV. All further citations from *The Guardian* are from this edition.

22. William Wycherley, *The Country Wife* (III, i), in *The Complete Plays of William Wycherley*, ed. Gerald Weales (New York: Norton, 1966), p. 293.

23. *Weekly Journal* (19 April 1718).

24. See *The Memoirs of Casanova*, trans. Arthur Machen (New York: G. P. Putnam's, 1959), IV, p. 557. On the history of masquerade costume, see Aileen Ribeiro, *The Dress Worn at Masquerades in England, 1730 to 1790, and its Relation to Fancy Dress in Portraiture* (New York: Garland, 1984), and my study, *Masquerade and Civilization: The Carnivalesque in Eighteenth-Century English Culture and Fiction* (Stanford: Stanford University Press, 1986), Ch. 2.

25. Griffin, *The Masquerade*, I, i.

26. See Horace Walpole's letter to Mann, 3 March 1742, in *Horace Walpole's Correspondence*, ed. W. S. Lewis, *et al.*, (New Haven: Yale University Press, 1954) 17, p. 359. *Connoisseur* (1 May 1755) described "one gentleman above six foot high, who came to the Masquerade drest like a child in a white frock and leading-strings, attended by another gentleman of a very low stature, who officiated as his nurse." The "two great Girls, one in a white frock, with her doll," described in *Gentleman's Magazine* (February 1771), were also undoubtedly female impersonators.

27. *Lady's Magazine* (February 1773).

28. At a magnificent masquerade given by her husband in 1769, the Duchess of Bolton appeared first in "a Man's Black Domino," then, later in the evening, as a Persian princess. See *The Diaries of a Duchess: Extracts from the Diaries of the First Duchess of Northumberland (1716–1776)*, ed. James Greig (London: Hodder & Stoughton, 1926), p. 91. Elizabeth Inchbald, who had appeared as Bellario on the London stage, went to a masquerade in male dress in 1781. See James Boaden, *Memoirs of Mrs. Inchbald* (London, 1833), I, pp. 140–41. On Judith Milbanke's male impersonation, see *The Noels and the Milbankes, Their Letters for Twenty-Five Years*, ed. Malcolm Elwin (London: Macdonald, 1967), p. 93. For other cases of eighteenth-century female cross-dressing, see Dianne

Dugaw, "Balladry's Female Warriors: Women, Warfare, and Disguise in the Eighteenth Century," *Eighteenth-Century Life*, IX, n.s. 2, 1985, pp. 1–20; Lynn Friedli, "'Passing Women'—A Study of Gender Boundaries in the Eighteenth Century," in G. S. Rousseau and Roy Porter, eds., *Sexual Underworlds of the Enlightenment* (Manchester: Manchester University Press, 1987), 234–60; and Rudolf M. Dekker and Lotte C. Van de Pol, *The Tradition of Female Transvestism in Early Modern Europe* (New York: St. Martin's Press, 1989).

29. Miss Milner, the heroine of Inchbald's *A Simple Story* (1791), is described by another character as wearing "mens cloaths" when she appears as the goddess Diana at a masquerade in that novel. Ribeiro comments on the features of the Diana costume in *The Dress Worn at Masquerades*, pp. 261–64.

30. *The Noels and the Milbankes*, p. 93.

31. Harriette Wilson, *The Memoirs of Harriette Wilson Written by Herself* (London: The Navarre Society, 1924), II, pp. 607–11.

32. Charles Johnson, *The Masquerade: A Comedy* (London, 1719), II, ii.

33. E. J. Climenson, ed., *Elizabeth Montagu, The Queen of the Blue-Stockings* (London: John Murray, 1906), I, p. 264. One of the many satiric engravings commemorating Miss Chudleigh's exploit is the plate entitled "Miss Chudley in the Actual Dress as she appear'd in ye character of Iphigenia at ye Jubilee Ball or Masquerade at Ranelagh," British Museum, Print Room no. 3031.

34. Ribeiro, *Dress Worn at Masquerades*, p. 32.

35. *Gentleman's Magazine* (March 1770).

36. Margaret Leeson, *Memoirs of Margaret Leeson, Written by Herself* (Dublin, 1797), III, pp. 4–10.

37. *Select Trials for Murders, Robberies, Rapes, Sodomy, Coining, Frauds, and Other Offences at the Sessions-House in the Old Bailey* (London, 1742), II, pp. 257–58. Gerald Howson comments on Margaret Clap in *Thief-Taker General: The Rise and Fall of Jonathan Wild* (London: Hutchinson, 1970), pp. 63–64.

38. James Ralph, *The Touchstone: or, a guide to all the reigning diversions* (London, 1728), p. 191.

39. *A Seasonable Apology for Mr. H———g—r* (London, 1724).

40. See, for example, Eliza Haywood's warnings in *The Female Spectator*, 3rd ed. (London, 1750), I, pp. 32–33. In a letter to Lady Bradshaigh, 17 August 1752, Samuel Richardson complained that "the sex is generally running into licentiousness; when home is found to be the place that is most irksome to them; when Ranelaghs, Vauxhalls, Marybones, assemblies . . . and a rabble of such-like and amusements, carry them out of all domestic duty and usefulness into infinite riot and expense." See *Correspondence*, ed. A. Barbauld (London, 1806), VI, p. 25.

41. *Weekly Journal* (18 April 1724).

42. Addison, *Spectator* 8.

43. Wilson, *Memoirs*, II, p. 616.

44. *Lady's Magazine* (February 1773).

45. Wilson, *Memoirs*, II, p. 616.

46. Lady Mary Wortley Montagu wrote that the Venetian custom of going about in masks led to "a universal liberty that is certainly one of the greatest *agremens* in life." She likewise believed that the amorous freedom of Turkish women was due to the "perpetual masquerade" of the veil. See Robert Halsband, *The Life of Lady Mary Wortley Montagu* (Oxford: Clarendon Press, 1956), pp. 71 and 185. For Fanny Burney's description of a 1770 masquerade, see *The Early Diary of Frances Burney 1768-1778*, ed. A. R. Ellis

(London, 1889), I, pp. 64–65. Boaden describes Inchbald's early love of "frolics" in the *Memoirs*, I, pp. 140–41. Inchbald herself spoke nostalgically of masquerades and other "exploded fashions" in her preface to Cowley's *The Belle's Stratagem* in the *British Theatre* series (London, 1808), XIX, pp. 4–5.

47. Henry Fielding, *The Female Husband* (London, 1746), reprinted in *The Female Husband and Other Writings*, ed. Claude E. Jones (Liverpool: Liverpool University Press, 1960). On the historical and rhetorical dimensions of Fielding's pamphlet, see Chapter 5, "'Matters Not Fit to be Mentioned': Fielding's *The Female Husband*."

48. See Randolph Trumbach, "London's Sodomites: Homosexual Behavior and Western Culture in the Eighteenth Century," *Journal of Social History*, II, 1977, pp. 1–33. On the eighteenth-century molly club, see Alan Bray, *Homosexuality in Renaissance England* (London: Gay Men's Press, 1982), pp. 81–114.

49. Boaden, *Memoirs of Mrs. Inchbald*, I, p. 140.

50. *Weekly Journal* (18 April 1724).

51. Tobias Smollett, *The Adventures of Peregrine Pickle*, ed. James L. Clifford, rev. Paul-Gabriel Boucé (Oxford: Oxford University Press, 1983), pp. 244–45.

52. John Cleland, *Memoirs of a Woman of Pleasure*, ed. Peter Sabor (Oxford: Oxford University Press, 1985), pp. 154–56. On Cleland's own rumored homosexuality, see Sabor's introduction, p. xiii.

53. On the concept of the "backstage" area, see Erving Goffman, *The Presentation of Self in Everyday Life* (Garden City, N. Y.: Anchor Books, 1959), pp. 112–20.

54. Trumbach discusses the emergence of sexual subcultures in eighteenth-century London in "London's Sodomites," p. 23. See also Lawrence Stone's comments on the "relaxed" nature of sexual attitudes in mid-eighteenth-century London in *The Family, Sex and Marriage in England 1500–1800* (New York: Harper & Row, 1977), pp. 332–35. One may dispute, of course, the extent of this tolerance; the punishments for sodomy become progressively harsher in England over the course of the century. Yet the intensifying official attack on homosexuality also suggests its growing prominence as a subcultural phenomenon.

55. On the role of the masquerade topos in eighteenth-century popular culture, see Chapter 7, "The Carnivalization of Eighteenth-Century English Narrative."

56. John Richetti, *Popular Fiction Before Richardson: Narrative Patterns 1700–1739*, (Oxford: Clarendon Press, 1969), p. 59.

57. *Gentleman's Magazine* (December 1754).

58. *The Masquerade: or, The Devil's Nursery* (Dublin, 1732).

59. Jean Starobinski, *The Invention of Liberty*, trans. Bernard C. Swift (Geneva: Albert Skira, 1964).

60. See *The History of Sexuality: An Introduction*, trans. Robert Hurley (New York: Pantheon, 1978), for Foucault's most influential statement on the post-Enlightenment proliferation of "discourses" on sexuality. To be sure, Foucault is sometimes contradictory on the subject of whether the new descriptions of sexuality entailed new practices: in the "Preface to Transgression" in *Language, Counter-Memory, Practice: Selected Essays and Interviews*, ed. and trans. Donald F. Bouchard (Ithaca: Cornell University Press, 1977), Foucault denies that the eighteenth century proffered "any new content for our age-old acts" (p. 30). However, in a posthumously published interview, Foucault speaks of the modern "eroticization of the body" as a concrete expansion of the "possibilities of pleasure." See Bob Gallagher and Alexander Wilson, "Michel Foucault—An Interview: Sex, Power, and the Politics of Identity," *The Advocate* (7 August 1984), p. 27.

61. Christopher Pitt, "On the Masquerades," lines 17–20.

Chapter 7

1. Joseph Addison, *The Works of Joseph Addison,* ed. Richard Hurd (London, 1811) 2:39. On Mary Wortley Montagu's fondness for masks and masquerades, see Robert Halsband, *The Life of Mary Wortley Montagu* (Oxford: Clarendon Press, 1956), p. 185. Writing to Horace Walpole in 1741, Horace Mann speaks enthusiastically of the outdoor carnivals of Florence. See Mann's letter to Walpole, July 30, 1741, in W. S. Lewis et al., *Horace Walpole's Correspondence* (New Haven: Yale University Press, 1937–79), 1:97.

2. Typical masquerade tales include Eliza Haywood's *The Masqueraders; or, Fatal Curiosity* (London, 1724), her history of Erminia in *The Female Spectator* (London, 1750), 32–35, and an anonymous "Affecting Masquerade Adventure," *Gentleman's Magazine,* December 1754. The masquerade was also a popular dramatic topos: Benjamin Griffin's *The Masquerade; or, An Evening's Intrigue* (1717), Charles Johnson's *The Masquerade; A Comedy* (1719), the anonymous *The Masquerade; or, The Devil's Nursery* (1732), Fielding's *Miss Lucy in Town* (1742), Francis Gentleman's *The Pantheonites* (1773), and Hannah Cowley's *The Belle's Stratagem* (1781) are representative masquerade plays and farces.

3. At the time this essay was first published (1984), only two literary critics had looked in any detail at eighteenth-century masquerade scenes: David Blewett, in a chapter on Defoe's *Roxana* in *Defoe's Art of Fiction* (Toronto: University of Toronto Press, 1979) and Robert Folkenflik in "Tom Jones, the Gypsies, and the Masquerade," *University of Toronto Quarterly* 44 (1975): 224–37. I subsequently published my own longer study *Masquerade and Civilization: The Carnivalesque in Eighteenth-Century English Culture and Fiction* (Stanford: Stanford University Press, 1986). Since then several other scholars have taken up the masquerade theme—notably Mary Anne Schofield in *Masking and Unmasking the Female Mind: Disguising Romances in Feminine Fiction 1713–1799* (Cranbury, N. J.: Associated University Presses, 1990) and Catherine Craft-Fairchild in *Masquerade and Gender: Disguise and Female Identity in Eighteenth-Century Fictions by Women* (University Park: Pennsylvania State University Press, 1993). Craft-Fairchild offers an interesting critique of a number of my ideas about the masquerade (particularly with regard to its use as a topos by women novelists), as does G. J. Barker-Benfield in *The Culture of Sensibility: Sex and Society in Eighteenth-Century Britain* (Chicago: University of Chicago Press, 1992), pp. 182–190.

4. See Mikhail Bakhtin, *Rabelais and his World,* trans. Hélène Iswolsky (Cambridge: MIT Press, 1968), esp. Chap. 1, "Rabelais in the History of Laughter."

5. On the varieties of masquerade dress, see Aileen Ribeiro, *The Dress Worn at Masquerades in England, 1730 to 1790, and its Relation to Fancy Dress in Portraiture* (New York: Garland, 1984) and "The Elegant Art of Fancy Dress," in Edward Maeder, ed., *An Elegant Art: Fashion and Fantasy in the Eighteenth Century* (New York: Abrams and Los Angeles County Museum of Art, 1983). Horace Walpole's correspondence contains numerous descriptions of costumes worn at contemporary masquerades; see also the *Weekly Journal,* January 25, February 8, and April 18, 1724; the *Universal Spectator,* April 5, 1729; *Gentleman's Magazine,* June 1769, February 1771, January 1773, and April 1774; and *Lady's Magazine,* February 1773.

6. Griffin, *The Masquerade,* I:i.

7. On the persistent association between the masquerade and illicit forms of sexual behavior, see Chapter 6, "The Culture of Travesty: Sexuality and Masquerade in Eighteenth-Century England." The moralistic diatribe against the masquerade lasted throughout the century. Typical attacks included the Bishop of London's *Sermon Preached to the Societies for the Reformation of Manners* (London, 1724), Fielding's poetic satire *The*

Masquerade (London, 1728) and *Charge to the Grand Jury* (London, 1749), and the anonymous pamphlets *The Conduct of the Stage Consider'd, With Short Remarks upon the Original and Pernicious Consequences of Masquerades* (London, 1721) and *Essay on Plays and Masquerades* (London, 1724).

8. According to contemporary accounts, attendance at Heidegger's weekly masquerades at the Haymarket averaged about seven hundred persons. Later in the century masquerades became larger still: *Town and Country Magazine* for May 1770 reports that twelve hundred gathered for a masquerade at Carlisle House on May 7 and that "near two thousand persons" had attended an assembly at the Pantheon the month before. Besides Horace Walpole and Mary Wortley Montagu, celebrated devotees included George II and numerous members of the English aristocracy, and, later in the century, Garrick, Goldsmith, Burney, and Boswell.

9. Samuel Richardson, *Pamela* (London: Dent, 1914), 2:262.

10. Samuel Richardson, *Sir Charles Grandison*, ed. Jocelyn Harris (London: Oxford University Press, 1972), 1:116.

11. Elizabeth Inchbald, *A Simple Story*, ed. J. M. S. Tompkins (London: Oxford University Press, 1967), p. 151.

12. Daniel Defoe, *Roxana: The Fortunate Mistress*, ed. Jane Jack (London: Oxford University Press, 1964), p. 173.

13. Henry Fielding, *Tom Jones*, ed. Sheridan Baker (New York: Norton, 1973), p. 543.

14. Henry Fielding, *Amelia*, ed. William Ernest Henley (New York: Cass, 1967), 1:301 and 2:11–59.

15. Frances Burney, *Cecilia: or, Memoirs of an Heiress* (London, 1784), 1:169.

16. For Addison's satiric comments on masquerade "promiscuity" see *Spectator* 8 and 101, in Joseph Addison and Richard Steele, *The Spectator*, ed. Donald F. Bond (Oxford: Clarendon Press, 1965), 1:35–38, 1:423–26, and *Guardian* 154, in Addison and Steele, *The Tatler and Guardian* (Edinburgh, 1880), pp. 225–26.

17. Tzvetan Todorov, *The Fantastic: A Structural Approach to a Literary Genre*, trans. Richard Howard (Ithaca, N. Y.: Cornell University Press, 1975), p. 163.

18. Todorov, *The Fantastic*, pp. 165–66.

19. Richardson, *Sir Charles Grandison*, 1:119.

20. *Ibid.*, 1:137.

21. *Ibid.*, 1:145.

22. Grete Ek comments on this subversion of sex roles in "Glory, Jest, and Riddle: The Masque of Tom Jones in London," *English Studies* 60 (1979): 148–58.

23. Fielding, *Amelia*, 2:227.

24. Richardson, *Pamela*, 2:320.

25. R. S. Crane's comments in his classic essay on *Tom Jones* typify critical displeasure with the episode: he suggests that it is impossible not to be "shocked" by Tom's entanglement with Lady Bellaston and that the masquerade sequence as a whole represents one of the few "faults" in Fielding's novel. Crane complains in particular about the inconsistency in the characterization. "It is necessary, no doubt," he writes, "that [Tom] should now fall lower than ever before, but surely not so low as to make it hard to infer his act from our previous knowledge of his character . . . for the moment at least, a different Tom is before our eyes." See "The Plot of *Tom Jones*," *Journal of General Education* 4 (1950): 112–30.

26. In the preface to *Amelia*, Fielding announces that his work is "sincerely designed to promote the cause of virtue, and to expose some of the most glaring evils, as well public as private, which at present infest the country." See *Amelia*, ed. William Ernest Henley (New

York: Cass, 1967), 1:12. J. Paul Hunter comments on this hypertrophy of didactic intention in Chapter 9 of *Occasional Form: Henry Fielding and the Chains of Circumstance* (Baltimore: Johns Hopkins University Press, 1975), as do I in *Masquerade and Civilization*, pp. 177–252.

27. On the complex role of the carnivalesque in *Madame Bovary*, see Barbara Babcock, "The Novel and the Carnival World," *Modern Language Notes* 89 (1974): 911–37.

28. Bakhtin, *Rabelais and His World*, pp. 32–33.

29. *Ibid.*, pp. 117–19.

30. On the increasing commercialization of popular entertainment in the eighteenth century, see J. H. Plumb, "Commercialisation and Society," in Blewer, McKendrick, and Plumb, *The Birth of a Consumer Society: The Commercialisation of Eighteenth-Century England* (London: Europa, 1982).

31. Late set pieces include the masquerade scenes in Maria Edgeworth's *Belinda* (1801) and Pierce Egan's *Life in London* (1821). On the Continent, where carnival tradition itself had a longer life, the masquerade remained a fictional topos well into the nineteenth century. Notable scenes occur in Balzac, in *La Peau de chagrin* (1831) and *Splendeurs et misères des courtisanes* (1843), and in Flaubert, in *L'Education sentimentale* (1869). The masquerade scene makes interesting vestigial appearances too in nineteenth-century opera. Verdi's *Un Ballo in maschera* (1859) remains the best-known "masquerade opera," but other works also invoke the topos—Johann Strauss's *Der Karneval in Rom* (1873), *Die Fledermaus* (1874), and *Eine Nacht in Venedig* (1883); Heuberger's *Der Opernball* (1898) and Nielsen's *Maskarade* (1906). Twentieth-century writers return to the masquerade scene primarily in the context of exoticism or self-conscious nostalgia. A striking costume ball occurs in Lawrence Durrell's *Balthazar*, in *The Alexandria Quartet* (1962), while in Brigid Brophy's *The Snow Ball* (1964), characters attend a sixties London masquerade party dressed in eighteenth-century (Mozartean) costume. In Isak Dinesen's posthumously published "Carnival" (1970), erotic intrigues develop among eight persons on the night of the Copenhagen Opera masquerade ball.

32. Tony Tanner, *Adultery in the Novel: Contract and Transgression* (Baltimore: Johns Hopkins University Press, 1979), pp. 3–4.

Chapter 8

1. Philippe Ariès, *The Hour of Our Death*, trans. Helen Weaver (New York; Alfred A. Knopf, 1981), p. 606. All citations are from this translation; parenthetical notation refers to page numbers in this edition.

2. Sir Walter Scott, *Lives of Eminent Novelists and Dramatists* (London: Frederick Warne, 1887), p. 568.

3. Because Austen made it so difficult to take certain aspects of *Udolpho* seriously, modern critics have often refused to take any aspect of the novel seriously. Certainly Radcliffe can be vulgar in the extreme, but her impact on the modern life of the emotions cannot be dismissed. It is one aim of the present essay to read Radcliffe against the current Austenian caricature, and to restore to view the powerful current of feeling in her work, however awkwardly or crudely this feeling is expressed.

4. See Montague Summers, *The Gothic Quest: A History of the Gothic Novel* (New York: Russell & Russell, 1964), p. 139; J. M. S. Tompkins, *The Popular Novel in England 1770–1800* (Lincoln: University of Nebraska Press, 1961), p. 261; and Andrew Lang, *Adventures Among Books* (London: Longman's, Green & Co., 1905), p. 127.

5. All citations are from the World's Classics edition of *The Mysteries of Udolpho*, ed.

Bonamy Dobrée, notes by Frederick Garber (Oxford: Oxford University Press, 1966). Parenthetical notation refers to page numbers in this edition.

6. See, for example, Robert Kiely, *The Romantic Novel in England* (Cambridge: Harvard University Press, 1972), p. 78; and among psychoanalytic and feminist critics, Norman Holland and Leona Sherman, "Gothic Possibilities," *New Literary History* 8 (1976–77): 279–94; Claire Kahane, "The Gothic Mirror," in *The (M)Other Tongue: Essays in Feminist Psychoanalytic Interpretation*, ed. Shirley Nelson Garner, Claire Kahane, and Madelon Sprengnether (Ithaca, N. Y.: Cornell University Press, 1985), pp. 334–51; Mary Poovey, "Ideology and 'The Mysteries of Udolpho,'" *Criticism* 21 (Fall 1979): 307–30; and Cynthia Griffin Wolff, "The Radcliffean Gothic Model: A Form for Feminine Sexuality," *Modern Language Studies* 9 (1979): 98–113. For other recent commentary on *Udolpho*, see Deborah Rogers, ed., *The Critical Response to Ann Radcliffe* (New York: Greenwood Press, 1993).

7. See Robert Darnton, "Readers Respond to Rousseau: The Fabrication of Romantic Sensitivity," in *The Great Cat Massacre and Other Episodes in French Cultural History* (New York: Random House, 1985), pp. 215–56. On *Udolpho's* contemporary appeal, see J. M. S. Tompkins, *Ann Radcliffe and Her Influence on Later Writers* (New York: Arno Press, 1980) and the Dobrée introduction to the Oxford edition.

8. Tzvetan Todorov, *The Fantastic: A Structural Approach to a Literary Genre*, trans. Richard Howard (Ithaca, N. Y.: Cornell University Press, 1975), p. 114.

9. Todorov, *The Fantastic*, pp. 116–17.

10. Todorov, *The Fantastic*, p. 118.

11. D. W. Winnicott, *Home is Where We Start From: Essays by a Psychoanalyst*, ed. Clare Winnicott, Ray Shepherd, and Madeleine Davis (New York: Norton, 1986), p. 30.

12. Sigmund Freud, "The 'Uncanny'" (1919), in *The Standard Edition of the Complete Psychological Works*, ed. and trans. James Strachey (London: Hogarth Press, 1955), XVII, 218–52.

13. In "Imagery of the Surface in the Gothic Novel" (*PMLA* 96 [March 1981]: 255–70), Eve Kosofsky Sedgwick suggests that Gothic fiction typically presents "a (novelistic) world of faces where the diacritical code is poor"—i.e., where the differences between characters' physiognomies are so slight as to challenge the "fiction of presence" the novel also tries to ensure. One effect of this impoverished physiognomic code, she writes, is to create "unbounded confusions of identity along a few diacritical axes: any furrowed man will be confusable with any other furrowed man (Schedoni with Zampari with Zeluca, for example), and so forth" (p. 263). Sedgwick's rigorously poststructuralist perspective forbids her to interpret this phenomenon in any psychological sense (she treats it instead as a formal convention—part of the play of the "surface" in Gothic fiction), but a fruitful connection might nonetheless be made, following the developmental model of Freud and Piaget, between such "confusability" and the early stages of cognitive perception in the human infant.

14. Todorov, *The Fantastic*, p. 148.

15. See Ariès, *Hour of Our Death*, Chaps. 10 and 11, esp. pp. 409–11 and 475–99. On the relocation of cemeteries see also Richard A. Etlin, *The Architecture of Death: The Transformation of the Cemetery in Eighteenth-Century Paris* (Cambridge, Mass.: MIT Press, 1985).

16. In *The Coherence of Gothic Conventions* (New York: Arno, 1980), Sedgwick takes modern critics like Lowry Nelson and Robert Heilman to task for speaking of the sinister ambiance of Gothic fiction as "mere decor," "stage-set," "claptrap," and so on. In so doing, she argues, they fail to see that objects such as bloodstained veils, burial crypts, and open

graves actually serve complex formal functions in the fictions in which they appear. While this is certainly true, Sedgwick misses a more obvious point: that the twentieth-century urge to trivialize may have something to do with the fact that the typical Gothic setting foregrounds precisely those artifacts—tombs, corpses, shrouds and so on—that modern society now views with particular fear and revulsion. The very assertion that such details are silly or melodramatic—or even as Sedgwick herself puts it, merely "formal" elements—suggests something of the extreme emotional defensiveness that the death-obsessed Gothic milieu now inspires. We have accustomed ourselves to finding hidden sexual plots in Gothic fiction (and indeed delight in them); we have still not reconciled ourselves, however, to its far more obvious concern with death and dissolution.

17. Ariès's description of romantic mourning, it should be noted, is very close indeed to the picture of chronic or disordered mourning familiar to modern psychology. Freud spoke of the inability to let go of mental images of a dead loved one ("loss of interest in the outside world—in so far as it does not recall the dead one") as one of the classic symptoms of normal grief in his famous essay "Mourning and Melancholia" (1917). He also noted, however, that this obsessional state might be unnaturally prolonged if the mourner possessed strongly ambivalent feelings toward the dead loved one. Modern clinicians, notably in Britain, have enlarged on this Freudian notion of chronic grief in a number of classic case studies. See in particular Geoffrey Gorer's *Death, Grief and Mourning in Contemporary Britain* (London: Tavistock Publications, 1965) and John Bowlby's magisterial *Attachment and Loss* (New York: Basic Books, 1980), 3 vols.

18. Samuel Richardson, *Clarissa: or, the History of a Young Lady*, ed. Angus Ross (New York: Viking Penguin, 1985), p. 1403. Compare also Tony Tanner's comments on the theme of sentimental reunion in Rousseau in *Adultery in the Novel: Contract and Transgression* (Baltimore: Johns Hopkins University Press, 1979), pp. 144-46.

19. Emily St. Aubert's sensation that her father's corpse still moves resembles the fantasy frequently held by children faced with death—i.e., that the dead body can somehow be made to move again. Likewise, the vision of the tomb as a home is also close to the projections of young children, who, as Bowlby points out, often believe that by dying themselves they can be reunited with a dead parent. See *Loss: Sadness and Depression* (Vol. 1 of *Attachment and Loss*), pp. 274 and 354–58.

20. Sigmund Freud, "Psychoanalytic Notes Upon an Autobiographical Account of a Case of Paranoia" (1911), in *Three Case Histories*, ed. Philip Rieff (New York: Macmillan Publishing Co., 1963), p. 155. For a further development of the notion that the cultivation of sublime emotion can be a paradoxical psychic mechanism for obviating loss or threats to the self, see Thomas Weiskel, *The Romantic Sublime: Studies in the Structure and Psychology of Transcendence* (Baltimore: Johns Hopkins University Press, 1976), pp. 17–18, 137–45, and 157–58; and Neil Hertz, "The Notion of Blockage in the Literature of the Sublime," in *The End of the Line* (New York: Columbia University Press, 1985), pp. 40–60.

21. On Aquinian notions of mental imagery see Jonathan D. Spence, *The Memory Palace of Matteo Ricci* (New York: Viking Penguin, 1984), p. 13.

22. See Frances A. Yates, *The Art of Memory* (New York: Penguin Books, 1969); and Spence, *Memory Palace*, pp. 1–23.

23. Keith Thomas, *Religion and the Decline of Magic* (New York: Charles Scribner's Sons, 1971), p. 587.

24. John Locke, *An Essay Concerning Human Understanding*, ed. and abr. A. D. Woozley (London: Wm. Collins Sons, 1964), pp. 123–25.

25. See M. H. Abrams, *The Mirror and the Lamp: Romantic Theory and the Critical*

Tradition (London: Oxford University Press, 1953), pp. 62–63; and Weiskel, *The Romantic Sublime*, pp. 17–19.

26. Burke, as Radcliffe probably knew, also wrote of the curious satisfaction to be found in grief: "The person who grieves, suffers his passion to grow upon him; he indulges it, he loves it; but this never happens in the case of actual pain, which no man ever willingly endured for any considerable time." And Burke too connected this pleasure with certain self-affirming mental operations: "It is the nature of grief to keep its object perpetually in its eye, to present it in its most pleasurable views, to repeat all the circumstances that attend it, even to the last minuteness." See Edmund Burke, *A Philosophical Enquiry into the Origin of our Ideas of the Sublime and Beautiful*, ed. J. T. Boulton (Notre Dame: University of Notre Dame Press, 1958), p. 37.

27. I purposely echo the title of Fredric Bogel's *Literature and Insubstantiality in Later Eighteenth-Century England* (Princeton: Princeton University Press, 1984). This rich discussion of "the perception of insubstantiality" in later eighteenth-century English literature relates in interesting ways to the concerns of the present essay.

28. Iconic images have always been used to inspire visions of the dead or absent. What have changed are the forms of commemorative imagery and the technological means by which such images are produced. In *Udolpho* characters habitually use small painted portraits of loved ones to evoke nostalgic thoughts: Du Pont steals a miniature picture of Emily and uses it throughout the novel as a sentimental *aide-mémoire*; St. Aubert keeps a miniature of his dead sister for a similar purpose; the nun Agnes has yet another miniature of the same woman, with whom she is obsessed. Because of its size and portability, the miniature had become the natural accessory to romantic mourning by the late eighteenth century: a talismanic device, so to speak, through which one might enter the idealizing space of the memory. As the capacity for image-reproduction improved in the nineteenth and twentieth centuries, with the invention of photography and similar processes, so undoubtedly was the spectralizing habit itself reinforced. What I am suggesting, however, is that the preference for mental imagery may in some sense have preceded and conditioned this new technology: that the very pattern of human invention was determined by preexisting emotional needs. On the role of commemorative objects in modern bourgeois culture, see also Susan Stewart, *On Longing: Narratives of the Miniature, the Gigantic, the Souvenir, the Collection* (Baltimore: Johns Hopkins University Press, 1984).

29. Sigmund Freud, *The Interpretation of Dreams*, trans. James Strachey (New York: Avon Books, 1965), p. 439.

30. The phrase "a conjuring into existence of a piece of real life" is from the essay "Recollection, Repetition and Working Through" (1914), trans. Joan Rivière, in *Therapy and Technique*, ed. Philip Rieff (New York: Macmillan, 1963), p. 162. Freud also uses the conjuring metaphor at several points in "Analysis Terminable and Interminable" (1937), reprinted in the Rieff volume. The phrase "psychical underworld" is from this last essay, p. 249.

31. Freud, "Dynamics of the Transference" (1912), trans. Joan Rivière, in *Therapy and Technique*, p. 114.

32. Freud, *An Outline of Psychoanalysis*, trans. James Strachey (New York: Norton, 1949), p. 31.

33. Freud, "Dynamics of the Transference," pp. 108–9.

34. Freud, *Outline of Psychoanalysis*, p. 34.

35. See Freud, "Analysis Terminable and Interminable," on "the still unresolved residues of transference," pp. 236–38.

36. Freud, "Analysis Terminable and Interminable," p. 242.

Chapter 9

1. Thomas Carlyle, *The French Revolution,* 3 vols. (London, 1837), 1:165; hereafter abbreviated *FR.*

2. Lawrence Sulivan, "Epilogue to *Julius Caesar,* performed at Mr. Newcome's School, Hackney, in May 1802," *Gentleman's Magazine* (June 1802): 544. The term *phantasmagoria,* apparently invented by Etienne-Gaspard Robertson, was probably derived from the Greek *phantasma* (phantom) and *agoreuein* (to speak in public), on the model of *allegory.* According to Paul Robert, *Le Grand Robert, Alphabétique et analogique diction-naire de la langue française* (Paris, 1985), however, the word may be a fanciful hybrid of *phantasma* and *gourer, agourer* (to deceive). See also G. Gougenheim, "L'Inventeur du mot *fantasmagorie,*" *Vie et Langage* 49 (April 1956): 160–62.

3. Arthur Rimbaud, "Night in Hell." *A Season in Hell, Rimbaud: Complete Works, Selected Letters,* ed. and trans. Wallace Fowlie (Chicago, 1966), p. 184.

4. Robertson (originally Robert) was born in Liège. On his colorful career, see his *Mémoires récréatifs, scientifiques, et anecdotiques d'un physicien-aéronaute* (Paris, 1830–34). I have used the modern reprint, introduced by Philippe Blon, 2 vols. (Paris, 1985); hereafter abbreviated *M.* Stendhal describes one of Robertson's provincial shows in his *Mémoires d'un touriste* (1838), in the section entitled "Nivernais, le 18 avril."

5. There are a number of nineteenth-century writings on the history and uses of the magic lantern. See, for example, letter 67 of Sir David Brewster's *Letters on Natural Magic* (London, 1833), or the anonymous manuals from later in the century, *The Magic Lantern: How to Buy and How to Use It. Also How to Raise a Ghost* (London, 1866) and *The Magic Lantern: Its Construction and Management* (London, 1888). For a modern account of Kircher's invention and its role in the history of cinematography, see Martin Quigley, Jr., *Magic Shadows: The Story of the Origin of Motion Pictures* (New York, 1960).

6. This description, from *L' Ami des lois,* is one of several newspaper accounts cited in Robertson's autobiography. Unless otherwise noted, all translations from the French are my own.

7. The account here is from an article by Armand Poultier, *L' Ami des lois,* 8, Germinal Year VI (28 March 1798).

8. A surviving program from early 1800 entitled "Fantasmagorie de Robertson," containing a list of experiments and illusions performed at the Cour des Capucines, is located in the University of Illinois library.

9. On Philipstal and the English phantasmagoria shows, see Richard D. Altick's magisterial history of nineteenth-century popular entertainments, *The Shows of London* (Cambridge, Mass. 1978), pp. 217–20. Additional information may be found in two works by Thomas Frost, *The Lives of the Conjurors* (1881, Ann Arbor, Mich., 1971), pp. 164–67 and 205–6, and *The Old Showmen, and the Old London Fairs* (London, 1875), pp. 311–12; and in E. Beresford Chancellor, *The Pleasure Haunts of London during Four Centuries* (1925: New York, 1969). Stanley Mayes discusses Philipstal's association with Madame Tussaud in *The Great Belzoni* (London, 1959), pp. 65–66.

10. William Nicholson, "Narrative and Explanation of the Appearance of Phantoms and other Figures in the Exhibition of the Phantasmagoria," *Journal of Natural Philosophy, Chemistry, and the Arts* I (February 1802), 148. Sir David Brewster's famous description of the phantasmagoria in *Letters on Natural Magic* (cited by Frost and others as an eyewitness account) appears to be a plagiarism of Nicholson's essay.

11. Mayes, *The Great Belzoni,* p. 49.

12. Altick, *The Shows of London,* p. 218.

13. Frost, *The Lives of the Conjurors*, p. 170.

14. Henry Crabb Robinson, *The London Theatre 1811–1866, Selections from the Diary of Henry Crabb Robinson*, ed. Eluned Brown (London, 1966), p. 47.

15. Frost, *The Old Showmen*, p. 311.

16. After succumbing to the "powerful effect" of the phantasmagoria at the Royal Mechanical and Optical Exhibition in 1812, Crabb Robinson observed that "in an age in which the process was familiar but not known to the people it must have been very easy to raise spirits from the dead apparently by means of good likenesses" (Robinson, *The London Theatre*, p. 47). A number of literary works of the period contain episodes in which magic lanterns are used to deceive credulous would-be ghost-seers. Friedrich Schiller's fragment *Der Geisterseher* (1789), translated into English as *The Ghost-Seer: or, The Apparitionist* (1795), is the best known of such works. See also the anonymous Gothic tale *Phantasmagoria: or, The Development of Magical Deception* (London, 1803).

17. Brewster, *Letters on Natural Magic*, p. 85.

18. *Ibid.*, p. 86.

19. Frost, *The Lives of the Conjurors*, p. 315.

20. On the Zoopraxiscope, Edison's peep-show, and other later nineteenth-century innovations, see Quigley, *Magic Shadows*, pp. 115–38.

21. Traveling motion-picture shows in rural England before 1914 often took the form of ghost-shows. The showman Randall Williams was among the first to exhibit moving pictures as part of his Ghost Show in the 1890s. See Ian Starsmore, *English Fairs* (London, 1975), pp. 65–66. Besides producing phantasmagorical illusions for the theatre, the pioneering early filmmaker Georges Méliès (1861–1938) made hundreds of shorts between 1896 and 1912 in which he used trick photography and other special techniques to create startling fantastic and comical effects. His subjects—*La Dame fantôme, Le Cauchemar, Apparitions fantômatiques, Les Transmutations imperceptibles, Le Spectre, La Lanterne magique*—suggest his profound connection with the Robertsonian ghost-show tradition. See Paul Hammond, *Marvellous Méliès* (London, 1974). On larger theoretical connections between film and the fantastic, see Artaud's essays, especially "Witchcraft and Cinema," *Collected Works*, trans. Alastair Hamilton, 4 vols. (London, 1968–), 3: 65–67, and Stanley Cavell, "What Becomes of Things on Film?" *Themes Out of School: Effects and Causes* (San Francisco, 1984), pp. 173–83.

22. *The Magic Lantern: How to Buy, and How to Use It*, pp. 9–10.

23. *Ibid.*, p. 7.

24. Marcel Proust, *Swann's Way*, vol. 1 of *Remembrance of Things Past*, trans. C. K. Scott Moncrieff and Terence Kilmartin (New York, 1981), pp. 9–11.

25. Honoré de Balzac, *Un Épisode sous la Terreur*, vol. 7 of *La Comédie humaine*, ed. Marcel Bouteron (Paris, 1955), p. 434. Victor Hugo, *Notre-Dame de Paris*, ed. Jacques Seebacher and Yves Gohin (Paris, 1975), p. 355.

26. George Gordon, Lord Byron, *The Vision of Judgment*, stanzas 76–77, *Byron*, ed. Jerome J. McGann, Oxford Authors (Oxford, 1986), p. 961.

27. Sir Walter Scott, *Letters on Demonology and Witchcraft, Addressed to J. G. Lockhart, Esq.* 2d ed. (London, 1831), p. 58; Eusèbe Salverte, *The Occult Sciences: The Philosophy of Magic, Prodigies, and Apparent Miracles*, trans. Anthony Todd Thomson, 2 vols. (New York, 1847), 1:255.

28. William Gell, *Pompeiana: The Topography, Edifices and Ornaments of Pompeii, the Result of Excavations Since 1819*, 2 vols. (London, 1832), 1:78.

29. Edward Bulwer-Lytton. *The Last Days of Pompeii* (1834, London, n. d.), p. 153.

30. Johann Wolfgang von Goethe, *The Sorrows of Young Werther* and *Novella*, trans. Elizabeth Mayer and Louise Bogan (New York, 1971), pp. 47–48; hereafter abbreviated *S*.

31. Mary Wollstonecraft, *Maria, or, The Wrongs of Woman* (New York, 1975), p. 49.

32. The poem appears on the final unnumbered page of the June 1802 volume. It is somewhat mysteriously dated 30 June 1801. The year may be a misprint for 1802, since Philipstal's shows did not begin at the Lyceum until late 1801. Mayes cites an unidentified London newspaper account from 4 September 1801 describing the erection of "a theatre for the representation [of phantoms] at the Lyceum Strand, where it will shortly open" (*The Great Belzoni*, p. 65). On Henry Lemoine, see the long article in the *Dictionary of National Biography*.

33. The lines appear in the first manuscript version of canto 2, stanza 134. See Byron, *Don Juan*, ed. T. G. Steffan, E. Steffan, and W. W. Pratt (New Haven, Conn., 1982), p. 599.

34. Thomas De Quincey, *Confessions of an English Opium-Eater*, ed. Edward Sackville-West (1822, London, 1950), p. 257.

35. Carlyle, *Sartor Resartus* (1908, London, 1973), p. 39.

36. Matthew Arnold, *Literature and Dogma* (Boston, 1873), p. 85.

37. *Newstead Abbey, Crayon Miscellany*, vol. 22 of *The Complete Works of Washington Irving*, ed. Dahlia Kirby Terrell (Boston, 1979), pp. 217–18.

38. *The Blithedale Romance* and *Fanshawe*, ed. William Charvat et al., vol. 3 of *The Centenary Edition of the Works of Nathaniel Hawthorne* (Columbus, Ohio, 1964), p. 1.

39. Bulwer-Lytton, *A Strange Story*, Lord Lytton's Novels, Knebworth Edition (1862; London, n.d.), p. 154, hereafter abbreviated *SS*.

40. Joseph Henry Shorthouse, *John Inglesant: A Romance* (1881; New York, 1897), pp. 252–53.

41. William Butler Yeats, "A General Introduction for my Work," *Essays and Introductions* (New York, 1961), p. 509. On the general relationship between early nineteenth-century optics and the language of romanticism, see C. J. Wright, "The 'Spectre' of Science: The Study of Optical Phenomena and the Romantic Imagination," *Journal of the Warburg and Courtauld Institutes* 43 (1980), 186–200. Interesting later uses of the phantasmagoria image may be found in Chateaubriand's *Essai sur la littérature anglaise* (1836); the Goncourt brothers' *Soeur Philomène* (1861); Lautréamont's *Les Chants de Maldodor* (1868); Loti's *Pêcheur d'islande* (1886); Apollinaire's *Alcools* (1913); Valéry's *Variété II* (1929), and Artaud's film scenario "Trente-deux," from the 1920s. Besides being a favorite Yeatsian metaphor, the phantasmagoria appears in Pound's *Hugh Selwyn Mauberley* ("Mauberley," canto 2). In "The Love Song of J. Alfred Prufrock" (1915), Eliot has the following ironic invocation of romantic optical machinery:

> But as if a magic lantern threw the nerves in patterns on a screen:
> Would it have been worth while
> If one, settling a pillow or throwing off a shawl,
> And turning toward the window, should say:
> 'That is not it at all,
> That is not what I meant, at all.'
> [*The Complete Poems and Plays, 1909–50* (New York, 1971), p. 6]

42. See, for example, one critic's comment on Gérard de Nerval: "Mais il est ce songeur et ce poète qui ne peut trouver de connaissance que fantasmagorique et de l'ordre du mythe" ["But he is the dreamer and poet who can only find knowledge in the phantasmagorical and the order of myth"](Marie-Jeanne Durry, *Gérard de Nerval et le mythe* [Paris, 1956], p. 62).

43. "The Fall of the House of Usher," *Collected Works of Edgar Allan Poe, Tales and Sketches 1831–1842*, ed. Thomas Ollive Mabbott, 3 vols. (Cambridge, Mass., 1978), 2:400; hereafter abbreviated *CW*.

44. I do not wish to gloss over the unsettling ambiguity of Poe's endings. Is Madeline Usher dead or alive? Is she present in the flesh or merely a figment of the narrator's imagination? Of course, we cannot finally decide. Tzvetan Todorov has defined this type of predicament—in which the reader is forced to "hesitate" between rational and supernatural explanations for the same narrated event—as the sign of the fantastic. Poe's stories are unquestionably *fantastic* in the general Todorovian sense. Yet they are also *phantasmagorical* in that they focus specifically on the epistemological problem of apparitions. See Todorov, *The Fantastic: A Structural Approach to a Literary Genre,* trans. Richard Howard (Ithaca, 1975), pp. 24–40.

45. An excellent short summary of the traditional theology of specters may be found in Rodney M. Baine, *Daniel Defoe and the Supernatural* (Athens, Ga., 1968), pp. 73–90. Keith Thomas has forcefully described the decline of ghost belief in the seventeenth and eighteenth centuries in his classic study of secularization in early modern Europe, *Religion and the Decline of Magic* (New York, 1971), pp. 587–606. One should not underestimate, however, the atavistic power of traditional thinking, even after 1800. Edmund Jones, Dissenting minister of Aberystruth, wrote a fervent *Relation of Apparitions of Spirits in the Principality of Wales* as late as 1780, claiming that "he must be a Deist and deny the word of God before he can deny Apparitions." Similarly, ghost-believers continued to publish stories of celebrated apparitions—often borrowed from such classic sources as Joseph Glanvill's *Saducismus Triumphatus* (1681), Richard Baxter's *The Certainty of the World of Spirits Fully Evinced* (1691), and Defoe's *Essay on the History and Reality of Apparitions* (1727)—well into the nineteenth century. Typical late eighteenth- and early nineteenth-century apparition books included *A View of the Invisible World, or, General History of Apparitions* (1752); *Life after Death: or, The History of Apparitions, Ghosts, Spirits, or Spectres* (1758); *Visits from the World of Spirits: or, Interesting Anecdotes of the Dead* (1791); *Apparitions, Supernatural Occurrences, Demonstrative of the Soul's Immortality* (1799); *New Lights from the World of Darkness: or, The Midnight Messenger, with Solemn Signals from the World of Spirits* (1800); *Phantasmagoria: Authentic Relations of Apparitions and Visions* (1805); and Thomas Ottway's *Spectre: or News from the Invisible World* (1836). *Visits from the World of Spirits* was published by none other than Henry Lemoine, author of the poem "Phantasmagoria" in *Gentleman's Magazine.*

46. The case of "Scratching Fanny," who terrorized the inhabitants of a house in Cock Lane, Smithfield, with knocking, scratching, and other poltergeist activity in 1762, has provoked controversy since the eighteenth century. Though the noises were subsequently attributed to a young girl living in the house (and several adults, who were prosecuted for fraud), the episode is still occasionally cited as a real haunting. For a summary of the episode and its aftermath, see Douglas Grant, *The Cock Lane Ghost* (London, 1965). Thomas Lyttelton, second Baron Lyttelton (1744–79), commonly known as "the wicked Lord Lyttelton," was reportedly visited by a ghost on 24 November 1779, who predicted that he would die at midnight three days hence. He indeed died mysteriously at the appointed hour. The sensational history became a staple in apparition books of the early nineteenth century, despite numerous attempts to debunk it. A typical version of the story appears in a pamphlet by Mary Knowles, *Brief Account of the Vision and Death of the Late Lord Lyttelton; to which is added, an anecdote of Lord Kames, and the melancholy end of a profligate young man* (Stanford, N. Y., 1804). On the Hammersmith Ghost of 1804, see Peter Haining, *Ghosts: The Illustrated History* (London, 1974), pp. 62–65.

47. Scott, *Letters,* p. 342.

48. See, for example, Brewster's comments on "Science used as an instrument of imposture," in *Letters on Natural Magic,* rev. ed. with additions by J. A. Smith (London,

1883), pp. 137-39. Salverte likewise gave an exhaustive account of the impositions of ancient necromancers in his *Sciences occultes*. On the history of charlatanism, see Grete de Francesco, *The Power of the Charlatan*, trans. Miriam Beard (New Haven, Conn., 1939).

49. The melancholiac, according to Burton, "imagineth a thousand chimeras and visions. . . .talks with black men, ghosts, goblins, etc." (Burton, *The Anatomy of Melancholy*, ed. Holbrook Jackson, 3 vols. [London and New York, 1964], 1:387).

50. Thomas Hobbes, *Leviathan*, ed. C. B. Macpherson (1651; Harmondsworth, 1968), p. 91.

51. Actually 1799 is the crucial watershed, for it was in that year that the Berlin bookseller and polemical writer Christoph Friedrich Nicolai presented his influential "Memoir on the Appearance of Spectres or Phantoms occasioned by Disease, with Psychological Remarks" to the Royal Society of Berlin. In this bizarre autobiographical memoir, Nicolai described how for a period of almost a year he was visited by hundreds of apparitions daily—the result, he concluded, of foregoing his annual bloodletting. An English translation appeared in Nicholson's *Journal of Natural Philosophy, Chemistry, and the Arts* 6 (Nov. 1803): 161–79. In subsequent decades virtually every anti-apparition writer from John Ferriar to Brierre de Boismont cited the Nicolai case in support of the theory of hallucination.

52. John Ferriar, *An Essay Towards a Theory of Apparitions* (London, 1813), p. 95. See also Ferriar's long historical essay on ancient apparition beliefs, "Of Popular Illusions, and particularly of Medical Demonology," *Memoirs of the Literary and Philosophical Society of Manchester* 3 (1790): 31–116. The term *hallucination* (from the Latin *alucinari*, to wander in mind) had of course been used before Ferriar: in *Pseudodoxia Epidemica* (1646), Sir Thomas Browne observed, "if vision be abolished, it is called *caecitas*, or blindness; if depraved and receive its objects erroneously, Hallucination" (*Works of Sir Thomas Browne*, ed. Geoffrey Keynes, 4 vols. [Chicago, 1964], 2:221). It appeared in philosophical and nosological treatises in the mid-eighteenth century as a synonym for illusion or false perception. The term was not in popular use, however, until around 1800. Alexandre Brierre de Boismont concluded that the word did "not appear to trace to a period far back," and credited the alienist Alexander Crichton with defining hallucination in his *Inquiry into the Nature and Origin of Mental Derangement* (1798) (Brierre de Boismont, *A History of Dreams, Visions, Apparitions, Ecstasy, and Somnambulism* [1845, Philadelphia, 1855], p. 31; hereafter abbreviated *HD*). (I have cited the first American translation of *Des Hallucinations: ou, Histoire raisonnée des apparitions, des visions, des songes, de l'extase, des rêves, du magnétisme et du somnambulisme*, based on the revised Paris edition of 1852). I have been unable to find the actual word *hallucination* in Crichton's work, however, and I am inclined to take Ferriar as the person mainly responsible for its popularization.

53. Ferriar, *Theory of Apparitions*, p. 15; see also pp. 16–20, 63, 99–100, 109–10.

54. Anonymous, "Phantasmagoriana," *Blackwood's Magazine* 3 (Aug. 1818); 590. The essay is a review of a French collection of supernatural tales translated from the German, entitled *Phantasmagoriana: ou Receuil d'histoires d'apparitions, de spectres, de revenans, fantômes, & c.* This would appear to be Jean-Baptiste Benoît Eyriès' *Fantasmagoriana* (Paris, 1812), the book of tales that supposedly inspired the famous ghost-story competition between Byron, the Shelleys, Claire Clairmont, and Polidori on the night of 16 June 1816 at the Villa Diodati. Yet the title *Phantasmagoriana* is also suggestive in a general sense. It was common practice in the early nineteenth century to name literary works of a miscellaneous or feuilletonistic nature—collections of tales by divers hands, books of light essays or satirical portraits—after the machinery of the spectre show. The underlying idea seems to have been that the constant shifting of topics and "scenes" in such works re-

created the pleasantly disorienting experience of watching a magic-lantern exhibition. See the Countess of Blessington's satirical sketches of London life, *The Magic Lantern: or, Sketches of Scenes in the Metropolis* (London, 1822), or Maria Jane Jewsbury's *Phantasmagoria: or, Sketches of Life and Literature,* 2 vols. (London, 1825). But there was also a growing sense in the period that reading in general was a phantasmagorical process. Medical writers like Crichton frequently warned that excessive reading—and especially reading books of a romantic or visionary nature—could send one into morbid hallucinatory states. Thus, besides referring to the mental ghost-show itself, *phantasmagoria* was sometimes used metonymically to refer to the kinds of literature likely to inspire phantasmata. Not surprisingly, in his garbled version of the Villa Diodati episode Walter Cooper Dendy used the word in precisely this way: "In imaginative minds, under peculiar conditions, intense reading may so shut out the real world, that an effort is required to re-establish vision. In Polidori's 'Vampyre' it is recorded that they had been reading phantasmagoria, and ghost stories in German, thereby highly exciting the sensitive mind of Percy Bysshe Shelley. Anon, on Byron's reading some lines of Christabel, Shelley ran from the room, and was found leaning on a mantel-piece bedewed with cold and clammy perspiration" (Dendy, *The Philosophy of Mystery* [London, 1841], p. 73).

55. Ferriar, *Theory of Apparitions,* p. 100.

56. William Newnham, *Essay on Superstition: Being an Inquiry into the Effects of Physical Influence on the Mind, in the Production of Dreams, Visions, Ghosts, and other Supernatural Appearances* (London, 1830), p. 41.

57. Samuel Hibbert, *Sketches of the Philosophy of Apparitions, or, An Attempt to Trace Such Illusions to their Physical Causes* (London, 1825), p. 251.

58. Dendy, *The Philosophy of Mystery,* pp. 55–56.

59. The spectral metaphor occurs prominently in the later nineteenth-century psychological writings of Sir Francis Galton. In a famous section on visionaries, Galton described the phantasmagoria as a "common form of vision" characterized by "the appearance of a crowd of phantoms, sometimes hurrying past like men in the street" (Galton, *Inquiries into Human Faculty and Its Development* [London, 1883], p. 166).

60. See my comments in Chapter 8, "The Spectralization of the Other in *The Mysteries of Udolpho*," on the atavistic intrusion of supernatural terms into the Freudian description of transference.

Chapter 10

1. Reginald Scot, *The Discoverie of Witchcraft,* ed. Hugh Ross Williamson (Carbondale: Southern Illinois University, 1965), p. 382.

2. Andrew Lang, *The Book of Dreams and Ghosts* (London: Longman's, Green & Co., 1897), p. x.

3. Keith Thomas, *Religion and the Decline of Magic* (New York: Charles Scribner's Sons, 1971), p. 606.

4. Thomas, *Decline of Magic,* p. 600.

5. I leave out here, obviously, many of the details and secondary themes of Thomas's richly elaborated account. Changing symbolic relations between the living and the dead, he argues, also contributed to the decline of ghost belief. In the increasingly atomistic society of the late seventeenth and eighteenth century, the dead no longer exerted such a powerful emotional influence over the living. It became easier to ignore the wishes of the dead. The Reformation and the waning of the belief in Purgatory assisted in this break with the past, but demographic changes also played a part. The breakup of rural communities, along with

changing forms of inheritance and property distribution, severed physical connections with the dead. At the same time it became more common for people to live out a full life-span, and to die only after they had "withdrawn from an active role in society," thus reducing the "social vacuum" they left behind. In earlier periods, by contrast, writes Thomas, "it was commoner for men to be carried off at the prime of their life, leaving behind them a certain amount of social disturbance, which ghost-beliefs helped to dispel" (p. 605).

6. Alexandre Brierre de Boismont, *A History of Dreams, Visions, Apparitions, Ecstasy, Magnetism, and Somnambulism* (Philadelphia: Lindsay and Blakiston, 1855), pp. 295–96. This is a slightly expurgated American edition of Brierre de Boismont's *Des Hallucinations: ou Histoire raisonnée des apparitions, des visions, des songes, de l'extase, des rêves, du magnétisme et du somnambulisme*, first published in Paris in 1845. The remark quoted here, according to Brierre de Boismont, is out of "Hutchinson . . . speaking of Boudin." It is largely Brierre de Boismont's invention, however, based on Francis Hutchinson's own citation of Samuel Harsnett's *Declaration of Egregious Popish Impostures* (1603) in his *An Historical Essay Concerning Witchcraft* (1720). In the dedication to the latter work, Hutchinson quotes Harsnett's description of the madness of the sixteenth-century demon-ologist Jean Bodin, who was so overcome by melancholia that his brain became "the Theatre and Sport-House for Devils to dance in." The reference to enemies and the police does not appear in Harsnett or Hutchinson.

7. Thomas, *Decline of Magic*, p. 595.

8. Complaining in his journal in May 1768 about new men of learning who took tales of witches and apparitions for "old wives' fables," John Wesley warned that "giving up witchcraft is, in effect, giving up the Bible." Yet if only one account of the intercourse of men with separate spirits were to be admitted, he continued, the "whole castle in the air (Deism, Atheism, Materialism) falls to the ground." See *The Journal of John Wesley*, ed. Nehemiah Curnock (London: Epworth Press, 1938), V, 265. Similarly, later in the century, in *A Relation of Apparitions of Spirits in the Principality of Wales* (1780), Edmund Jones, the Dissenting minister of Aberystruth, blamed the "Irreligion and Atheism" of the present age on those who denied the reality of spectres; "for men who come to deny the being of Spirits, the next step is to deny the being of God who is a spirit, and the Father of Spirits" (p. iii). But many orthodox laymen shared such views. Though contemptuous of superstitious excesses, Joseph Addison affirmed the traditional pneumatological view when he confessed in *Spectator* 12 (March 14, 1711) that he was "apt to join in Opinion with those who believe that all the Regions of Nature swarm with Spirits; and that we have Multitudes of Spectators on all our Actions, when we think our selves most alone." This belief in spirits in turn implied faith "in him who holds the Reins of the whole Creation in his Hand, and moderates them after such a Manner, that it is impossible for one Being to break loose upon another without his Knowledge and Permission." See Joseph Addison and Richard Steele, *The Spectator*, ed. Donald F. Bond (Oxford: Oxford University Press, 1965), I, 54.

9. See "Apparitions," *Encyclopédie: ou Dictionnaire raisonné des sciences, des arts et des métiers* (Paris, 1751), III, 546.

10. Since the sixteenth century skeptics had suspected that many notorious spirit-raisings recorded in ancient times had actually been produced using hidden optical devices. In *The Discoverie of Witchcraft*, from 1584, Reginald Scot had identified the famous Biblical apparition of the Witch of Endor as a sham vision produced using optical tricks and smoke effects. After 1790, the technological debunking of apparitions became even more common. Improvements in the magic lantern, and the development of the magic-lantern spectre show—or phantasmagoria—in London and Paris in the years around 1800 focused public attention on the ease with which spectacular "ghosts" might be raised using mirrors,

concave lenses, and candles. In the section entitled "Science used as an instrument of imposture" in his 1832 *Letters on Natural Magic,* Sir David Brewster described the magic lantern devices supposedly used by Greek and Egyptian necromancers, as did Eusèbe Salverte in his *The Occult Sciences: The Philosophy of Magic, Prodigies, and Apparent Miracles* (1847). On the history of the spectre show and its relation to ghost beliefs, see the companion essay in this volume, "Phantasmagoria."

11. Sir Walter Scott, *Letters on Demonology and Witchcraft,* 2nd ed. (London: John Murray, 1831), pp. 37–38.

12. The anecdote appears in Essay III of "The First Landing-Place" in *The Friend* of 1818. See Samuel Taylor Coleridge, *The Friend: A Series of Essays* (London: George Bell and Sons, 1880), pp. 89–90.

13. Mary Weightman, *The Friendly Monitor: or, Dialogues for Youth against the Fear of Ghosts, and other Irrational Apprehensions, with Reflections on the Power of the Imagination and the Folly of Superstition* (London, 1791), p. 62.

14. Weightman, p. 106.

15. John Abercrombie, *Inquiries Concerning the Intellectual Powers and the Investigation of Truth* (Boston: Otis, Broaders & Co, 1844), p. 134. Abercrombie offers here a slightly edited version of Imlac's famous attack on the imagination in Chapter 44 of *Rasselas.*

16. Daniel Defoe, *An Essay on the History and Reality of Apparitions* (London, 1727). For a general summary of Defoe's views on apparitions, see Rodney M. Baine, *Daniel Defoe and the Supernatural* (Athens: University of Georgia Press, 1968).

17. Parenthetical notations refer to page numbers in the 1727 edition.

18. Scott, *Letters on Demonology and Witchcraft,* pp. 358–59.

19. See Sir Humphrey Davy, *Researches, Chemical and Philosophical* (London: Smith, Elder & Co., 1839), pp. 269–330.

20. John Ferriar, *An Essay Towards a Theory of Apparitions* (London, 1813), p. 138.

21. J. H. Brown, *Spectropia: or Surprising Spectral Illusions* (London, 1864), p. 9.

22. "Spectral Illusions," *Chambers' Miscellany of Instructive and Entertaining Tracts,* ed. William and Robert Chambers, rev. ed. (London and Edinburgh: W. and R. Chambers, 1872), X, 3. Alexandre Brierre de Boismont used the same metaphor in 1845: a hallucination, he wrote was but the "daguerreotype," or "corporeal portion," of an idea deeply fixed in the mind. See Brierre de Boismont, *History of Dreams,* p. 282.

23. Locke's attack in Chapter 33 of Book II of *An Essay Concerning Human Understanding* (1690) on the "foolish maid" who infects her charges with superstitious tales about night-walking goblins and sprites was cited approvingly by later eighteenth-century skeptics. The example appears in a crucial passage on the association of ideas: a man who is told at an early age that spirits walk at night, Locke argues, will ever afterwards associate "darkness" with spirits and be afraid of the dark. The unfolding of Lockean epistemology is thus linked from the start with the drama of demystification. Locke's ghost-story anecdote in turn provides a kind of allegory or founding myth for modern scientific rationalism: human understanding—reason itself—depends on the primal internalization of the spectral.

24. Samuel Hibbert, *Sketches of the Philosophy of Apparitions; or, An Attempt to Trace Such Illusions to their Physical Causes* (London, 1825), p. 123.

25. Hibbert, *Philosophy of Apparitions,* p. 135.

26. See Ferriar, *Theory of Apparitions,* p. 33 and "Spectral Illusions," X, 28.

27. Sir David Brewster, *Letters on Natural Magic,* rev. ed. with additions by J. A. Smith (London, 1883), p. 123.

28. Ferriar, *Theory of Apparitions*, p. 100.

29. Cited by Hibbert, *Philosophy of Apparitions*, p. 251.

30. John Netten Radcliffe, *Fiends, Ghosts, and Sprites: Including an Account of the Origin and Nature of Belief in the Supernatural* (London, 1854), p. 174.

31. Brierre de Boismont, *History of Dreams*, p. 42.

32. See "A Memoir on the Appearance of Spectres or Phantoms occasioned by Disease, with Psychological Remarks. Read by Nicolai to the Royal Society of Berlin, on the 28th of February, 1799," in William Nicholson's *Journal of Natural Philosophy, Chemistry, and the Arts*, n.s. 6 (November 1803), 161–79.

33. Robert Macnish, *The Philosophy of Sleep* (Glasgow, 1834), pp. 264–65. Macnish's description of Miss S. L.'s visions is reprinted in "A Case of Spectral Illusion Confirmatory of Phrenology," *American Phrenological Journal*, I:6 (1838), p. 141.

34. Washington Irving, *Newstead Abbey*, in *The Complete Works of Washington Irving*, ed. Dahlia Kirby Terrell (Boston: G. K. Hall, 1979), 22, pp. 224–38. That women, owing to the innate excitability of their natures, saw apparitions more often than men did was a commonplace, of course, in eighteenth- and nineteenth-century apparition writing. Women were especially prone to imagining ghosts, wrote the Abbé Lenglet Dufresnoy in 1751, "parce qu'elles ont l'imagination plus forte & plus vive; une bagatelle est capable de les détourner, le moindre crise les effraye, le moindre mouvement les occupe." See Dufresnoy, *Traité historique et dogmatique sur les apparitions, les visions & les révélations particulières* (Paris, 1751), I, 246–47.

35. Alexander Crichton, *An Inquiry into the Nature and Origin of Mental Derangement* (London, 1798), II, 6.

36. Crichton, *Mental Derangement*, I, 8–9.

37. William Newnham, *An Essay on Superstition: Being an Inquiry into the Effects of Physical Influence on the Mind, in the Production of Dreams, Visions, Ghosts, and other Supernatural Appearances* (London: J. Hatchard and Sons, 1830), pp. 44, 109.

38. Johnson Grant, "Reverie; considered as connected with Literature," in William Nicholson's *Journal of Natural Philosophy, Chemistry, and the Arts*, 15 (October 1806), p. 116.

39. Erasmus Darwin, *Zoonomia: or, The Laws of Organic Life* (London, 1794–96), I, 222.

40. See Grant, "Reverie," pp. 113–16, 119, 122–23, and 125.

41. *Ibid.*, p. 124.

42. Abercrombie, *Intellectual Powers*, p. 131.

43. Grant, "Reverie," p. 121.

44. Freud cites two nineteenth-century works on the apparition problem in *The Interpretation of Dreams*: Robert Macnish's *The Philosophy of Sleep* (Glasgow, 1834) and James Sully's *Illusions: A Psychological Study* (New York, 1891). Macnish's treatise, a phrenological explanation of hallucinations, contains chapters on trance, voluntary waking dreams, spectral illusions, and reverie. Macnish defined reverie as a mental disorder proceeding from a "want of balance in the faculties," aggravated by too much solitude. This "quiescence of the brain" (characteristic of persons with a small organ of "concentrativeness") inevitably led, he thought, to mental "extravagancies." Sully's study deals with perceptual illusions, dreams, and "illusions of introspection"—the confusion of internal and external experience. A number of passages likewise anticipate Freudian themes.

45. Hibbert, *Philosophy of Apparitions*, p. 330.

46. Sigmund Freud, "Notes upon a Case of Obsessional Neurosis" (1909), trans. Alix

and James Strachey, in *The Collected Papers of Sigmund Freud* (London: Hogarth Press, 1948), III, 291–383. Parenthetical notations refer to page numbers in this volume.

47. Sigmund Freud, *The Psychopathology of Everyday Life*, ed. James Strachey, trans. Alan Tyson (New York: Norton, 1960), pp. 258–59.

Chapter 11

1. Sir Walter Scott, *Letters on Demonology and Witchcraft, Addressed to J. G. Lockhart, Esq.*, 2d ed. (London, 1831), pp. 344–45.

2. Sigmund Freud, *Group Psychology and the Analysis of the Ego*, trans. and ed. James Strachey (New York, 1959), p. 22.

3. In synopsizing the background to *An Adventure* I have drawn on Lucille Iremonger's *The Ghosts of Versailles: Miss Moberly and Miss Jourdain and Their Adventure: A Critical Study* (London, 1957), hereafter abbreviated *GV,* and Joan Evans's "An End to *An Adventure:* Solving the Mystery of the Trianon," *Encounter* 47 (October 1976): 33–47, hereafter abbreviated "E." Moberly's family memoir, *Dulce Domum: George Moberly, His Family and Friends* (London, 1911), provides additional information about her upbringing and milieu; further information about Eleanor Jourdain can be found in Hilary Spurling's *Ivy: The Life of I. Compton-Burnett* (New York, 1984), pp. 312–19.

4. Elizabeth Morison and Frances Lamont [Charlotte Moberly and Eleanor Jourdain], *An Adventure*, 2d ed. (London, 1913), p. 17, hereafter abbreviated *A. An Adventure* went through five editions in all—in 1911, 1913, 1924, 1931, and 1955. Each edition was also reprinted. The different editions vary considerably; some, for instance, include the appendices and "A Rêverie," while others do not.

5. There were uncanny moments during this second visit: Jourdain remembered feeling "the swish of a dress" close by her at one point, and later thought she heard eighteenth-century music being played somewhere by an unseen orchestra. She wrote down twelve bars of this music from memory afterwards and in 1907 showed them to an unnamed "musical expert" who said they dated from "about 1780." After researching the matter further at the Conservatoire de Musique in Paris, Jourdain concluded that "the twelve bars represented the chief motives of the light opera of the eighteenth century" and could be found in different variations, in the works of "Sacchini, Philidor, Monsigny, Grétry and Pergolesi" (*A,* pp. 94–95). Her findings were rudely satirized by a writer in the *Musical Times* of 1 September 1912, who pointed out that she had conveniently neglected to print the "ubiquitous twelve bars" in *An Adventure*. In a subsequent letter about *An Adventure* to the same journal, the distinguished music critic, Ernest Newman—referring to "those wildly ludicrous pages dealing with the phantom music"—dismissed Jourdain's musicological claims as "grotesque" (quoted in *GV,* pp. 293–94).

6. Moberly and Jourdain drew most of their basic historical information about Marie Antoinette and her court from various late nineteenth-century popular histories: Pierre de Nolhac's *La Reine Marie-Antoinette* (Paris, 1890), Julie Lavergne's *Légendes de Trianon, Versailles et Saint-Germain* (Paris, 1879), Gustave Adolphe Desjardins's *Le Petit Trianon: Histoire et description* (Versailles, 1885), and the Comte de Reiset's, *Modes et usages du temps de Marie Antoinette* (Paris, 1885). That these sources gave a somewhat romantic, unscholarly, and anecdotal picture of life at the Trianon was pointed out by several of Moberly and Jourdain's critics. "What is Julie Lavergne's *Légendes de Trianon,*" asked Iremonger dismissively, "but a charming imaginative creation, built upon the bones of fact

perhaps, but the merest rainbow tissue of flights of fantasy? What is de Nolhac's *Marie Antoinette the Queen* but a gorgeous picture-book with all the difficulties of considering France under the Revolution made easy and engaging, a chocolate eclair for a serious student?" (*GV,* p. 286).

7. Both Iremonger and Evans credited the effusions of "A Rêverie" to Moberly; her prose style was purportedly more "emotional" than Jourdain's. Moberly's brother Robert, it is worth noting, won the Newdigate Prize in 1867 for a poem about Marie Antoinette, the lachrymose sentimentality of which may well have influenced "A Rêverie":

> In simple peace she moves; more joyously
> Here 'mid the shame, and on the road to die—
> Than when of old her royal beauty shone
> Mid the triumphant splendour of a throne. . . .
> —Naught rests but heaven—no form of woman this—
> It is a spirit divine that moves to bliss. (quoted in *GV,* p. 287)

8. Mrs. Sidgwick's anonymous review appeared in the June 1911 supplement to the *Proceedings of the Society for Psychical Research*. It is also reprinted in full in chapter 12 of *GV*.

9. W. F. Barrett, *Psychical Research* (London, 1911), pp. 200, 201.

10. The first case mentioned by Barrett is described in the *Journal of the Society for Psychical Research* 13 (June 1907), 90–96. The young woman in question had nightly visions of Marie Antoinette during her childhood and subsequently developed such an obsession with the dead queen that she spent most of her waking hours at the South Kensington Museum "gazing at Marie Antoinette's bust, examining her toilet table with its little rouge pots, etc." On the renowned Swiss medium Hélène Smith, who claimed to be the reincarnation not only of Marie Antoinette but also of Cagliostro, several "Hindoo" sheiks and princesses, and a mysterious personage from Mars named "Pouzé Ramié," see Theodore Flournoy, *From India to the Planet Mars: A Study of a Case of Somnambulism,* trans. Daniel B. Vermilye (1900; New York, 1963). For a further discussion of these cases, and the Marie Antoinette "obsession" of numerous late nineteenth- and early twentieth-century women, see my study *The Apparitional Lesbian: Female Homosexuality and Modern Culture* (New York, 1993), pp. 107–49.

11. In the appendix to the 1913 edition Moberly and Jourdain called their original accounts, respectively, "A1" and "A2" and the subsequent "fuller" accounts "B1" and "B2." Confusingly, later writers—following W. H. Salter—referred to the first accounts as "M1" and "J1" and the second as "M2" and "J2." In this obsession with alphabetical nomenclature, *Adventure* scholarship often reads like a parody of Biblical textual scholarship.

12. Moberly and Jourdain's authorship was publicly revealed for the first time in the fourth edition of *An Adventure,* ed. Edith Olivier, with a note by J. W. Dunne (London, 1931). Yet the fact of their authorship was already by then widely known. Moberly and Jourdain had told officials at the Society for Psychical Research about the Trianon apparitions in 1902. In later years they shared their story with virtually anyone who would listen. Thus Evans's assertion—in the preface to the 1955 edition of *An Adventure*—that even in 1911 the identity of the book's authors was largely a *"secret de Polichinelle"* (p. 20), that is to say, no secret at all.

13. See Moberly and Jourdain, *Les Fantômes de Trianon (Une Aventure),* trans. Julliette and Pierre Barrucand (Monaco, 1959). As well as the preface by Cocteau, the French edition includes a lengthy (mostly skeptical) introduction by Robert Amadou.

14. Moberly and Jourdain were not entirely without defenders: following the unexpected death of Jourdain in 1924, Olivier, a former protegée of Moberly's from St. Hugh's, took on the task of preparing the third edition of *An Adventure* and remained a lifelong partisan. A few scientific writers were also sympathetic. J. W. Dunne, the author of *An Experiment with Time* (New York, 1927), suggested that Moberly and Jourdain's story confirmed Einstein's theory of relativity; G. N. M. Tyrrell, an electrical engineer and later president of the Society for Psychical Research, reviewed the case, apparently seriously, in a book on apparitions in 1942. Rather more tongue-in-cheek was the advocacy of Cocteau: in the preface to the 1959 French translation of *An Adventure*, he eulogized "les dames d'Oxford" (Moberly had died in 1937) for their futuristic assault on conventional notions of space and time. Despite the fact that Moberly and Jourdain hailed from "Grande Bretagne"—"où les histoires de fantômes abondent"—their book, Cocteau wrote, constituted "une manière de scandale nonconformiste de la plus haute valeur" (*Les Fantômes de Trianon*, p. 9).

15. See J. R. Sturge-Whiting, *The Mystery of Versailles: A Complete Solution* (London, 1938), pp. 125–34.

16. *Ibid.*, pp. 147, 158, 146.

17. See W. H. Salter, "'An Adventure': A Note on the Evidence," *Journal of the Society for Psychical Research* 35 (January–February 1950), 178–87. His findings are also reviewed at length in *GV*. Salter's reasoning was as follows: in the second edition of *An Adventure* (1913), the first edition in which all four of the accounts were published, Moberly and Jourdain claimed that the first accounts (M1 and J1) had been written on "November 25" and "November 28," and the second (M2 and J2) in "November 1901" and "December 1901," respectively. Yet, he observed, when the two of them wrote to Mrs. Henry Sidgwick at the Society for Psychical Research about the Versailles apparitions in October 1902, they sent only M1 and J1 as evidence. Why, he asked, if the more detailed accounts M2 and J2 were already then in existence, having supposedly been written "'for those who had not seen the place'" (p. 181), had Moberly and Jourdain not sent them instead? When asked later what had happened to the original manuscripts of M2 and J2, Moberly and Jourdain said only that they had destroyed them, after copying them along with "a few introductory sentences" into an exercise book in 1906. Concluded Salter, as summed up by Iremonger, "it does look rather as if M2 and J2, instead of having been written, as Miss Moberly claims, a matter of days after M1 and J1, were written *at best a year afterwards*, and perhaps much later than that!" (*GV*, pp. 190–91). Tellingly, almost all of the additional information provided in M2 and J2 served to strengthen Moberly and Jourdain's claim that they had seen eighteenth-century personages.

18. Though she never once used the word *lesbian* to describe them, Iremonger's interest in her subjects' emotional predilections verged on the prurient. Quoting an unnamed St. Hugh's source, she described Jourdain's "unhealthy" relationships with various students in the college, who reciprocated by falling in love with their principal. "An illuminating punning phrase which had currency at that time," wrote Iremonger, "was, 'Have you crossed Jordan yet?' In other words, have you fallen under the sway of this woman who is acknowledged to be consciously exercising her charm to bind students to her?" According to "the Mistress of Girton," Iremonger noted, "'a lot of kissing went on'" (*GV*, p. 88).

19. See Philippe Jullian, *Robert de Montesquiou, un prince 1900* (Paris, 1965); trans. John Haylock and Francis King, under the title *Prince of Aesthetes: Count Robert de Montesquiou, 1855–1921* (New York, 1968).

20. *An Adventure*'s critics were especially fond of invoking racial or occupational

stereotypes as evidence. Iremonger, for example, attributed Moberly's mystical and excitable streak to the fact that she was supposedly of Russian extraction. (Moberly claimed to be descended from Peter the Great.) Moberly's face, wrote Iremonger, was "perfectly Slavonic. She might have been Mr. Molotov's twin sister" (*GV,* p. 59). Somewhat differently, though equally disparagingly, Evans described Moberly as having "the narrow square head often found in the middle ranks of the Anglican clergy"—thus explaining, presumably, her lack of critical intelligence (Evans, preface, *An Adventure,* p. 14). Even the commonsensical Salter was inclined toward ruminations of this nature: explaining, in 1950, the strange clothing worn by the people described in *An Adventure,* he spoke of the typically "French" predilection for unusual uniforms. Likewise he added, "the cloaks and sombreros (or slouch hats) of the sitting and running men were, unless my recollection of that period is wholly wrong, an attire much affected by contemporary artists" (Salter, "A Note on the Evidence," p. 185).

21. Even some of Moberly and Jourdain's defenders, paradoxically, managed to discredit them. In "Is There a Case for Retrocognition?" a bizarre essay published in the *Journal of the American Society for Psychical Research* 44 (April 1950), 43–64, W. H. W. Sabine—while willing to accept Moberly and Jourdain's story whole hog—argued that they had not in fact gone back in time; they had simply had a "precognition," or foreglimpse, of the results of their future research. Their "hallucinatory visions," he maintained, "did not contain any information not ascribable to clairvoyant awareness of documents and books, and/or precognition of the coming experience of looking them up" (p. 63). Why, then, were their visions specifically of Marie Antoinette? Because, Sabine argued, they suffered from "lingering schoolgirl sentimentality" (p. 61). They were already obsessed with the dead queen in 1901; they "precognized" the future researches they would undertake regarding her, and through a kind of maudlin, back-to-front ESP, thought they *saw* her.

22. In April 1990 this "mania" led me, like Sturge-Whiting and others before me, to visit the Trianon and retrace Moberly and Jourdain's steps in the hope—unrealized—of seeing an apparition.

23. See Charles Lasègue and J. Falret, "La Folie à deux (ou folie communiquée)," *Annales Médico-Psychologiques* 18 (Nov. 1877); trans. Richard Michaud, under the original title, *American Journal of Psychiatry (Suppl.)* 121 (Oct. 1964), 1–23; hereafter abbreviated "F."

24. The alienist D. Hack Tuke was the first British clinician to appropriate Lasègue and Falret's term; see his essay "Folie à Deux," *Brain: A Journal of Neurology* (January 1888): 408–21. On the subsequent history of the concept, see Alexander Gralnick, "Folie à Deux—The Psychosis of Association. A Review of 103 Cases and the Entire English Literature," *Psychiatric Quarterly* 16 (Apr. 1942): 230–63, 491–520; Berchmans Rioux, "A Review of Folie à Deux, the Psychosis of Association," *Psychiatric Quarterly* 37 (July 1963): 405–28; and Robert A. Faguet and Kay F. Faguet, "La Folie à Deux," in *Extraordinary Disorders of Human Behavior,* ed. Claude T. H. Friedmann and Robert Faguet (New York, 1982), pp. 1–14.

25. Later clinicians sometimes substituted the terms *parasite* and *infected one, inductor* and *inductee, transmitter* and *receiver, activator* and *victim, aggressor* and *recipient,* or *sadist* and *masochist* for Lasègue and Falret's *active* and *passive* partners. See Gralnick, "Folie à Deux—The Psychosis of Association," pp. 235, 237.

26. The theme of double suicide, usually between sisters, crops up frequently in the *folie à deux* literature. Tuke in 1887 described the case of the baronesses Anna and Louisa Guttenburg, who "committed suicide by drowning themselves in the Starnberg Lake, on the identical spot where the King of Bavaria was found dead eleven months before" and were discovered the next day "in the soft clay, firmly clasped in each other's arms" (Tuke,

"Folie à Deux," pp. 414–15). A case of sororal double suicide (with distinctly lesbian overtones) occurred, interestingly enough, in the family of Ivy Compton-Burnett, the novelist and companion of Margaret Jourdain, Eleanor Jourdain's younger sister. Compton-Burnett's sisters Primrose and Topsy committed suicide together in 1917 by taking an overdose of Veronal. Later it was suggested that the two had been involved in an incestuous affair, having been found dead in one another's arms in the bed they always shared. See Spurling, *Ivy*, pp. 234–36.

27. Freud's silence on the subject of *folie à deux* is intriguing. The closest he came to touching on it was in a striking passage on identification in *Group Psychology and the Analysis of the Ego*. "Supposing," he wrote,

> that one of the girls in a boarding school has had a letter from someone with whom she is secretly in love which arouses her jealousy, and that she reacts to it with a fit of hysterics; then some of her friends who know about it will catch the fit, as we say, by mental infection. The mechanism is that of identification based upon the possibility or desire of putting oneself in the same situation. The other girls would like to have a secret love affair, too, and under the influence of a sense of guilt they also accept the suffering involved in it. (p. 39)

Later psychoanalytic writers inevitably cited this passage when explaining *folie à deux*. "Freud's basic example of the mechanism of identification," wrote Oberndorf, "concerns related hysterical manifestations involving several boarding-school girls when one of their number goes through a crisis in a blighted love affair. Such a group situation, transient and evanescent in its character, bears a psychological resemblance to the more profound and continued disturbances grouped under *folie à deux*" (C. P. Oberndorf, "Folie à Deux," *International Journal of Psycho-Analysis* 15 [January 1934]: 15). What the Freudian paradigm also reinforced, obviously, was the longstanding psychiatric connection between "mental infection" and women—particularly women living in all-female environments.

28. Helene Deutsch, "Folie à Deux," *Psychoanalytic Quarterly* 7 (April 1938): 307–18; reprt. Deutsch, *Neuroses and Character Types: Clinical Psychoanalytic Studies* (New York, 1965), pp. 237–47; hereafter abbreviated "FD."

29. Gralnick, "Folie à Deux—The Psychosis of Association," pp. 239–40.

30. Jourdain was the first of the two women to return to the Trianon—in January 1902. Unlike Moberly, Jourdain spoke some French and had something of an obsession (disavowed in *An Adventure*) with French history and culture. That she had imposed her fancies on Moberly was clearly Iremonger's conclusion: Iremonger quoted a St. Hugh's source who remembered Jourdain saying that she had difficulty distinguishing between "the dream world and reality" and that she believed in second sight and auras (quoted in *GV*, p. 99).

31. Spurling, *Ivy*, p. 314.

32. In his 1933 biography of the queen, Stefan Zweig discussed rumors about her "Sapphic inclinations" at length. Owing to Louis XVI's inability "to gratify her physiological requirements," as Zweig quaintly put it, Marie Antoinette turned to female companions to "relieve her spiritual and bodily tensions." " 'There have very generally been ascribed to me two tastes,' " she was supposed to have written to her mother, " 'that for women and that for lovers.' " The Comtesse (later Duchesse) de Polignac was her most notorious favorite: Zweig described their passion as "a sudden and overwhelming interest, a clap of thunder, a sort of superheated falling in love" (Zweig, *Marie Antoinette: The Portrait of an Average Woman*, trans. Eden and Cedar Paul [New York, 1933], pp. 119–21). The rumors about Marie Antoinette have always had particular currency among lesbians; an early issue of *The Ladder*, the underground lesbian periodical published in the United States between 1956 and 1972, contained an essay about the relationship between Marie Antoinette and the Comtesse de Polignac. See Lennox Strong, "The Royal Triangle: Marie Antoinette and the

Duchesse de Polignac," in *Lesbian Lives: Biographies of Women from "The Ladder,"* ed. Barbara Grier and Coletta Reid (Oakland, Calif., 1976), pp. 180–85.

33. Sabine hinted at a psychoanalytic interpretation when he spoke of *An Adventure's* dreamlike, "story-book" aspects. "This definitely 'bad man' [the kiosk man] who is awaiting the women in a lonely spot has to be escaped from. So—as though in response to the wish—on the scene runs the young and handsome page, quite an incipient story-book hero, and the two ladies are saved from a most disagreeable encounter" (Sabine, "Is There a Case for Retrocognition?" p. 54). What Sabine's reading neglects, however, is precisely the "feminocentric" pull of the story—toward the queen and her symbol, the Petit Trianon. On the role of the "pavilion" as an emblem of female erotic and intellectual independence in eighteenth- and nineteenth-century fiction, see Nancy K. Miller, "Writing from the Pavilion: George Sand and the Novel of Female Pastoral," *Subject to Change: Reading Feminist Writing* (New York, 1988), pp. 204–28.

34. See Michael Baker, *Our Three Selves: The Life of Radclyffe Hall* (New York, 1985), pp. 84–97. Hall and Troubridge's relationship paralleled Moberly and Jourdain's in interesting ways. Not least was the fact that both couples felt themselves profoundly susceptible to occult influences: in Brighton in 1920, Hall, in the company of Troubridge, saw the apparition of a mutual friend inspecting an automobile in a garage. The two published an account of their experience in the *Journal of the Society for Psychical Research* 20 (Apr. 1921): 78–88.

35. The British socialist and freethinker Edward Carpenter (1844–1929) was one of the first writers to call for homosexual emancipation; his pamphlet *Homogenic Love, and Its Place in a Free Society* appeared in England in 1894. In Germany the homosexual emancipation movement developed under the leadership of the sexologist Magnus Hirschfeld (1868–1935), who founded a group called the Scientific-Humanitarian Committee in Berlin in 1897. His periodical devoted to the homosexual cause, *Yearbook for Sexual Intermediate Types,* appeared between 1899 and 1923. On the involvement of lesbians in Hirschfeld's movement, see *Lesbians in Germany, 1890's–1920's,* ed. Lillian Faderman and Brigitte Eriksson (Tallahassee, Fla., 1990).

36. Arthur W. Wilcox, "Communicated Insanity," *Journal of Mental Science* 56 (July 1910), 481. Along the same lines, at the conclusion of his 1887 essay on the subject, Tuke warned that "we should discourage susceptible young women, and especially hysterical ones, from associating with persons having delusions, or even entertaining wild eccentric notions short of insane delusions" (Tuke, "Folie à Deux," p. 421).

37. In "A Study of *Folie à Deux,*" *Journal of Mental Science* 85 (Nov. 1939): 1212-23, Stanley M. Coleman and Samuel L. Last argued that economic distress was "the ground upon which *folie à deux* flourishes . . .[It] is a most potent reason for causing dissatisfaction with reality." This same "dissatisfaction with reality" on a grander scale, they argued, led to the creation of "new creeds and religions" and political ideologies such as "Communism and fascism" (p. 1220). On the association between *folie à deux* and blacks, see J. W. Babcock, "Communicated Insanity and Negro Witchcraft," *American Journal of Insanity* 51 (Apr. 1895): 518–23. Babcock, who was the superintendent of the South Carolina Lunatic asylum in Columbia, described a case in which a white man, "B. S.," became "infected" with religious delusions after meeting a black faith healer, "Doctor" George Darby, who claimed to effect magical cures with the assistance of "Little Solomon," a bundle of roots tied up in cloth. B. S. in turn passed his delusion on to his wife and brother and "five Negro men." After B. S. was committed to an asylum, his wife and brother recovered; the five black men apparently did not. What is especially striking about the case history is the author's implicit assumption that blacks are more prone to collective delusions than whites, and that once infected, become incurable.

38. Oberndorf, "Folie à Deux," p. 17.

39. See Marjorie Wallace, *The Silent Twins* (New York, 1986).

40. See Faguet and Faguet's "La Folie à Deux," in *Extraordinary Disorders of Human Behavior*. The authors, both professors of psychiatry at the University of California, Los Angeles, repeat without dispute Laségue and Falret's one-hundred-year-old observation that women suffer from *folie à deux* more than men (p. 7; see "F," p. 16). The *folie à deux* diagnosis has occasionally been invoked—with mixed results—as a legal defence. In a celebrated murder trial in Auckland, New Zealand, in 1954, two teenaged girls, Juliet Hulme and Pauline Parker, were accused of bludgeoning Parker's mother to death because she opposed their lesbian relationship. Lawyers for the defense argued that Parker and Hulme suffered from *folie à deux* and were not responsible for their actions, but the jury rejected the defence and both girls were sent to prison. For a fascinating account of the case by two New Zealand lesbians, see Julie Glamuzina and Alison J. Laurie, *Parker and Hulme: A Lesbian View* (Auckland, N.Z.: New Women's Press, 1991).

WORKS CITED

Abercrombie, John. *Inquiries Concerning the Intellectual Powers and the Investigation of Truth*. Boston, 1844.

Abrams, M. H. *The Mirror and the Lamp: Romantic Theory and the Critical Tradition*. London: Oxford University Press, 1953.

Ackroyd, Peter. *Dressing Up—Transvestism and Drag: The History of an Obsession*. New York: Simon & Schuster, 1979.

Adams, George. *A Short Dissertation on the Barometer, Thermometer, and other Meteorological Instruments*. London, 1790.

Addison, Joseph. *The Spectator*. 5 vols. Ed. Donald F. Bond. Oxford: Clarendon Press, 1965.

———. *The Tatler and Guardian*. Edinburgh, 1880.

———. *The Works of Joseph Addison*. 6 vols. Ed. Richard Hurd. London, 1811.

"Affecting Masquerade Adventure." *Gentleman's Magazine*, December 1754, pp. 560–66.

Altick, Richard D. *The Shows of London*. Cambridge, Mass.: Harvard University Press, 1978.

"Apparitions." *Encyclopédie: ou Dictionnaire raisonné des sciences, des arts et des métiers*. Paris, 1751, III, 546.

Apparitions: Supernatural Occurrences, Demonstrative of the Soul's Immortality. London, 1799.

Arbuthnot, John. *The History of John Bull*. Ed. Herman Teerink. Amsterdam: H. J. Paris, 1925.

Ariès, Philippe. *The Hour of Our Death*. Trans. Helen Weaver. New York: Alfred A. Knopf, 1981.

Arnold, Matthew. *Literature and Dogma*. Boston, 1873.

Artaud, Antonin. "Witchcraft and Cinema." In Alastair Hamilton, ed. and trans., *Collected Works of Antonin Artaud*, 3:65–67. 4 vols. London: Calder & Boyars, 1968.

Ashley, Leonard, ed. *A Narrative of the Life of Mrs. Charlotte Charke*. Gainesville, Fla.: Scholar's Facsimiles and Reprints, 1969.

Ashton, John. *Chapbooks of the Eighteenth Century*. London, 1882; rpt. with introduction by Victor Neuburg. New York: Augustus M. Kelley, 1970.

———. *Eighteenth-Century Waifs*. London: Hurst and Blackett, 1877.

Babcock, Barbara A. "The Novel and the Carnival World." *Modern Language Notes* 89 (1974): 911–37.

———, ed. *The Reversible World: Symbolic Inversion in Art and Society*. Ithaca, N. Y.: Cornell University Press, 1978.

Babcock, J. W. "Communicated Insanity and Negro Witchcraft." *American Journal of Insanity* 51 (April 1895): 518–23.

Backscheider, Paula R. *Daniel Defoe: His Life*. Baltimore: Johns Hopkins University Press, 1989.

Baine, Rodney M. *Daniel Defoe and the Supernatural*. Athens: University of Georgia Press, 1968.

Baker, Michael. *Our Three Selves: The Life of Radclyffe Hall*. New York: William Morrow, 1985.

Baker, Sheridan. "Henry Fielding's *The Female Husband*: Fact and Fiction." *PMLA* 74 (1959): 213–24.

Bakhtin, Mikhail. *Rabelais and his World*. Trans. Hélène Iswolsky. Cambridge, Mass.: MIT Press, 1968.

Balzac, Honoré de. *Un Épisode sous la Terreur*. Vol. 7 of *La Comédie humaine*. Ed. Marcel Bouteron. Paris: Bibliothèque de la Pléiade, 1955.

Barber, C. L. *Shakespeare's Festive Comedy: A Study of Dramatic Form and its Relation to Social Custom*. Princeton, N. J.: Princeton University Press, 1959.

Barbin, Herculine. *Herculine Barbin*. Trans. Richard McDougall. New York: Pantheon Books, 1980.

Barker-Benfield, G. J. *The Culture of Sensibility: Sex and Society in Eighteenth-Century Britain*. Chicago: University of Chicago Press, 1992.

Barney, Natalie. *Adventures of the Mind*. Trans. John Spalding Gatton. New York: New York University Press, 1992.

Barrett, William F. *Psychical Research*. New York: H. Holt, 1911.

Barthes, Roland. *Littérature et réalité*. Paris: Éditions du Seuil, 1982.

Battestin, Martin. *Henry Fielding*. London: Routledge, 1989.

Baudelaire, Charles. *Oeuvres complètes*. 2 vols. Ed. Claude Pichois. Paris: Gallimard, 1975–76.

Baxter, Richard. *The Certainty of the World of Spirits Fully Evinced*. London, 1691.

Beaune, Jean-Claude. "The Classical Age of Automata: An Impressionistic Survey from the Sixteenth to the Nineteenth Century." In Michel Feher, ed., *Zone: Fragments for a History of the Human Body*, 3:1 (1989): 430–80.

Bender, John. "A New History of the Enlightenment." In Leo Damrosch, ed., *The Profession of Eighteenth-Century Literature*, pp. 62–83. Madison: University of Wisconsin Press, 1992.

Birch, Thomas. *The History of the Royal Society of London*. 4 vols. London, 1756.

Blessington, Countess of. *The Magic Lantern: or, Sketches of Scenes in the Metropolis*. London, 1822.

Blewett, David. *Defoe's Art of Fiction*. Toronto: University of Toronto Press, 1979.

Boaden, James. *Memoirs of Mrs. Inchbald*. 2 vols. London, 1833.

Bogel, Fredric. *Literature and Insubstantiality in Later Eighteenth-Century England*. Princeton, N. J.: Princeton University Press, 1984.

Bolle, Bert. *Barometers*. London: Argus Books, 1984.

Boswell, John. *Christianity, Social Tolerance, and Homosexuality*. Chicago: University of Chicago Press, 1980.

Boucé, Paul-Gabriel, ed. *Sexuality in Eighteenth-Century Britain*. Manchester: Manchester University Press, 1982.

Bowlby, John. *Attachment and Loss*. 3 vols. New York: Basic Books, 1980.

Braudel, Fernand. *The Structures of Everyday Life: The Limits of the Possible*. Vol. 1 of *Civilization and Capitalism*. Trans. Sian Reynolds. New York: Harper & Row, 1981.

Braudy, Leo. "Daniel Defoe and the Anxieties of Autobiography." *Genre* 6 (1973): 76–97.

——. "Penetration and Impenetrability in *Clarissa*." In Phillip Harth, ed., *New Approaches to Eighteenth-Century Literature* (Selected Papers from the English Institute), pp. 177–206. New York: Columbia University Press, 1974.

Bray, Alan. *Homosexuality in Renaissance England*. London: Gay Men's Press, 1982.

Brewer, John, and Neil McKendrick and J. H. Plumb, eds. *The Birth of a Consumer Society: The Commercialisation of Eighteenth-Century England*. London: Europa, 1982.

Brewster, David. *Letters on Natural Magic*. Rev. ed. with additions by J. A. Smith. London, 1883.

Brierre de Boismont, Alexandre. *A History of Dreams, Visions, Apparitions, Ecstasy, Magnetism, and Somnambulism*. Philadelphia: Lindsay and Blakiston, 1855.

Bristol, Michael D. *Carnival and Theatre: Plebeian Culture and the Structure of Authority in Renaissance England*. London: Methuen, 1985.

Brooke, Frances Moore [Mary Singleton]. *The Old Maid*. London, 1764.

Brown, Homer O. "The Displaced Self in the Novels of Daniel Defoe." *ELH: Journal of English Literary History* 38 (1971): 562–90.

Brown, J. H. *Spectropia: or Surprising Spectral Illusions*. London, 1864.

Browne, Sir Thomas. *Pseudodoxia Epidemica*. In Vol. 2 of *The Works of Sir Thomas Browne*. Ed. Geoffrey Keynes. Chicago: University of Chicago Press, 1964.

Bullough, Vern L. *Sexual Variance in Society and History*. Chicago: University of Chicago Press, 1976.

Bulwer-Lytton, Edward. *The Last Days of Pompeii*. London, 1834.

———. *A Strange Story*. London, n.d.

Burke, Edmund. *A Philosophical Enquiry into the Origin of Our Ideas of the Sublime and Beautiful*. Ed. J. T. Boulton. Notre Dame: University of Notre Dame Press, 1958.

Burke, Peter. *Popular Culture in Early Modern Europe*. New York: Harper & Row, 1978.

Burnet, Gilbert. *History of His Own Times*. 4 vols. Ed. Thomas Burnet. London, 1818.

Burney, Frances. *Cecilia: or, Memoirs of an Heiress*. 5 vols. London, 1784.

———. *The Early Diary of Frances Burney 1768–1778*. 2 vols. Ed. A. R. Ellis. London, 1889.

Burton, Robert. *The Anatomy of Melancholy: What it is, with all the kinds, causes, symptoms, prognostickes & severall cures of it*. Ed. Holbrook Jackson. New York: Random House, 1977.

Byrd, Max. *London Transformed: Images of the City in the Eighteenth Century*. New Haven: Yale University Press, 1978.

Campbell, Jill. *Natural Masques: Gender and Identity in Fielding's Plays and Novels*. Stanford, Ca.: Stanford University Press, 1995.

Carlyle, Thomas. *The French Revolution*. 3 vols. London, 1837.

———. *Sartor Resartus*. London: J. M. Dent, 1908.

Casanova, Jacques. *History of My Life*. Trans. Willard R. Trask. New York: Harcourt, Brace & World, 1967.

"Cases of Spectral Illusion Confirmatory of Phrenology." *American Phrenological Journal* I:6 (1838): 135–41.

Castle, Terry. *The Apparitional Lesbian: Female Homosexuality and Modern Culture*. New York: Columbia University Press, 1993.

———. *Clarissa's Ciphers: Meaning and Disruption in Richardson's 'Clarissa.'* Ithaca, N. Y.: Cornell University Press, 1982.

———. "Eros and Liberty at the English Masquerade 1710–1790." *Eighteenth-Century Studies* 17 (1983-84): 156–76.

———. *Masquerade and Civilization: The Carnivalesque in Eighteenth-Century English Culture and Fiction*. Stanford, Ca.: Stanford University Press, 1986.

Cavell, Stanley. "What Becomes of Things on Film?" In *Themes Out of School: Effects and Causes*, pp. 173–83. San Francisco: North Point Press, 1984.

Cawte, E. C. *Ritual Animal Disguise*. Cambridge: D. S. Brewer, 1978.

Centlivre, Susannah. *The Gamester*. London, 1723.

Chalmers, Alexander, ed. *British Essayists*. 38 vols. London, 1823.

Chancellor, E. Beresford. *The Pleasure Haunts of London during Four Centuries*. London, 1925; rpt. New York: Benjamin Blom, 1969.

Charke, Charlotte. *A Narrative of the Life of Mrs. Charlotte Charke*. London, 1755; rpt. Gainesville, Fla.: Scholar's Facsimiles and Reprints, 1969.

Cleland, John. *Memoirs of a Woman of Pleasure*. Ed. Peter Sabor. London: Oxford University Press, 1985.

Climenson, E. J., ed. *Elizabeth Montagu, The Queen of the Blue-Stockings*. 2 vols. London: John Murray, 1906.

Cocteau, Jean. Introduction to *Les Fantômes de Trianon* by Charlotte Anne Moberly and Eleanor Jourdain. Trans. Julliette and Pierre Barrucand. Monaco: Editions du Rocher, 1959.

Coleman, Stanley M., and Samuel L. Last. "A Study of *Folie à Deux*." *Journal of Mental Science* 85 (November 1939): 1212–23.

Coleridge, Samuel Taylor. *The Friend: A Series of Essays*. London: George Bell and Sons, 1880.

———. *Selected Poetry and Prose*. Ed. Donald A. Stauffer. New York: Modern Library, 1951.

The Conduct of the Stage Consider'd, with Short Remarks upon the Original and Pernicious Consequences of Masquerades. London, 1721.

Craft-Fairchild, Catherine. *Masquerade and Gender: Disguise and Female Identity in Eighteenth-Century Fictions by Women*. University Park: Pennsylvania State University Press, 1993.

Crane, R. S. "The Plot of *Tom Jones*." *Journal of General Education* 4 (1950): 112–30.

Crichton, Alexander. *An Inquiry into the Nature and Origin of Mental Derangement*. 2 vols. London, 1798.

Crompton, Louis. "The Myth of Lesbian Impunity: Capital Laws from 1270–1791." In Salvatore J. Licata and Robert P. Petersen, eds., *Historical Perspectives on Homosexuality*. New York: Haworth Press, 1981.

Cross, Wilbur L. *The History of Henry Fielding*. 3 vols. New Haven: Yale University Press, 1918.

Darnton, Robert. "Readers Respond to Rousseau: The Fabrication of Romantic Sensitivity." In *The Great Cat Massacre and Other Episodes in French Cultural History*, pp. 215–56. New York: Random House, 1985.

Darwin, Erasmus. *Zoonomia or, The Laws of Organic Life*. 2 vols. London, 1794–96.

Davis, Natalie Zemon. "Women on Top: Symbolic Sexual Inversion and Political Disorder in Early Modern Europe." In Barbara A. Babcock, ed., *The Reversible World: Symbolic Inversion in Art and Society*, pp. 147–90. Ithaca, N. Y.: Cornell University Press, 1978.

Davy, Sir Humphrey. *Researches, Chemical and Philosophical*. London: Smith, Elder & Co., 1839.

Defoe, Daniel. *Colonel Jack*. Ed. Samuel H. Monk. London: Oxford University Press, 1964.

———. *An Essay on the History and Reality of Apparitions*. London, 1727.

———. *Roxana: The Fortunate Mistress*. Ed. Jane Jack. London: Oxford University Press, 1981.

———. *A True Relation of the Apparition of one Mrs. Veal*. London, 1706; rpt. in Manuel Schonhorn, ed., *Accounts of the Apparition of Mrs. Veal*. Los Angeles: Augustan Reprint Society and William Andrews Clark Memorial Library, 1965.

Dekker, Rudolf M. and Lotte C. Van de Pol. *The Tradition of Female Transvestism in Early Modern Europe*. New York: St. Martin's Press, 1989.

Dendy, Walter Cooper. *The Philosophy of Mystery*. London, 1841.

De Quincey, Thomas. *Confessions of an English Opium-Eater*. Ed. Edward Sackville-West. London: Cresset Press, 1950.

Deutsch, Helene. "Folie à Deux." *Psychoanalytic Quarterly* 7 (April 1938): 307–18. Rpt. in Deutsch, *Neuroses and Character Types: Clinical Psychoanalytic Studies*, pp. 237–47. New York: International Universities Press, 1965.

Diderot, Denis. *The Nun*. Trans. Leonard Tancock. Harmondsworth, Middlesex: Penguin Books, 1974.

————. *Sur les femmes*. Paris: Léon Pichon, 1919.

Dijkstra, Bram. *Defoe and Economics: The Fortunes of 'Roxana' in the History of Interpretation*. London: Macmillan, 1987.

Donaldson, Ian. *The World Upside-Down: Comedy from Jonson to Fielding*. Oxford: Clarendon Press, 1970.

Donoghue, Emma. *Passions Between Women: British Lesbian Culture 1668–1801*. London: Scarlet Press, 1993.

Doody, Margaret. *A Natural Passion: A Study of the Novels of Samuel Richardson*. Oxford: Clarendon Press, 1974.

Douglas, Anne. *The Feminization of American Culture*. New York: Knopf, 1977.

"Dream Romances." *Journal of the Society for Psychical Research* 13 (June 1907): 90–96.

Dryden, John. *Three Plays*. Ed. George Saintsbury. New York: Hill & Wang, 1957.

Duberman, Martin, Martha Vicinus and George Chauncey, Jr., eds. *Hidden from History: Reclaiming the Gay and Lesbian Past*. New York: Meridian, 1990.

Dudden, F. Homes. *Henry Fielding: His Life, Works, and Times*. 2 vols. London: Oxford University Press, 1952.

Dufresnoy, Abbé Lenglet. *Traité historique et dogmatique sur les apparitions, les visions & les révélations particulières*. Paris, 1751.

Dugaw, Dianne. "Balladry's Female Warriors: Women, Warfare, and Disguise in the Eighteenth Century." *Eighteenth-Century Life* 9 (1985): 1–20.

————. *Warrior Women and Popular Balladry 1650–1850*. Cambridge: Cambridge University Press, 1989.

Durry, Marie-Jeanne. *Gérard de Nerval et le mythe*. Paris: Flammarion, 1956.

Eagleton, Terry. *The Rape of Clarissa*. Minneapolis: University of Minnesota Press, 1982.

Eaves, T. C. Duncan, and Ben D. Kimpel. *Samuel Richardson: A Biography*. London: Oxford University Press, 1971.

Edgeworth, Maria. *Belinda*. 3 vols. London, 1801.

Egan, Pierce. *Life in London*. London, 1821.

Ek, Grete. "Glory, Jest, and Riddle: The Masque of Tom Jones in London." *English Studies* 60 (1979): 148–58.

Eliot, T. S. *The Complete Poems and Plays 1909–50*. New York: Harcourt Brace, 1971.

Elwin, Malcolm, ed. *The Noels and the Milbankes, Their Letters for Twenty-Five Years*. London: Macdonald, 1967.

Epstein, Julia and Kristina Straub, eds. *Body Guards: The Cultural Politics of Gender Ambiguity*. New York and London: Routledge, 1991.

Etlin, Richard A. *The Architecture of Death: The Transformation of the Cemetery in Eighteenth-Century Paris*. Cambridge, Mass.: MIT Press, 1985.

Evans, Joan. "An End to *An Adventure*: Solving the Mystery of the Trianon." *Encounter* 47 (October 1976): 33–47.

Eyriès, Jean-Baptiste Benoit. *Fantasmagoriana: ou Receuil d'histoires d'apparitions, de spectres, de revenans, fantômes, &c.* Paris, 1812.

Faderman, Lillian. *Surpassing the Love of Men: Romantic Friendship and Love Between Women from the Renaissance to the Present.* New York: William Morrow, 1981.

Faguet, Robert A. and Kay F. Faguet. "La Folie à Deux." In Claude T. H. Friedmann and Robert Faguet, eds., *Extraordinary Disorders of Human Behavior*, pp. 1–14. New York and London: Plenum Press, 1982.

Ferriar, John. *An Essay Towards a Theory of Apparitions.* London, 1813.

———. "Of Popular Illusions, and Particularly of Medical Demonology." *Memoirs of the Literary and Philosophical Society of Manchester* 3 (1790): 31–116.

Fielding, Henry. *Amelia.* 2 vols. Ed. William Ernest Henley. New York: Cass, 1967.

———. "An Essay on the Knowledge of the Characters of Men." In Vol. 1 of *Miscellanies.* Ed. Henry Knight Miller. Oxford: Clarendon Press, 1972.

———. *The Female Husband.* London, 1746. Rpt. in Claude E. Jones, ed., *The Female Husband and Other Writings.* Liverpool: Liverpool University Press, 1960.

———. *Joseph Andrews.* Ed. Martin C. Battestin. Boston: Houghton Mifflin, 1961.

———. *Juvenalis Satyra Sexta.* In Vol. 1 of *Miscellanies.* Ed. Henry Knight Miller. Oxford: Clarendon Press, 1972.

———. *The Masquerade.* London, 1728. Rpt. in Claude E. Jones, ed., *The Female Husband and Other Writings.* Liverpool: Liverpool University Press, 1960.

———. *Tom Jones,* Ed. Sheridan Baker. New York: W. W. Norton, 1973.

Flaubert, Gustave. *Bouvard and Pécuchet.* Trans. A. J. Krailsheimer. Harmondsworth, Middlesex: Penguin Books, 1976.

———. *Madame Bovary.* Trans. Mildred Marmur. New York: New American Library, 1964.

Flournoy, Theodore. *From India to the Planet Mars: A Study of a Case of Somnambulism.* Trans. Daniel B. Vermilye. New York and London: Harper & Bros., 1900.

Folkenflik, Robert. "Tom Jones, the Gypsies, and the Masquerade." *University of Toronto Quarterly* 44 (1975): 224–37.

Foster, Jeannette. *Sex Variant Women in Literature.* 3rd ed. Tallahassee, Fla.: Naiad Press, 1985.

Foucault, Michel. *The History of Sexuality: An Introduction.* Trans. Robert Hurley. New York: Pantheon, 1978.

———. Introduction to *Herculine Barbin.* Trans. Richard McDougall. New York: Pantheon, 1980.

———. *Language, Counter-Memory, Practice: Selected Essays and Interviews.* Ed. and trans. Donald F. Bouchard. Ithaca, N. Y.: Cornell University Press, 1977.

Francesco, Grete de. *The Power of the Charlatan.* Trans. Miriam Beard. New Haven: Yale University Press, 1939.

Freud, Sigmund. "Analysis Terminable and Interminable." In Philip Rieff, ed., *Therapy and Technique*, pp. 233–71. New York: Macmillan, 1963.

———. "The Dynamics of the Transference." In Philip Rieff, ed., *Therapy and Technique*, pp. 105–15. New York: Macmillan, 1963.

———. *Dora: An Analysis of a Case of Hysteria.* Ed. Philip Rieff. New York: Macmillan, 1963.

———. *Group Psychology and the Analysis of the Ego.* Ed. and trans. James Strachey. New York: W. W. Norton, 1959.

———. *The Interpretation of Dreams.* Trans. James Strachey. New York: Avon Books, 1965.

———. *An Outline of Psychoanalysis*. Trans. James Strachey. New York: W. W. Norton, 1949.

———. "Psychoanalytic Notes Upon an Autobiographical Account of a Case of Paranoia." In Philip Rieff, ed., *Three Case Histories*, pp. 103–86. New York: Macmillan, 1963.

———. *The Psychopathology of Everyday Life*. Ed. James Strachey. Trans. Alan Tyson. New York: W. W. Norton, 1960.

———. "Recollection, Repetition and Working Through." In Philip Rieff, ed., *Therapy and Technique*, pp. 157–66. New York: Macmillan, 1963.

———. *The Standard Edition of the Complete Psychological Works of Sigmund Freud*. Ed. James Strachey. 22 vols. London: Hogarth Press, 1959.

———. "The 'Uncanny.'" In Vol. 17 of the *Complete Psychological Works*, pp. 218–52.

Friedli, Lynn. "'Passing Women'—A Study of Gender Boundaries in the Eighteenth Century." In G. S. Rousseau and Roy Porter, eds., *Sexual Underworlds of the Enlightenment*, pp. 234–60. Manchester: Manchester University Press, 1987.

Friedman, Martin. *Hockney Paints the Stage*. New York: Abbeville Press, 1984.

Frost, Thomas. *The Lives of the Conjurers*. London, 1881.

———. *The Old Showmen, and the Old London Fairs*. London, 1875.

Frye, Northrop. *Anatomy of Criticism*. Princeton, N. J.: Princeton University Press, 1957.

Gallagher, Bob, and Alexander Wilson. "Michel Foucault—An Interview: Sex, Power, and the Politics of Identity." *The Advocate*, August 7, 1984, pp. 27–28.

Galton, Sir Francis. *Inquiries into Human Faculty and Its Development*. London, 1883.

Garber, Marjorie. *Vested Interests: Cross-dressing and Cultural Anxiety*. New York: Routledge, 1992.

Gell, William. *Pompeiana: The Topography, Edifices and Ornaments of Pompeii, the Result of Excavations Since 1819*. 2 vols. London, 1832.

Glamuzina, Julie and Alison J. Laurie. *Parker and Hulme: A Lesbian View*. Auckland, N. Z.: New Women's Press, 1991.

Glanvill, Joseph. *Saducismus Triumphatus*. London, 1681.

Goethe, Johann Wolfgang von. *The Sorrows of Young Werther*. Trans. Elizabeth Mayer and Louise Bogan. New York: Random House, 1971.

Goffman, Erving. *The Presentation of Self in Everyday Life*. Garden City, N. Y.: Anchor Books, 1959.

Golden, Morris. "*Clarissa*'s Debt to the Period." Paper read at the Northeastern American Society for Eighteenth-Century Studies, October 1981, New York City.

Goldsmith, Oliver. *The Works of Oliver Goldsmith*. 10 vols. Ed. Peter Cunningham. New York: G. P. Putnam's, 1908.

Goodison, Nicholas. *English Barometers, 1680–1860*. Woodbridge, Suffolk: Antique Collectors' Club, 1977.

Gordon, George, Lord Byron. *Don Juan*, Ed. T. G. Steffan, E. Steffan, and W. W. Pratt. New Haven: Yale University Press, 1982.

———. *The Vision of Judgment*. In Jerome K. McGann, ed., *Byron*. London: Oxford University Press, 1986.

Gorer, Geoffrey. *Death, Grief and Mourning in Contemporary Britain*. London: Tavistock Publications, 1965.

Gougenheim, G. "L'Inventeur du mot *fantasmagorie*." *Vie et Langage* 49 (April 1956): 160–62.

Gralnick, Alexander. "Folie à Deux—The Psychosis of Association: A Review of 103 Cases and the Entire English Literature." *Psychiatric Quarterly* 16 (April 1942): 230–63, 491–520.

Grant, Douglas. *The Cock Lane Ghost*. London: Macmillan, 1965.

Grant, Johnson. "Reverie; considered as connected with Literature." *Nicholson's Journal of Natural Philosophy, Chemistry, and the Arts* 15 (October 1806): 108–26.

Greig, James, ed. *The Diaries of a Duchess: Extracts from the Diaries of the First Duchess of Northumberland (1716–1776)*. London: Hodder & Stoughton, 1926.

Griffin, Benjamin. *The Masquerade: or, An Evening's Intrigue*. London, 1717.

Gubar, Susan. "The Female Monster in Augustan Satire." *Signs: A Journal of Women in Culture and Society* 3 (1977): 380–94.

Haining, Peter. *Ghosts: The Illustrated History*. London: Sidgwick and Jackson, 1974.

Hall, Jane. "Sex and the Senior Girls: NBC's Golden Girls Are the Toast of TV with their Mid-Life Miami Spice." *People*, January 6, 1986, p. 55.

Hall, Radclyffe, and Una Troubridge. "A Veridical Apparition." *Journal of the Society for Psychical Research* 20 (April 1921): 78–88.

Halsband, Robert. *The Life of Mary Wortley Montagu*. Oxford: Clarendon Press, 1956.

Hammond, Paul. *Marvellous Méliès*. London: St. Martin's Press, 1974.

Hawthorne, Nathaniel. *The Blithedale Romance and Fanshawe*. In vol. 3 of *The Centenary Edition of the Works of Nathaniel Hawthorne*. Ed. William Charvat et al. Columbus: Ohio State University Press, 1964.

Hayles, Nancy K. "Sexual Disguise in *As You Like It* and *Twelfth Night*." *Shakespeare Survey* 32 (1979): 63–72.

———. "Sexual Disguise in *Cymbeline*." *Modern Language Quarterly* 41 (1980): 231–47.

Haywood, Eliza. *The Female Spectator*. 4 vols. 3d ed. London, 1750.

Hertz, Neil. "The Notion of Blockage in the Literature of the Sublime." In *The End of the Line: Essays on Psychoanalysis and the Sublime*, pp. 40–60. New York: Columbia University Press, 1985.

Hibbert, Samuel. *Sketches of the Philosophy of Apparitions; or, An Attempt to Trace Such Illusions to their Physical Causes*. London, 1825.

Hilles, Frederick. "The Plan of *Clarissa*." In John Carroll, ed., *Samuel Richardson: A Collection of Critical Essays*, pp. 80–91. Englewood Cliffs, N. J.: Prentice-Hall, 1969.

Hobbes, Thomas. *Leviathan*. Ed. C. B. Macpherson. Harmondsworth, Middlesex: Penguin Books, 1968.

Hoffmann, E. T. A. *The Best Tales of Hoffmann*. Ed. E. F. Bleiler. New York: Dover Books, 1966.

Holland, Norman, and Leona Sherman. "Gothic Possibilities." *New Literary History* 8 (1976–77): 279–94.

Hollander, Anne. *Seeing Through Clothes*. New York: Viking, 1978.

Horkheimer, Max, and Theodor Adorno. *The Dialectic of Enlightenment*. New York: Continuum, 1989.

Howson, Gerald. *Thief-Taker General; The Rise and Fall of Jonathan Wild*. London: Hutchinson, 1970.

Hugo, Victor. *Notre-Dame de Paris, 1482; Les Travailleurs de la mer*. Ed. Jacques Seebacher and Yves Gohin. Paris: Gallimard, 1975.

Hume, David. *Political Discourses*. London, 1752.

Hunt, Leigh. *Essays and Sketches*. Ed. R. Brimley Johnson. London: H. Frowde, 1916.

Hunt, Lynn. "The Many Bodies of Marie Antoinette." In Hunt, ed., *Eroticism and the Body Politic*, pp. 108–30. Baltimore: Johns Hopkins University Press, 1991.

Hunt, Margaret. "Hawkers, Bawlers, and Mercuries: Women and the London Press in the Early Enlightenment." In Phyllis Mack. ed., *Women and the Enlightenment*, pp. 41–68. New York: Haworth Press, 1984.

Hunter, J. Paul. *Occasional Form: Henry Fielding and the Chains of Circumstance*. Baltimore: Johns Hopkins University Press, 1975.

Hutchinson, Francis. *An Historical Essay Concerning Witchcraft*. 2nd ed. London, 1720.

Inchbald, Elizabeth, ed. *The British Theatre: or, A Collection of Plays, which are acted at the Theatres Royal, Drury Lane, Covent Garden, and Haymarket. With Biographical and Critical Remarks by Mrs. Inchbald*. 25 vols. London, 1808.

———. *A Simple Story*. Ed. J. M. S. Tompkins. London: Oxford University Press, 1967.

Iremonger, Lucille. *The Ghosts of Versailles: Miss Moberly and Miss Jourdain and Their Adventure: A Critical Study*. London: Faber & Faber, 1957.

Irving, Washington. *Newstead Abbey*. In Vol. 22 of *The Complete Works of Washington Irving*. Ed. Dahlia Kirby Terrell. Boston: G. K. Hall, 1979.

Jewsbury, Maria Jane. *Phantasmagoria; or, Sketches of Life and Literature*. 2 vols. London, 1825.

Johnson, Charles. *The Masquerade: A Comedy*. London, 1719.

Johnston, David Landale. *The Trianon Case: A Review of the Evidence*. Ilfracombe: A. H. Stockwell, 1945.

Jones, Edmund. *A Relation of Apparitions of Spirits in the Principality of Wales*. London, 1780.

Jullian, Philippe. *Prince of Aesthetes: Robert de Montesquiou, 1855–1921*. Trans. John Haylock and Francis King. New York: Viking, 1968.

Juvenal. *Juvenal: The Sixteen Satires*. Trans. Peter Green. Harmondsworth, Middlesex: Penguin Books, 1974.

Kahane, Claire. "The Gothic Mirror." In Shirley Nelson Garner, Claire Kahane, and Madelon Sprengnether, eds., *The (M)Other Tongue: Feminist Psychoanalytic Interpretation*, pp. 334–51. Ithaca, N. Y.: Cornell University Press, 1985.

Kahn, Madeleine. *Narrative Transvestism: Rhetoric and Gender in the Eighteenth-Century English Novel*. Ithaca, N. Y.: Cornell University Press, 1991.

Katz, Jonathan Ned, ed. *Gay/Lesbian Almanac: A New Documentary*. New York: Harper & Row, 1983.

———. *Gay American History: Lesbians and Gay Men in the U.S.A.* New York: Crowell, 1976.

Keats, John. *The Complete Poetry and Selected Prose of John Keats*. Ed. Harold E. Briggs. New York: Modern Library, 1951.

Kiely, Robert. *The Romantic Novel in England*. Cambridge, Mass.: Harvard University Press, 1972.

Kinkead-Weekes, Mark. *Samuel Richardson: Dramatic Novelist*. Ithaca, N. Y.: Cornell University Press, 1973.

Knowles, Mary. *A Brief Account of the Vision and Death of the Late Lord Lyttelton; to which is added, an anecdote of Lord Kames, and the melancholy end of a profligate young man*. Stanford, N. Y., 1804.

Kunzle, David. "World Upside Down: The Iconography of a European Broadsheet Type." In Barbara A. Babcock, ed., *The Reversible World: Symbolic Inversion in Art and Society*, pp. 39–94. Ithaca, N. Y.: Cornell University Press, 1978.

Laqueur, Thomas. *Making Sex: Body and Gender from the Greeks to Freud*. Cambridge, Ma.: Harvard University Press, 1990.

Lang, Andrew. *Adventures Among Books*. London: Longman's, Green & Co., 1905.

———. *The Book of Dreams and Ghosts*. London: Longman's, Green & Co., 1897.

Lasègue, Charles, and J. Falret. "La Folie à deux (ou folie communiquée)." *Annales Médico-Psychologiques* 18 (November 1877); trans. Richard Michaud and rpt. *American Journal of Psychiatry (Suppl.)* 121 (October 1964): 1–23.

Lecky, W. E. H. *History of the Rise and Influence of the Spirit of Rationalism in Europe*. 2 vols. Rev. ed. New York: D. Appleton, 1919.

Leeson, Margaret. *Memoirs of Margaret Leeson, Written by Herself*. 3 vols. Dublin, 1797.

Lettsom, John Coakley. *Hints Designed to Promote Beneficence, Temperance, and Medical Science*. London, 1801.

——. *On the Effects of Hard Drinking*. London, 1791.

Lewis, W. S., ed. *The Correspondence of Horace Walpole*. 39 vols. New Haven: Yale University Press, 1937–79.

Licata, Salvatore J. and Robert P. Petersen, eds. *Historical Perspectives on Homosexuality*. New York: Haworth Press, 1981.

Life After Death: or, The History of Apparitions, Ghosts, Spirits, or Spectres. London, 1758.

Locke, John. *An Essay Concerning Human Understanding*. Ed. A. D. Woozley. London: Collins, 1964.

Macaulay, Thomas Babington. *The History of England from the Accession of James the Second*. 5 vols. Harper & Brothers, 1879.

Mack, Maynard. *Alexander Pope: A Life*. New York: W. W. Norton, 1985.

Macnish, Robert. *The Philosophy of Sleep*. Glasgow, 1834.

The Magic Lantern: Its Construction and Management. London, 1888.

The Magic Lantern: How to Buy and How to Use It. Also: How to Raise a Ghost. London, 1866.

Mann, Horace. Letter to Horace Walpole, July 30, 1741. In *Horace Walpole's Correspondence*.

Marchand, Leslie A. *Byron: A Portrait*. Chicago: University of Chicago Press, 1970.

Marx, Karl. *The German Ideology*. In Robert C. Tucker, ed., *The Marx-Engels Reader*, 2nd ed., pp. 146–204. New York: W. W. Norton, 1978.

The Masquerade: or, The Devil's Nursery. Dublin, 1732.

Mayes, Stanley. *The Great Belzoni*. New York: Walker, 1961.

McGuigan, Hugh A. "Medical Thermometry." *Annals of Medical History* 9 (1937): 148–54.

Middleton, W. E. Knowles. *A History of the Barometer*. Baltimore: Johns Hopkins University Press, 1964.

——. *A History of the Thermometer and Its Uses in Meteorology*. Baltimore: Johns Hopkins University Press, 1966.

Miller, Karl. *Doubles: Studies in Literary History*. Oxford: Oxford University Press, 1985.

Miller, Nancy K. *The Heroine's Text: Readings in the French and English Novel, 1722–1792*. New York: Columbia University Press, 1980.

——. "Writing from the Pavilion: George Sand and the Novel of Female Pastoral." In Miller, *Subject to Change: Reading Feminist Writing*, pp. 204–28. New York: Columbia University Press, 1988.

Moberly, Charlotte Anne. *Dulce Domum: George Moberly, His Family and Friends*. London: J. Murray, 1916.

——, and Eleanor Jourdain [Elizabeth Morison and Frances Lamont]. *An Adventure*. 2nd ed. London: Macmillan, 1913.

——. *An Adventure*. 5th ed. Ed. Joan Evans. London: Faber & Faber, 1955.

——. *Les fantômes de Trianon*. Trans. Julliette and Pierre Barrucand. Monaco: Editions du Rocher, 1959.

Monk, Samuel H. Introduction to *Colonel Jack* by Daniel Defoe. Oxford: Oxford University Press, 1965.

Morgan, Fidelis. *The Well-known Troublemaker: A Life of Charlotte Charke*. London: Faber & Faber, 1988.

Mullan, John. *Sentiment and Sociability: The Language of Feeling in The Eighteenth Century*. Oxford: Clarendon Press, 1988.

Napier, Elizabeth. "'Tremble and Reform': The Inversion of Power in Richardson's *Clarissa*." *ELH: Journal of English Literary History* 42 (1975): 214–23.

New Lights from the World of Spirits; or, The Midnight Messenger; with Solemn Signals from the World of Spirits. London, 1800.

Newnham, William. *An Essay on Superstition: Being an Inquiry into the Effects of Physical Influence on the Mind, in the Production of Dreams, Visions, Ghosts, and other Supernatural Appearances*. London, 1830.

Nichols, John. *Hogarth's Complete Works*. Edinburgh, 1883.

Nicholson, William. "Narrative and Explanation of the Appearance of Phantoms and other Figures in the Exhibition of the Phantasmagoria." *Nicholson's Journal of Natural Philosophy, Chemistry, and the Arts* 1 (February 1802): 148–50.

Nicolai, Christoph Friedrich. "Memoir on the Appearance of Spectres or Phantoms occasioned by Disease, with Psychological Remarks." In *Nicholson's Journal of Natural Philosophy, Chemistry, and the Arts* 6 (November 1803): 161–79.

Novak, Maximillian E. "Crime and Punishment in Defoe's *Roxana*." *Journal of English and Germanic Philology* 65 (1965): 445–65.

Oberndorf, Clarence P. "Folie à Deux." *International Journal of Psycho-Analysis* 15 (January 1934): 14–24.

Ottway, Thomas. *Spectre: or News from the Invisible World*. London, 1836.

Ovid. *Metamorphoses*. Trans. Rolfe Humphries. Bloomington: Indiana University Press, 1955.

Parker, Gustavus. *An Account of a Portable Barometer, with Reasons and Rules for the Use of It*. London, 1710.

Partridge, Eric. *A Dictionary of Historical Slang*. Harmondsworth, Middlesex: Penguin, 1972.

Patrick, John. *A New Improvement of the Quicksilver Barometer*. London, 1700.

Paulson, Ronald. *Hogarth's Graphic Works*. 2 vols. New Haven: Yale University Press, 1965.

Phantasmagoria: Authentic Relations of Apparitions and Visions. London, 1805.

Phantasmagoria: or, The Development of Magical Deception. London, 1803.

"Phantasmagoriana." *Blackwood's Magazine* 3 (August 1818): 589–96.

Philosophical Transactions of the Royal Society. London, 1694.

Pitt, Christopher. "On the Masquerades." London, 1727. Rpt. in Samuel Johnson, ed., *The Poets of Great Britain*. London, 1807.

Plato, *The Dialogues of Plato*. 3rd ed. 5 vols. Trans. Benjamin Jowett. New York: Macmillan, 1875–1892.

Plumb, J. H. "Commercialisation and Society." In John Brewer, Neil McKendrick, and J. H. Plumb, eds., *The Birth of a Consumer Society: The Commercialisation of Eighteenth-Century England*. London: Europa, 1982.

Poe, Edgar Allan. *Collected Works of Edgar Allan Poe, Tales and Sketches 1831–1842*. 3 vols. Ed. Thomas Ollive Mabbott. Cambridge, Mass.: Harvard University Press, 1978.

Poovey, Mary. "Ideology and *The Mysteries of Udolpho*." *Criticism* 21 (Fall 1979): 307–30.

Proust, Marcel. *Swann's Way*. Vol. 1 of *Remembrance of Things Past*. Trans. C. K. Scott Moncrieff and Terence Kilmartin. New York: Random House, 1981.

Quigley, Martin, Jr. *Magic Shadows: The Story of the Origin of Motion Pictures*. Washington, D. C.: Georgetown University Press, 1948.

Rabb, Melinda. "Underplotting, Overplotting, and Cor-respondence in *Clarissa*." *Modern Language Studies* 11 (Fall 1981): 61–71.

Radcliffe, Ann. *The Mysteries of Udolpho*. Ed. Bonamy Dobree. London: Oxford University Press, 1966.

Radcliffe, John Netten. *Fiends, Ghosts, and Sprites: Including an Account of the Origin and Nature of Belief in the Supernatural*. London, 1854.

Ralph, James. *The Touchstone: or, a Guide to All the reigning Diversions*. London, 1728.

Redgrove, Peter. "To the Habitués." In *The Mudlark Poems & Grand Buveur*. London: Rivelin Grapheme Press, 1986.

Reed, Arden. *Romantic Weather: The Climates of Coleridge and Baudelaire*. Hanover, N. H.: University Press of New England, 1983.

Rey, Léon. "Une Promenade hors du temps." *Revue de Paris*, December 1952.

Ribeiro, Aileen. *The Dress Worn at Masquerades in England, 1730 to 1790, and its Relation to Fancy Dress in Portraiture*. New York: Garland, 1984.

———. "The Elegant Art of Fancy Dress." In Edward Maeder, ed., *An Elegant Art: Fashion and Fantasy in the Eighteenth Century*. New York: Abrams and Los Angeles County Museum of Art, 1983.

Rich, Adrienne. *The Dream of a Common Language*. New York: Norton, 1978.

Richardson, Samuel. *Clarissa: or, The History of a Young Lady*. 4 vols. New York: Dutton, 1979.

———. *Correspondence*. 6 vols. Ed. A. Barbauld. London, 1804.

———. *Pamela; or, Virtue Rewarded*. Ed. Peter Sabor. New York: Penguin Books, 1979.

———. *Pamela*. 2 vols. Ed. George Saintsbury. London: J. M. Dent, 1914.

———. *Sir Charles Grandison*. 3 vols. Ed. Jocelyn Harris. London: Oxford University Press, 1972.

Richetti, John J. *Defoe's Narratives: Situations and Structures*. Oxford: Clarendon Press, 1975.

———. *Popular Fiction Before Richardson: Narrative Patterns 1700–1739*. Oxford: Clarendon Press, 1969.

Rimbaud, Arthur. *A Season in Hell*. In Wallace Fowlie, ed. and trans., *Rimbaud: Complete Works, Selected Letters*. Chicago and London: University of Chicago Press, 1966.

Rioux, Berchmans. "A Review of Folie à Deux, the Psychosis of Association." *Psychiatric Quarterly* 37 (July 1963): 405–28.

Robert, Paul. *Le Grand Robert: Alphabétique et analogique dictionnaire de la langue française*. 2nd ed. Rev. by Alain Rey. Paris: Le Robert, 1985.

Robertson, Etienne-Gaspard. *Mémoires: récréatifs, scientifiques, et anecdotiques d'un physicien-aéronaute*. 2 vols. Ed. Philippe Blon. Langres: Clima, 1985.

Robinson, Henry Crabb. *The London Theatre 1811–1866: Selections from the Diary of Henry Crabb Robinson*. Ed. Eluned Brown. London: Society for Theatre Research, 1966.

Rogers, Deborah, ed. *The Critical Response to Ann Radcliffe*. New York: Greenwood Press, 1993.

Rogers, Pat. "The Breeches Part." In Paul-Gabriel Boucé, ed., *Sexuality in Eighteenth-Century Britain*, pp. 244–58. Manchester: Manchester University Press, 1982.

———. *Henry Fielding: A Biography*. London: Paul Elek, 1979.

———. *Literature and Popular Culture in Eighteenth-Century England*. Brighton: Harvester Press, 1985.

Rose, June. *The Perfect Gentleman: The Remarkable Life of James Miranda Barry*. London: B. Hutchinson, 1977.

Rousseau, George S. "Nerves, Spirits and Fibres: Towards the Origins of Sensibility." In R. F. Brissenden and J. C. Eade, eds., *Studies in the Eighteenth Century* (Proceedings of the David Nichol Smith Memorial Seminar), 3:137–57. Canberra: Australian National University Press, 1976.

———, and Roy Porter, eds. *Sexual Underworlds of the Enlightenment*. Manchester: Manchester University Press, 1987.

Rousseau, Jean-Jacques. *Reveries of a Solitary Walker*. Trans. Peter France. Harmondsworth, Middlesex: Penguin Books, 1979.

Sabine, W. H. W. "Is There a Case for Retrocognition?" *Journal of the American Society for Psychical Research* 44 (April 1950): 43–64.

Sacks, Oliver. *Awakenings*. Rev. ed. New York: E. P. Dutton, 1983.

Salter, W. H. "'An Adventure': A Note on the Evidence." *Journal of the Society for Psychical Research* 35 (January 1950): 178–87.

Salverte, Eusèbe. *The Occult Sciences. The Philosophy of Magic, Prodigies, and Apparent Miracles*. 2 vols. Trans. Anthony Todd Thomson. New York, 1847.

Saul, Edward. *An Historical and Philosophical Account of the Barometer, or Weather-Glass*. London, 1725.

Schiller, Friedrich. *The Ghost-Seer: or, The Apparitionist*. London, 1795.

Schofield, Mary Anne. *Masking and Unmasking the Mind: Disguising Romances in Feminine Fiction 1713–1799*. Cranbury, N. J.: Associated University Presses, 1990.

Scot, Reginald. *The Discoverie of Witchcraft*. Ed. Hugh Ross Williamson. Carbondale: Southern Illinois University Press, 1965.

Scott, Sir Walter. *Letters on Demonology and Witchcraft, Addressed to J. G. Lockhart, Esq*. 2nd ed. London, 1831.

———. *Lives of Eminent Novelists and Dramatists*. London: Frederick Warne, 1887.

———. *The Waverley Novels*. 12 vols. Edinburgh, 1844.

A Seasonable Apology for Mr. H———g—r. London, 1724.

Sedgewick, Owen. *The Universal Masquerade: or, The World Turn'd Inside Out*. London, 1742.

Sedgwick, Eve Kosofsky. *The Coherence of Gothic Conventions*. New York: Arno, 1980.

———. "Imagery of the Surface in the Gothic Novel." *PMLA* 96 (March 1981): 255–70.

Select Trials for Murders, Robberies, Rapes, Sodomy, Coining, Frauds, and Other Offences at the Sessions-House in the Old Bailey. 2 vols. London, 1734–35.

Shinagel, Michael. "The Maternal Paradox in *Moll Flanders:* Craft and Character." In Edward Kelly, ed., *Moll Flanders*, pp. 404–14. New York: W. W. Norton, 1973.

Shorthouse, Joseph Henry. *John Inglesant: A Romance*. 8th ed. New York: Macmillan, 1903.

Sinclair, George. *Observations Touching the Principles of Natural Motions; Especially Touching Rarefaction and Condensation*. London, 1677.

Singer, Charles, and E. Ashworth Underwood. *A Short History of Medicine*. New York: Oxford University Press, 1962.

Smith, John. *Horological Disquisitions*. London, 1694.

Smollett, Tobias. *The Adventures of Peregrine Pickle*. Ed. James L. Clifford. Rev. Paul-Gabriel Boucé. London: Oxford University Press, 1983.

"Spectral Illusions." *Chambers' Miscellany of Instructive and Entertaining Tracts*, pp. 159:1–32. Rev. ed. Ed. William and Robert Chambers. London and Edinburgh: W. and R. Chambers, 1872.

Spence, Jonathan D. *The Memory Palace of Matteo Ricci*. New York: Viking Penguin, 1984.

Spence, Joseph. *Letters from the Grand Tour*. Ed. Slava Klima. Montreal: McGill-Queens University Press, 1975.

Spitzer, Leo. "Milieu and Ambiance: An Essay in Historical Semantics." *Philosophy and*

Phenomenological Research 3 (1942): 1–42, 169–218. Rpt. in Spitzer, *Essays in Historical Semantics*. New York: S. F. Vanni, 1947, pp. 179–316.

Spurling, Hilary. *Ivy: The Life of I. Compton-Burnett*. New York: Knopf, 1984.

Starobinski, Jean. *The Invention of Liberty*. Trans. Bernard C. Swift. Geneva: Albert Skira, 1964.

Starr, G. E. *Defoe and Spiritual Autobiography*. Princeton, N. J.: Princeton University Press, 1965.

Starsmore, Ian. *English Fairs*. London: Thames & Hudson, 1975.

Steele, Richard. *The Tatler*. London: J. M. Dent, 1953.

Stephen, Sir Leslie. *History of English Thought in the Eighteenth Century*. 3rd ed. 2 vols. New York: G. P. Putnam's Sons, 1902.

Stewart, Susan. *On Longing: Narratives of the Miniature, the Gigantic, the Souvenir, the Collection*. Baltimore: Johns Hopkins University Press, 1984.

Stone, Lawrence. *The Family, Sex and Marriage in England 1500–1800*. New York: Harper & Row, 1977.

Straub, Kristina. "The Guilty Pleasures of Female Theatrical Cross-Dressing and the Autobiography of Charlotte Charke." In Julia Epstein and Kristina Straub, eds., *Body Guards: The Cultural Politics of Gender Ambiguity* pp. 142–66. New York and London: Routledge, 1991.

Strong, Lennox. "The Royal Triangle: Marie Antoinette and the Duchesse de Polignac." In Barbara Grier and Coletta Reid, eds., *Lesbian Lives: Biographies of Women from 'The Ladder,'* pp. 180–85. Oakland, Calif.: Diana Press, 1976.

Sturge-Whiting, J. R. *The Mystery of Versailles: A Complete Solution*. London: Rider & Co., 1938.

Sulivan, Lawrence. "Epilogue to *Julius Caesar,* performed at Mr. Newcome's School, Hackney, in May 1802." *Gentleman's Magazine* (June 1802): 544.

Sully, James. *Illusions: A Psychological Study*. New York, 1891.

Summers, Montague. *The Gothic Quest: A History of the Gothic Novel*. New York: Russell & Russell, 1964.

Swift, Jonathan. *The Complete Poems*. Ed. Pat Rogers. New Haven: Yale University Press, 1983.

———. *The Prose Works of Jonathan Swift*. 14 vols. Ed. Herbert Davis. Oxford: Basil Blackwell, 1939–68.

Sydney, William Connor. *Social Life in England from the Restoration to the Revolution*. New York: Macmillan, 1892.

Tanner, Tony. *Adultery in the Novel: Contract and Transgression*. Baltimore: Johns Hopkins University Press, 1979.

Thomas, Keith. *Religion and the Decline of Magic*. New York: Charles Scribner's Sons, 1971.

Todd, Janet. *Sensibility: An Introduction*. London: Methuen, 1986.

———. *Women's Friendship in Literature*. New York: Columbia University Press, 1980.

Todorov, Tzvetan. *The Fantastic: A Structural Approach to a Literary Genre*. Trans. Richard Howard. Ithaca, N. Y.: Cornell University Press, 1975.

Tompkins, J. M. S. *Ann Radcliffe and her Influence on Later Writers*. New York: Arno Press, 1980.

———. *The Popular Novel in England 1770–1800*. Lincoln: University of Nebraska Press, 1961.

Trumbach, Randolph. "London's Sapphists: From Three Sexes to Four Genders in the Making of Modern Culture." In Julia Epstein and Kristina Straub, eds., *Body*

Guards: The Cultural Politics of Gender Ambiguity pp. 112–41. New York and London: Routledge, 1991.

———. "London's Sodomites: Homosexual Behavior and Western Culture in the Eighteenth Century." *Journal of Social History* 11 (1977): 1–33.

Tuke, D. Hack. "Folie à Deux." *Brain: A Journal of Neurology* (January 1888): 408–21.

Unger, Roberto Mangabeira. *Passion: An Essay on Personality*. London: Free Press, 1984.

Urquhart, Thomas. *The Jewel*. Ed. R. D. S. Jack and R. J. Lyall. Edinburgh: Scottish Academic Press, 1983.

Van der Meer, Theo. "Tribades on Trial: Female Same-Sex Offenders in Late Eighteenth-Century Amsterdam." *Journal of the History of Sexuality* 1 (January 1991): 424–44.

Van Sant, Ann Jessie. *Eighteenth-Century Sensibility and the Novel*. New York: Cambridge University Press, 1993.

Vicinus, Martha. "'They Wonder to Which Sex I Belong': the Historical Roots of the Modern Lesbian Identity." *Feminist Studies* 8 (Fall 1992): 602–28.

A View of the Invisible World: or, A General History of Apparitions. London, 1752.

Visits from the World of Spirits, or, Interesting Anecdotes of the Dead. London, 1791.

Wallace, Marjorie. *The Silent Twins*. Harmondsworth, Middlesex: Penguin Books, 1987.

Walpole, Horace. *The Correspondence of Horace Walpole*. 39 vols. Ed. W. S. Lewis. New Haven: Yale University Press, 1937–79.

Warner, William B. *Reading Clarissa: The Struggles of Interpretation*. New Haven, Conn.: Yale University Press, 1979.

Weightman, Mary. *The Friendly Monitor: or, Dialogues for Youth against the Fear of Ghosts, and other Irrational Apprehensions, with Reflections on the Power of the Imagination and the Folly of Superstition*. London, 1791.

Weiskel, Thomas. *The Romantic Sublime: Studies in the Structure and Psychology of Transcendence*. Baltimore: Johns Hopkins University Press, 1976.

Wesley, John. *The Journal of John Wesley*. 8 vols. Ed. Nehemiah Curnock. London: Epworth Press, 1938.

Wheelwright, Julie. *Amazons and Military Maids*. London: Pandora, 1989.

Wilcox, Arthur W. "Communicated Insanity." *Journal of Mental Science* 56 (July 1910): 480–85.

Wilson, Harriette. *The Memoirs of Harriette Wilson, Written by Herself*. 2 vols. London: The Navarre Society, 1924.

Winnicott, D. W. *Home Is Where We Start From: Essays by a Psychoanalyst*. Ed. Clare Winnicott, Ray Shepherd, and Madeleine Davis. New York: W. W. Norton, 1986.

Wolff, Cynthia Griffin. "The Radcliffean Gothic Model: A Form for Feminine Sexuality." *Modern Language Studies* 9 (1979): 98–113.

Wollheim, Richard. *The Thread of Life*. Cambridge, Mass.: Harvard University Press, 1984.

Wollstonecraft, Mary. *Maria: or, The Wrongs of Woman*. New York: W. W. Norton, 1975.

———. *A Vindication of the Rights of Woman*. Ed. Miriam Kramnick. New York: Penguin, 1975.

Woolf, Virginia. *To the Lighthouse*. New York: Harcourt Brace, 1927.

Wordsworth, Dorothy. *The Journals of Dorothy Wordsworth*. Ed. Helen Darbishire. Harmondsworth, Middlesex: Penguin, 1971.

Wright, Andrew. *Henry Fielding: Mask and Feast*. London: Chatto & Windus, 1965.

Wright, C. J. "The 'Spectre' of Science: The Study of Optical Phenomena and the Romantic Imagination." *Journal of the Warburg and Courtauld Institutes* 43 (1980): 186–200.

Wunderlich, Carl. *On the Temperature in Diseases: A Manual of Medical Thermometry*. London, 1871.

Wycherley, William. *The Complete Plays of William Wycherley*. Ed. Gerald Weales. New York: W. W. Norton, 1966.

Yates, Frances A. *The Art of Memory*. New York: Penguin, 1969.

Yeats, William Butler. "A General Introduction for My Work." In *Essays and Introductions*, pp. 509–26. New York: Macmillan, 1961.

Zimmerman, Everett. *Defoe and the Novel*. Berkeley: University of California Press, 1975.

Zweig, Stefan. *Marie Antoinette: Portrait of an Average Woman*. Trans. Eden and Cedar Paul. New York: Viking, 1933.

INDEX

Pages in *italics* refer to illustrations.